THIRTY YEARS WITH THE SILENT BILLION

THIRTY YEARS WITH THE SILENT BILLION

Adventuring in Literacy

FRANK C. LAUBACH

FLEMING H. REVELL COMPANY

Westwood, New Jersey
London E.C.4—29 Ludgate Hill
Glasgow C.2—229 Bothwell Street

Library of Congress Catalog Card Number: 60-5516

Printed in the United States of America

1.1

The first eight chapters of this book were originally published in the book *The Silent Billion Speak*, copyright 1943, 1946 by Frank C. Laubach, and are reproduced here with minor revisions.

This book is dedicated to the men and women who, at untold sacrifice, have taught the "Silent Billion" in all corners of the earth, and who are writing now, in a thousand tongues, the priceless truth these underprivileged must have to live the more abundant life.

INTRODUCTION

FRANK LAUBACH—RESTLESS MAN

THIS IS THE saga of one of the world's most restless men, a globe-trotter with an accordion passport. There are few countries to which Frank Laubach has not gone. Even at seventy-six he is planning to include any he may have missed up to now. By camel and canoe, jet, river boat, elephant, oxcart and shanks' mare, he has been a unique missionary with a world-wide parish.

Some journey in the hope of exploring where no man has been. Some go forth as ambassadors of commerce. Many roam the globe out of sheer curiosity. The urge that causes men to take the open road is often hard to define. From cosmic rays to oceanography, the reasons for travel are many, and some are unusual. But Laubach's motive is unique. A Kipling fan, he once remarked that he would like to make a journey through Khyber Pass. Some friends took him there, but little did he see of that historic gorge through which so many invasions have swept on the way from Central Asia to the fecund plains of Hindustan. During most of the trip Laubach had his nose buried in a literary chart of the Pushtu language; his thoughts were not on the fabulous Pass, but on the people, the picturesque Pathans.

People! The underprivileged, the sullen, the 700,000,000 illiterates who are ill-fed and ill partly because they are illiterate—the millions who can neither read nor write—these are the people to whom he has devoted more than thirty years.

How he went to them, and what happened when he got there, he tells here. "When I first started," he says, "they had their heads down."

His purpose was to bring their heads up—to give them the dignity to which all men are entitled, by teaching them to read and write. He has worked out, in 262 languages, a simple system of phonetic charts—a picture-language method—through which (sometimes in as little as three or four days!) they have entered the rich world of previously forbidden letters and books. He has been called the foremost teacher of our times. Surely he is, if it is true that he performs this miracle at the rate of ten million a year, that many through his "Each One Teach One" plan becoming literate.

Frank Laubach has also been called the "One-man Point Four Program." At home and abroad he battled endlessly for food, medicines, ploughs, seeds and scientific help from his fellow Americans. All this he passes on to the seething, submerged 700,000,000. That there is seething he has no doubt. He sees the world in fiery flux, the masses boiling with unrest. He tells us time is running out; that world unrest will break into global flame unless the Christian West wakes up.

To all who see our world as a race between compassion and suicide, who believe that hunger has spawned communism, and that hunger's senior partner is illiteracy, to those shocked at the thought that nearly half the world's population is *still* illiterate, to those who have any hope for such a world, here is the thrilling story of a man who has had the courage to attempt the impossible and make it seem possible.

LOWELL THOMAS

CONTENTS

THIRTY YEARS WITH THE SILENT BILLION

CHAPTER I

AFTER THE SILENCE OF THE CENTURIES

THREE OUT OF five of the human race cannot read or write—this was the startling revelation made in 1927 by James F. Abel, of the United States Bureau of Education. In Asia and Africa alone over a billion people are illiterate, nine persons out of every ten—half the human race. This cold type cannot tell you what that means. You think it is a pity they cannot read, but the real tragedy is that they have no voice in public affairs, they never vote, they are never represented in any conference, they are the silent victims, the forgotten men, driven like animals, mutely submitting in every age before and since the pyramids were built. It is a human weakness not to become aware of suffering unless we hear a cry. The illiterate majority of the human race does not know how to make its cry reach us, and we never dream how these millions suffer.

The most bruised people on this planet, the naked, the hungry, the fallen among thieves, the sick, the imprisoned in mind and soul, are the 1,200 million illiterates, three-fifths of the human race. At least a billion are virtual slaves. Take India for illustration. She had over 340 million illiterates at the time the 1941 census was taken, 88 per cent of her people; and almost every illiterate is in debt all his life—and his children and his children's children after him. He does not know how much his debt is nor whether the interest is correct. The money-lender takes all he can take and still keep his victim alive—for it would be silly to kill the animal that makes him rich! In one form or another this is the black sorrow of nearly every illiterate in the world. More than half the human race is hungry, driven, diseased, afraid of educated men in this world and of demons in the next.

I have not only seen these people across Asia and Africa, but have sat beside many of them and taught them one by one, and have seen a new light kindle in their eyes; love and hope began to dawn as they stepped out of blindness and began to read. I know that we could free this multitude from their tragic bondage; indeed, their emancipation has already begun.

The curve of literacy, which has been nearly stationary in Asia and Africa and Russia for centuries, has turned upward recently, especially in the past thirty years. Two hundred million more adults read today than thirty years ago. If that curve follows its present trend, within fifty years we shall have 500 million new readers stepping out of the silent ranks of illiteracy to speak for the first time. This is not only exciting news. It is the most stupendous, the most arresting, and it may be the most ominous fact on this planet. Nothing can stop it now.

It will be wonderful or terrifying, depending upon whether these vast multitudes awaken with their hearts full of Christ's love or with their hearts full of hate. They will bless or blast the world. That is why the church must step to the front and take a leading share in the mighty upsurge of the sunken half.

We must not only help them rise but we must also put reading in their hands, the right kind of reading; and that is a staggering task. The literacy campaigns now under way are going to double the world's readers! In China and India, where through recent decades more than nine-tenths of the people have been illiterate, a mighty tide is now rising. Eight hundred millions in those countries alone will be reading before we are ready. Over eighty-five out of a hundred Africans are still illiterate. But campaigns are starting all over that continent. Africa will be reading—before we are ready. A billion people now illiterate will be reaching out with hungry minds for something to read. Will they be fed with the message of Christ or with atheism? Will they read love or hate? Whatsoever is sown in their minds, the world will reap. And what will happen when these hundreds of millions shall speak "after the silence of the centuries"?

For ages Asia and Africa, with 300 million more people than all the rest of the world together, have been sunk in apathy and stagnation. They followed in the footsteps of their ancestors, ignoring the rest of the world. They believed it was wrong to break with any of the customs of the past. But with our imperialism, our business invasions, our missions, our radios, our airplanes, our armies, we have stabbed these peoples awake, and now the passion for progress burns like fire in their veins. They make more changes now in ten years than they used to make in a thousand years.

But as Asia and Africa attacked their enormous handicap of illiteracy they were confronted with a surprising difficulty. Modern medical science has been more successful than education. We helped them stamp out smallpox, cholera, bubonic plague, malaria, typhus, and other diseases that had kept their populations stationary, and now their populations are multiplying with ever-increasing rapidity, faster than they can be educated. In India, between the 1921 and 1931 censuses, the number of literate persons increased by five millions, but the population increased by the staggering total of thirty-three millions, six times as fast as they could be taught to read.

This inability to catch up with their rising populations is making governments desperate. They eagerly welcome any suggestions that promise relief. It is here more than at any other point that they feel the need of missionary help. In India in 1939 every state, province, and presidency followed the lead of missions in establishing literacy campaigns. Those of us traveling over India in this cause found maharajahs, prime ministers of Indian states, college presidents, governors, Mr. Gandhi, Mr. Nehru, important leaders of all communities —Hindu and Moslem as well as Christian—giving this movement their personal support and many of them attending literacy conferences conducted by missionaries. The leaders of Africa were equally cooperative. It was the same in China. Here is a cause in which every country believes. If the Christian church will help these countries out of their dilemma, it will win their cooperation and their hearts. I know many missionaries who are permitted to teach illiterates in prisons and other places that have been closed to them for any other purpose.

Teaching illiterates is proving to be a wonderful way to bring people to Christ. If you sit down beside an illiterate as your equal, your heart overflowing with love for him, and with a prayer on your lips that you may help him to a new vision; if you never frown nor criticize, but look pleased and surprised, and praise him for his progress, a thousand silver threads wind about his heart and yours. You are the first educated man who ever looked at him except to swindle him, and he will be so mystified by your unusual kindness that he is likely to stop and ask: "How do you expect to get paid for this? I have no money." Then you have your chance to say:

"I do not want any pay. I have learned this from Jesus. He spent all His time helping people free of charge. From the moment He awoke in the morning until He closed His eyes at night, He was looking around asking whom He could teach, or heal, or encourage, or defend, or save. I think that is a beautiful way to live. If we were all like Jesus, this world would be a paradise. So I thought I would try helping people just because I love them. And I have discovered the secret of happiness! When I am teaching you it makes my heart sing. When I have finished teaching you, I want you to go and teach your neighbors. Don't take any money for it, and your heart will sing! Brother, we have found the secret of happiness."

He goes out and teaches others, his heart sings, and he learns to love Jesus. The only irresistible gospel is love in action—helping people where they are in desperate need. If we serve the illiterates and then tell them the gospel after we have won their hearts, they will believe in Christ because they believe in us.

Teaching illiterates is a means of extending the gospel, moreover, because every Christian needs to read his Bible. Wherever a church contains many illiterates, it feels weak and unhappy until it has taught them to read. It finds that illiterates just emerging from non-Christian habits need constant personal attention to keep them from sinking back into the old life. They could gain new power to overcome if they could read the gospels, and hymns, and Sunday school journals, and prayer books. Moreover, illiterates have no influence with the educated people among whom they live. For these and other reasons it is universally recognized that literacy is a first objective in every Protestant mass movement.

The belief that everyone has a right to read and write is modern; it came out of the Protestant reformation. In ancient and medieval times, perhaps one in twenty, perhaps one in a thousand, could read. It varied in different countries. When the leaders of the Protestant reformation taught their followers to search the Scriptures instead of consulting a priest, reading became a practical necessity for anybody who tried to be a first-rate Christian. Johannes Gutenberg met an acute need in 1450 when he invented moveable type, and thereafter every well-to-do home could afford to have a family Bible instead of only one Bible for a town or province. Then Luther, Tyndale, and other heroes flew in the face of orthodoxy by actually translating the Bible from sacred Latin into vulgar German and English so that people could learn to read it without learning Latin. Then came democracy with its radical teaching that everybody had a divine right to rule and therefore to have a little education. So democracy, Protestantism, and literacy are triplets. The first Sunday schools in England were established to teach people how to read the Bible and to do easy numbers. In Wales the Sunday school still teaches reading, writing, and 'rithmetic.

In the United States our literacy picture is still spotty. In various parts of the country illiteracy ranges from a low of 1.4 per cent to a high of 9.6 per cent of the population over ten years of age; and among certain racial groups in some sections as many as 22 per cent are still unable to read. In 1900 the illiteracy for our whole country was 10.7 per cent. Vigorous campaigns by government and private teachers reduced this to 4.3 per cent by 1930. Estimates for 1941 further lowered it to 3 per cent. This is still higher than the Netherlands, Germany, Denmark, Norway, Sweden, and Switzerland, all of which claim less than 1 per cent of illiteracy. These countries had a simpler problem than ours, however. They can teach reading in half the time it takes us, because their alphabets are regular and phonetic, while our English alphabet is "confusion worse confounded."

Japan also has better literacy statistics than ours. She claims that her illiteracy is below 1 per cent. Nobody knows the genius who invented the Japanese *kana* syllabary a thousand years ago. There is a symbol for every syllable and these are arranged in perfectly logical sequence so they are easy to memorize. *Kana* was already waiting to make literacy easy when Admiral Perry opened Japan to the West in 1854. Japan soon started to take mighty strides in progress and education. Every registered child was compelled to go to school. The fact that everyone reads books and newspapers is one of the secrets of her power. No other country in Asia is over 20 per cent literate, while most of them are less than 10 per cent.

The Chinese did not, until recent years, have an alphabet of their own. Their characters represented ideas instead of sounds, while our Roman letters represent sounds and not ideas. The Chinese talk in monosyllables, which not only saves their breath but gives them a language simple in the extreme. They have twenty-four consonant sounds to start off or end their words and sixteen vowel and diphthong sounds to use with consonants. Because of their use of monosyllables and the fact that some letters are never found except at the beginning while others are found only at the end of the words, they can have only about 500 words so far as sound is concerned. Fortunately, by using a variety of tones or inflections, they multiply this number to well over 2,000. Nevertheless, each word often has from ten to twenty possible meanings. Laugh at them if you will, only remember that we have some of these same troubles with our Anglo-Saxon monosyllables. For example, to ("to" has at least ten meanings) two, too; or do, due, dew; or u, you, ewe; or hew, hue, whew! We indicate different meanings by very bad spelling. When Chinese talk, they show what they mean by tones, and glides, and looks, and gestures. Obviously they cannot very well write tones and gestures with an alphabet. So they have shorthand pictures called ideographs—separate characters for every meaning of every word. A few years ago the Chinese did adopt an alphabet; it is useful to help illiterates to pronounce, but, as in Japanese, the characters have to be printed beside the spelled words to show what they mean. There is a New Testament in Mandarin with the words spelled down the left column and the characters beside them down the right column.

In spite of these difficulties of language, China, in the past quarter-century, has been the scene of one of the world's outstanding movements for literacy. It will always be associated with the name of Dr. James Yen, a Yale graduate—one of those brilliant Chinese who absorbs all America has and takes it back to China for the good of his people. In 1914, during the First World War, he was called to Europe by the Young Men's Christian Association to work for the 200,000 Chinese laborers building trenches in France. "Jimmy" Yen started a paper for them, the *Laborer's Weekly,* confining his articles as far as possible to the thousand most commonly used Chinese characters. These thousand characters he arranged in four books, each book containing twenty-five lessons, with ten characters in each lesson. By learning ten characters a day, the student could master 240 characters in one month or all the thousand characters in four months. These lessons were so popular that the coolies began to think themselves lucky to have been brought to France.

When the war was over Dr. Yen returned to China where he found the illiterates in every province eager to learn his thousand characters.

One of the fine things about his literacy program in China was that at least nine different kinds of experiments were undertaken in different provinces at the same time, so that the results might be compared—how many were taught in a year, how much it cost for each pupil, how many enrolled, how many kept coming, and how long it took them to learn.

In Hunan Province in 1922 Dr. Yen and the group of young experts whom he had enlisted in his cause began the campaign by trying to create what they called a "climate of willingness to go to school." They printed 1,500 posters picturing how China is hindered by ignorance. They distributed thousands of handbills urging education. The governor put up on hundreds of street corners proclamations that the people must learn to read. A law was passed that every illiterate should be taxed until he had learned one thousand characters and could pass the examination. There were meetings of shop-masters. There was a general parade by college and middle school students bearing banners saying, "An Illiterate Is a Blind Man," "Is Your Son Blind?" "Can You Stand It To See Three-Fourths of China Blind?" They had huge mass meetings. Eighty teachers were recruited from the government and from mission schools; all they received was $4 a month for transportation. Then seventy-five teams set out to visit shops, homes, and streets, and in three afternoons 1,400 persons volunteered to study—ricksha pullers, beggars, scavengers, fuel gatherers, pig buyers, and peddlers. Classes were opened in sixty places, sometimes two classes under one roof. Of the original number, 1,200 stayed through, and 967 passed the examinations.

Shansi Province, using equally original methods, raised its literacy by 10 per cent in ten years, and several other provinces claim to have done as well. It is estimated that since 1926, ten million persons have learned the 1,200 characters considered necessary for simple reading. The average cost for all China was $1.40 per pupil.

The invasion of China by Japan in 1937 did not stop this mass education, but rather stimulated it. The whole program was taken over by what was called the People's Military Training Corps. In the city of Kweilin the boys and girls of middle schools taught their elders while they were crowded into caves near the city during airplane bombardments. It helped keep their minds off their worries. Later they said that, thanks to the Japanese bombs, illiteracy was wiped out of the city.

Far and away the largest literacy campaign carried on in all history has been that by Russia since 1921—though China and India together will teach seven times as many before their campaigns are finished! Russia under the czars was far behind other European nations in literacy. In 1920 her literacy was given as 31.9 per cent in government reports, but less than 9 per cent really were able to read intelligently, as they now confess. This illiteracy ran directly across Lenin's idea of government by the masses. On every occasion he placed literacy among the first necessities for a communist government. "An illiterate people cannot build a communist state," he said. "An illiterate person is outside the sphere of politics. The first thing he needs is to be taught the alphabet!"

In a dictatorship things can be accomplished swiftly by government orders. Lenin began by ordering all spelling changed. Russian spelling had been as bad as ours is in English. A perfectly phonetic alphabet was adopted in place of the old one. The second change Lenin made was to teach the languages that people spoke. The old czarist government had refused to teach any but the official Russian language. Lenin saw that Russia would not be literate in a hundred years if he tried to teach only one language, for there are fifty-eight important languages in the U. S. S. R. (282 if all subdialects are counted). Some of the Russian languages had used Arabic script, but many had never been written at all—they were only spoken. The Communists reduced these fifty-eight principal languages to writing, using the new alphabet, and prepared textbooks in them. In 1922 they made education free for everybody, irrespective of race or color. Children were put into vocational schools and every child was taught to read and to do something useful with his hands.

Adults, both men and women, were also taught to read in Russia-wide campaigns. Two and a half million "cultural soldiers" were recruited to teach without pay, and these were commanded by hundreds of thousands of special paid teachers. School children were organized into "Down with Illiteracy Societies," which surveyed their towns to find out how many illiterate adults there were. After August, 1931, illiteracy became a legal offense!

The campaign gathered momentum with astonishing speed: in 1927, 1,300,000 persons were taught; in 1928, 2,700,000; in 1929, 10,500,000; and in 1930 the number more than doubled—22,000,000 persons were officially recorded as having learned to read. In 1933 Stalin announced that 90 per cent of the U. S. S. R. could read and write. There were several tribes that began with a literacy level as low as eight-tenths of 1 per cent and that became wholly literate. A nation of 160 million people had been made literate in fifteen years!

As Dr. John R. Mott once declared, "The alphabet is the most dangerous weapon ever put in human hands." It is like science—it may bless the world or destroy it. It is like science in another respect—nobody can stop either science or literacy now: all we can do is to guide them. This is why people with the ideals of Christ must take a leading part in teaching illiterates and in producing literature.

I had an interesting conversation with Mahatma Gandhi in 1935 when I first visited India. We had just completed a reading chart in the Marathi language and I took it to Wardha to show Mr. Gandhi what we were attempting. He was sitting on the floor. I sat down cross-legged in front of him and unrolled the Marathi chart. He glanced at it, then looked up, and, to my amazement, said: "I doubt whether India ought to become literate."

"You are the first person I ever heard say that," I said, hardly believing my ears. "What do you mean?"

"The literature you publish in the West is not fit for India to read. Look at what you are writing and selling us on any railway stand." He was right about that—I had looked! Without waiting for my reply, this man, revered as a saint by millions, gave me a second punch before

I had recovered from the first—and don't you agree that this was "the most unkindest cut of all" to a Christian missionary?

"Many of the greatest benefactors of the human race have been illiterate—Mohammed, for example." My answers, I think, came out of heaven. At least I haven't been able to think of any others as good.

"Mr. Gandhi," I said, "you are right. But on the other hand, millions of us admire you and have read your books with great blessing. If you had not written these books and if we had not learned to read, we should never have heard of you."

Mr. Gandhi dropped his head and said meekly, "I think I would have done a little good."

The other answer came to me that instant and I let him have it: "The greatest single blessing that ever came to this world was the life and teaching of Jesus Christ. If Christ's life had not been written and if we had not been able to read the gospels, we would know very little about him."

Mr. Gandhi shook his head up and down slowly and silently for a few moments, and he looked through me every time his head came up. I wish I knew what he meant by that head shake. He changed the subject.

"I really do believe in literacy for India," he said at last. "Indeed, I have probably been instrumental in teaching thirty thousand indirectly myself. But by far the largest question for India is how to feed her hungry multitudes."

"This," I said, "is exactly why India needs to become literate. The right way to lift the masses above hunger is to teach them to lift themselves. Your illiterates have been the victims of educated scoundrels who have kept them in debt all their lives. Literacy is the only road I see to their complete emancipation."

The truth is that Mr. Gandhi, like nearly all Indian leaders in those years, was in despair about teaching a people as underfed and as overworked as the masses of India, and believed that economic relief had to come before they could take even the first step toward education. But in subsequent years, first in one corner of India, then in another, ever larger literacy movements began to appear, indicating that perhaps, after all, literacy is the horse that should come before the cart. In his later years Mr. Gandhi became more and more emphatic in saying that illiteracy could and had to be wiped out in India. In 1939 he wrote in the papers: "I am converted, and now believe that literacy should be required for the franchise. If each one of us will teach one illiterate, we can make India literate in no time!"

And now all India is on the march to become literate!

But before I tell that story, I shall first go back to 1929, when a new approach to adult literacy was developed under the American flag among the Moros of Mindanao in the Philippines, and then I shall trace the spread of that "Philippine method" over the world. I came from these experiences with my faith unwavering in the very face of the Second World War because I have seen how easy it is to win the love of peoples of any race when we really love and serve them unselfishly.

CHAPTER 2

1929-30: A LITERACY CAMPAIGN FROM THE INSIDE

THE LITERACY CAMPAIGN that began among the Moros of Lanao Province of Mindanao in 1930 attracted some attention in the United States, but much more in Asia, Africa, and Latin America. This chapter is an intimate tale of that campaign: why it started, how it felt as we carried it on, and what it did to the Moros. During those years I wrote weekly letters to my father, and in this book I have quoted frequently from them.

When Effa Seely and I were married in 1912, we chose as our field for foreign service the great island of Mindanao in the southern Philippines. It appealed both to our religion and to our patriotism. We had first become interested in this island when Effa's cousin, Harry Edwards, and another fellow-townsman, Joe Albertson, went there as teachers in 1901, among the first 600 teachers sent to the Philippines by our government on the famous transport *Thomas*. Harry and Joe wrote back vivid accounts of the Moros of Mindanao and Sulu, the worst troublemakers American soldiers had ever faced.

In 1915, just before we left for Mindanao, there was a farewell meeting at the Harvard Church in Brookline, Massachusetts, and several of us departing missionaries gave five-minute speeches. I remember as though it were yesterday what I said, for I had reached my decision only after a struggle with selfish ambition:

"If I were in a battle and with no orders from my captain, I would be a coward if I fought where we were winning; I would be a man if I fought where our ranks were thin and we were losing the battle. We *are* in a battle for Jesus Christ, to conquer the world, and the ranks are thinnest and the battle hottest in the Orient. So we are going where we are needed most."

When we reached Mindanao that year we found its mountains and lakes as beautiful as we had expected. We visited lovely blue Lake Lanao, which lay in the crater of an ancient volcano half a mile above sea level, with a raging river plunging twenty miles to the ocean. But the atmosphere of the place was tense. The government was having continuous trouble with the Moros.

Army officers whom we met on arriving told us that an inexperienced missionary talking religion to the Moros would only make matters worse and they did not think the Moros would be ready to hear us for several years. So we moved on and settled at Cagayan, a hundred miles away, where conditions were more favorable. However, we returned to Lanao a month every summer to enjoy the cool air and to watch for the time when work could begin with the Moros.

The Moros, in point of fact, had been fighting and hating Christians ever since Magellan discovered the Philippines in 1521. It happened that just twenty-nine years before that date, in the famous year 1492, back in Spain, the Moors (or Moros as they are called in Spanish) had been hurled across the Strait of Gibraltar into Morocco. When the Spaniards went down around South America, crossed the Pacific Ocean, and ran into Mindanao in the southern Philippines, they found people practising the Moslem religion, and so made the big mistake of calling them "Moros," just as Columbus had made the mistake of calling American natives "Indians."

But the Spaniards made the far worse mistake of waging war on these Filipino "Moros" just because they had been fighting the African Moros. What consummate stupidity! They gave them the wrong name, then said, "Now you are Moros, too, so we will fight you!" It was almost the silliest war on record. In 377 years the Spanish troops never conquered the Moros of Mindanao. When the United States took the Philippines in 1898, the Moros resisted the new rulers as fiercely as they had resisted the Spaniards. General Pershing became famous fighting these Lanao Moros. Not until 1917 did the American troops regard the situation sufficiently under control to permit them to move out of Lanao and leave in the hands of Filipino soldiers the camp that Pershing had built.

It was not until 1929 that the time seemed ripe to open the Lanao station. Leaving my wife and my son Bob in a school north of Manila, I went to Lanao alone. My colleagues, the Reverend and Mrs. Frank J. Woodward, who had reached Mindanao a year after our arrival and who were working along the coast of that island, had built a little summer cottage close to the military camp. They invited me to make their cottage my home. I took my meals at the officers' club. With me were the superintendent of schools, the principal of the high school, and the captain of the Philippine constabulary, three fine men—and all of them, like myself, lonesome. While they drowned their loneliness in whiskey, I drowned mine in religion. Every evening at five when the other Americans were at MacSmith's store for their evening comforter, I would climb Signal Hill, back of my cottage, with no one but my black dog Tip, and talk to God and the sunset.

The first month in Lanao was the hardest of my life. One evening I was sitting on Signal Hill looking over the province that had me beaten. Tip had his nose up under my arm trying to lick the tears off my cheeks. My lips began to move and it seemed to me that God was speaking.

"My child," my lips said, "you have failed because you do not really love these Moros. You feel superior to them because you are white. If you can forget you are an American and think only how I love them, they will respond."

I answered back to the sunset, "God, I don't know whether you spoke to me through my lips, but if you did, it was the truth. I hate myself. My plans have all gone to pieces. Drive me out of myself and come and take possession of me and think Thy thoughts in my mind."

In that terrible, wonderful hour on Signal Hill I became color-blind. Ever since, I have been partial to tan, the more tan the better! Every missionary goes through some such experience as that—or comes home defeated.

My lips spoke again to me: "If you want the Moros to be fair to your religion, be fair to theirs. Study their Koran with them."

I went down the hill and told some *panditas* (priests) that I wanted to study their Koran. The next day they crowded into my little cottage, each with a Koran under his arm. They were bent upon making a Moslem out of me! So we went to work with great zeal.

A few days later they brought me a pamphlet published by an Islamic propaganda society in India, to show me how to be a good Moslem. It said that Islam has four Holy books: the Torah, the laws of Moses; the Zabur, the psalms of David; the Kitab Injil, the gospel of Jesus Christ; and the Koran of Mohammed.

I sang the doxology under my breath. They had built a bridge across which I might some day be able to lead them to Christ! I said to them, "I have studied these first three books since I was a boy, and you have studied the Koran. We will exchange our knowledge!"

We began a search for more common ground. They brought me a book that said the Moslems believe Jesus was born of the Virgin Mary, but do not believe He was crucified! "When Jesus was praying in Gethsemane God looked at him and said, 'He never did anything wrong. It would not be just to allow him to die.' So God quickly snatched Jesus up to heaven. Then God came back and snapped his finger and made Judas look like Jesus. So they seized Judas and crucified him as he deserved. Even today Jesus Christ is sitting on a throne at the right hand of God, pleading with God to be merciful to us because we are ignorant. Jesus is our best friend in heaven!" Their book also said that in Medina there are four graves—one the grave of Mohammed, another of Fatima his daughter, the third that of Mohammed's greatest missionary, Omar, and the fourth grave is empty. They are saving it for Jesus, who they think will return to the world and reign for a thousand years and then be buried beside Mohammed.

I did not try immediately to correct their theology. For the time being, I was only too glad they had Jesus beside God, no matter how they got Him there.

I soon realized that I must have a more thorough knowledge of the Moro language, so I asked an American officer, Lieutenant Cramer, whether he knew any Moro whom I could trust to teach me. Cramer replied:

"There is a Moro here who was convicted of murder and sentenced to twenty years' imprisonment. I thought this sentence was too heavy, so I helped him appeal to the supreme court on a plea of self-defense.

I was dumb-founded when he was acquitted. Pambaya is now my loyal friend, and, if I recommend you to him, he will do anything you say."

So this man Pambaya, who so narrowly escaped spending twenty years in prison, became a close friend and was the strongest bulwark against all opposition. He helped us prepare our dictionary and translate thousands of pages into Maranaw, including the Gospel of Luke and the Book of Acts.

Donato Galia, a Filipino with an M.A. from Teachers College, Columbia University, came to Lanao with his wife to cooperate in our mission. He was a born educator and deserves much credit for the discoveries in literacy that were made that year.

Our murderer friend, Pambaya, began to teach Galia and myself the Maranaw language. Not a page of it had ever been printed. The priest knew Arabic letters, as did some of the *datos* (chiefs), but Arabic was too hard for most people. Galia and I adopted a Roman alphabet, one letter to a sound and only one sound to a letter—perfectly phonetic.

When we tried to write the words we heard, nobody could tell us where one word began and another ended! If I asked Pambaya, "What is the Maranaw word for 'go'?" he did not know. But if I asked how to say, "Where are you going?" he answered at once, *"Andakasoong."* By many trials and errors we discovered that *anda* was "where," *ka* was "you," and *soong* was "go"—"Where you go?" We had to make some hard decisions also about spelling. We decided to use *w* for *oo,* pronounced as in *two*. Then we always used *u* for the sound of *u* pronounced as in *cup*—never two sounds for the same letter.

In six weeks we had a box ten inches long filled with cards recording thirteen hundred words. The words were in the box but not in our heads! Galia learned much more quickly than I did and was talking to everybody in a few weeks. He was bright and besides he was born with a Filipino language, Visayan, in his mouth. All Filipino and Malay languages seem backwards to us Americans. Instead of "What have you?" they say, "What is had by you?" Instead of "Let me see it" they say, "I will be let by you to have it seen by me." It's easy in Maranaw when you get the knack of thinking in roundabout fashion!

After that night on Signal Hill, when God killed my racial prejudice and made me color-blind, it seemed as though He were working miracles at every turn. Galia and I became positively superstitious about it. We needed a schoolhouse. William MacSmith, the rough but big-hearted American merchant and liquor dealer, said: "Here is a building nobody is using. I reckon you can buy it for $250. The owner went back to God's country [he meant America, not heaven!]. But anyhow you can use it free while we find out what he wants for it."

Thus we had a huge building that had once been a dance hall and motion picture theater, for $250. Later we got MacSmith's store that had once been a saloon. We "converted" it into a church.

We prayed, "Lord, we are grateful for this big school building. But we need a printing press, too." A friend in Cagayan wrote us a letter: "You don't need a press, do you? We could sell two presses and lots of type, altogether worth about 3,000 pesos, for 250 pesos, and Silvino Abaniano, the printer, will come with it." Galia and I nearly wept as we read that letter. "God is working ahead of us," he whispered.

So I took the press and the printer to Lanao. "Where shall we put this press?" I asked Donato. "This old floor will not hold up a thousand-pound machine." We examined our big building and there we discovered a concrete base exactly the right shape and size! "Man," I said to Galia, "God put it here for us, twenty years ago!"

Silvino, the printer, began to set up the first page of Maranaw ever put into type. The Moros buzzed with excited curiosity. None of them could read their own language with our alphabet. When the *imams* (chief priests) saw the Roman letters they insisted that we must have Arabic type, which, they said, was the "holy" script of the Moslems. They had an idea that "Roman" type belonged to the Roman Catholic church—that types went with religions! So our teacher Pambaya wrote our newspaper out in Arabic for stencils that the superintendent of schools loaned us. We had Arabic text on one side of each sheet and Roman text on the other. We called it *The Story of Lanao*. Here is a translation of the opening paragraphs:

> This is the beginning of a story paper in the Moro language, to be distributed around the four sides of Lake Lanao. All Moros feel delighted because this paper is being started. The leading *datos* will furnish stories for the newspaper, telling of the famous ancestors of early days, and the events in Mecca and other important places.
>
> Our paper will also be helpful for business. It will tell the price of rice, corn, beans, various kinds of cloth and thread, of silk and woven hemp, of lumber, brass, silver and gold articles, and betel nuts.

At last the great day came when we were ready to distribute the first issue. I wrote my father all about it:

February 16, 1930

Tomorrow morning will be an important morning in the history of this province, I believe, for we are going to distribute our first paper. Personally, I am not very well pleased with its appearance. We tried to stencil on newsprint, and the ink came through so much that the printing on the other side is not clear. But the Moros who have seen the proof copies are as pleased as though it were bound in gold! They all prophesy that our paper will be a grand success. I hope so, for it involves enough labor to deserve results! We had first to find something they would like; then we had to put it into Maranaw in Roman letters, which has never been done before; then we had to have Pambaya write it in Arabic letters, and a priest had to decide whether it could be understood, and another priest copied it off on a stencil.

Now we have to teach everybody how to read the paper. No Moro but Pambaya can read the side with Roman letters. We have prepared a chart full of short sentences with very large letters. To make this the superintendent of schools loaned us his box of hand-printing letters. We did our best to teach some Moros these sentences but it hasn't worked well, so Galia and I have gone into a huddle to devise some better way. We revised and re-revised, and shortened and re-shortened our charts until there was nothing else we could think of to do. We asked the Moros to help us and tried out all the ideas that they submitted. They are helping us look for "key words" that will contain all their twelve consonants. They found some rather good "keys," but we are seeking better ones. We keep telling ourselves that this chart must be worked over like an automobile road, until every step is smooth and the grade so easy that the poorest car could slip along without getting stuck or even jolted. The teacher corresponds to the chauffeur. All he needs to do is to learn to keep the car on the road and to regulate his speed and the road will carry him through. This is our ideal.

Thus we were stumbling into the beginnings of a literacy campaign —although this was the farthest thing in the world from our intentions. Galia and I had come intending to start a teachers' normal school. We had never dreamed of teaching the ABC's to adults! But one of the lessons every missionary must learn is to be adaptable, to give up his cherished dreams, and do whatever he finds can be done. This crashing of our plans was harder on poor Galia than on me, for he had spent a year in Teachers College writing a thesis on a normal school for Moros!

But the doors opened so wide for a literacy campaign that neither Galia nor I had time to weep over shattered hopes.

One of these doors had been opened by General Pershing twenty-five years before when he gave a gold-headed cane to Dato Pandi-in, who ever after was a loyal friend to Americans. In 1941 I carried an ebony and ivory cane to General Pershing as a return gift from Dato Pandi-in. General Bullard opened another door. He studied the Koran until he knew it so well that he surprised the Moslem scholars. A terrible cholera epidemic was killing the Moros but no American soldiers were stricken. Bullard told a one-eyed Moro *hadji* (one who has made the pilgrimage to Mecca) named Kakairan that the water contained little devils, "just as the Koran said," and that the Americans roasted the little devils to death over a fire. The *hadji* took the secret back to his people, the cholera stopped, and America had made one more friend.

When, twenty-five years later, General Bullard's one-eyed friend, Hadji Kakairan, heard of our literacy campaign, he came over from Tamparan bringing his nephew, Gani Noor, whom he offered me as a teacher. Gani Noor became our first Moro literacy expert. How General Bullard's study of the Koran bore fruit is revealed in a letter written to my father during my first spring in Lanao:

May 14, 1930

I have just been having one of the most marvelous times of my life—with four Moros, my fine young teacher, Gani Noor, and three of his friends, one named Kakairan, a prominent *hadji*. They have been traveling over this province telling the people that I am the Moros' friend and will help them. One *hadji* asked me why I had come to help the Moros, so I told him:

"I have but one life to live. If I were to acquire a million pesos I could not take them with me to heaven. All we ever take with us to heaven is the gratitude of people we have helped; and I think the Moros need a friend at this time.

"You have been helping me in Lanao, for here I have learned that 'Moslem' means 'one who does the will of God in every smallest detail,' and since I have been here I have been trying harder than ever before in my life to keep God in my mind all day. Wherever I find a man like yourself who is trying to submit to the will of God, then he is my dearest friend. You and I shall be friends forever."

The *hadji* replied, "Although you may say you wish to learn about Islam from us, you tell us more about Islam than we have ever heard before."

To my amazement he shamelessly wiped tears from both his eyes with his sleeve. Then I came in for the most astounding bombardment of compliments that I have ever heard or hope to hear. There were too many for me to remember, but here are a few samples: "Your words are like luscious fruit, which make us want more. We hope that you will promise to live among us forever. We will write our friendship upon iron."

These people here need a friend, and that is why they talk like this.

The next day I was still full of open-eyed amazement as I wrote:

Such a marvelous morning that I have almost lost my breath! Gani Noor called together all the leading priests and sultans and *hadjis* and *datos* of Lanao. The governor came and made a welcoming speech. The program lasted for hours. I do not know exactly what they all thought, but I tried through Gani as interpreter to make them all understand that while I knew nothing much about Islam, I was anxious to do the will of God and believed God wanted me in Lanao. They all promised to study how to read and write and to bring their children and buy our newspaper.

Never, it seems to me, was there such evidence that God was doing nine-tenths of the work. Gani Noor seems to be the man God has been preparing for just this work.

During the long forenoon of speeches and questions from these leading Moros, I spent my time thinking of God. I felt that something would go wrong if I let up for a minute. As a result, this had been perhaps the most successful day in keeping God in mind since we began the experiment in March.

Gani Noor and I have nearly finished with the translation of the epic song (*darangan* is what the Moros call it) of the famous ancient Moro hero, Bantugan. Gani Noor tells me that this song is learned by heart by thousands of people. Indeed, in every home the mothers lull their children to sleep with it, and the old men sing it far into the night. At every fiesta and at every wedding, able reciters repeat this tale by the hour.

It is hard to preserve the original beauty in the translation. I am finding it especially difficult to throw into choice English the statement that "Bantugan expectorates a stream of red betel-nut juice." I cannot find any English word that makes this act seem noble; I fear it may detract from your sense of awe at the hero. If we all chewed tobacco or betel nut, we might feel differently. Perhaps I shall take the liberty of omitting the betel nut from the translation, for the rest of the poem possesses restrained dignity like the *Iliad* and *Odyssey*. It ends in a manner that would be a true and thrilling climax to a Moslem, but which I fear cannot be used by the public schools, for Bantugan triumphantly returns from a great fight bringing fifty wives with him! If this poem is to become literature in Christian lands, it will need a little expurgating—although we have never expurgated the scandal about Solomon's seven hundred wives.

When you realize that the unwritten lyric and epic poetry sung by the Moros would make thousands of printed pages, you see that this work of recording becomes highly important to them. It is also important to anthropology as the only survival of the ancient Filipino literature. When Spanish friars reached the Philippines, they stamped out with fire and sword all the folklore of the Filipinos—but they could not stamp out the Moros or their culture. That this Moro folklore is ancient is proved by its strange obsolete language and by the fact that the ideas go back to a period long before the Moslem religion reached the Philippines. The heroes worshipped the spirits of rocks, clouds, and crocodiles and never mentioned God or Mohammed. So we are at last bringing to light something that has been hidden in Lanao for perhaps a thousand years.

June 1, 1930

Six months since I came to Lanao! How fast time flies when one is busy! And I am busy! For now that the Moros have become fast friends, I have little time to myself. They are here morning, noon, and afternoon—fortunately not yet at night. They are afraid of ghosts, and Galia and I are careful not to change that belief!

This forenoon after church, when I wanted to sleep for a few minutes, there was a rap at my door and in walked three distinguished *gooros* (teachers of Islam), and with them three other men. They came, so they said, to pay me a visit on Sunday because all my time was taken during the week and they were afraid I was working too hard. It did not strike them as rather funny to come and awaken me from sleep in order to tell me that they were afraid I was overtired. But I saw the funny side of it, for they were so kindly about it.

I told these religious teachers, "I am trying a little experiment with myself today to see how many minutes I can keep my mind on God, and how many minutes I forget Him in spite of myself."

One of the *gooros* replied, "Any man who tries to remember God all the time is not only a good Moslem but he is like Mohammed himself, and when he dies he will be carried up to the seventh heaven."

Then he added what to me was the most pathetic word of all, "We never heard anybody talk like this before, and so we have decided to make you our leader in religion because you are always giving us the loveliest things in the Koran."

"I learned all these things from Jesus," I said. "Jesus and Mohammed agreed that we must do God's will."

"Yes," said the delighted *gooros,* "they said the very same words."

Does it not seem to you that we are getting somewhere when we can have the strong moral backing of all the leading priests and *datos* in Lanao, and can tell them that these ideals are the ideals that we learned from Jesus? Doesn't this justify the method of approach we are trying?

Just at noon today a Moro from Togaya—where all the fighting has taken place during the past few weeks—came to ask us to establish a school there so that the people might learn good customs and stop fighting. Then, to my great surprise, he produced a New Testament and said he wanted to study it and that he wanted to have a copy in Maranaw. I promised that some day we would print it, and now we must make good.

Excerpts from letters written during the following year reveal the new problems that were arising and give the high points of our progress. I have not attempted to give their respective dates, for they form a running narrative of events.

Our problem is now going to be to print enough literature in Maranaw to keep up with the demand. This week a man came and asked whether the next issue of our magazine was out, and when I offered him a back number he said proudly, "I have read all the old ones and everything else your press has printed in our language." Is there another press in the world that can boast that anybody has read everything it has turned out? Here, many Moros have done so. But that is not saying very much, for our total output to date is about twenty pages!

When one sees the vile trash that appears in some of the books and magazines in English that reach these outposts of civilization, one feels sure we can make better Moros out of those who never learn to read English than out of those who acquire a taste for this low reading. So perhaps we may be able to mold this Moro nation far more than we realize through the pages we shall print and circulate among the people.

Two Moros just came in to show me how they are learning to read. Very, very slowly but correctly one read a paragraph; perhaps in another month he will attain fair speed. He has passed the first, and hardest, achievement, for he knows that letters can be so pronounced together that they form themselves into words and convey the ideas that he wants to express.

During the past months we have devised a system that is so easy that the brightest Moros can repeat every letter within ten minutes. We start with three words that contain all the consonants used in the Maranaw language. These three words are as familiar to them as "mother," "hand," and "work" are to us.

They are *Malabanga,* name of a town in Lanao; *ḳaratasa,* paper; *paganada,* study or learn. We cut the words up like this: *ma la ba nga, ḳa ra ta sa, pa ga na da.*

Then we begin with *ma ma,* which means man; *a ma,* which means father; *ma la,* which means big, and so on. The combination of these

a	ma	la	ba	nga
i	mi	li	bi	ngi
o	mo	lo	bo	ngo
u	mu	lu	bu	ngu

ma ma man	a ma father	la la to pat	a la God	ma la large	la ma yard
mi mi girl	a mi our	li li name	a li name	li ma hand	li o outside
mo mo chewed	a mo monkey	lo lo dull	a lo hello	ma lo pretty	o lo head
ba ba short	ba ba i woman	la ba profit	ba la pair	ba li a receipt	ba lo clang
bi bi duck	bi ba i push	la bi more	i bi itch	o bi a vegetable	lo bi cocoanut
bo bo to pour	ba bo aunt	la bo prefer	bo la ball	bu la wide	bu l smoke
nga nga open mouth	ba nga island	bo nga fruit	lu nga plural	ma nga a fly	o nga fruit
ngi ngi corner of mouth	la ngi wait	li ngi to turn	lu ngi allow	lu ma smooth	lu mi make flat

FIRST MARANAW READING CHART (LESSON 1)

consonants with the other vowels in the language is a simple additional step. Learning to read from the chart [p. 35] is so easy that the most stupid person can do it. And they love it so much they hardly give us time to eat.

It is like a miracle for a man who never knew a letter to walk out of our school in an hour able to read a whole page of his own language with Roman letters. We see that miracle happen over and over, every day. But the joy of seeing people learning ten times as fast as they expected to learn and all set up about their own brilliance does not lose its edge.

Mr. Galia says that he taught nine Moros to read in a half hour. That is better than any record that I have thus far made with a large group. A half dozen Moros interrupted this letter. They came in and said they could not wait until tomorrow but had to be taught right away! They had only an hour to spare and wanted all the education they could get in that time. So I have stopped this letter to teach them. While I concentrated on one of them, the rest listened. They have just left the house. I do not expect you to believe me, but here is the fact: this man had finished reading three pages of our newspaper, and could read everything I put before him with fair speed. One hour! Every time that happens I feel as though a miracle had happened. It is possible only because these people are hungry mentally and spiritually.

Nine-tenths of our job is sitting close beside the people who flock to us and getting thrills of delight with them as they emerge from ignorance. Just this morning we drove forty kilometers, stopping to teach crowds of Moros and to distribute the newest chart. The speed with which the people learned was even more astonishing to them than it was to me, for they had not had opportunity to see the thing happen before.

Yesterday an old *hadji* came to see me, and though he thought he was too old to learn to read a new way, we assured him that it was easy and he started. We kept him roaring with laughter and in fifteen minutes he knew every letter and could read. A letter a minute! When he went up the road he was still laughing and reading. This sounds incredible, yet we are doing it daily. Fifteen minutes is the time we expect a bright man who knows Arabic letters to require to learn to read Roman letters. Those who never knew how to read anything before require from an hour to a week.

One of the outlaws (I had better not name him for he's now my friend) came at five in the evening and I taught him in a half hour. He was unusually bright and very much pleased with himself, and I praised him and told him I wanted him to be a teacher in his village. When we had finished he took me over where nobody else could hear us and said, "You taught me to read, and you are the best friend I have in the world. I want to do something for you. Is there anybody in Lanao you want me to put out of the way?" I said, "No, thank you, brother. But you are certainly a very big-hearted man. Go home and teach others and that will make me happy."

I have been trying to teach a boy to read this afternoon, but his mind was so slow the task seemed like pouring water into a mosquito net. I often wonder when I am working with a stupid man whether he is worth all this effort. But then when that same man fondly runs his fingers through my hair and fairly beams with gratitude while he calls me "good uncle," I know that a little love is created. If, as we believe, this entire universe is a desperate attempt of love to incarnate itself, then "important duties" that cut us off from helping little people are not duties but sins.

On market day twice a week, I stand from seven to twelve before a chart in the market place while people crowd around trying to get near enough to learn to read, always threatening to push me off my stool in their eagerness to be next. I do not see how my teachers get time to record the names of their students; I seldom do.

As I finished breakfast about six-thirty and arose from the table there came a knock at the door. I turned the knob and there crowded into my little house sultans and *hadjis* and *datos;* sixty tried to get in, but some had to stay outside for want of room. They had hired a launch and had come twenty miles to be examined, for they had learned to read Moro with English letters. We marched down the road a mile to our school, and there we spent the whole forenoon in joyously throwing compliments at one another. Everybody in the province seems caught up with the same gladness. They think the whole world will be surprised at their achievement, and I think they are right! This thing may have had parallels, but I have neither seen them nor heard of them. On our school wall is a motto: "In five years, Lanao the most literate province in the Philippines." These men declared, "Less than five years, much less!"

But there is a price to pay for all this—one cannot get any time alone. Three men, very intimate friends and splendid workers, have just been here and in spite of my hints and insistences that I needed to work, they stayed a long time. One of them is writing a letter about our campaign to the President of the United States at this moment; and he did not relent until we promised to translate it into English and send it to President Hoover.

Any executive will say, "You ought to organize your time and have it understood that visitors are welcome only at certain hours." Something, at least, must be done about it; but not something that will nip our tender promising plant in the bud. What a beautiful frail thing it is!

The Moros know that we love them, but they do not realize what a gulf —at least historically—separates us. If they did, would they be so affectionate? Yes, if they knew all, if they knew the love of God in all its wondrous fervor, they would!

And to think that less than a year ago we were writing about "the most difficult place under the American flag, if not in the world!"

I think now that America is the most difficult place in the world, for there you demand ability, unusual ability, while here in Lanao they demand only love.

It is the end of a day as nearly perfect as any I have ever seen, and so I write about it at once. It has been exasperatingly busy, for Moros have come to the house from early morning to dark. They were all so loving and grateful that I think I never saw anything like it before in the whole world. As darkness approached, I sent them home, telling them I must walk off alone. As I climbed Signal Hill, God began to use my tongue to speak to me:

"My child you have at last struck your pace. Here in Lanao you will accomplish something with me for the human race. You will broaden the circle of their minds, which is good, and you will help them to a new comradeship with me, which is the most wonderful thing that can happen to any man. This very minute, while you are walking with me and listening to me, you are doing the last highest thing a human being can ever do. You must not fret because you have not done more in your life. Only live close to me minute by minute as you have done so much of the day today, and what you *are* will speak. You need not worry about what you do, but only what you are. And what you are depends upon whether you *are holding on to me.*"

The Moros come and watch our Sunday services with ever-increasing interest and appreciation. To our great delight we have found that they like Jesus. It is Christians they hate because Christians have mistreated and misunderstood them. They love Jesus and claim Him for their own. So we are going to try to write a series of tracts on "Jesus as a Good Friend," to be distributed in Maranaw in the market place. If we can untangle Christ from the terrible handicap of Christendom, which has kept so many millions from Him, we will be doing the Moros a priceless service.

When we came here in 1915 for the first time, we heard an officer say that the only good Moro was a dead one, and I have heard this very statement repeated by government officials this year. Perhaps the only good Moros they come in contact with are dead ones, but our program has attracted a group of young men who in my estimation are as big-hearted and as splendid as any young men you could find in any country. My heart is all bound up with them. I never had friends whom I felt I could rely upon to be more loyal and who understood my own motives better than these Moros. Neither they nor I feel that the boundary of religion or race can keep us apart.

A swift, wonderful year has gone by [I wrote in January, 1931], and yet it would not be counted much of a success in many mission circles. There has not as yet been a single baptism of a Moro. They do not even know that baptism is our custom.

On the other hand, we can claim one victory. Almost 100 per cent of the Moros are now our friends. It has been encouraging, too, to hear so many visitors in Lanao say, "This is what I call true missionary work!"

Some months ago the Sultan of Samoi collected over a thousand signatures of prominent *datos* and sent them along with a beautiful silver box to hold betel-nuts to Mayor Charles G. Phillips of Montclair, New Jersey. Today Mayor Phillips' reply arrived. I showed it to the men who are helping us make a dictionary, and they were so delighted they could not sit still. Mayor Phillips had pictured "a university to be established at your capital—an institution where boys and girls from all over the island might come for intellectual training, and then go back as teachers to their own localities." These men kept saying, "My goodness, that is just the thing. Just think what that would do for Lanao."

Sheik Bogabong, the very highest scholar of all the Moros, came this morning and this afternoon, followed by his retinue, to help us and to discuss religious problems. He is so genuine and friendly and so interested in the quest for God, which means everything to me, that I enjoyed the conversations greatly.

He said that the chief difference between Islam and Christianity was that the Moslem can pray anywhere, while Christians have to go to church! One of my fellow workers objected to this, and said that I prayed on top of Signal Hill at sunset. Sheik Bogabong replied, "That is just where Mohammed and Jesus liked to pray best—on a hilltop!" Then Campong, my helper, said, "Ah, the Bible and the Koran are much alike on the question of prayer."

Yesterday Effa and I went with Lieutenant Alviola and his wife to Ramain and visited a number of homes. Abolais, the teacher, had a *ba-i* or princess from the royal family read for us in each house. They all could read rapidly and beautifully. It was market day in Ramain and men were learning to read all about the market. Hundreds of men and about fifty women have learned to read here in the past two months.

We all wanted to know how Abolais had secured such a stampede of Ramain ladies to learn to read, so he told us his secret. He had a handsome young man write a love lyric to one of the young ladies who had already learned, telling her that her education made her the most charming lady in Lanao. She read the love song to the other young ladies, and the scramble to learn to read was on—a perfect illustration of the use of love as an educational instrument! When we told the other teachers how Abolais did it, they all declared they would adopt the same method and now we have to print a love lyric every week in *Lanao Progress*.

In the whole province 600 Maranaw women and girls have thus far been reported as having learned to read. Every week some high *dato* brings his daughter and asks us to keep her in our school, which we are not yet equipped to do. You see what a wonderful opportunity is opening here.

We now have twenty literacy teachers, most of them high school students and some of them graduates, scattered through the main districts. Their average pay is $10 a month. Besides these twenty who are in the employ of the *madrasa,* as our folk school is called, there are at least fifty others who are doing more or less regular teaching without pay. They reported having taught 930 this month, which is at the rate of 11,160 a year.

We have just come home from high adventure in Togaya, the home of notorious outlaws. It is our first visit since the soldiers destroyed their stone fort. Mr. McKinley, who was with us, tried to become friendly with one *imam* but received only black looks in return. This man was probably a close friend of the outlaws. As soon as we pulled out our lesson sheets there was a buzz of excitement. The old *imam* suddenly became friendly and said he had heard of the "American *madrasa*." Every person in the party was soon surrounded by a crowd of Moros, all of them learning to read. When you consider that they burned down the only school they ever had, ten years ago, you can see what this new doorway to civilization may mean to them.

Campong Basman said, as we were leaving Togaya, "Our poor Moro people do not know in which direction to go and are in need of leaders. They follow anybody who knows what to do."

Campong is a keen-minded young Moro who graduated from Muños Agricultural College and began to teach, but was dismissed from the bureau of education for carrying firearms without a license. He is a tireless worker and a high-grade translator. He has just completed the translation of a little booklet on the care of babies, and has translated about a hundred pages of the Old Testament. From our pulpit on Sunday morning, he has been reading the stories of the Prophets to the Moros.

The Christian Endeavor meeting is just out. Down the street tonight goes somebody singing and whistling, "Out of the darkness into the light, Jesus, I come, Jesus, I come." It sounds like Campong Basman. Though still a Moslem, he takes a leading part in Christian Endeavor every week.

I think we could have imposing statistics in the way of church membership this year, but if we did so we might sacrifice the wonderful good will that now exists toward our enterprise. If we can be of great service to the Moros during the next four or five years educationally, medically, and in other ways, then they will think of our Christianity in terms of loving service rather than in terms of doctrine. Hitherto, Christians have seemed chiefly enemies of Mohammed and Islam. We do not want to be thought of as enemies of any other religion, but as lovers of all men.

Last Sunday was a turning point for our church here. We abandoned our room at the military camp and went to the Moro school in Dansalan to hold our Christian services. The windows were all filled with Moros listening to the service from start to finish. I spent a couple of minutes preaching to the Moros in their own language. What I said was about as follows:

"Friends, we use a different language and worship with somewhat different forms, but we worship the same God. These songs that we sing today could all be sung by you with as much earnestness as they are sung by us. The story of Joseph, which we read, is well known to you, for Joseph is one of your great prophets. Come in and worship with us if you wish. We call you our dear friends."

The life of the pioneer missionary can be thrilling! Never did I enjoy any other work as I do this. It is literally true that the missionaries on the very front lines are the ones who are getting the greatest fun out of their experiences. If anybody is going to be a missionary, let him plunge into the farthest frontiers. Never pity Livingstone again. Envy him, loneliness, malaria, and all!

Livingstone never had an experience like mine yesterday! We have five automobiles in Dansalan now, great curiosities to the people across the lake, where there are neither roads nor autos. Kakai (pronounced Cockeye) Dagalangit brought six of his thirteen wives, with their daughters and maid-servants, yesterday to see our auto and beg for a ride. So fourteen queens and princesses piled into our Ford, two or three deep, every princess saturated with perfume from Cairo. They giggled incessantly until we reached the corkscrew road down the mountain, when some of them began to get sick. A few got out, two leaned out, and one leaned on my shoulder. I did not hesitate for an instant to turn homeward, for there was a hole in one tire and I trembled for it every minute. Think of fourteen sick royal ladies, a flat tire, and no spare! Harems have lost their glamour.

Everywhere I turn I see people teaching each other to read, or else reading the papers that we have printed.

We have doubled our force of Moro typesetters, all inexperienced but eaten up with zeal. They are putting forced draught on our printing presses —we bought another old press—so that we may catch up with the rising demand for literature.

Yesterday a young man came and said, "We have now read everything you have printed. Are you finished with a new issue of the paper?"

"Not until next Monday."

He began to walk the floor in consternation as he said, "What will the young ladies do? They will be discouraged if they have nothing to read. They will finish this paper in a day. Then what?"

Then what! That is the question we are now trying to solve!

Lieutenant Carlton of the U. S. Army and Mrs. Carlton have been visiting Lanao for a week. They were deeply interested in our program and spent a long while watching us teach the Moros to read. They watched us make these large charts by hand, since of course our presses are too small for them. The day before they left, Lieutenant Carlton said, "Mrs. Carlton and I have noticed how much you need more charts, and how slow the present process is. If you will give us a sample of just what you want, we will make them on better paper than you have so that they will last longer; we will send you one thousand."

I visualized what it meant in an instant—a large lovely chart in every chieftain's house—and was so happy I felt stunned.

"Lieutenant," I said, "this means that we shall win! This will be the most literate province in the Philippines in five years—and perhaps the most literate in Asia." So every day has new wonders; God *is* doing this.

Before I opened my front door this morning I heard some men outside. One was a *dato* from Waw, a distant corner of the province. He said, "We have no public school in our district. The people are all ignorant, not even one man who can teach the rest of us. We want you to send us a teacher."

"There is no money to send you a teacher," I replied. "But Mr. Presidente (he was the mayor of his town), suppose you learn right now and go back and teach the people yourself."

So he went at it and in an hour he could read—slowly, it is true, but perfectly. Then he started in to learn to write. We teach them to print their letters, so they are easy to learn. He went away with a large, brilliantly decorated chart in his hand, a diploma under his arm, and a broad grin on his face. "I graduated from the *Madrasa* yesterday," he will say when he gets home. "Now I am your teacher."

This morning early a group of *datos* came to give us land. They wanted us to have a beautifully situated piece of land, which we had regarded as the most desirable in Dansalan, for a Moro girls' dormitory and school. They told me that they absolutely would not sell it to anybody else for it was too precious, but for our school they wanted to give it without a cent. And they were so excited about it that one of them said, "If anybody else ever tries to build a house on that land, we will murder him!"—and they meant it. These fellows have pretty tough ways with their enemies, but what marvelous friends they can be! The wife of one owner crowded up and cried in a high voice, "I told my husband if he did not give that property to you, I would cut his throat while he was asleep." The husband smiled proudly. It was his wife's gentle hint that she agreed with him entirely.

The financial situation in America has hit some of our supporters so hard that I shall have to cut my budget to less than one-half. I have gone over our meager resources and looked for money until I am about sick, but will have to drop twelve of our staff and cut the salaries of all the rest. This will reduce our total budget by $100 a month. I have worked over these names a hundred different ways to make the operation as painless as possible—they are such splendid, loyal fellows. Tomorrow they must be told; it will be a very critical day. If I fail in tact and wisdom everything may smash up, or worse. When one has a painful job like this to face, one needs to be alone. I am really scared about that meeting, and feel like a cur after all those boys have done.

I am so keyed up this evening that I cannot relax. It has been a wonderful and a terrible day. I have had nothing in all my life like it.

I tried to prepare our teachers for the shock by giving them the Friendship treasure chests filled with school supplies that were sent from the children in America. Then I told the teachers to write letters to those who sent the chests, explaining our terrible dilemma and the necessity of cutting our expenses in half. They all promised to write.

Then we heard the reports of their literacy work. Man alive, some of them made me weep! I know from experience what labor is involved in teaching fifty, sixty, eighty people, one by one, how to read. One man, Santos Gangawa, taught forty-one women and seventy-one men to read during this one month. How the crowd applauded his description! Something in my eyes would not behave, and all over that room I felt the same deep emotion almost ready to break out. The room became tense and silent as man after man came forward with his magnificent achievement for the salvation of his province.

I felt swept on by a power that I could neither explain nor control. I was a little part of it, and so were all the others. I know it was the spirit of God in a strange new form. At last the names of all who had learned to read were counted and there were 1,521, over 300 of them women. Then fifty-one young men arose and volunteered to be teachers, making 110 volunteers in all. I felt as though I were passing through an incredible dream. Somebody moved that we have a gigantic fiesta, and the sultans and *datos* who crowded that room voted with a mighty roar that a month from today Dansalan is to see such a fiesta as was never seen here in Lanao. And all that amazing morning a tragic secret was in my breast and I was afraid.

Then came the terrible afternoon. I had to call in the paid teachers and tell them one by one that I could not pay them any longer. These same magnificent fellows that had felt such a thrill in the morning had to hear that my money was exhausted. I told them the truth, that it would be much easier to jump in the lake than to face them with this news. I expected some of them, at least, to go into a rage, but they saw that I was suffering and so they rose to it like men. Some of them hung their heads and turned pale, but not a man showed any resentment. Because they saw how sick I was about it myself I think they learned a new sympathy, and we are better friends because of the things we are suffering together.

Kakai Dagalangit, a tall chieftain with fierce black eyes, stood up. He has thirteen wives and all he has to do is to look at them and they behave. He looked at me with those fierce eyes and said, "This campaign shall not stop. It's Lanao's only hope." Then he looked at those teachers with his fierce eyes and said, "I'll make everybody who knows how to read teach somebody else, or I'll kill him."

Everybody taught. Nobody died. Everybody liked it. I did not like the motto "teach or die" and so changed it to "Each One Teach One," and this method, started by the Moro chieftain, has gone around the world.

CHAPTER 3

1930-34: THE "EACH ONE TEACH ONE" IDEA SPREADS

In the ten years following the opening of the Lanao station the attitude of the Moros toward Christianity swung from one pole to the other. It was unmitigated hatred when we arrived; love, good will, and cooperation when we departed. As one after another of the younger generation was baptized during the last two years not a word of opposition reached our ears. The members of our church were trying to keep God in their thoughts every minute of the day so that, as they said, "the Moros will see Christ in us." This was why we developed the "Game with Minutes," which is our adaptation of Brother Lawrence's effort to practise the presence of God all day long. The daughter of the Sultan, who was attending our girls' school, said openly that she was going to be baptized. The Sultan himself had too many wives to become a Christian, but he always came and had his picture taken right in the center of our church photographs.

The beginning of this Lanao transformation had repercussions in other parts of the Philippines almost from the first. In 1930 the pastors of the United Evangelical Church of the Philippines came to Dansalan for a retreat to pray and plan. Before they left they made a Cebuan chart, like our Maranaw chart, and just as easy to learn. Our printer, Silvino Abaniano, himself a Cebuano, worked night and day to print the new chart so that every preacher could take a supply home with him. These preachers went away in high spirits and started literacy campaigns in other parts of Mindanao and in the central Philippines.

Then came one of those miraculous interventions that make me sure God is working for the forgotten illiterates. It happened (or did it just happen?) that my old friend Dr. Sidney L. Gulick, of the Committee on World Friendship among Children in New York, thinking I still lived in Manila, appointed me American representative to help distribute the 28,000 beautiful Friendship treasure chests sent by the children of America to the children of the Philippines. This was the third and last of Dr. Gulick's great friendly gift adventures. The first, in 1926-27, was when American children sent thousands of dolls to Japan. These were distributed in nearly every village in Japan amid a great wave of pro-Americanism. The second, in 1928-29, a shower of schoolbags from the children of America to the children of Mexico, had great influence in counteracting the Mexican's dislike for Yankee *gringos*. The Friendship chests for the Philippine children were very attractive. They were of metal, decorated with pictures of Washington, Rizal, Columbus, Magellan, gods of the sea, and maps of the world, in imitation of ancient Spanish treasure chests. Inside they were crammed with a variety of articles that the children of America had thought would please the children of the Philippines.

At the end of 1930 I spent ten days in Manila helping direct the formal reception of the chests and the great celebration before Rizal's monument on the Luneta. This responsibility brought me into contact with many officials from the governor-general to the director of education. All of them were interested in literacy.

It was while I was in Manila that Mr. E. K. Higdon, then secretary of the National Christian Council, arranged for me to make an exploratory literacy expedition through the northern Philippines. So the following October found me again aboard ship on the way from Mindanao to Manila. In the midst of a storm—and with everybody seasick!—I tried to write my father about the start of my voyage:

October 18, 1931

I am on my way to the northern part of the Philippines to help prepare lessons like those we made for the Moros in several Filipino dialects.

We are now out from behind the shelter of Mindanao and the waves are becoming uncomfortable. A sudden storm has struck us. Bump, rattle, bang go the doors. Good-by until it is over.

Three hours later: The tables are tied against the wall. The floor is streaked with rain, which is driving through the closed windows. At this moment a window was shaken loose with a loud clatter. There goes the hardest shock we have had yet. I wonder how much water poured into the lower deck of this little steamer.

Mindanao Sea is an ugly piece of water, because storms like this pile up against the tidal currents that pour in from the Pacific Ocean to the China Sea.

The wind howls worse every minute. I wonder whether the hearts of all the passengers are behaving as strangely as mine. I am reminded of Bob's remark after he was in an airplane: "I wasn't scared, but my stomach was." I wonder whom I shall see first in heaven if this ship capsizes or goes down. I read somewhere that if one prays for others he can forget himself. Can I pray for all the passengers on this ship while we toss about on this enraged sea?

Yes! It works! Praying for others has brought my heart back to its normal beat again. There goes a wave clear over the ship, but I have not stopped praying for the Filipinos and my heart behaves perfectly.

The captain has surrendered to the storm and is trying to keep it on our stern. We must be going at a terrific rate, yet the spray blows over the ship from stern to stem each time we pitch up, down, up.

Two hours later: Behind Siquijor Island—safe, and almost calm.

When we reached Manila, there on the dock was the energetic Mr. Higdon, who hurried me to Union Seminary, to the university, to the bureau of education, and to the newspaper reporters. The report went over Manila that we could teach people to read in a day—some said an hour; and an article entitled "Lightning Literacy" appeared in the best journal in the islands. It was a month before I had time to do any writing. Paragraphs from my next two letters to my father reveal what had been accomplished:

To date we have completed charts in nine languages—Visayan, Tagalog, Ibanag, Ilocano, Gaddang, Isinay, Pampangan, Pangasinan, and Bicol. It is proving easier than we had feared to find the key words for each of these languages. We have trained 150 young people to teach and have given them certificates.

A young Kalinga at the American Bible Society helped prepare a chart in his dialect. The Kalinga tribe lives in the northernmost mountains of Luzon. My curiosity was excited by the striking differences between Kalinga and all other Philippine dialects. It has no *r* as the others have; also, unlike the others, it does have the letter *j*. Governor Early, who lived among them for several years, has an explanation. He says that an ancient colony of Japanese was driven into the mountains and intermingled with the natives, introducing Japanese sounds. Certainly their features bear more resemblance to those of the Japanese than do those of any of their neighbors.

We are taking steps to teach illiterates in the leper colony on Culion Island. This will bring the Bible, and thus comfort and enrichment of life, to those pitiful unfortunates—there are six thousand of them—who are least able to care for themselves.

During this tour I felt more strongly than ever that we could sweep the world with this scheme of key-word teaching if it were not for one obstacle—the spelling of the English language! If we spelled English phonetically, American children could be taught to read in a week. We needed only a day with the Philippine dialects. I can see only one thing to do—start a strike against the way English is misspelled—become a spelling Bolshevist! I suppose that unless we revolt we shall be handing on this same accursed orthography to our children, and our children's children, to the crack of doom.

Back in Lanao, in the meantime, larger and larger numbers of Moros had been learning to read. We made a "literacy thermometer" to place on our school wall. It was ten feet high and recorded percentages from zero to one hundred. The left side showed the literacy percentages of the leading nations of the world; the right side, where Lanao stood each month. In 1931 the "mercury"—red paint!—showed a literacy of 20 per cent. It had grown steadily since our campaign had begun in January 1930, when we estimated the literacy of Lanao to be 4 per cent. A year later it had risen to 8 per cent, and during 1931 it increased at the rate of 1 per cent a month.

Several of the little boys became as expert in teaching as any of the men, and we could not refuse them certificates when their work was perfect. Besides, they were favorites with the women, who were timid about allowing any men except their husbands to teach them. Hundreds of women in all parts of the province were being taught by small boys, while thousands more were learning to read from other women. We knew that we could not get 100 per cent of the men unless we got 100 per cent of the women.

I have never found such genuinely grateful people as the Moros. We lived under a spell of continuous benediction. Nor have I ever felt so utterly safe in my life. I knew that if anybody tried to harm us, he would first have to deal with a hundred thousand Moros. They have qualities of fidelity and independence that every American honors. I am frank to confess that I lost my heart to the Moros.

Every Friday, in the Moslem mosques, Pambaya (now a *hadji*) preached the ideals that he learned in our mission. He told the Moros that God expected them to be honest; that it was God's will for every man to forget his own selfish interests and devote his life to serving his fellow man. The *hadji* returned from the mosque one day and told me that he had been pleading with the Moros to resist the idea of opening a cabaret, as some had planned to do. "We must not adopt everything we see in Western countries," he told them, "for many things there are bad. Though they call themselves Christian, some Western countries do not follow the teachings of Nabi Isa (Jesus). The Protestant mission is opposed to the cabaret. We are not going to admit that our religion does not have ideals as high as the ideals of these missionaries, are we?"

In the spring of 1932 I was filled with joy by the arrival of a staunch Moro Christian, and I wrote my father of what it would mean for our work!

March 13, 1932

The Moro Christian from Jolo, Matias Cuadra, whose story, you will remember, is in *Seven Thousand Emeralds,* is here with his family. He has come to work with us! Today he preached his first sermon. The church—the one that was once a saloon—was crowded, with more Moslems than Christians. Matias produced a profound impression as he talked about "Youth Movements Around the World." He made the babies cry with his mighty shout, while the rest of the audience gasped and trembled. As I sit tonight I can remember nearly every word he said—sure proof that he said it well.

The first day Matias arrived he began to mix with the people of the town. To the delight of the *hadjis,* he talked with them in Malayan, which is almost as sacred to them as Arabic. Mrs. Cuadra has a sweet voice, and is teaching the Moros Christian tunes. The new day has dawned for Lanao, and we are unutterably grateful.

Another very important event took place that spring. The new governor-general of the Philippines, Theodore Roosevelt, Jr., visited

Lanao and made a lasting impression upon the Moros and upon our school.

We went down to Iligan to meet him as he came in on the boat. Fine arches had been erected over the entrance to the dock, and the people of Iligan presented him with the "key to the city." He lived up to all their highest expectations for cordiality, making them feel that he was really glad to meet each person who came to shake hands with him. When he was given the key, he made a short but telling address.

The following day Mr. Roosevelt came to our school in Dansalan intending to stay only a few minutes, but he stayed half an hour. He showed deep interest and made some very helpful suggestions. He was enthusiastic about the eighteen Societies of Educated Youth that we had organized around Lake Lanao, and listened attentively while some of these young Moros told him that they were meeting every week to answer the question, "How can we help our town, our province, our country, and the world?"

"This is not mere theory," they told him. "We have found thirty needs in our province and we have set our shoulders with all our power to meet these needs. Each of us has charts in his home and has promised to teach as many people as he can. We are distributing seeds around the four parts of Lanao. We are showing people how to keep well. We are encouraging people to send their children to school. Hitherto we have thought the only use of education was to become a clerk or errand boy in a government office, but we have discovered so many ways to be useful to humanity that we are intoxicated with enthusiasm."

Their eyes flashed and their voices had a new ring. These boys were dreaming dreams far beyond the borders of Lanao. They were tingling with eagerness to do something for all the world. One day I had read to them from Professor Fleming's book, *Marks of a World Christian,* that "two out of three inhabitants of our globe have still to be taught to read and write. The United States may send its hundreds of teachers to the Philippines and make those islands a world model for educational progress, but there are a billion more who need this help."

"Boys," I had burst forth, "you and I are in the biggest undertaking we ever heard of. This book says that two-thirds of the people of the world cannot yet read. Let's start a world campaign! Tell the literacy teachers I'll have my eye on them and very likely some may be called to foreign countries to establish literacy campaigns like ours. Write to the *datos* and tell them that I believe that a world literacy movement is beginning in Lanao and I am on fire with the idea."

The boys had caught fire, too. We started at once to see what improvements we could make in our chart and in our methods of teaching. When we finished there was roaring in my ears the assurance that we were going to arouse the enthusiasm of many leaders in this literacy enterprise, and that it would sweep around the world.

We had made a large map of the world, with Dansalan, Lanao, Mindanao, in the very center. Whenever a letter came from some other part of the world, we would stick on a bright red silk thread running from that country to Lanao Province. The *datos* would come and ask what the threads meant, and while we explained to them, they would cluck their tongues and say, "See how important we are becoming all over the world! We'll certainly have to go and help those other people." How their eyes popped when Governor-General Roosevelt studied that map and asked me to send charts of Moro lessons to Puerto Rico, where he had been governor-general before coming to the Philippines.

At one of our meetings, called to enable the young men to explain to the *datos* about our dream of helping the world, Kakai Dagalangit stood up and said, "If we are going to do that for the world, we will first have to change our name. People think that Moros do nothing but murder and steal and spit betel nut. But now we have stopped being foolish and are getting educated. Why, most of us can read already! Please go to Manila and ask Governor-General Roosevelt to change our name. Tell him to call us 'Islam,' for that means we are trying to do the will of God."

Some of our young men wanted to be baptized, but we were leaning over backward in that respect to avoid fanatical opposition. So far we had baptized only one Moro boy and two Moro girls. We had achieved something, however, that should not be underestimated. There was a new friendliness toward our religious services so marked that the Moros came and watched us worship with open sympathy. I returned their visits by accepting their invitations to worship with them in their mosques every Friday noon. And after the prayers were finished, we would sit around in a circle in the center of the mosque, talking about the prophets and Nabi Isa Rokola (Jesus Christ)—ours and theirs!

In the autumn of 1932 I was off on another tour to the north, to the island of Luzon—a journey that lasted until almost Christmas. Early in my travels Mrs. Josefa Jara Martinez, one of those wonderful Protestant Filipina leaders, took me to Welfareville, where she conducted government homes for delinquent minors, orphans, and destitute aged. I trained about twenty teachers, and later they sent me a splendid letter, pledging themselves to teach four illiterate inmates each before I returned in two weeks' time.

At the invitation of Colonel Santos, director of prisons, I went with Dr. George William Wright to Bilibid Prison in Manila, where a large majority of the prisoners were unable to read or write. The director said the prison needed to teach literacy because it would give the prisoners mental occupation and make them better citizens when they were discharged. I stayed there over seven hours—my longest prison sentence to date!—and trained about forty prisoners, most of them Moros, to teach. One prisoner told me, "Half the murders in the Philippines are committed by your Moro friends!"

At the church in Cavite, I taught a servant girl to read, and the next day she taught the entire chart beautifully to another servant, in front of some thirty people. She was so overcome with joy that she wiped the tears from her eyes with her red handkerchief as she taught. The women who watched her wept, and the men turned their backs or bowed their heads and blew their noses. When the girl finished teaching, the pastor asked us to sing "Praise God from whom all blessings flow," and the meeting turned into a service of thanksgiving. Thereafter Pastor Cruz held literacy classes in that church at five every afternoon and evangelistic campaigns at night. "My little army," he boasted, "will teach 500 persons within the next year. You'll see!"

We had developed a splendid chart in the Ilocano dialect. The three key words we selected were: *carabasa*—"calabash" (squash); *mangalata*—"let us take it"; and *nagapada*—"they had a fight." We associated the three words with this story: "Two boys found a 'squash' and said, 'Let us take it'; but 'they had a fight.'" On the chart were pictures of (1) a calabash, (2) two boys running, and (3) pulling each other's hair. Everywere we traveled in northern Luzon people shouted, *"Carabasa! Mangalata! Nagapada!"* And we shouted back, *"Wen apo!"* which literally is "Yes, sir!" but has the flavor of "Oh, boy, you've said it!"

In Bangued, the capital of the province of Abra, the *presidente* was an ex-teacher and deeply interested in literacy. He himself learned our method, then he required his secretary, his clerks, his councilors, the captain of his constabulary, and a number of his lieutenants to learn. I taught practically all the government employees in the town. A map of Bangued with every house drawn in was prepared and hung on the wall of the big, dirty, old *municipio*. The *presidente* and his force, together with the constabulary, planned to visit all the homes, recording the number of male and female illiterates in each house, and then to send teachers to teach in every home. A gold star was to be pasted on each house that became 100 per cent literate.

At Lagangilang Agricultural School in Abra my heart went out especially to two boys of the primitive Apayao tribe of northern Luzon. They had black tattoos covering their bodies and wore bright red G-strings—a tribal custom. The boys were so eager to learn to teach their people that they would not let me go to lunch; they had heard that I was to leave in an hour and they felt that their learning to teach was infinitely more important than anyone's meal. They said that no one in their mountain tribe was able to read or write and they made me promise to go to those remote mountains above Baguio to prepare Apayao lessons.

At Baoguen, in Ilocos Sur, fifty people gathered from the hills and mountains, some walking thirty kilometers. We taught twelve who had never read before, and the second day passed six of them as qualified teachers. The whole community was abuzz with excitement. As we ate our dinner we could hear people in the neighboring houses repeating the chart—*carabasa* and all the rest, syllable by syllable. "Nobody in those houses knows how to read," said our hostess.

The *presidente* of San Fernando told me, "In all our family I am the only man who has been able to read. Think what a struggle it has been for me to get an education." He brought his own brother to be taught, and in an hour the brother knew all the syllables and could read very slowly. The man's face was radiant, and the *presidente* was astonished beyond measure. "It took me two years to learn to read even a little English," he said. We all laughed as I patted the young man on the back and said to the *presidente,* "See how much brighter your brother is!"

In all my life I have never engaged in work that brought to the surface so much genuine gratitude and such pathetic longing for help. For thirty years my heart had ached for these multitudes, and now that the way was opened to help them, I was most grateful to God.

I was introduced to the students of Muños Agricultural School by Professor Ambrosio Torres, a fine Christian gentleman, who said, "Boys, do you remember how our martyred hero, Dr. José Rizal, risked his life to return to the Philippines in order to cut the cataracts from his mother's eyes? You can be Rizals and cut the cataracts of illiteracy from the eyes of your mothers and fathers and neighbors." The effect of this speech was electric. To a man the students promised that when they went home for vacation they would try to teach their relatives and neighbors to read and write.

Upon returning to Manila from this tour through the Ilocos provinces, I found our leading Protestant layman, Jorge Bocobo, president of the University of the Philippines, intensely interested. He called in the hundred leading students of the university and looked on while I showed them how to teach the Tagalog chart. "I am going home tonight," said President Bocobo, "and teach our cook. I challenge these students to make somebody literate before I do." He said he was trying to put a bill through the legislature to provide for a department of adult literacy.

Dr. Bocobo, Representative Fabian de la Paz, and Dean Francisco Benitez took me to see Governor-General Roosevelt, who had been keeping in touch with our progress ever since he had visited Lanao. The governor-general said he had heard the fear expressed that our campaign would be used as Protestant propaganda. I replied that the only way to meet the objection was to take the movement out of missionary hands.

"At present," I told Mr. Roosevelt, "there is no government committee, and no non-religious committee of any kind, to which people can turn for information and literacy lessons. We have already set up five campaigns with municipal *presidentes* as their heads. For all their lesson material they must write to the National Christian Council, a Protestant organization. In Bangued the priest sent his principal teacher to learn our method. He must buy charts from the National Christian Council. Scores of high schools are taking up this cause with enthusiasm. They must write to the National Christian Council. Either the legislature or yourself should create a non-sectarian committee to study, stimulate, counsel, and coordinate the agencies interested in literacy and to furnish them books. I am sure that the Roman Catholic churches will cooperate with such a committee."

At the suggestion of the governor-general, the Philippine Education Company agreed to print and sell packets containing the necessary teaching material. We devoted several days to writing instructions for teachers and organizers in seven dialects.

Governor-General Roosevelt also sent me to see Dr. Luther Bewley, director of education. "We have started literacy campaigns in ten of your high schools," I told him. "If all your high school and intermediate students will learn this method and teach their parents, they can wipe illiteracy out of this nation."

"You are right," Dr. Bewley replied, "but it takes time to get a huge organization like ours to undertake such a tremendous task. Meanwhile I hope you will visit all the schools in the Philippines."

When I reached San José, Antique, on the island of Panay—the last stop in my two months' tour—the Reverend E. F. Rounds took me to visit his friend, the Dutch priest. The padre was extremely cordial, offered us his best wine and cigars, and took us to see the eight Catholic sisters in the convent. These nuns, six of them Spanish and two of them Filipina, were lovely, spiritual women with a deep eagerness to help the illiterates who, they said, were very numerous in the province of Antique. For two hours they studied our charts and methods with keen interest.

As I traveled toward Lanao once more I listed the languages in which we had prepared key-word lessons. I counted twenty-one:

Maranaw	Ilocano	Joloano
Cebuan	Ibanag	Subano
Ilongo	Manobo	Bukidnon
Tagalog	Isinay	Bontoc Igorot
Bicol	Gaddang	Ifugao
Pampangan	Samarino	Kalinga
Pangasinan	Magindanao	Visayan

This was the beginning of the Philippine literacy campaigns. "But," you will ask, "did they continue?" Indeed they did and for this the National Christian Council deserves much of the credit. It appointed Miss Maria Dayoan general director of literacy in 1935, and until she came to America in 1938 she achieved astonishing results. At one of her early demonstrations before a huge crowd at the Philippines Normal School, the leading teachers' institution of the islands, the illiterates learned to read so quickly that the crowd again and again broke into applause, and every student and teacher volunteered to teach. The Federation of Women's Clubs, one of the most powerful organizations in the Philippines, sent Miss Dayoan everywhere to train their leaders.

Her reports are full of happy experiences:

As I discovered how quickly people learned, I became more and more enthusiastic about literacy and was able to convince other people because of my own personal experience. Illiterates were taught far more rapidly than I had ever believed could be possible. In one demonstration before public school teachers, a woman was taught to read in twenty-five minutes. She was very much pleased and went home full of delight to tell her neighbors. Not long after she left, people flocked into the building. Many wanted to learn how to read and write, and others wanted to know how to teach their brothers, sisters, parents, or other relatives.

I have explained literacy and have trained teachers, not only in churches and women's clubs but also in parent-teacher associations, community assemblies, public and private schools, colleges, secondary and elementary schools, in lodges, municipal councils, dormitories, and student centers. The fact that I was representing the Federation of Women's Clubs enabled me to work with all sorts of organizations, with both Roman Catholic and Protestant groups as well as with those connected with no church.

The Moros themselves were becoming deeply concerned with the progress of their people, and soon after the first Independence Act was passed by Congress in 1932 I wrote of the hopes it had aroused:

January 27, 1933

I wish you could have been with me the other night as our head printer, Macaindeg, poured out his passionate longing to save his people. The passing of the Independence Bill by Congress is having a profound influence upon these young Moros. They know that their province is behind the rest of the Philippine Islands. Macaindeg realizes that unless the Moros put forth a tremendous effort to lift themselves educationally and economically during the next ten years, they will be ruined when independence comes.

Meanwhile, the governor-general took first steps toward a government department of adult education by instituting a series of community assemblies. Over a hundred lectures on vital topics were sent throughout the islands to be delivered in all important languages.

Just as soon as the Philippines became a commonwealth, the National Supreme Council established a division of adult education. This important development in the progress of literacy took place in 1936. Thereafter, the literacy campaign became a government enterprise and reached out to every province and village. Literacy wagons were sent over the islands to attract all the illiterate adults and give them reading lessons. Adult night schools were established nearly everywhere.

The March, 1940, number of the government publication called *Adult Education* announced that the prize for the greatest number of illiterates taught to read that month had gone to the Davao Penal Colony. "The prisons," it said, "are becoming universities."

Matias Cuadra eventually became a chaplain in the Philippine army, and because of his experience in Lanao was given full charge of the literacy campaign among the armed forces. He pushed the campaign with such vigor that the army was nearly 100 per cent literate when Japan struck.

No account of our Lanao mission would be complete without a tribute to the magnificent men and women who worked with us during those years. They had come to the Philippines for sheer love of Christ and the romance of this great literacy adventure.

First, in 1930, came Mrs. David Lund, who opened our Moro girls' dormitory, paying her own salary and contributing $50 a month to aid poor Moro girls. Mrs. Laubach came in 1931 to teach Moro women and keep our books, and with her came our thirteen-year-old son Bob and the Reverend and Mrs. Irving M. Channon, for years missionaries in the Caroline Islands and later at Silliman University, situated on Negros Island within sight of Mindanao. They gave us an extra year before retiring. Irving Channon could do more things than any other man I ever knew. With the aid of our Japanese neighbor, Mr. Matsui, he actually built us a home.

Late in 1931 the Woodwards, in whose home I had stayed on my first visit to Mindanao, moved to Lanao so that, while Mr. Woodward continued his evangelistic work along the coast of the island, his wife could help in the huge task of compiling a dictionary and translating the Bible.

In the summer of 1932 I was overjoyed to receive a letter from Miss Minnie K. Schultz in Pennsylvania. Her interest had been aroused by the magazine articles she had read about our literacy campaign, and she wanted to come out to help us. Friends in America contributed funds to cover her salary, and in January of the following year she arrived to act as secretary and librarian. She won our hearts by her splendid spirit and by the intelligence with which she grasped the work. She was the first person of our acquaintance to go out and secure her own salary before starting out into the field—a wonderful thing to accomplish during those years of depression.

Mrs. Pearl Spencer, one of the famous early government teachers—"best principal in the Philippines," the director of education told me—also joined our mission group for educational work at one-sixth of her previous salary. In 1941 she became the first head of our Moro high school.

In 1940 the American Board of Commissioners for Foreign Missions sent us the Reverend Alvin H. Scaff and his wife, both of them members of Phi Beta Kappa; and in the fall of 1941, when the situation in Japan grew tense and the Japanese Christian leaders urged the missionaries to leave, the Reverend Darley Downs came to our Lanao station. When the tragic war struck the Philippines, Darley Downs, Marion Woodward, and Pearl Spencer were still in Lanao, all three of them separated from their families, who happened to be in the United States. All of them were marvelous Christians, warm friends of the Japanese, Chinese, and Filipinos as well as of the Moros, and their influence was tremendous as they gave witness to the love of Christ in Lanao.

While our mission force was thus growing, there was coming over the Moros a change so profound that it was nothing less than miraculous. When we arrived in 1929 the atmosphere was tense with hatred between the Moros and the constabulary. The government was trying to "keep the boat from rocking" as much as possible. Everyone except the missionaries carried guns—even in the daylight in the military camps—in 1929. But in thirteen years this had nearly all disappeared.

And in 1942 these same Moros who had so hated us signed a solemn pledge that they would die rather than allow the Japanese to overthrow the good government established by the United States. Ten thousand Moros signed their names to this pledge—most of them men whom we had taught to read. They had stopped glorying in being outlaws and were proud of being good citizens. Fourteen years before they had burned fifty school buildings, determined to root education out of Lanao. In 1941 we left them clamoring for schools faster than the government could provide them, and sending girls as well as boys to be educated.

At the time of the Japanese invasion we still had the only press printing Maranaw literature. We were producing close to a million pages a year, although it had to be set up by hand or mimeographed. In the ten-year period preceding we had published booklets with stories of the Old Testament prophets, running both the Bible and Koran accounts in the same volume. We had printed Luke in Maranaw; and when the war broke out the American Bible Society was in the process of printing the Acts. We had printed three editions of an English-Maranaw dictionary, with definitions of ten thousand words. And we were issuing *Lanao Progress,* a sixteen-page fortnightly.

We had specialized in paper-bound booklets and pamphlets, which we sold and gave away by tens of thousands. The non-religious pamphlets were on such varied subjects as "Care of the Skin," "Motherhood and Baby Care," "The New Miracle Rice," "Moro Folklore in Prose," and "History of the World." The bureau of education took the entire edition of a hundred-page volume containing a compilation of Moro lyrics. The religious pamphlets besides the Bible were on such themes as "Life on Its Highest Levels," "Three Hundred Objectives of Character," "God Is Beyond Us All," "Why Does God Permit Suffering?," "Where Christians and Moslems Are Brothers," "Secrets of a Student's Success," "Game with Minutes" (later published in America), and sixty four-page tracts on "The Friendship of Jesus" for distribution in the Moro markets. In 1942 these tracts formed the basis for a book published by Harper & Brothers, New York, under the title *You Are My Friends.*

During all these adventures we were developing a science and technique in adult literacy that we believed would be distinct contributions to education. This was in part the art of building easy lessons, to be sure, but it was far more than that—more than anything that could be written on paper. It was a thing of the spirit—the art of applying to education that mysterious love power that held together the early followers of Jesus.

Experience has shown us that it is necessary to produce a congenial spiritual climate if a campaign is to flourish. So the training of teachers involves far more than teaching them to say the right words. It is helping them to be warm friends of their students, to pray for them, to rejoice in their progress—in a word, to radiate a Christlike atmosphere.

One day after I had taught a half-dozen women and children to read while fifty teachers looked on, the chairman rose and said, "I have watched this remarkable exhibition and I believe I have found the secret. It is love." He was at least 50 per cent right. The psychological principles that we explain to all our teachers are the "highest" secret, not only of the literacy enterprise described in this book, but of life.

We prefer to teach one by one so that we may sit down beside our students; a teacher of a class is too much like a superior person. Every illiterate has an inferiority complex—he thinks we feel above him. The very first thing is to remove the gap between us. When we sit beside him we disarm his feeling of inferiority. Then we proceed to treat him not like a student but like a rajah! We try to make ourselves humble and him important. He thinks he is too old to learn. We must prove that he can learn easily, quickly, and delightfully, no matter how old he is. Every step is so short that an ordinary man can take it easily. The chart provides for this; but occasionally the teacher must say just the right word to help a dull student over a hard spot. There must be no embarrassing pauses, never a question the student cannot answer, no examination to find out what he knows!

We must keep out of the student's way, neither pushing him nor retarding him. An illiterate is happy only when he feels free to take his own natural gait.

On every line of the chart the student finds himself saying something surprising. An atmosphere of expectancy is thus developed; we can see it in the bright, open-mouthed eagerness of our illiterate learner. The chart becomes a Pandora's box of glad surprises, appealing to the emotions and drawing forth peals of laughter.

There is never a frown nor a rebuke nor a loud tone of voice. Students remember a whisper better than a howl because it is pleasanter. In teaching an illiterate there must be no unpleasant moments. Never a gesture of impatience nor a yawn. Upon the slightest justification we pat him on the shoulder and say, "That's fine." The student strives to maintain this charmed spell, perhaps the most thrilling hour of his life! He is getting along much better than he had expected because the lesson is easy and we teach correctly. He attributes it to his brilliance. What everybody craves, of all things on earth, is to have some hidden genius discovered in him. If you become the discoverer of that genius, he is yours, body and soul.

We have seen hundreds of men and women going out from their first lessons wreathed in smiles, saying, "Very easy! He was surprised at my bright mind." And after that all the others in the village are eager to have their brilliance discovered! We never forget that while we are teaching one man we are selling the idea to his neighbors.

Then, when the student has learned lesson one, we set him to teaching somebody else. We look delighted at his teaching and say when he finishes, "You are going to be a splendid teacher. Teach about five more as you did now. Then I'll give you the next lesson." His teaching others has these obvious advantages:

1. The lesson is well fixed in his mind by the time he has taught it five or six times. We never really know a thing until we have used it.

2. He is at once given a new status in society, a new self-respect. He becomes a member of the teaching profession. It is astounding how his shoulders go back, his face beams, his eyes gleam—he has arrived!

3. By making every student a teacher, the teaching is done at small cost, and the increase in readers is very rapid. We educate by geometrical progression.

4. Our student comes to realize that he is learning in order to help others. The spirit of sharing is fostered.

Nothing I have ever seen begets friendship so effectively as thus teaching illiterates and sending them out to teach others; not even a doctor, caring for the sick, has quite the same chance. For while the doctor and nurse do something *for the patient,* they do not request him to *go and cure others.* On the other hand, when we teach we ask our student to pass it on. He goes out with the feeling that he has surprised us, and that now we expect big things of him. Warm with gratitude, he tries to merit our further praise, and there is established a bond of affection that will last a lifetime. The student emulates our warm kindliness, so that it begins to permeate the entire community like some beneficent contagion. The spirit of sharing is taught, not by talking about it, but by doing it, and—what is even more vital—recruiting others to do it.

CHAPTER 4

1935: A LITERACY TOUR ACROSS SOUTHERN ASIA

Malaya, India, Cairo, Turkey

OUR MORO TEACHERS kept asking, "Do you suppose we can really make lessons as easy as these in other languages?" We knew it could not be done in English with its hopeless spelling. But what we were all eager to know was how many of the languages of the world were spelled regularly enough to be taught by our method.

Matias Cuadra, our Moro preacher, had lived in Borneo for several years and fortunately spoke Malay. He went to work preparing lessons in our front schoolroom while a hundred Moros looked on with mouths agape. In two days he had a Malay chart completed and the whole Moro tribe clamored to read it, for they think Malay is nearly as sacred as Arabic. Cuadra almost became their god. Having tasted that triumph, we were all eager for more.

Many missionaries wrote us from India, men who had beaten their heads against the stone wall of illiteracy for twenty or thirty years. These men asked us to visit them, though one of them warned us to expect "a task about equal to shoveling the Himalayas into the Indian Ocean." "We shall never have a strong indigenous church in India," he wrote, "until more of its members can read the Scriptures; and so

I am keenly interested. Even though I fear that your visit will be a disappointment to you in the way of definite results, I do believe you will stir up interest in the subject."

It was our irrepressibly enthusiastic secretary, Minnie Schultz, who really pushed us over the brink into world literacy tours. She persuaded me to prepare a letter for persons along our route to America via India and Suez, which we would be taking when we left on furlough. Before I realized it Miss Schultz had mimeographed and mailed five hundred copies of this letter! Many of those who received it sent us most urgent invitations to visit them.

We wrote accepting invitations from Singapore, Ceylon, parts of India, Cairo, Palestine, Syria, and Turkey, and on January 20, 1935, I set out alone, half frightened at my own audacity! We had no resources except a furlough travel allowance, so, to save expenses, Mrs. Laubach, our son Bob, and Miss Schultz remained in Lanao two months longer and met me in Colombo after I had finished my visit in India.

On shipboard from Lanao to Manila I wrote to my father telling him all about the farewell celebrations the Moros had held for us:

January 20, 1935

At last I am on the way home. What a farewell we had! For days we had felt excitement in the air as we packed our baggage to leave, but we did not expect a *despedida* as overwhelming as those dear Moros gave us.

Five big trucks filled with them followed our car down to Iligan, the seaport twenty-five miles away. They swarmed on the ship and spilled over on the wharf. Every high *dato* in Lanao wanted to make a speech on how they were sending me to bring light to mankind and how this was to be the beginning of emancipation for the human race, the turning point in world history! At ten that night the captain blew his whistle to warn that he was about to cast off, but the Moros laughed and went on talking. The captain subsided for fear they would cut his head off. When every *dato* had made his speech the sheik said: "We are going to pray for you." They could not bow to the deck for they were crowded together like sardines, so they held out their hands and kept turning them over, palms up, palms down, while their highest *imam* prayed that this American friend, whom they had helped to make the easiest lessons in the world, should have the blessing of Allah as he went around the world introducing their method to the less fortunate nations. Then they kissed me and hugged me and one-eyed Hadji Kakairan cried on my shoulder as he said: "We will pray for you in every mosque in Lanao while you go around the world spreading the glory of Lanao." They declared they would have gone along if only they could have sold their brass pots for cash! A dozen Moros did go as far as Manila.

When later I told the Moslems in Malacca, India, Palestine, Syria, Dar es Salaam, and Zanzibar that these Moslem friends in Lanao were praying for us, they laughed with delight and hugged me as only Moslems hug brothers. When anybody tells me that it is hard to make friends among Moslems I know better. They do get angry when we throw stones at their religion, but who can blame them when we ourselves are so horribly unlike our Christ? I have found among Moslems as loyal and true friends as among any Christians in the world, and some Moslems, especially the Sufis, are truly saints.

The expectancy with which Christians and Moslems received us across southern Asia was not only astonishing, it was embarrassing! We were thrown at once into the limelight, although we were still timid explorers and our methods were in the experimental stage, changing from one week to the next. So greatly did people feel the need of literacy help that they wanted to believe we were infallible.

Malaya

The first place I touched was Singapore. The missionaries told me that the Malay language is not much used in that city, which is largely made up of Chinese, Indians, and whites, so they packed me off to Malacca, a hundred miles to the north. The Reverend and Mrs. Robert A. Blaisdell collected a dozen Moslem boys in a few minutes, and since I had only two days to work before returning to Singapore to catch the boat, we toiled with feverish haste, day and night, taking out an hour for church, until Sunday noon. We were still working while we ate our last meal together, papers in hand, and were past the hardest points when I ran to catch the mail car. Later the Blaisdells sent me a beautiful set of Malay lessons exactly like those in the Philippines, and just as easy, for Malay belongs to the same language family and has many of the same words.

Three years afterward one of the leaders in Singapore wrote:

> We are going ahead in Malay with the method of teaching illiterates that you worked out with Mr. and Mrs. Blaisdell. There are great possibilities here, for the statistics show that only 25 per cent of the people are literate, and in the village districts and the jungle not 10 per cent can read.

One difficulty is the fact that all Malay education is officially in the hands of the British Department of Education, which is naturally a bit nervous about a mission crashing into a field where they have had the monopoly. Moreover, the government is afraid we may use literacy as an entering wedge for Christian missions among the Malays.

Of course literacy is an opening wedge for any idea or movement, good or bad, among a backward people. But the British fear that it might start a wave of religious fanaticism in Malaya was groundless. Our experience in Mindanao had demonstrated that a literacy campaign, far from causing unrest, was the best possible way to bring loyal cooperation.

We found another curious complication at Singapore. The British spell the Malay language the English way, and the Dutch in Sumatra, within sight of Singapore, spell it the Dutch way! So whenever Malays in British territory desire to write to Malays in Dutch Sumatra, they have to use Arabic letters because the English and Dutch spellings are so far apart. I told the inspector of schools in Singapore that I thought this was ridiculous, and he replied, "Oh, not at all, not at all! Variety is the spice of life, don't you know? It would be a pity to have the monotony of spelling Malay only one way." Later, I suppose, they were spelling it the Japanese way, which would still further relieve the monotony.

India

On the steamer from Singapore to India was an Indian, Mr. G. D. Mehrottra, who became very keen to help make Hindi lessons without waiting to reach Bombay. Another passenger, Miss Caroline Pope, who was a missionary from India, caught Mehrottra's enthusiasm. Using her Hindi dictionary we three labored and wrestled every day to find key words—or rather they labored and I wrestled.

The very first day it became evident that we could not make lessons as easy as those we had made in the Philippines because the Hindi alphabet was far more complicated. In Lanao we had sixteen letters, but Hindi had fifty. Moreover, they have the split and spliced letters, half of one letter on top of half another. The reason for this is that every consonant has a vowel sound understood. We went through the dictionary twice and could not find good key words for all their consonants—they just did not exist.

"Mehrottra," I said, "I'm going to cable my wife to come on the next ship and sail right on past India. I'm licked."

But Mehrottra never lost his courage. "This," he said, "is what India needs most of all. Our people are 90 per cent illiterate, and somebody has got to help us out. Let's try again. Put the letters that sound alike in families, then we can find key words. Let's put *p* and *b* in one family, *t* and *d* in another, and so on."

We tried that and had fifteen families and five beautiful key words in half an hour! By the time we reached Bombay we had finished the first set of key-word lessons ever made in an Indian language. We walked down the gangplank into India feeling like Hannibal plunging out of the Alps into Italy on his elephant. Little did I dream what Himalayas lay ahead! It is providential that they were hidden from my eyes. India had known them too well and they had defeated her so long that she was deep in a "slough of despond." She needed easier lessons, it is true, but even more she needed new faith. As I took the train from Bombay to Nagpur to meet the National Christian Council, I rashly supposed that I had one answer to India's problems already tucked under my arm.

The evening I arrived in Nagpur, Mahatma Gandhi was dining with the secretary of the National Christian Council, Dr. J. Z. Hodge, who arranged for me to call upon the Mahatma at Wardha the following week. We had nothing to show Mr. Gandhi, so we had to work fast. Three Indian women and one man, all of them teachers, poured themselves with intense enthusiasm for six days into preparing Marathi charts in colors to lay before their famous leader.

At his little house in Wardha Mr. Gandhi received me courteously, but, like all the other leaders at the time, he despaired of making India literate so long as she was hungry and destitute. Our conversation on this occasion has been briefly reported in the first chapter. As we drove home that evening my British companion said, "Gandhi thinks you are attempting the impossible." "Fools rush in where angels fear to tread," I replied and we both laughed. If you can't laugh at yourself, don't set out to reform the world.

One of the tricks a traveler in India has to learn is to provide his own bedding in winter. The inexperienced newcomer on his first journey is likely to get into a train that is stifling hot at five o'clock in the evening, without blankets or overcoat, and then wake up at midnight with teeth chattering. I took a night train from Nagpur without enough blankets and long before daybreak tumbled out of my bunk shivering, wishing I were in Lanao and tempted to blame God for getting me into this "fix."

At the station at Raipur a man in shorts walked up and said, "My name is Moyer. Is your name Laubach?"

"Moyer! Why, I thought you lived a hundred miles from here."

"I do," said Moyer, "but I just drove in to meet you and take you on down to Dhamtari."

"And you got here at four A.M.! Did you get any sleep?"

"Yes, plenty. I slept on the station benches."

I put my arm around him and said, "Man, you make me weep. If you hadn't been here, I would have taken the next train right back to Bombay. I'm scared about your expectations."

"Never mind," said Moyer. "We are all praying, and God wants this done more than anybody else. You'll win."

That is the way the missionaries were all over India; there is no more wonderful group of Christians on this planet. But then, I've felt the same way about the missionaries in every country I ever visited!

Dhamtari is on the edge of an Indian jungle where the tigers love to lie across the road at night and worry belated auto drivers. Every missionary has seen them. The big cats look into the headlights, stretch, move lazily off the road, and try to peer into the windows while the cars pass, but they have never struck a car yet. Americans at this Mennonite mission at Dhamtari, together with their Indian colleagues, worked on the Hindi lessons for a month, and each evening we all went to a nearby village of outcastes to try out our lessons on illiterate leather workers, the Chamars. The lessons worked well on them, so we tried them at a camp of three hundred lepers, and then had them printed. The Reverend J. D. Graber took over the supervision of these experimental lessons and improved them until they were really good.

The following month I went with Dr. Mason Olcott, of the Union

Teachers Training School near Katpadi, and about sixteen of his teachers into another remote region a hundred miles northwest of Madras, where Dr. Olcott worked with eight teachers on Tamil lessons and the other eight teachers worked on Telugu. I acted as the guinea pig on which both groups tried their lessons. Tamils can say longer words and say them faster than any other people on earth—like a rapid-fire gun. Tamil is spoken by more than twenty million people. Telugu, used by upwards of twenty-six millions, is a lovely language, often called the "Italian of India." We went out every evening to a Tamil or Telugu mud village to experiment, and had illiterates teaching one another as far as the rays of our powerful Mazda lantern would reach. We all slept in a hot schoolroom. It was cooler outside, but panthers lived in the nearby rocks.

The third week we became a three-ring circus. The headmaster of the Moslem Government School of Vellore brought his staff of teachers to our country schoolhouse to make Urdu lessons, but they shouted and argued so zealously that the Tamil and Telugu gangs had to move off thirty yards to hear themselves talk.

The president of the Arabic College in Madras took me home with him, gathered the Moslem leaders to his college in a great meeting, staged a successful demonstration of our method, put wreaths of fragrant flowers around my neck, and made such speeches as I had never heard before.

At the lovely summer residence center of Kodaikanal, 7,000 feet above the sea, a hundred deeply interested missionaries met me one afternoon for a demonstration of the Tamil charts. As we closed, one of the men took my hand and said with deep feeling, "If I had a million dollars, I would give it to you for this work in India!" That is exactly what somebody ought to do for literacy in India—give it a million dollars.

Those missionaries ordered 5,000 sets of Tamil and Telugu lessons, sight unseen. When I left them I was weak and frightened. The lessons were very rough and imperfect; they would need long months or years of patient improvement to be very successful. I had told everyone this. But would they believe it, or would they cast them aside at the first trouble? It was with those misgivings and with my task hardly begun that I left India. People would be trying these first hastily prepared lessons in Hindi, Marathi, Telugu, Tamil, and Urdu—would they, I wondered, ever want to see me again?

Cairo

I met Mrs. Laubach, Bob, and Miss Schultz at Colombo and together we sailed on to Cairo, where there awaited us one of the most surprising welcomes we have ever had. This, too, was connected with Signal Hill, and it was God pushing me into deep water! Here is what happened.

A friend in New York had kept a scrapbook of letters to my father as they came out each week in the Benton *Argus*. He had sent them the previous year to Miss Constance Padwick, secretary of the Central Literature Committee for Moslems in Cairo. Miss Padwick had mimeographed selections from those letters and sent them to missionaries and Christian workers throughout the Near East.[1] So when we reached Cairo, they hurried me off to a Near East Christian conference timed especially for the occasion, and everyone treated me like a long-lost brother. The Egyptians greeted me in Oriental fashion and said, "We have read about you and your Moro friends. Do the same thing for us in Egypt that you did for them."

Forty missionaries and nationals volunteered to take turns in shifts of ten each to prepare Arabic lessons. Miss Padwick had a book called *Phonetics of Arabic,* which arranged the letters into families exactly as we had been doing in India. We took this arrangement to our committee and asked them to find key words. In all my life I have never seen such brilliant work. They found three key words in ten minutes! The committee then made lessons with such wit and skill and joy that people couldn't wait for their shift—they did not want to miss the fun. In two days we had completed five charts. The press mimeographed thirty copies each of all five lessons, so that people could experiment with them.

All that week I had no time for sightseeing—only one swift look at the pyramids by moonlight. Miss Padwick and our family ate supper in the dusk under the ghostly shadows of the oldest pyramid in the

[1] These were printed in the United States under the title *Letters by a Modern Mystic* (Westwood, N. J., Fleming H. Revell Company, 1937, 1958).

world. The air seemed full of the spirits of millions of those slaves who had toiled in that sand 5,000 years ago. We were told that they had piled up the sand and dragged the stones to the very top of that lofty pyramid and then had dug all the sand away again, leaving the most stupendous mass of masonry on earth towering above the desert.

The doctor in the hospital in Old Cairo invited us to try our new charts on his convalescent patients. Forty missionaries and Egyptians gathered to see the experiment. The hospital doctor brought in thirty illiterate convalescents, and each member of the audience was given one illiterate to teach for twenty-five minutes.

They returned with grave faces, and Miss Padwick's face looked as sick as my heart felt. I realized that I had made a major mistake in allowing all those forty people to teach instead of teaching them how to do it first. And I should have tested the students' eyes first. For the doctor arose and informed us that every convalescent in his hospital had eye disease, and probably could not see the letters anyhow! What did he think we had—a Braille system? Everybody laughed, but the beans had been spilled. The whole overexpectant gathering had hoped for a miracle and an easy victory. They did not realize that persistence is our only secret; that months, perhaps years, of hard work with the Arabic language would be necessary before we could claim success.

One of the chief advantages of traveling from region to region is that when one committee is worn to a frazzle or becomes discouraged, you find the next group fresh and eager to begin. And you never breathe a word about your last troubles. For an inner voice tells you it is not defeat, only delay.

Jerusalem

At Jerusalem the principal of the Newman School of Missions invited fifty missionaries and Palestinians, some of them members of the bureau of education, to a meeting the first afternoon we arrived. This was followed by nine more addresses that week—and in between we revised the lessons that had just been made in Cairo.

I showed them to the British director of education and eight of his staff. Some of the Palestinians did not like the words we had used, said they were not classical words. A hot debate broke out as to whether colloquial words ought ever to be used. I was horrified. "Of course," I told them, "people must learn to read familiar words first, before they attempt unknown words." "No, no, no, no!" the pundits objected. "Our scholars would never tolerate such degradation of literature!" There in the Holy City I had my first battle with the fastidious scholar who would have classical words or none, no matter whether illiterates learned to read or not. This stupid mistake, I learned later, was Asia's worst foe to literacy. They ended the debate by deciding to try to prepare a list of all the classical words the illiterates used in conversation —if there were any—and use these "pure" but well-known words in building lessons.

The next day the two leading primary school specialists of Palestine were sent by the director of education to Ain Karim, the birthplace of John the Baptist, five miles west of Jerusalem, to experiment with me on illiterate Moslems. One of them, Mr. Hannosh, taught the first boy, he the second, the second the third; all of them behaved brilliantly. To my deep delight, Constance Padwick arrived in the very middle of the experiment. She had come all the way from Cairo "to see whether we were yet killing the giant illiteracy." Her cheeks flushed with pleasure as she saw the giant at least dealt a severe blow under the chin. And I breathed a prayer of thanksgiving for her sake.

Beirut

My family tarried another week to see Jerusalem while I hurried on to Beirut to make more charts. I was in such a frenzy to improve those Arabic charts that I felt few regrets at missing the most wonderful land in the world for any Christian to visit. The Jerusalem experiment had been an improvement over the Cairo failure, but already my head was buzzing with new ideas, and I needed a fresh committee on which to try them.

On the way I went to visit the ruins of Capernaum alone, and stood a long while in the very synagogue where Jesus had taught and outside whose doors He had cured so many sick. I could not help repeating over and over, "Master, you really stepped here and sat here as you spoke," and I caressed the stones as I fairly felt Him walking there unseen again.

My stay in Beirut was nothing short of breathless—twenty-five different addresses during six days. Such excellent plans had been made by friends in the American University and the Near East School of Theology that we also found time for rebuilding the Arabic lessons. There were only two members in my committee, but they were a joy. Professor Tannus was a Syrian in the American University. Miss Nejla Izzadin, Ph.D., a graduate of Vassar College with her doctorate from the University of Chicago, was a Druse. My notes say: "She eats original research of this kind as though it were chocolate candy."

No doubt the keen interest of Miss Izzadin was due to her desire for her own people, the Druses, to become literate. They are a strange, proud, wonderful race of people, who believe themselves to be superior, never changing their religious convictions, and never intermarrying with outsiders. Miss Izzadin, with all her travels and education, seemed as much a Druse as ever. We could not complete the charts before I was compelled to leave, but those two Syrian scholars finished and printed them after I was gone—the best Arabic lessons for adults ever made. That summer Miss Izzadin and a camp of students from the Junior College in Beirut taught the illiterates in some Syrian villages. This is what she wrote me about that experience:

> This may mean much to Syria, 90 per cent of whose population is still illiterate. Cordially and enthusiastically the Nusaireyeh villagers welcomed us; the women wanted to know when the children were to be taught—but having the adults learn to read was too entirely unheard of! Had they not existed all these years without knowing how to read and write? Why trouble themselves now? Even Sheik Ali shook his head. "No, some are born to be educated like the sheiks, and others must work and till the soil. What respect would the workers have for us, if they, too, could read?"
>
> Grudgingly permission was given that the older girls and women might come, but these, long used to being told that they were too stupid to learn, said they dared not leave their work. Nevertheless, three came, more from curiosity than interest, and, pleased with their rapid progress, brought three others the second day, and twenty the third! Possibly the unexpected opposition was the best way to get the movement going, for Sheik Ali has now sent word that next week his whole village will be ready to start.

Every summer since then, student camps from Beirut have carried on campaigns among the illiterate villagers of Lebanon and Jordan.

While I was in Beirut Mr. Uwum Seadat published an article that is loaded with truth:

Dr. Laubach's lectures and illustrations fill me with great hopes and they also arouse in me great fears. I am afraid that here is another blessing that God has bestowed upon the world that will be used for evil ends.

To teach the Syrians to read and write means to release a great new power in Syria. But for what? So that Syria may advance in the direction in which it is moving at the present time? It is hardly worth the effort. It seems to me that we need to set our goal first. What can be done to bridge the tremendous gap that exists and is widening between Christians and Moslems, or what can we do about the great hatred that the Arabs have for the Jews? Can we utilize this great new power of literacy to bridge those gaps?

Unless persons with a spiritual motive take hold of it and further it for specific spiritual ends, the whole movement will be a curse. People who have experienced love, sacrifice, and service must take this great task upon their shoulders.

What Uwum Seadat said about Syria applies to all Asia and Africa—and the world.

Turkey

Turkey is changing with incredible rapidity, like her neighbor Russia. A republic in form, Turkey became in reality a dictatorship under President Mustafa Kemal—Kemal Ataturk, as he chose in 1934 to be called ("Ataturk" means "Father of the Turks"). He was a highly efficient dictator with good ideas and enormous capacity to get things done. In 1928 he threw Arabic out of the schools and replaced it with a splendid Latin phonetic alphabet. It all happened during the summer vacation period. No textbooks with the old script were permitted in the schools when they reopened that fall. The children had to start all over like first graders with these unknown letters. No religious teaching was permitted in the school programs because Kemal Ataturk believed the Moslem priests were obstructing education. John Dewey and other well-known educators were asked to come and introduce the latest education ideas. Turkish teachers were sent abroad to glean the world's best ideas. All education became free and compulsory.

Night schools for adults were opened everywhere. Kemal Ataturk himself became a teacher to set the educated people an example. The government announced that jobs would go only to those who could read and write. In four years two millions were taught. The coffee houses began to lose business and the seventeen hundred libraries of the country were crowded.

The atmosphere in Turkey in 1935 was unlike any we have ever experienced. One could fairly feel the iron hand of Kemal Ataturk as he crashed through old customs to achieve his idea of progress. He had been breaking the power of the Moslem church leaders by one edict after another, even compelling priests to read the Koran in Turkish instead of in the sacred Arabic language. While we were there the priests and nuns, Moslem as well as Christian, were forced to abandon clerical garb, to adopt Western costumes and cut their hair *à la Parisienne*. Dr. F. W. McCallum said one evening as we strolled through Istanbul, "Take your last look at the priests and nuns, for tomorrow you'll not see any." And we didn't! But we could spot the priests by the awkward way they wore Western trousers!

My old friend the Reverend John Kingsley Birge, with whom I had worked at Spring Street Neighborhood House in New York City in 1910, had been in Turkey for many years as a missionary. His most important contribution to the new Turkish education was a scientific word count to determine the one thousand "basic" Turkish words, the ones that would be needed in order to teach illiterates. He counted words from five sources—government reports, conversation, school readers, village literature, and Turkish newspapers—and found these startling facts: *four* Turkish words make up *12* per cent of the word occurrences, one-eighth of all the words in the Turkish language; *twenty-seven* words make up *24* per cent of the word occurrences. In the Turkish New Testament he found that *fifty-eight* words make up *33* per cent of the word occurrences; *303* words make up *70* per cent of the word occurrences.

King Birge's first five hundred and his first thousand most used Turkish words are now in use in the government primary schools.

Unfortunately Birge was out of Turkey on his furlough in 1935 when we paid our visit, but he had given me helpful introductions to government officials. Dr. Paul Monroe, then president of Robert College, also introduced me to important educational leaders.

Director of Education Husein Bey, asked me to make a set of lessons and submit them to his government. I was also invited in Ankara to the headquarters of the *Halk Evi* or People's Party (the only political party they had in Turkey), which was responsible for adult literacy. They entertained me like the Shah of Persia, and told me one of the strangest stories that ever came to my ears. The Turkish leaders, they said, were feeding their people a new language in spoonfuls—five new words a day, which everybody must memorize. They were making the people believe that these words had been rescued from the ancient Hittite civilization from which, so they told the people, the modern Turks had descended. Hundreds of scientific words like "electricity," "radio," and "telegraph" did not come from Europe—perish the thought! They came from "our ancestors, the Hittites."

In Istanbul we found an excellent committee of scholars and in three days we had finished fifteen lessons by working many hours overtime every day. Just before our ship was to sail, we sent them off to the director of education. From Mindanao to Turkey we had built charts in thirty languages.

I shall never forget one member of that fine Turkish committee—a Persian by birth. He was blind and had to be led to our meetings by his daughter. He possessed such fine spiritual insight that I told him, "We are the blind ones and you alone can see into reality." He begged me to go to Iran, where, he told me, "not one person in a hundred can read." But I lacked time and—what I did not tell him—money. Indeed, this whole venture was coming out of a missionary's meager allowance. So we left on the last lap of our long journey to America before our pockets were empty.

CHAPTER 5

1936-37: AROUND THE WORLD AND BACK TO INDIA

WHEREVER AMERICANS HEARD the story of the world's enormous need for literacy, as I traveled over the country during my furlough year 1935-36, their response was always the same. They were stunned to learn that China and India together have over 700 millions of illiterates —more than one-third of the human race—and that of the whole world's population, the greater part are still illiterate.

In the autumn of 1935, a group of interested friends, chiefly in my own church in Upper Montclair, New Jersey, formed what we called The World Literacy Committee. In 1941, the Foreign Missions Conference invited our Committee to join them, since our work was being done with missions throughout the world, and we formed the "Committee on World Literacy and Christian Literature of the Foreign Missions Conference of North America." It is now called "World Literacy and Christian Literature, a Committee of the Division of Foreign Missions, National Council of the Churches of Christ in the USA." It represents more than thirty-five "Member Boards." I continued to make literacy lessons around the world for this Committee until I retired at the age of seventy, in 1954.

In the summer of 1936 I left the United States for the Orient and on my way attended a seminar on Pacific Education held at Honolulu. Three hundred leading educators in countries bordering on the Pacific were present. Mr. I. J. Brugmans, director of education in the Dutch East Indies, Mr. Georges A. Bernard, assistant to the director of public instruction in Hanoi, French Indo-China, and all the other delegates from Pacific areas listened to the story of our Philippine experiment with eager interest and urged me to visit their countries. There was not then, to my knowledge, a country on earth that remained closed to this movement. The organizer of the seminar, the late Professor Charles T. Loram of the Yale Graduate School, went on with me to study at firsthand the progress of our literacy campaign in the Philippine Islands.

I had planned to stay in the Philippines only a few days and then push on as rapidly as possible to India, but I was delayed in Manila for two months. Before leaving the islands in 1934 I had showed the University Press an unfinished manuscript of a biography of José Rizal, the greatest Filipino known to history. The Press now urged me strongly to remain in Manila long enough to complete this, and I spent wonderful days with Rizal's three sisters—old ladies of eighty-four, seventy-eight, and seventy-four—coaxing from them many anecdotes of their brother. By great concentration I was able to finish the manuscript, but before I could complete the reading of the proofs I had to take ship for India.

When I finally reached my destination in November, I was distressed to find that my delay had disrupted a crowded and carefully planned program in southern India. They had closed some schools, they had brought people in for many miles, and I had failed to arrive.

All I could say in amazement was, "I never dreamed that anybody cared whether I came back or not." "Cared!" they replied. "Stanley Jones has gone all over India, demonstrating what you showed him at Kodaikanal and insisting that we must make every Christian literate with all possible speed."

Other things, too, made my cheeks burn. The Tamil chart that we had prepared in Dr. Olcott's country school, wrote Lloyd Lorbeer of Madura frankly, "has not really taken hold. It is cheap, but except for that merit, it offers no improvement over books and charts now in the field. Many of the words used in your chart are unknown here in Madura." Reading those words gave me cold chills. I felt especially sorry for Mason Olcott and other friends who had invested so much money and so much time on those charts, only to have them fail. Had I been attempting the impossible? Had Gandhi been right?

But splendid Mason Olcott, with his bulldog under jaw, was as resolved as ever. He said it was true that the Tamil charts had not succeeded, but then never mind, why should we expect success in such a brief time? We had not yet begun to fight. We would find the trouble and rectify it. He brought two Indian teachers to his home and the four of us spent seven days in a huddle around a table looking for our mistakes. We found it all too true that many of the words in our lessons were unfamiliar to illiterates and, what was worse, several were Telugu words. As though you had put French or Latin words in English primers—like *non compos mentis,* for example, which is precisely what it would be!

How did this happen? We had prepared the lessons in the border region between the Tamil and the Telugu country where the illiterates understood both languages. It did not take us long to weed out the Telugu and make sure every word was familiar.

At our conference with missionaries and Indian Christians in Madras the next week, we met two Indians who had devoted their long lives to literacy. Mr. S. G. Daniel, a lovable saint of seventy years, a born teacher, had been teaching men, women, and children for forty-five years and had developed the most widely used primer in the Tamil language. We watched him teach, his low, mellow, slightly tremulous voice holding the illiterates like magic. He spent one hour telling them about the letter *ee,* which means "fly." An entire hour on one letter, and they have two hundred and forty-seven letter forms to learn in Tamil! But then nobody is in a hurry in south India—it is too warm for speed.

The other was Mrs. A. Devasahayam, a gray-haired woman with a radiant face. She, too, had spent many years of her life teaching the Tamil alphabet. Her scheme was to arrange the letters that were shaped nearly alike into families and teach about ten letters at a time, as though we were to group *p, b, d, g, h* because they look alike. To prove that it would work she taught some illiterates for us, and on the third day they all knew their letters and thought it was fun. By many years of practice Mrs. Devasahayam had streamlined her teaching so that not a word was wasted.

It was not mere accident that Mr. Daniel and Mrs. Devasahayam, the two who had worked harder than any other Indians to make Madras literate, were both Christians. It was from Christ that they had received their deep passionate love for unfortunates and their perseverance in the face of the "impossible."

Bezwada, in the heart of the Telugu-speaking region 150 miles north of Madras, is one of the famous mass movement areas, where tens of thousands, especially from the depressed classes, had joined the church. Here the leaders reported that the Telugu lessons that we had made at Mason Olcott's school the year before had proved successful. They did not want us to discard the lessons but only to leave out the unfamiliar words. There were a hundred Anglican missionaries and Indians assembled for our all-day meetings, their minds alert to find ways of helping their thousands of converts to learn to read.

I went to the Lutheran College in Guntur with unusual eagerness because its president was Dr. Roy Strock, the man who more than any other person had influenced me in my pre-college days to become a student volunteer. He had been a teacher at Perkiomen School near Philadelphia, had coached our football team during the week, and had held a mission study class in his own room on Sunday. It was not the heroism in the books that impressed us so much as the heroism of Roy Strock. He had lost one eye through an accident only a few months before, but this did not prevent him from playing high-grade tennis, nor volunteering to go to Africa as a missionary. The way he rose above his misfortune made me love him—and his cause. He finally was sent to India, where the same power to make good in spite of handicaps pushed him to the front until he became secretary for the National Christian Council of all India. And now I was being entertained by my boyhood hero in his own home!

Another heart-moving experience awaited me in Guntur. We were hard at work on the revision of Telugu lessons when in walked a woman of about thirty, who was introduced to me as Miss Grace Chapman. She had an unmistakable Australian accent. This is what she told that group while I went limp with amazement:

"I have been a missionary teaching Moslem women in their homes in Sholapur. When I read in various journals about the success of the literacy movement among the Moslems in Mindanao, I made up my mind to go to the Philippines and see what they were doing. As it was my furlough time, I returned home to Australia, intending later to go from there to Mindanao. It happened that the Bishop of Dornakal was also visiting Australia and he told me that Dr. Laubach was returning to India and had probably reached there by now. So I packed my belongings and came right back to India as fast as I could travel without taking my furlough. The millions of illiterates in India are more important than my vacation."

Through the following months Grace Chapman went from one end of India to the other, stimulating literacy efforts among the Christians, who were her first interest. She wanted the Bible used for the very first lessons—and this was sound practice among Christians, because they were more eager to read the Bible than any other one book. She had already prepared a very beautiful *Gospel Primer* with limited word lists and it had been translated into many languages. Before Miss Chapman's untimely death a year later, she had stirred all Christian India with her passionate crusade. When my soul needs new courage I think of dear Grace Chapman, who would rather see India literate than take a furlough in her home country. Her spirit broods over her beloved India, and I pray that her vision may be captured in this book.

At Guntur, and at other points on this tour of India, there were debates over "story method versus the key-word method." We always came out at the same place—it is the language that determines which method is best.

In the English language, where *o,* for example, has as many sounds as the entire Moro alphabet, we get far less confused if we begin with words from the very first, teaching the children a few each day from a story like "The Little Red Hen," and postponing the sad news about our crazy spelling until several weeks later. Phonetics do not help much since we never know how to pronounce an English word until somebody tells us, and then we are not sure he knows.

In Maranaw, on the other hand, where there is only one possible sound for a letter and where there are only sixteen letters, it is easy to teach the adults all their sounds the first day, and a skillful teacher can do it in one hour. After that, the Moros can pronounce nearly every word for themselves, and the teacher has little need of saying much. Many have taught themselves to read after the first session. This is "lightning literacy" indeed, as compared to the story method, if you have a perfectly phonetic alphabet, because you have to teach only twenty to forty sounds instead of a thousand words.

The question we discussed at Guntur was whether Telugu was phonetic enough so that the key-word method would work—a very important question. If it would work, we could adopt the "each one teach one" idea, for anybody could spare a few hours to start students one by one so they could go on teaching themselves. But if the key-word method would not work, then students would have to be taught constantly for a year or two, and nobody would teach that long without being paid for it. There was room for a real difference of opinion. Some of our delegates at Guntur were from teachers' colleges in New York and Chicago. They said, "Argument will not prove this question. Let us try both ways for a year, and compare notes." This they did; a year later everyone voted for the key-word method.

The Telugu language is not only the pleasantest to hear but the most beautiful to look at in all India, with the graceful curves of figure skating. It could be a perfect alphabet, if only a few dozen irregularities were omitted. But when you suggest this to a scholar, he tells you, "There is a tremendous literature in Telugu that has been written on palm leaves through the past three thousand years." "A far greater literature," declared one pundit, "than you have in English. Who dares change this sacred writing for mere simplicity in learning!" The obvious answer is, "Nobody dares."

After the Guntur meeting Mr. K. G. Sundaram, principal of the teachers training school at Dornakal, prepared an excellent key-word primer in Telugu. He later became one of the five or six great literacy leaders of India. Never discouraged and never satisfied, he persisted in experiments with tireless tenacity, until he developed a key-word adult primer as streamlined as a jet liner.

Sundaram took me home with him to Dornakal, where I had two never-to-be-forgotten days at the home of Dr. Azariah, bishop of Dornakal, one of those Anglican spiritual giants who remind one of the late great Bishop Brent. Azariah was black with the blazing sun of South India, but in every other respect like an English bishop, if anything more so! For years he has been recognized as the leader of

Indian evangelical Christianity. It was amazing to see groups of Indians, all of them from the depressed classes, stopping the bishop along the road to ask whether they might not be received into his church.

Another of the influential Christians of India was Professor Bhaskarao P. Hivale of Wilson College, Bombay. He received his Ph.D. degree at Harvard University and had long periods of residence in America. Full of energy and optimism, it was natural that he should be made chairman of nearly everything. I saw him at his best as chairman of a retreat at Poona that December. Nationals and missionaries combined prayer, eager dedication of self to the stupendous task, and clear, efficient planning in a remarkable synthesis of vision and hard work. Lillian Picken's face fairly shone when she told us how she longed to open the most priceless of all books to her illiterate Indian Christians as she carried forward her reconstruction program at Satara, in Bombay Presidency.

We went from that retreat in an ecstasy like that of the Christians after Pentecost, to prepare lessons in Marathi—a language used by more than twenty millions of people. Twenty people had been at work for a week before I arrived and had already discovered key-words. To finish the task required only a few more days of delightful if strenuous application. Dr. Hivale was brilliant throughout. He wanted the lessons printed at once, even though they were still only the first rough draft. He argued that the swiftest way to experiment was to have a large number of persons trying the lessons simultaneously and pooling their experiences.

"Yes," I said, "if you do not kill the enthusiasm of the experimenters by that process."

"Never worry about us," he answered. "Nothing can kill our zeal, for this has got to be done."

I yielded to his infectious faith, and he printed five hundred copies at his own expense and gave them away to everybody who would experiment with them.

The following week he delivered a stirring inaugural speech as president of the All-India Conference of Indian Christians at Delhi, in which he declared: "We can make every Christian in India literate by 1941 if we adopt the motto 'Each One Teach One' and go home to see that every literate Christian does his duty." Hivale's speech became the watchword for all Christian India. "Every literate Christian do his duty . . . Each one teach one . . . Indian Christians literate by 1941."

Christmas Eve, 1936, found me in a crowded third-class railway carriage alone among strangers. I might as well have been on Mars. No one, so far as I knew, was a Christian, and I could not ask them because I could not speak Marathi. Perhaps nobody else in that car even knew it was Christmas Eve! I was lonesome and unhappy, for in my heart I knew those lessons we had been preparing and which Dr. Hivale had been so anxious to print were not yet right—they would not prove to be the answer to India's need. It was the strangest, most painful, and before that sleepless night was over, the most blessed Christmas Eve of my life. For an invisible Friend crept up close to my aching heart and God and I passed the night talking to each other about the millions of India. We have all had the experience that the loneliest hours of life may prove to be the most precious. God sends us such lonely hours, so that He can fill the vacuum.

Christmas Day was as lighthearted as that night had been solemn. We enjoyed a wonderful celebration at Vadala, where Dr. Edward Fairbank and his family were conducting one of the famous agricultural colleges of India. To have seen us in the midst of our fun on that day, nobody on earth would have guessed that all of us were missionaries and that none of us had imbibed anything stronger than tea. We were intoxicated with the spirit of Christmas.

The next day a hundred delegates hurried together from all over India to attend the annual conference of the National Christian Council held at Nagpur. The chairman of the council was the bishop of Dornakal, and its secretary was President Roy Strock of Guntur. Out in front also sat the leader of the world Christian movement, Dr. John R. Mott. And there was Bishop J. W. Pickett, a foremost authority on the Christian mass movements of India. Indeed, I felt as if the gods on Olympus were holding a session. The discussion centered mainly around the depressed classes, who were clamoring to enter the Christian church and so to get out of their endless and hopeless depression.

Mr. Gandhi had written the council a letter accusing missionaries of enticing the outcastes by picturing to them the worldly advantages they would gain by becoming Christians. The council spent the entire last day trying to word a reply so that it would not sound as if they were over-urging the outcastes but that still would make them feel welcome.

All this postponed my presentation of literacy to the last half hour. It seemed to me that the real issue was not whether we should or should not receive the outcastes into the church, but what kind of Christians we would make of them. We in America could not be very satisfactory Christians if we never read our Bibles nor other Christian literature. How can we expect these outcaste peoples, struggling against all their old habits, to be good Christians unless they can go to the Gospels daily to get victory by the power of Christ? Because of the mass conversions of the depressed classes, the literacy of Christians in India had dropped 6 per cent in twenty years. This was something to worry about. If we received them illiterate and left them that way, we would be cheating them, and we would risk the quality of the church and its standing in India.

To all this, the council listened for the final twenty-five minutes, eyes on their watches, and then rushed off to catch their trains. They had at least done a little better by the then illiterate 92 per cent of India than any council that had ever gone before them.

Our next conference was at Baloda Bazar in the Central Provinces. Here two first-rate educators, the Reverend J. C. Koenig and the Reverend E. W. Menzel, and some of their Indian teachers fairly scintillated with bursts of genius as they prepared a delightful key-word set of lessons. I know no other fun like making lessons with a really brilliant team.

Mr. Koenig had already prepared a list of the thousand most used Hindi words to guide writers of primers for children. These had been adopted by the Central Provinces government. Koenig's list revealed the words that books print most frequently but not the words that illiterates speak—it is amazing how these differ in India. After my visit, Mr. Menzel prepared another list of words by listening to illiterates talk and writing down the words they used. Hindi writers will henceforth have two excellent guides for preparing the kind of literature that adults just learning to read will love—if the fastidious Hindi scholars will tolerate in print words taken directly from the speech of the people. I doubt if they will, for the vernacular is full of slang! In

America, being democratic, we soon adopt these words of lowly origin into the dictionary, but in India, never!

Koenig, Menzel, and I also tried another daring innovation—tampering with the Hindi alphabet; but we got into trouble. The reaction was like an erupting volcano. Hindi letters, the pundits let us know, have the most ancient and aristocratic lineage on earth, descending from sacred Sanskrit—a perfect alphabet handed down out of heaven. So we fled from holy ground like Adam from Eden, and never again ventured to tamper with alphabets. Somebody else can do that!

Mr. Jawaharlal Nehru, the most distinguished leader in the Indian National Congress, later came out boldly in favor of using the Roman letters in all Indian languages. Under the protection of his shadow, I venture to endorse this with all my heart, mind, and strength.

At Shantiniketan, north of Calcutta, I had the rare privilege of meeting one of the world's greatest poets, the late Rabindranath Tagore, who was then very aged and looking like Father Time, with his long, white, flowing beard. When he looked at me with those large brilliant eyes, I forgot everything except the lovely soul behind them and the music of his sweet voice. He was the most unhurried great man I have ever met. For an hour I listened in rapt silence while he told me of his dream for Shantiniketan and the education of India.

One mark of Tagore's genius was this: that he took the common spoken words of Bengal's masses and wove them together into sentences of breath-taking beauty. He did it so long and so bewitchingly that the spoken Bengali has become correct as well as popular, and the old, stilted, "learned," cloudy language of the pundits has lost its grip on literature.

Tagore was the first in India to break the backbone of literary prudery. He set an example that writers in other dialects now venture to follow. Mr. Gandhi was doing it in his magazine *Harijan* for all India; we were indeed witnessing the beginning of a literary revolution that would prove to be a godsend to our literacy program. All over India I preached about Tagore, India's greatest living poet, as proof that all writers ought to become simple, clear, and direct, and Tagore's name convinced even the pundits.

At Allahabad, 500 miles up the Ganges from Calcutta, Sam Higginbottom presided over his famous Agricultural Institute. One of the major concerns of Higginbottom and his colleagues from the first was the improvement of India's cattle. India has the largest cattle population of any country in the world. No Hindu ever kills a cow. They have homes for aged, weak, and helpless cattle. But India's cows, unfortunately, give little milk, barely enough for their calves, and are used chiefly as draught animals for plows and carts. Higginbottom got the idea of introducing strains of great milk-producing cattle like Guernseys or Holsteins. The 100 million cows that have been eating India into poverty would then become as much an asset as they have been a liability.

But Higginbottom's problem was that diseases in India killed foreign cows, whereas long exposure has rendered the Indian cattle almost immune to these diseases. So he had to find a way to cross native and foreign strains in such a manner as to produce milk and at the same time retain immunity from disease.

It will require many generations of skillful breeding to establish these new cattle strains throughout India, but when it is accomplished it will have done more to furnish food for the starving multitudes than any other single step ever taken.

This huge undertaking would require the intelligent cooperation of the common people. It is impossible to go around and explain the principles to 345 million men and women by word of mouth, but it would be easy to enlist cooperation if the people could read. This is why Sam Higginbottom said to his students at the end of my first lecture: "There has never been a more important subject discussed in this college than the one you have just heard."

Straight across the Jumna River from the Agricultural Institute is Ewing Christian College. Here were 500 students burning with passion to lift India out of poverty and ignorance. They crowded the platform after I had challenged them to join the army of literacy teachers, and offered themselves, not one by one, but in platoons and companies. The statement that struck fire in their young souls was this:

"In five years there is going to be a tremendous awakening of interest in literacy throughout India, such as we now have in Russia, Turkey, Mexico, and China. Then India will be looking for leaders trained to become directors of adult education. Only a handful as yet meet the requirements. Thousands of writers will be needed also who know how to say things clearly and in simple, beautiful language such as Tagore uses in Bengali. Over a quarter of a million educated men and women in India are at present looking in vain for suitable employment. The number of available jobs for educated men and women is not as great as the supply. But this swiftly expanding literacy movement is a new field of opportunity for those who are adaptable and farsighted enough to see what is ahead. You students will soon have a vacation; use it to gain the experience you will need by teaching illiterates in your community. Then you will be ready for the new day."

That appeal I found brought students to the platform in every part of India.

Dr. J. H. Lawrence of Mainpuri had had the longest experience in all northern India in teaching illiterates. He had a school for men, women, and children, from sixty down to six, and used his own key-word method similar to ours in Lanao. Dr. Lawrence was a genius as a story writer in the simplest Hindi dialect. He could write equally well for men, women, or children. Some of his tales were borrowed from foreign lands, but most of them were taken from Indian folklore. He had put the Gospel of Luke into Hindi without ever an unfamiliar word, and yet it was as faithful to the original as the difficult standard Hindi text.

"Indeed," he declared, "it is more faithful, for, as all Bible students know, the original New Testament was not written in the classical Greek. It was written in the spoken Greek of Christ's day—they called it *koinē,* but we call it 'lingo.' Unless we translate the New Testament so that it is equally simple in Hindi, we in turn are not being faithful to the lovely simplicity of the original. It is mistranslating clear writing into the unintelligible. We make people think the Bible is 'highfalutin' while in reality it was common folk's talk."

Lawrence was not only telling the truth, he was using good horse sense.

At Agra I had the unforgettable experience of visiting the Taj Mahal by moonlight. Gossamer clouds reached down out of the evening sky and hung over the tips of the Taj minarets as though one of the "many mansions" that Jesus spoke about had been let down out of heaven in a moonbeam net and might be lifted to heaven again.

Canon T. D. Sully, principal of St. John's College at Agra, went with me to see this loveliest of all human creations and entertained me in his home. The canon looked like Hoffman's pictures of Jesus Christ, and his gentle voice and loving thoughtfulness were as Christlike as his appearance. His students had caught much of his compassion and were as pathetically eager to help India's illiterate unfortunates as the students in Allahabad had been. The day I was there they started a four-page paper in the simple language used by illiterate people and have carried it on ever since.

The Training School for Village Teachers at Moga, south of Lahore, deserved its reputation as the most modern educational institution in all India. Here I found the finest educational skill and something far deeper. Dr. and Mrs. Arthur E. Harper, graduates of Teachers College at Columbia University, and their highly trained Indian and American staff radiated a Christian spirit that even in a pugnacious province like the Punjab was bringing divergent elements into loving cooperation. For our conference at Moga the Harpers had gathered Christians, Moslems, Hindus, and Jains, who worked in delightful companionship.

Here our aim was to make "each one teach one" lessons in Urdu, which employs an Arabic form of alphabet. Half the vowels in Urdu are omitted, much as we use the abbreviation "bldg.," which one has to learn stands for "building" and not "bulldog." Urdu is almost as bad as English. In such a language there seemed to be no choice but to use the story method, beginning with easy sentences and building up a vocabulary by frequent repetition of familiar words. This is how Moga was teaching children. They had not up to that time attempted to teach adults. While I was there we tried to make lessons that could be taught to adults merely by following the line in the text, as a correspondence school makes self-explanatory lessons that the student can study by himself.

When we broke up five days later, I knew in my heart that we had not found the perfect answer to the riddle of Punjabi Urdu, but all of us parted smiling and happy, confident that we had started right and would finally succeed. We were happy, too, at the memory of the heavenly days we had enjoyed together.

Of all the precious memories at Moga, the one that went deepest into my heart was a conversation with Mr. Sadr-ud-din, supervisor of schools at Ferozpore. This Moslem gentleman was a rare spirit, overflowing with love and with a desire to do a million times more for India, for the whole world, than he knew how to do. He wanted me to realize how profoundly he was impressed by the life and teaching of Jesus Christ.

"The greatest story in the world," Sadr-ud-din told me with his eyes full of tears, "is the story of Jesus and the woman at the well. It has every quality of greatness. Jesus breaks the customs by talking to a woman alone, and transforms her life. Jesus meets this stranger of a hated race and a different religion, but He does not hesitate to break through every convention and talk to her, alone, and then He leaves her better than He found her. The greatest need of the whole world is to break down all the walls that separate us, of race and religion and nationality and sex, so that the pure love of God can tie the world together. The idea of God the invisible who is worshipped in spirit and in truth is the loftiest idea of God ever uttered. This story is so wonderful that I have it repeated to every child in every grade of my school. It strikes straight at the worst curse in India—the caste system."

The morning before I was to leave Moga, a truckload of students from the Government Training School in Lahore came down to visit this famous school. When I challenged these Lahore students to become specialists in literacy, they responded with eagerness, as only youth can. Several of them followed me back to Dr. Harper's home and insisted on knowing just how they could prepare for this new profession. One young man begged me to change my plans and go with him to Jind State, where his father was superintendent of schools. Two young men from Afghanistan demanded that I go to their country beyond the Khyber Pass at once. "We are far worse off than India," they said, "for we are 100 per cent illiterate! We will make sure that our government sends you a special invitation." They stuck so close and pleaded so hard that I missed my lunch and had to carry it along to eat on the train. "God helping me," I told those boys, "I shall go to Afghanistan." And I resolved to keep that promise.

In the ashram founded by Dr. E. Stanley Jones at Lucknow was another of those "heavens on earth" that have made my journeys so delightful. People of several nationalities and castes live together in radiant fellowship, some of them studying, others teaching, others laboring. All worship together. The prayer hours morning and evening, while we sat on the floor listening to God, filled my heart with a strange ecstasy, which comes back as I write. We could recover the sense of God's presence in America if we had a shrine in every Christian home and spent an hour in morning and evening prayer.

Mr. J. Holmes Smith, head of the ashram, was working actively in an organization to rescue the masses from debt and ignorance. Practically all the illiterate people in India are in debt, and since they cannot read they do not know what the account says; they only know that they and their ancestors have always been in debt and that they must do exactly what the moneylenders tell them. If that terrible load is lifted from the illiterate half of humanity, it will be one of the most glorious liberations in history.

At Isabella Thoburn College in Lucknow I asked the women students to make themselves specialists in lifting Indian women out of illiteracy. At somebody's suggestion we asked how many would volunteer to teach at least two and how many of them would try to write easy articles for illiterates to read. The whole roomful rose as though the floor had been lifted under them. After my talk they stampeded to the platform to volunteer, all of them asking questions at once. The terrible eagerness of India's educated young men and women holds the promise of the making of a new nation—one of the mightiest on earth; and India's wonderful young women will have an immense part to play.

The National Christian Council had by this time determined to take up literacy as one of its large programs, and in February 1937 it called a national conference in Nagpur, the city where its headquarters was located. Many of India's leading educators were present. The findings of this conference were circulated over all India. Here there is space for only a few sentences from the stirring appeal with which the findings conclude:

> Without the loyal service of patriotic young men and women, India cannot become literate. The insistent demand of the times is for youth who will gladly devote their time and effort to teaching illiterates in village and town as a great labor of love. We urge them to learn the best methods and carry the torch of education to their villages during the coming summer.
>
> We pass on to them and to all our fellow workers the ringing words of Garibaldi: "I offer neither pay nor quarters nor provisions; I offer hunger,

thirst, forced marches, battles, and death. Let him who loves his country in his heart, and not with his lips only, follow me!"

I wrote in my diary on the final night of that conference: "Tired but thankful for the finish of a wonderful conference. Keep us humble and perfectly responsive, open wide toward Thee. This I pray for myself and all the delegates who are again scattering over India. God, all Thy will, for all of us!"

There was thrill after thrill in the visit the next week to the immense city of Bombay. Under Dr. John McKenzie's leadership a conference was held at Wilson College; then another under the auspices of the educational committee of the Bombay Representative Christian Council. At an official city mass meeting on literacy the chairman was Bombay's leading citizen, former Mayor K. F. Nariman. But the man who kindled our enthusiasm most was a Hindu visitor from the important city of Poona—its mayor, Mr. S. R. Bhagwat. God raised him up for this turning point in India's history. He was an engineer, but his leading passion was the salvation of the illiterate masses from their misery, and he was convinced that they must be taught to read and write so that they will be able to lift themselves. All over India I found such wonderful Hindus, aching to lift the load from their tragic country, men and women who have much to teach America in self-sacrificing devotion. Mr. Bhagwat was living in a modest little house and spending all his income for the masses.

These months had taught me that India needed a wholly different kind of lessons from those in our easy Moro language, but what the new thing was to be only God knew. I went to Godhra, north of Bombay, praying and nearly desperate. The faculty of the Teacher Training School there heartily cooperated and for two weeks concentrated on making lessons in Gujerati, the language of about twelve million people in the northern parts of Bombay Presidency and Baroda.

My diary reminds me how, like a drowning man, I was grasping at a straw. While I was praying at midnight an idea came to me and the next day we tried it. Fortunately at the training school there was a good Indian artist and he did his best. We found words that began with each of the Gujerati consonants, then made pictures for the

પાઠ ૧.

કલમ	ખડીઓ	ગધેડું	ઘડો		ક k	ખ kh	ગ g	ઘ gh	
ચકલી	છત્રી	જમાદાર	ઝભલું		ચ ch	છ chh	જ j	ઝ jh	
ટપાલી	ઠગ	ડબ્બો	ઢબુ		ટ ṭ	ઠ ṭh	ડ ḍ	ઢ ḍh	
તપેલી	થડ	દડો	ધજા	નગારૂં	ત t	થ th	દ d	ધ dh	ન n
પગ	ફળ	બકરી	ભમરો	મરચું	પ p	ફ ph	બ b	ભ bh	મ m
રસ્તો	ઇયળ	લસણ	વડ		ર ra	ય ya	લ la	વ wa	
શકોરૂં	સસલું	હળ			શ sh	સ s	હ h	ળ ṛ	

GUJERATI READING CHART

words and prepared the first "picture-word-syllable" chart of its kind in India—or the world. Some women and children illiterates tried it and loved it so much they came back earlier every day for more. We would find them waiting on the doorstep when we arrived. God had answered my prayer, for that week we turned a literacy corner not only for India but for many other nations.

At the urgent request of Mr. Ralla Ram, secretary of the Student Christian Movement of India, I postponed my sailing for Africa and hastened back to Allahabad for further experiments with our Hindi charts. He had collected several highly educated Indians, college professors with scientific training, men who were eager for new things, no matter how radical, if only they could save India.

My heart still warms at the memory of the magnificent spirit of that group, particularly Ralla Ram; I could feel him praying every minute we labored. Then there was Mr. Reyazul Hassan, a Moslem who worked all day in a government office. He would rush home from his office at five o'clock and work on with me in the evening until it was time to close the college buildings for the night. We rearranged the Urdu letters according to their shapes and then he made brilliant nonsense rhymes to assist our memories. After he got home at night Hassan tried these lessons on illiterates as long as they would stay awake, and returned every day thrilled at their success.

By the end of two weeks our committee had prepared one set of lessons in Hindi and another in Urdu unlike any we had ever done elsewhere. It is marvelous how working creatively on literacy lessons ties silver threads about our hearts. Time after time separating from my fellow workers was harder than pulling out an eye tooth. The last session at Allahabad was a love feast and a prayer meeting of thanksgiving. When I left they gave me a silver acanthus leaf picture frame shaped like a heart and told me, "With this we are giving you India's heart."

Pandit Jawaharlal Nehru lived in Allahabad and had sent word that he was very anxious for us to work on lessons in Urdu, so I had the joy of taking the Urdu lessons to his home. He gave me the impression of great refinement and sensitiveness to the highest spiritual values. He afterwards wrote me as follows:

Anand Bhawan, Allahabad

I am greatly interested in the literacy movement which is gathering momentum in India. With your wide experience in the liquidation of illiteracy, this movement should derive great profit by your cooperation. I hope that the provincial governments in India, who are pushing this literacy campaign, will take full advantage of your expert knowledge and experience and will seek your cooperation. I am glad to learn that the World Literacy Committee of New York is interesting itself in the work in India. Any help that they may give in this work will be very welcome and will bear fruitful results.

Yours sincerely,

JAWAHARLAL NEHRU

With less than two weeks to spare before leaving for Africa, I hurried down to Sholapur and worked at the home of the Reverend William Hazen with feverish haste to throw into Marathi the new discoveries in "picture-word-syllable" chart-making that we had improved at Allahabad. Every evening we went to a "criminal tribe" settlement to experiment and we found the new method gave better results than anything we had ever tried. Mrs. Hazen later wrote that "they work like a miracle."

With these lessons under my arm, I went back to Poona to show them to my friend, Mayor Bhagwat. Eager and impulsive as ever, he took me at once to his car and in fifteen minutes we were at the office of his printer! Mr. Bhagwat ordered 10,000 copies of the lessons made then and there, although I begged him to try out only a thousand first, for they most certainly needed improvement. "No, no," he said. "I can sell 10,000 as easily as 1,000." So I surrendered. You can't put your foot down and say "no" to a mayor!

I had only two more days before leaving Bombay and was irresistibly driven by some power beyond me to undertake the preparation of lessons in the form of Urdu, commonly used among the Moslems of that city and surrounding region. Urdu is written in the Persian character and is the language generally spoken in Moslem centers of population. It has a number of variant forms in different parts of India. I sought some competent Moslem to help me and was fortunate in being introduced to a distinguished lawyer, Mr. A. H. Fyzee. His wife and mother, both educated women, caught my enthusiasm at

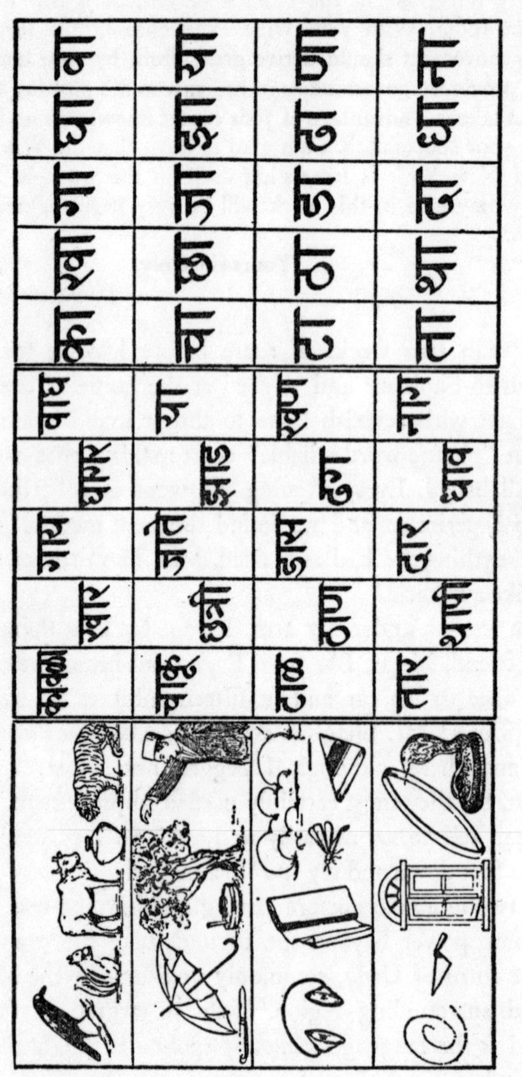

MARATHI READING CHART

once and worked with me all day Easter Sunday, except while I was in church. I felt that I had never pleased the Master more than that Holy Week, working all Good Friday with a Brahman and all Easter with two Moslem women. In two days' time we had completed our set of Bombay Urdu lessons.

Monday afternoon former Mayor Nariman and a large crowd of leading Indians met at the Gilder Tank School, the leading public school of Bombay, and listened to Mr. Bhagwat and myself describe the new lessons and tell them how Bombay might become literate. The government agreed to publish all of the new lessons in Marathi, Gujerati, Hindi, and Urdu. They began that afternoon to lay the foundation for what two years later was to be one of the most gigantic literacy campaigns in any city in all history.

As I sailed away from India that spring, bound for Africa, I wrote to my "prayer regiment," some hundreds of people scattered over all the world who have promised to pray for this literacy work every day: "Within five years a tremendous campaign against illiteracy will grip all India." And it did!

These are a few brief pictures of the second visit to India, but as I read over the diary that I was writing at the close of each day, I am reminded that the story you have read tells only of surface results, and that the deep secret of these remarkable days of discovery lies in surrender. On January 1, 1937, I had written in my diary:

> God, I want to give you every minute of this year. I shall try to keep you in mind every minute of my waking hours. I shall try to let my hand write what you direct. I shall try to let you be the speaker to direct every word. I shall try to let you direct my acts. I shall try not to act nor speak nor even think except in cooperation with you.

A few days later I was writing again to my "prayer regiment":

> These days have been closer to God than any five days of my life, and I want to make all 1937 like that, without a waking hour away from God. The thing that God has asked me to do for India and for the whole world will not be accomplished unless I make good on this new resolve. If God can only have His perfect chance, the thing He desires for India and for the illiterates of the world will come to pass.

CHAPTER 6

1937: A FIFTY-DAY ADVENTURE IN EAST AFRICA

LANDING AT MOMBASA, the principal port of Kenya, one takes an evening train for the long climb to Nairobi, the capital, a mile above sea level, and 300 miles inland. The next morning one awakes to look out over a vast grassy plain where thousands of zebras, wildebeests, gazelles, antelopes, and ostriches are grazing, unafraid of the train. One giraffe on the hillside towers against the sky—he looks tall enough to reach up and bite a piece out of the pale setting moon. On the south side of the track, extending for hundreds of miles, is a game preserve where nobody is allowed to hunt. The only enemies of these gentle-eyed grazing creatures are the lions, who, in defiance of the law, make a kill whenever they are hungry. Zebras are their delicacy, and they are never in want of fresh meat, for twenty-five million of these beautiful black and white striped ponies range the African plains.

On that April afternoon in 1937 when I reached Nairobi, Mr. E. G. Norris, the director of education, promptly dispatched one letter to the Catholic bishop and another to a representative of the Protestant missions, requesting each of them to appoint two language experts to help build adult lessons.

Mr. Norris then sent me on to Kisumu, some 200 miles west of Nairobi, with Archdeacon Owen, a leading missionary of the Church of England, a linguistic authority and a noted geologist. Once the archdeacon stopped his car to jump into a new excavation and study the stones. Presently he emerged in triumph, with a rough stone that he said was made by the most primitive people in the world.

"Are their descendants in Africa now?" I asked innocently, and he looked at me almost with pity.

"The lowest people on the earth today are highly civilized compared with those men of the rough Stone Age," he said. "They lived here a hundred thousand years ago. We may find that Africa was the cradle of the human race; this valley may have been the Garden of Eden." He chuckled at that.

In addition to his other gifts, the archdeacon had a fine sense of humor—a necessity for a missionary in Africa.

Kisumu is a town of shining white houses on the shore of Lake Victoria. My task was to make lessons in the Luo language, which belongs to the Sudan or Nilotic language group. There are three main language groups in Africa. The other two are Bantu and Hamitic. Archdeacon Owen introduced me to a great scholar of the Luo language, his friend Father Rolands of the Roman Catholic Society at Kisumu, and the kindly father gave me a copy of his new Luo grammar—and his blessing.

The committee appointed to work with me was the faculty of the Maseno School for Boys, on the edge of the densely settled Kavirondo Reserve.

At night I slept on one side of the equator and during the day our committee worked on the other—a marker showed exactly where it crossed the school grounds. One evening, after looking in all directions to be sure no one was watching, I stepped back and forth across the equator one thousand times—just so I could boast. It seemed that with the equator completely at one's mercy something had to be done about it. So, believe it or not, Mr. Ripley, I am the only living man—at least from Benton, Pennsylvania—who has crossed the equator one thousand times in twenty-five minutes.

At a wee place called Bunyori, in the bush north of Kisumu, the American Church of God has a mission among the Nyore people, who speak one of the Bantu languages. With a tiny hand-press and a small amount of type, an American woman and her faithful African helper had printed primers and booklets about geography and other subjects. They had translated the entire New Testament into Nyore, and it had been published by the American Bible Society. Their school was very practical, teaching the boys how to farm and build houses and the girls how to cook and weave and care for children.

Making lessons in Africa was much easier than in India, because the alphabets were so much simpler and more phonetic. There were almost no written languages south of the Sahara desert when the missionaries arrived; so they could choose their own alphabets. The only trouble is that there are many sounds in Africa for which we whites had no letters. You have doubtless read of the *kq* sound the Zulus use—a sound like saying "get up" to a horse by making a cracking sound behind your wisdom teeth. Spell that if you can! So if you had *three* cracking sounds to spell as the Zulus have, what letters would you use?

However, the big riddle in Africa is not how to spell, but what language to teach illiterates. "Their own language, of course," you say. Yes, but there are nine hundred languages and dialects that so shade into one another that it cannot be determined where one ends and the next begins. Some dialects are spoken by several million people, some by a few thousand. For example, in the section of Kenya where we were working, there are five different missionary societies from America and England, each working with a different dialect. All five dialects belong to the Bantu family and are enough alike for the native people to talk to one another with the aid of a few gestures. Did they need five different sets of lessons and five different newspapers? This was our problem. The saving in time and money would be enormous if we could use only one. The missionaries agreed to give their best scholars a year to compare their word lists and find out. By the end of the week we had made charts in Luo and in Nyore.

As I went a little farther south into the Kikuyu country I began to touch the most important of all the Bantu languages in Kenya. Kikuyu is spoken by over a million people. My heart was stirred by the hardships suffered by their women. As soon as she can walk, a baby girl begins to carry all her little back can stand, holding the load with a strap running over her forehead. She learns to walk leaning far forward and her neck muscles become so strong that by the age of fifteen she may be able to carry 200 pounds. This practice the government has tried to discourage by making sixty pounds the legal load for women as for men, but Kikuyu women refused to obey this, saying, "Who are we that we should be limited to the load a man is able to carry?" All over this land, one sees lines of these pack-carrying women leaning forward as they trudge along, up and down the steep hills. The Kikuyu never go around a hill. They prefer to go straight up and straight down to their destination.

Here among the Kikuyu we ran into another of those perplexing spelling questions. The Italian Fathers, who have a school and press at Nyeri, in north Kenya, have adopted the Latin spelling as used in Italy. The Protestants had sought the advice of German authorities and had adopted a very different spelling, especially for vowels. No one had ever succeeded in reconciling these two forms of spelling; so when I arrived, our committee had to choose between them.

The three educated Africans who constituted my committee for the Kikuyu language desired the Italian form of spelling, and I was quite satisfied, because there were only five vowels—the shorter the better, for quick learning. So we spelled our charts as words are spelled in Spanish and Latin.

These three Africans were on fire with eagerness for the education of their people. I want their names in this book: Mr. Eliud W. Mathu, president, and Mr. James S. Gechuru, secretary, of the Kikuyu African Teachers Union, both teachers in the Alliance High School; and Mr. Stevenson Githi, an educated evangelist of the Scottish Church missions on an adjacent hill.

Building lessons with these young men was a spiritual benediction, for they were intensely in earnest. We were four brothers together, getting an immense thrill out of our adventure. They brought some nearby illiterates every day, and the lessons proved easier than anybody had expected. The teachers and students laughed in sheer glee. When we reported our good results to the director of education, he said: "You do not surprise me, for to tell you the truth, the African children are doing better in our schools than the white children."

He called a literacy conference at the Jeanes School in Kabete, and thirty-six persons responded, most of them Protestant and Roman

Catholic missionaries. The three men who had helped build the Kikuyu lessons told the gathering that every African longs to become literate, and begged us to cooperate. "All we Africans ask of you whites is to give us your backing and financial help, and we will do the rest."

When the chief inspector took me to lunch later, he said, "You little realize how timely your visit to Kenya has been. These Africans are getting more and more insistent that the government educate adults. We cannot refuse much longer."

The memory of those three African teachers pleading with us to help their illiterate countrymen came back to me some days afterward as I chatted with a handsomely dressed European while waiting in a railway station. He told me he was an official of a gold mining company, and when I told him my mission, he said, "I have nothing whatever against you personally, but I will tell you frankly that professionally you are my enemy. If you teach these savages to read, they will soon think they are as good as we are. Can't you see that you will start unrest and labor troubles all over Africa?"

This man who called himself my "enemy" had helped me for the first time to realize all it could mean to be one more missionary laboring for the emancipation of Africa. That night I wrote in my diary:

April 30, 1937: Today, Father, closes the four most glorious months of my life. We are stepping into a new world, dear Lord, hand in hand, sailing together with thrilling eagerness toward unknown shores. At fifty-two, nothing I have ever done seems worth preserving or even recalling save this high adventure. God, help me to continue a gentle but incessant pressure of my will toward Thee on and on and on!

My hosts at the Alliance High School, Kikuyu, had been Principal Bruce Grieves and his wife, who had welcomed me like a long-lost son. When I was ready to leave they drove me all the way down to Nairobi, and waved to me as the train departed until we were out of sight. We had found each other on levels far deeper than common educational interests.

A short passage southward along the coast brought me to Zanzibar. This is the island to which, for centuries, most of the slaves taken in eastern Africa by Arab slave traders were brought to be auctioned off and shipped to various parts of the world. The Episcopal cathedral now stands on the site of the old slave market. Swahili is a Bantu language that contains many Arabic words. It was spoken on the coast and spread into the interior with the traders.

In 1890, when the British made Zanzibar a protectorate, they abolished slavery; but Swahili, the old slave drivers' language, has stuck. It has penetrated deep into the very heart of Africa and to this day it is the language people find it easiest to use when they visit tribes other than their own. The British are promoting Swahili as a *lingua franca* for East Africa. It has a comparatively simple grammar with few irregularities, and so is easy for Africans to learn—far easier for them than English. Yet the Africans outside Zanzibar prefer English, even if it is harder to learn, because one cannot secure advancement into the better paid government posts without command of it.

I discovered that Director of Education G. B. Johnson and his wife had traveled in the United States studying educational methods and knew something of American education, and that Mrs. Johnson had founded and was principal of the government school for Moslem girls, one of the best of its kind to be found anywhere. They immediately drew together a fine, live committee, which in three days prepared eight Swahili lessons, tested them, and found that they worked with natives.

But our work was interrupted during the week of the coronation of King George VI. In Zanzibar I was staying in the home of the British Resident, the senior British official. He took me with him to the cathedral for the coronation service, and, to my horror, conducted me up to the front row, the only man in this group not wearing a military or academic costume. "At least," I thought, "I can stand for democracy!" The rest of that day was spent with the Resident and his wife, listening over the radio to the coronation ceremonies in London.

In the evening we went out to the enormous military grounds where thirty-six different African tribes, each forming its own circle, were dancing, singing, and shouting to celebrate the crowning of the new king. This, shades of Mr. Barnum, *was* "The Greatest Show on Earth," a thirty-six ring circus, every ring different from every other, out of the heart of Africa; drums, shields, spears, gorgeous headdresses, hideous false faces, blood-curdling yells, war dances, love dances, spirit dances.

The coronation exercises interfered with our literacy efforts for nearly a week. Everybody celebrated; nobody felt in the mood to work. The only thing our energetic director Mr. Johnson could accomplish was to appoint committees.

As chairman of a special committee for work with women, Mrs. Johnson took me one day to the balcony of her school for a glimpse of the two hundred girls, rich and poor alike, some wearing fine dresses and jewelry, who came to school in tightly curtained motor cars.

"Now," she said, "I want you to prepare short-cut lessons with Arabic letters for these girls to use." So the next day a Moslem committee joined me and built up Swahili lessons with Arabic letters. The committee disagreed and scolded and shouted and ended up happy and triumphant, in true Arabian style.

The next stop on my voyage down the coast was Dar es Salaam, capital of the British mandated territory of Tanganyika. In the government school for African boys, three students helped build Swahili lessons several steps beyond any we had previously attempted. We gave them the name "Picture-Word-Syllable" lessons. (See *Toward a Literate World,* by Frank C. Laubach, pp. 128-131. New York, World Literacy Committee, 1938.) There were many more pictures than we had ever before used; indeed, one for every syllable in the Swahili language. The African boy who drew the pictures was only a fair artist, but his heart was in his task. He labored for many hours, patiently changing every picture as we changed our ideas. He felt that he was doing something enormously important for his needy people and insisted that he must give nothing but his best. Long before we had finished, this African boy had stolen my affections.

When we tried the Swahili lessons on illiterates, the pictures did so much of the teaching that after a few minutes of explanation the students could go on alone, discovering the sounds of the letters for themselves—and having great fun doing it.

My diary gives a better picture of the exciting days that followed at Dar es Salaam than I know how to show in any other way:

May 21, 1937: Yesterday and today have filled my heart with boundless gratitude to God. The new charts are working like magic! We have tried them on twelve or more persons with uniformly striking success. They are, I am sure, an improvement on anything we have ever before attempted. They contain sixty pictures and will involve a little more expense for cuts than I had hoped would be necessary, but they work!

I have a good place in which I can experiment with a large number of women. It is the African Girls' School, where a class for adult women is held every afternoon from two to four. These women seem to be even more eager to learn to read than the men are, and their progress has been astonishing.

They are not like the carriers of burdens that I saw in the Kikuyu hills. They are well clothed. But mentally and morally and spiritually they are pitiful. They are among the forty thousand natives who have been attracted from tribal life somewhere deep in Africa to live in this crowded city of Dar es Salaam. The men work, but their wives are cooped up in hot little rooms with nothing to do. Under these circumstances, they are under great temptation to break away from moral restraint, yet not one of them seems beyond hope if the vision of Christ can take possession of her life.

May 23: How eager they are to learn! Saturday afternoon came and the school was not to be open. The women begged me to return and arranged especially for the room. They don't want a holiday! I am weary after a two-hour session every afternoon, but they say, "We are not tired yet," and want to go on studying until dark.

The three leading African men of Dar es Salaam came to see this women's class this afternoon and showed great enthusiasm. These men are employed by the government but will give me their entire holiday, Monday. I am now teaching men in the forenoon in "The Old Comrades' Club House" and devoting the afternoon to this women's school. I have not seen such eagerness on the part of illiterates since I left Lanao!

May 27: Our Swahili lessons are all finished. Everyone, including two men over fifty years old, learned without the slightest difficulty. Eight men have reached the reading stage this week. One young fellow was learning the syllables when suddenly he discovered that he could pronounce new words alone. With victory gleaming in his eyes, he shouted: "Give me a book! I can read!" And he did, as elated as Columbus was when he first sighted the coast of the New World.

This forenoon Mr. Isherwood, director of education, called together sixty leaders, over half of them Africans, to "The Old Comrades' Club House" to hear the eight men who had studied there that week read and to lay plans for the future. I prayed and thanked God while those men demonstrated their brilliance before the meeting. "These men knew how to read before. They deceived you," insisted some of the English visitors, "for it is humanly impossible for anybody to read so soon." The faces of the new literates were radiant. When I said, "You may go now," they insisted on staying; and although they could not understand a word of English, they leaned forward and tried to learn it that afternoon. They had made up their minds that education was easy! "Look at the light in their eyes," whispered the director of education, and the light was in his eyes, too.

After that demonstration everybody was in favor of going ahead at once. The Africans, trembling with hope, said they would teach everybody in Dar es Salaam. We asked the men who had just learned to read if they would be teachers, too, and they nodded their heads and beamed like angels in heaven. Mr. Martin Kyamba, the outstanding African of all Tanganyika, clung to my hand and said in front of that whole gathering of foreigners, "I have watched you day by day teaching my countrymen, and I am convinced that this is the greatest hope that has come to Africa since Livingstone!"

We must have a newspaper for those newly literate men and women; we are agreed about that. The director told us that he had had an interview with the governor, who had expressed himself as in favor of the paper, under proper auspices.

June 1 (sailing from Africa for India): Mr. John, editor of the government school paper, *Mamba Leo,* came with me as far as Zanzibar to make plans. Within half an hour after our arrival there, I was captured by the Moslem committee, who were full of new ideas for making better lessons with Arabic script. We had time to examine a new arrangement of letters, and they promised that they would finish the lessons themselves. The intense and passionate zeal of these Moslems for their faith and their people is beyond praise.

Mr. Johnson called his Zanzibar committee, and Mr. John told them that the Tanganyika government was ready to go full speed ahead. Then the committee decided to have a hundred copies of our lessons duplicated so that teachers in Kenya, Zanzibar, and Tanganyika might experiment and present their opinions to the directors, who will then decide whether to release appropriations to print the lessons on a large scale. Only a hundred copies on a duplicator! But no African leader was there to weep!

Now I am steaming away from Africa with no doubt about our lessons but much doubt about our organization and the training of our leaders. To the last hour before the boat sailed, four of the men who are to do the real work remained with me on the ship's deck to learn all they could. A cold chill is gripping my heart lest red tape strangle our new-born campaign to death.

I almost got back to Africa in 1940, but not quite. The World's Sunday School Association had invited me to speak and train literacy leaders at its proposed convention in Durban, South Africa, and I had planned to visit all southern and central Africa during the six months following the convention. But meanwhile the Second World War broke out and the Durban convention was canceled.

This first visit to Africa, like my first visit to India, was little more than exploratory and altogether too brief. The infant campaign did not thrive alone. In Kenya it was nearly choked to death by a controversy over spelling. The Protestants stood firm for the spelling that they had adopted in 1931, while the Kikuyu African Teachers Union favored the spelling of the Italian Catholic Fathers. "The government," said the Union in a report, "was ready to print the lessons on a large scale . . . but unfortunately was unable to proceed on account of the orthography controversy." Behold what a great fire two letters can kindle! The Italian Fathers printed and used the new lessons without waiting for the government.

In spite of the disappointments, delays, and general indifference that checked the efforts for extending adult literacy in Africa, some amazing reports were received in the years following that visit. At least forty mission stations informed us that they built lessons generally similar to those developed in 1937 and that they were being used with excellent results. There were doubtless others of which we have no record. Experience in the war has made many Africans aware of the importance of reading. A missionary serving as a chaplain with native troops somewhere in East Africa wrote in 1942 to Miss Margaret Wrong of the International Committee on Christian Literature for Africa: "You would be amazed at the sale of literature among African soldiers. It beats anything I have ever seen in the villages. I simply cannot keep pace with the demand. When work is over, a walk round the camps would show groups of Africans here and there reading, singing, and some studying, the place littered with books. It is the finest extra-mural university I have yet seen in Africa."

The experience in lesson building at Dar es Salaam marked a real advance in our world literacy program because it registered a definite improvement in method, the principal features of which might be thus summarized:

In India our pictures had illustrated all of the consonants, but only one of the vowels. Each consonant was followed by the vowel sound *a;* pictures illustrated the syllables *ba, ma, sa,* and the rest, but not *be,* nor *bi,* nor *bo,* nor *bu.*

In the Swahili charts made in Dar es Salaam we had pictures of words that began with every possible combination: *ba, be, bi, bo, bu, ma, me, mi, mo, mu,* and so on to the end. While the Swahili charts required more pictures than the Indian charts used, they gave the student a picture for every syllable, so that if he forgot the sound, he could find it for himself. Our lessons in India had been like speeding down a fine asphalt road fifty miles an hour and suddenly running into mud holes. In Africa we had filled the holes. I left Zanzibar for Bombay determined that for our campaigns in India we would perfect lessons as smooth as those we had developed in Dar es Salaam.

I arrived in Bombay on June 12, 1937, with plans to meet Mrs. Laubach in Colombo sixteen days later and proceed with her to Manila. I was so consumed with eagerness to accomplish many tasks in these brief weeks that I could not sleep. First I hurried down to Sholapur and told my good friends the Hazens of my hopes for the coming days. In two hours I was at work with a teacher and an artist, who shared some of my excitement, though they did not know what it was all about. In two days we changed our earlier Marathi lessons to conform to the African type of charts. Without taking time to try them on illiterates I started east to Hyderabad, in my pocket a letter of introduction to the director of education, intending to attempt the preparation of lessons in Urdu.

The director was not there—providentially! From that point on I had the most astonishing experience of God's doing everything while I looked on that ever came to me. Walking toward the station I whispered, "Why did you bring me here, Lord? The director isn't here." An inner voice said, "Go into this store." I looked and saw it was the British and Foreign Bible Society. I told the clerk my name and he cried, "We all know you. Come with me to Dr. Frank Sackett's home. He is the Methodist superintendent."

The moment my name was mentioned, Dr. Sackett picked up *Letters by a Modern Mystic* from his table and said, "I was just reading this. Will you go with me to Medak, seventy-five miles north of here?"

"I have just three days," I said.

"Then," he replied, "we will start immediately."

Medak was in the center of one of the greatest mass movements toward Christianity and the seat of a normal training school. The faculty had not dreamed of my coming, but they stopped school at noon and set free eighteen missionaries and Indian teachers to make literacy lessons in Telugu. They made Miss Sallie Anstey, head of the Girls Training School, "general" of this literacy army, and she was a wonderful general of a wonderful army. She prayed every minute and worked while she prayed.

The "war" began right after lunch and was carried on with unflagging spirit until eleven that night. Though the whole plan for Telugu was new and difficult, we all seemed able to take every step without a moment's hesitation. If God ever in this world inspired human beings, He gave us those lessons. Eight of us prepared the material, ten copied the letters by hand (for no one has yet invented a typewriter that will hold all the Telugu letters), and two Indians drew pictures. Next day we worked all day until eleven at night, and on the third day we finished.

The air was electric; everyone felt sure that God was doing the work, using our hands and minds. The memory of those three days still makes me tingle. Later, when my co-workers tried the lessons on illiterates, they called them "miraculous," "perfect."

In that group was Frank Whittaker, who became secretary of the National Christian Council of India a few months later and who was responsible for setting up the splendid schedule for the literacy campaign of the following year. Its tremendous success is due more to his unquenchable zeal and infinite pains than to any other factors, and his zeal was born in Medak during those three days.

What God says to me through that miraculous experience is this: "You don't have to be bright; you don't have to be powerful; you don't have to see the whole way ahead. All you need is to be sure of what I want done, trust enough to venture, and obey every minute."

I now rushed on down to Bangalore in Mysore State to undertake the preparation of charts in Kanarese, an important language spoken by eleven million people, in which I had never before attempted lessons. I arrived unannounced, but the Methodist missionaries dropped everything else, found a drawing master, and set to work with me.

Indian Director of Education N. S. Subla Rao returned the next day from his vacation and immediately became excited when he saw the lessons we had made. It happened that one of the most brilliant educators in India, K. Srinivasa Achar, Hindu headmaster of the Government Normal School in Tumkur, Mysore, was visiting the office when I came in. The director appointed him on the spot to help me. He canceled his plans to return to his normal school and worked with us two more days. The Kanarese lessons were as fine as the Telugu, and the artist's work was better. That evening I left for Madras, my soul blazing with eagerness to throw just one more language, Tamil, into the new African type of lessons before leaving India.

The Christian Literature Society of Madras appointed their two best Tamil writers and critics and their expert artist to cooperate with me, and in two and a half days we had finished the Tamil lessons. That night I took the train for Colombo and could sleep! Between June 12 and 28 we had completed lessons in four languages along the new lines developed first in Dar es Salaam, and I knew it could be done all over India!

This is from a letter to my "prayer regiment," written after the ship left Colombo:

> I am most grateful to God and to the people everywhere who dropped their work and closed their classes in order to help make lessons. Everywhere people seem to have heard about literacy and to be on tiptoe with expectancy for the future. I can hardly wait two years to hear, or—as I ardently hope—to see what the results will be.

It must seem to you like sheer audacity for me to have undertaken to help other countries with only my Philippine experience. But, after all, God, who had planned it all, pushed me on when I hardly knew what I was doing—and He is working out the future far ahead of us. We have nothing to fear except our own deafness to His voice when He calls us to larger opportunities. This much I can see—our experiments will have a profound significance for three-fifths of the human race. We are now en route to the Philippines to resume our work among the Moros—we can hardly wait. . . .

CHAPTER 7

1938-40: THE INDIA-WIDE CAMPAIGN FOR LITERACY

UPON RETURNING to Lanao we developed a new series of lessons based on what we called the "picture-chain" method (p. 113), even simpler than those we had developed in Africa. I was eager to try these all over India. The opportunity came in December 1938, when the International Missionary Council met at Tambaram, near Madras.

Those two previous visits had sown more seed than any of us could have anticipated and this third visit found the harvest ripe. The newspapers all over India had been giving our aims and efforts large publicity. Thousands of leaders who had formerly despaired of making that vast country literate were now convinced that the way had been found, and at the top of the list were Mr. Gandhi and Mr. Nehru. The imagination of the country was captured by figures showing the speed with which India could achieve literacy, if only enough public spirit and altruism could be released so that each literate would teach one illiterate a year—or, failing that, if he would pay somebody to do it for him.

In 1938 8 per cent were literate. If each of the 8 per cent taught one that year, then in 1939 16 per cent would be literate, in 1940 32 per cent would be literate, in 1941 64 per cent would be literate, and in 1942 128 per cent would be literate! That extra 28 per cent would make up for the increase in population!

Of course this is pure idealism. We had not expected them to reach

	a	i	o	u
amo	a	i	o	u
mama	ma	mi	mo	mu
sapi	sa	si	so	su
karabao	ka	ki	ko	ku
tali	ta	ti	to	tu
babak	ba	bi	bo	bu
lapad	la	li	lo	lu
nanas	na	ni	no	nu
papanok	pa	pi	po	pu
gantang	ga	gi	go	gu
dado	da	di	do	du
rantai	ra	ri	ro	ru
ngari	nga	ngi	ngo	ngu

MARANAW PICTURE-CHAIN CHART

that perfect result, but they did better than ever before in their history. It is estimated on the basis of the 1941 census figures that the percentage of literates for the entire country increased from less than 7 per cent in 1931 to 12 per cent in 1941.

Frank Whittaker had arranged 218 meetings of various kinds preceding and following the Madras conference, and these proved to be the most wonderful experiences I had in India. An account of the meetings and a history of the literacy movement in India are contained in *India Shall Be Literate,* sponsored by the National Christian Council of India, Nagpur, 1940. Merely to name them, a line to a meeting, would take too many pages of this book. I shall ask you only to take grasshopper leaps with me to a score of the most interesting points, which must serve as samples for all the rest.

The early part of December 1938 found me packed in a small auto with my friend Mason Olcott and his wife and children, going west through the hills of Madras Presidency until at last we came to a huge valley across which the government had just completed a mile-long dam for one of its wonderful irrigation projects (Britain was building such dams in India before we began them in America). Mason Olcott had selected Mettur Dam as the site for a literacy conference because it was accessible from eastern and western cities and because every delegate would be so far from home that he would not be bothered by his neighbors!

One hundred leading Hindus, Moslems, and Christians had come great distances, some over 200 miles, to this remote place to plan the conquest of illiteracy. Religious differences were wholly forgotten while these men struggled with "public enemy number one"—as the vice-chancellor of the University of Madras called it in his opening speech. He had come 150 miles to preside.

We did not try to make lessons—with a hundred leaders, all eager to talk, we would never have finished. We were there to wrestle with the other problems to be solved in carrying a literacy campaign through to victory—questions that will interest and perhaps astonish you.

There was a debate on the question of whether "each one will really teach one." This gave us a chance to say that this would work if we could inject enough Christlike love into the campaign—and Hindus and Moslems believed it! We discussed the high art of making adults love their teacher and their lessons so much they would come back without compulsion.

Somebody objected that adults were too old to learn, whereupon Mason Olcott brought forth Professor Edward L. Thorndike's *Adult Learning* to prove that a man of forty can learn more quickly than a child of six. A whole half day was devoted to women—only 4 per cent of the women of India are literate as against 12 per cent of the men.

A forenoon was dedicated to explaining how to start campaigns, to get the people stirred up and eager, how to find teachers and generals, how to find the best time of day and the best places to teach, and how to get factories and schools and churches into the campaign.

But half the battle for literacy depends upon the literature that is prepared for the new literates. It must be *easy*. So the conference appointed language experts to prepare lists of the basic words the illiterates have been accustomed to using. It must be *interesting,* for semi-literates cannot read fast nor far—they want no scholarship, but simple, clear, high-powered news—every sentence packed with important facts. So we spent some hours in a fascinating and hilarious exploration of what illiterates talk about most. The list those men made astonishes and sometimes shocks Americans: debt and hate of moneylenders, Gandhi, jewelry for ladies' noses and ankles, fate, cows, cooking, cow dung for fuel, quarrels (especially of mothers and daughters) court trials, rice, pilgrimages and sacred rivers, ghosts, caste, everything about sex including birth control, riddles, sleight-of-hand and snake charming, eye diseases, itch, plague, purdah, weddings, water, selling girls, markets, snake bites, gossip, drowning, taxes, mud houses, rats.

We also discussed the question Mr. Gandhi had raised: Shall we fill people's stomachs and give them better homes first, or teach them to read first? The conference ended up unanimous on that question—if we make people literate, they will be able to help themselves, but if 12 per cent of India tries to lift the other 88 per cent, it will never get done. As a grand climax the committee on findings read such a challenge to India as sent us home bursting with confidence and eagerness to get at the job. Mason Olcott's face was beaming. He had spent endless hours and much money in the interests of literacy and now his day of triumph had come.

Conferences like that at the Mettur Dam were held in forty other places in India during the succeeding five months, each lasting from a day to a week. Always there was a premier or vice-chancellor or mayor or judge or some other distinguished citizen in the chair. Always we discussed alphabets, looked wistfully at the Roman letters—but only twice dared to adopt them! Always teachers sat open-mouth at the "revolutionary" idea that you can teach by love instead of by scolding. Always we had to prove the equally revolutionary idea that adults are not too old to learn. Always we had to answer the doubt as to whether people can be made unselfish enough to teach anyone else without pay. Often we had to face the doubt as to whether women ought to be allowed to read or had the brains to learn. Always the pundits insisted on using only those words to be found in classical literature—and always they were silenced by the example of Rabindranath Tagore and Gandhi. Between conferences were sessions for building lessons, making addresses of all kinds, holding interviews, and paying respects to officials.

This journey was broken between December 12 and 29 by the meeting of the International Missionary Council at Tambaram. Four hundred and sixty-four delegates from sixty-nine nations and areas here wrestled with the overwhelming religious and social problems of our age. It was the first international conference of evangelical Christians in which a full half of the delegates were from the non-white peoples of the world and represented the younger churches. Furthermore, it was the first great Christian convention that gave any attention to the illiterate three-fifths of the world as a class.

The literature committee included these paragraphs in its findings:

> Thus far we have discussed the needs of those who can read. But over 90 per cent of the adherents of non-Christian religions are illiterate. What is equally distressing is that in some lands many Christians, including some of their leaders, are unable to read their own Bibles and hymn books. It is futile to talk of distributing literature to these people until they can read.
>
> As medicine heals the bodies of men, literacy liberates their minds and has a legitimate place in the Christian program.
>
> To be successful, literacy campaigns must follow well tested scientific methods, and should have the best available expert advice on such matters

as lesson building, basic word lists, adult psychology and the training of leaders. Invaluable experience has accumulated from the lands now engaged in the intensive literacy campaigns and provision must be made for passing on the experience to all regions grappling with the problem of illiteracy.

Those who have just learned to read must be supplied with a literature simple in form and interesting to adults. The need for this is acute, for if Christian writers fail to provide it many anti-Christian forces will enter the field. Such a literature calls for expert authorship, and help in this matter should be afforded from one field to another.

The meeting was crowded with notable speeches that stirred one's very depths. The climax was Dr. John R. Mott's marvelous closing address, which sent us out silent with aching purpose.

Between sessions delegates came to the literature room where fifty literacy lessons were exhibited and where the beginnings were made of twelve more picture-chain charts in languages of Africa, Asia, and the Americas. At the same time a fine artist from the Christian Literature Society of Madras prepared on masonite a large picture-chain chart in the Tamil language. It was beautifully painted in three colors and shimmered with a special kind of varnish, the loveliest chart any of us had ever seen. This I carried with me all over India and it sold the picture-chain method by its sheer beauty.

The first place we showed this chart following the Madras conference was at Bangalore, Mysore State. Dr. Fred Field Goodsell, executive vice-president of the American Board of Commissioners for Foreign Missions, went with me to show it to Dewan (Premier) Sir Mirza M. Ismael, B.A., K.C.I.E., O.B.E. The dewan was an engineer whose remarkable development of Mysore State makes one feel he deserved all those honors. He was a lover of beauty and was charmed by our beautiful chart. "Make one of these for us in Kanarese," he said, "and we will have it made up on green Mysore marble with inlaid letters in silver and placed in every village in our dominion!"

The dewan requested me to go to Mysore City, of which he is tremendously proud. These Indian States are totalitarian, and the request of a dewan is a command! I obeyed, and was entertained like a prince at the government palace. In the evening I was taken to see the most marvelous system of illuminated, colored fountains in all India, or, so far as I know, in all the world—the dewan's cherished creation. The fountains are located below the great dam that furnishes lights to all Mysore cities and would soon, the dewan said, be lighting every village home in the state. The sheer ability of these government officials in Mysore, and the clip, clip with which they were running everything was marvelous. There was here no sign of democracy, but a most competent and benevolent dictatorship, if one may judge by material progress.

Early in January, 1939, I returned to Madras to meet fifty-five of the élite gathered at the beautiful home of Mrs. Ammu Swamanathan. The premier of the Madras provincial government, C. Rajagopalachari, was chairman. Later he came into wider fame for his independent utterances in the Indian Congress. The president of every leading college in Madras was present. This literacy adventure, which two years before had been confined almost wholly to missionaries and Christian laymen, was now drawing hearty support from leaders of all the Indian communities. Wholly overwhelmed at the hospitality of Madras society, I wrote in my diary that evening:

> O God, O God, these twenty millions of illiterate Tamils hang now upon that group who have met here with the Premier to organize the Adult Education Movement of Madras Presidency. Thou knowest how to prepare their hearts to do what Thou dost desire. Please, God, take such possession of me that Thy will, exactly, all and nothing but Thy perfect will, may be accomplished. This is Thy work and it must go on. Others are now seeing the vision and they will continue it. Thank thee, dear Friend, for letting me have a share in this stupendous undertaking.

In the magnificent buildings of Madras University was held the South India Adult Education Conference. The presiding officer was the minister of education. Educators of every religion spoke, but above them all the Christian leaders—Mrs. A. Devasahayam, Mr. S. G. Daniel, and Dr. Mason Olcott—shone like stars. These three, one felt, represented the passion of Christ spending itself for the oppressed. But the undying fire in their hearts was matched by a young Hindu, Mr. T. J. R. Gopal, a passionately patriotic youth who had organized this conference and who later wrote a book about it. Heaven had set his young heart literally on fire with passion to get the Tamil people literate, and with the impatience of youth he wanted no time lost in doing it!

As we journeyed north again we stopped at Raichur in Hyderabad State, where a hundred Christians and a dozen missionaries were gathered to do further work on our Kanarese lessons, and to learn to teach them. I told them the dewan of Mysore said he would make our charts on marble if we prepared good ones. Two students were artists. A dozen others were chosen to work. It was one of the most exciting weeks of this breath-taking year. No, not a week—only three days! We all worked until midnight every night and until three in the morning the last day, to get the pictures done in colors before my departure. Everyone was so happy with the results that we nearly wept on each other's shoulders. Before I left they put a lovely blue Kashmir shawl around my shoulders and said, "With this shawl we adopt you. Now you are an Indian!" For years I carried that shawl with me everywhere and wrapped it around me when I prayed for India. They sent Mrs. Laubach a lovely red one to match it.

The director of education of the little state of Aundh, near Hyderabad, telegraphed that their *rajkumar* (prince) wanted me to come. There was not a day available, so I had to say "no." But Aundh State, prince and all, had caught the literacy epidemic and went ahead so effectively that they outdistanced every other state in India so far as percentages were concerned. The school children were all dismissed for three months to help teach the illiterates. Their slogan was: "Everybody in the state literate in twelve weeks!" The *rajkumar* took a leading part in the campaign, going with his princess from village to village, singing *kirtans* (long musical narratives) on literacy. There were large phonetic charts posted in conspicuous places in every village. All the villagers gathered round these centers at night to study. In two months 12,000 learned to read out of a total population of 76,000. Literacy had been doubled in eight weeks. If a little state could do that, why not a big one?

At Jubbulpore, in the Central Provinces, I found a hundred literacy students gathered on the veranda of Leonard Theological Seminary, teaching one another. As soon as they learned a lesson they had to teach it to the newest students. This school had begun with about ten pupils who had brought others each evening until they spilled all over the seminary yard.

The students of eight other schools in that city responded to a challenge to overthrow India's illiteracy by volunteering almost to the last man. A professor of Robertson College took me and twenty students with him to a village a few miles from Jubbulpore where his class was helping in social reconstruction. The students learned how to use the new charts for teaching illiterates, while all the village folk were eager and excited with the prospects of learning to read. Thereafter literacy was central in their village uplift project, as it was in fifty other college projects in India.

In the hill country of Chota Nagpur, at Ranchi, we made picture-chain lessons in the Mundari language and showed them to 500 representatives from Lutheran, Anglican, and Roman Catholic churches, and the government schools. All came together in the Anglican church —Catholics as well as Protestants. It seemed as if the millennium were at hand. The very fact that Christians who had never spoken to one another before had found a common task to perform for India gave them a new sense of oneness.

In St. John's Hall, a Roman Catholic school at Sindega, near Ranchi, I demonstrated the Mundari lessons to 300 people. They said they already had 15,000 illiterates under instruction. The Catholic fathers were eager and excited about the possibilities of literacy.

Patna, capital of Bihar Province, which I visited in February, was the buzzing scene of one of the world's greatest literacy campaigns. Mr. B. B. Mukherjee had started it and was its secretary. He told me how he had "caught the literacy bug." His wife had attended a Girl Guides convention at Calcutta, where she had heard about the Philippine method of teaching and about the rapid progress of the Moros. On fire with enthusiasm, she returned home and aroused her husband's interest in the cause of literacy. That is one of the amazing aspects of India, that so many men and women become aflame with an unquenchable passion to make their people literate and to lift them out of poverty.

The city of Patna was alive with literacy campaigns. Mr. Mukherjee took me from one to another until I was nearly dead and then said we had barely started! I saw classes in Hindustani and Urdu being taught side by side. These two languages are really the same language in Bihar, only the alphabets are different, for Moslems will have nothing but Persian letters and Hindus will have nothing but those derived from Sanskrit. All they had to do was to use the same lesson text in different alphabets! I saw some of the students learning both alphabets at once and having fun doing it. Everywhere in Bihar the literacy classrooms were packed to suffocation with students. As I looked into their pathetic faces, I could think only of the helpless, defeated look of cattle in a slaughter house. India does not know how to smile, for she has had so little to smile about.

With Mr. Mukherjee I attended a huge gathering where the volunteer teachers were wedged in against each other, as everybody tried to see the instruction of illiterates. The climax at Patna was a meeting in a gigantic hall where I had to shout to be heard by the crowd of a thousand people who were present, the élite of Patna. The literacy campaign in Bihar province was so big that it resembled a stampede. No one had ever attempted to handle an educational problem as large as this, and it had burst all bounds. It was education run wild!

Mr. Mukherjee took me also to Gaya Prison, where I saw 1,700 prisoners studying in classes on the floor of sixty prison buildings, and nearly all the prisoners already literate. I seldom get stage fright, but I didn't know how to act as these prisoners rose from their seats, shouted my name, and burst into terrifically loud singing. The superintendent, Colonel J. Chandra, M. D., had wonderful ideas for prison reform. He had the prison almost wholly self-managing, with a government elected by the prisoners. Very little attention was paid to the gate, Dr. Chandra said, for the prisoners would rather live inside the prison than out! I saw what love and light can do with a prison. Toward the end of that incredible day, the prison cabinet met and their best poet, Syed Abdul Mannan Shayar, sang a song, while I wept with the prisoners who listened. This was the poem, as written down by one of the officials with not a word changed:

The spring season has set in for our souls and the name of God has a new charm and the garden of my heart a fresh beauty. Praise be to God for His grace to the prisoners of our jail, for He has been exceedingly gracious in dealing with us. Oh, kind Lord of goodness, I will sacrifice myself for your sake, for I have discovered what kindness and graciousness really mean. The days of my sighs and groans are over and another voice is in my life. I was not free inside this jail, nor was I free even before I came; but today there is a new longing in my heart. We Indians have been living in the prison of utter ignorance, but now the good news has reached us that a new day is dawning. No longer shall we be slaves of black ignorance. Who am I that I dare dream such new aspirations as I now cherish? Why should we not entertain our guest in this prison? My prayer is different altogether, O Shayar. Everybody is praying for the happiness of our august guest, but my prayer surpasses all others and exceeds all measure. How fortunate we are that we should have him in our midst as our guest, for he hails from the land of the free! His kindness to us prisoners beggars all description. It is the heart's magnet that has drawn him from far-off America and brought him to us who are in jail. How can the atoms praise and do justice to the sun? Pray convey this humble message of ours to America, that all Indians are full of praise for the Americans. Please tell your countrymen that the unique discoveries of Americans have opened our eyes and that we are only taking a leaf out of your books and faithfully following in your footsteps.

I went home that night limp with emotion, and for most of the night I lay awake in bed, thinking of the vast multitude, nearly three-fifths of all the people in the world, in the prison of ignorance. I knew that they all would stampede toward the light the moment they saw hope, as did the pathetic multitudes I had seen in Bihar.

There was no sleep on the train from Calcutta down to the province of Orissa. The track was so rough one had to hold on to one's bunk and hope that the wheels would also hold on to the rails. They did, and the next day the train arrived intact at the city of Cuttack, the capital. I was taken at once to the office of the minister of education in the provincial government, who said, "You shall have the best artists and educators we have and all the money you need. Go ahead."

We set immediately about the arduous task of preparing lessons in the Oriya language with an alphabet I had never set eyes on before. We got on wonderfully, though our artists grumbled at working twelve hours a day. The finished lessons were shown to the prime minister, who commended them highly and promised his support in a literacy campaign.

Besides building lessons I spoke to twelve assemblies in five days, one an evening meeting in the open air at which an amplifying system enabled me to reach the vast crowd trailing off into the distant darkness. Furthermore, mission schools, teacher-training schools for men and for women, and colleges all had to be given instructions in between lesson-making hours! The campaign that followed my visit to Orissa became "immense," in the words of their director of education.

At the end of that strenuous week I returned to Calcutta, and went from there by train and boat to Biri Siri in Assam, far to the northeast. Here the language with which we worked was called Garo. We began chart building with nationals and Australian and American Baptist missionaries, keen, energetic, and thorough. Our Garo artists were not clever, but they were tireless and determined not to stop until they had done their best. They not only worked on pictures all day but stayed up for two nights practically without sleep. In two days we had finished a set of Garo lessons in Roman letters for the mountain people of Assam and another set in Bengali letters for the lowland people. Similar lessons were subsequently made by missionaries in six other languages of Assam.

The last night at Biri Siri keeps returning to mind with a strange persistency. A wandering Christian *sadhu,* or religious devotee, had come to the church to sing the story of Christ. As he sang, his eyes were lifted to heaven and his face was transformed like that of an angel. As his high tenor voice floated out over that audience, holding the people in breathless attention, he seemed lost in the bliss of heaven. Though I did not understand his words I was sure I could understand his lovely soul. If Christ does sometimes come back to earth, He was there in the humble Garo church on the edge of Assam that night, for the *sadhu* looked and sounded and acted like a reincarnation of Jesus all during his rapturous singing. I rushed up to him at the close and said to the interpreter, "Tell him I saw Christ in him as he sang. Oh, tell him that, please, in Bengali." The *sadhu* looked at me for a second, then turned away toward the children. He saw Christ in the children but not in me.

Jamshedpur—also called Tatanagar or Tata City—is the home of the gigantic Tata Iron and Steel Works, largest in the British Empire. The whole city is owned and ruled by the company. Here early in March I found a first-rate literacy campaign was already in full swing under a secretary of mass literacy, who showed me twenty adult literacy classes being taught at night. Mr. J. J. Ghandy, general manager of the company, was so interested that he had printed a lengthy address urging every laborer to learn to read.

At Ghaziabad, 700 miles to the northwest, near Delhi, in the heart of a huge mass movement, were gathered a hundred delegates, men and women of great earnestness. Though we worked as usual on new lessons in Hindustani, this was no ordinary conference.

They took me to a *mela*—a religious festival—where thousands of Christians, all former outcastes, had gathered from the surrounding region. While we were eating dinner I heard weird music and stole away alone to the large central tent to see what was going on. One of the outcastes was dancing and chanting while hundreds of others swayed and shouted their approval. Feeling grew ever more intense as the frantic dancer gesticulated, his mood swiftly changing from hatred to anguish and grim resolve. Suddenly he seized a boy in front of him, held him aloft a moment, and hurled him to the ground in one violent gesture of desperation. "What is it? What do they mean?" I asked of J. Holmes Smith, a great friend of the outcastes, who had slipped in beside me. "They are depicting the despair of the outcastes in their struggle for emancipation," he explained, "and the triumph of Jesus Christ over untouchability."

After the tense drama, presented with such moving realism, the missionaries conducted a service of Christian worship. We felt the very spirit of Christ to be with us in that tent. A hundred persons received baptism and nearly the entire throng participated in the celebration of the Lord's Supper. Their clothes were still the same, but their hearts were new and their faces shone! Oh, you who despair of Christ's transforming the human race, if only you could see a *mela* in India where the titanic epic of man's transformation into the divinity of sons of God is telescoped into one brief, tense hour! If you could see that, you would never again doubt that Christ is the world's hope!

At Lahore—the capital of the Punjab, a night's journey farther north—my heart went out to a group of fiery students called the "Anti-Illiteracy War Council," who had the bureau of education worried sick because they wanted to cut all the red tape and go ahead and make the Punjab literate immediately by geometrical progression! They wanted to cajole, bully, buy, and force all the educated people to teach illiterates or make them pay a fine. They were telling the whole city of Lahore that the bureau of education was asleep.

The radical steps these boys wanted were:

1. Fifteen days of intensive propaganda, with handbills, posters,

radio broadcasts, leaflets from airplanes, songs about literacy on the streets, processions.

2. A pledge from every literate man either to teach one person each month or to pay a rupee for that month until Lahore was literate.

3. All schools to have vacations of three months, but every student required to teach during school hours every day instead of studying.

The honorable minister of education was thoroughly vexed and asked me what I thought could be done to suppress such rash youth. I replied, "It seems to me the safest thing is to give them all the rope they want and then try to keep up with them!"

At the Gakhar Normal School for Moslem Teachers, 200 Moslem students were being trained to teach adults. Principal Yamini had already caught the idea of our picture-chain lessons and had prepared a good set when I arrived. Only, being a classical scholar, he insisted on using words the illiterates did not understand. In the Punjab the Moslem scholars were convinced that the illiterates ought to learn to read Urdu, the language of culture, or nothing! They were unanimous against teaching the despised Punjabi, which everyone speaks and almost no one who is anyone reads! Even the professors speak Punjabi among themselves.

The students of the Gakhar Normal School practised on the village of Kot Nura, two miles away. Here before a crowd of a thousand peasants I was asked to give fifty new literates their certificates. Perhaps 200 others were studying in little classes of five to ten in number. Classes like these were springing up in nearly every corner of India.

Swinging far south again and west we found at Rutlam, in central India, a tremendous mass movement in progress. Thirty thousand Bhils, an aboriginal people, had been baptized in three years! The nerves of the missionaries from the United Church of Canada were taut to the point of snapping—they were exhausted with success. Now this multitude of illiterate and half-civilized Christians needed to be taught to read and write. "They are 100 per cent illiterate," I was told, "and there is no literature in their language except some of the Gospels." We asked a pastor how many of his members could read. The pastor said, "I have 3,000 members and have taught twenty-six so they can read the Bible."

It was now late March and the thermometer reached 102° every day. In the noon sun a government Packard came one day and carried me a hundred blistering miles to the government guest house at Indore. In ten minutes I was at the bottom of a tub of cool water, and in that tub I stayed until my hosts came to take me to tea.

That night, in spite of the heat, we opened a conference with 800 people, many of them in full dress and many in government uniforms. A profuse letter was read from the premier, containing extravagant adjectives about myself that fitted the facts about as well as a horse collar would have fitted my neck. But I had begun to understand the psychology of India and made no effort to correct exaggerations. The leaders of India had made up their minds to launch an onslaught on illiteracy, and they needed a figurehead from some distant land to give the signal—someone about whom they knew nothing and who thus made it possible for them to give limitless range to their imaginations. I had succeeded somewhere, which was all that mattered. The one thing India needed above all else was faith to believe it could be done. So the Indore literacy campaign was launched that night with a blare of trumpets.

The next morning 600 Indore teachers gathered for instructions; as though they could receive a course in two hours! I gave them two hours' worth of faith that India can be literate and a few principles of the psychology of teaching an illiterate: "Never scold nor frown nor yawn; say 'yes' when you mean 'no'; look surprised and pleased and pat the student on the back and tell him how bright he is; tell him he will make a wonderful teacher and that you want him to help you teach the rest of the village; treat him like a rajah, and make him like you; don't say a single unnecessary word, but let the student talk all he will; never ask a question the illiterate cannot answer; never tell him what he already knows."

This psychology of teaching—all of it directly contrary to Indian custom, where they believe the old maxim, "Spare the rod and spoil the child"—is about 50 per cent of the art of teaching illiterates. It sounded like an educational revolution to the teachers of India. They thought being so kind might work with adults if you taught only one at a time—but with children, God forbid!

In this vast central and western region of India with its many native states is Daly College for the training of princes, which I was invited to visit. Every one of the sixty princes wore a sky-blue turban. They had smooth handsome faces and great black eyes, just like the princes of the story books. I had a queer sensation of unreality while talking to them. They all promised to do their part to make their states literate, but they did not have a passion for the poor in their eyes, and I wondered whether any of my words would really sink in. I got not half the sense of irresistible power that came when I talked to Isabella Thoburn College, for example, or the wonderful educational committee of the Indian National Congress.

As I rolled into the station at Baroda the next morning at 1:45 I was met by four Hindu students and a Christian missionary. They said they had come to invite me to the literacy conference they were holding that afternoon in an Indian school. Then to my amazement the students tossed a garland of jasmine about my neck. How can one help loving people who meet you at 1:45 A.M. with invitations and jasmine!

It was Sunday morning when I reached Ahmedabad, the great industrial city north of Bombay, and spoke to a thousand Christians at eight o'clock in a united service arranged by several churches and missions. I told them that since so many people in India lacked the Christian passion to teach without pay, each Christian ought to teach four to make up for the slackers who would not teach at all. When I asked how many in that audience would volunteer, they all stood up.

At the service for all religions that evening I told them that that morning a thousand Christians had each promised to teach four others. Six hundred more rose to promise that they would teach at least two illiterates during that year. Even though most of them were not Christians, I think they would have promised four instead of two, if they had been asked. I felt there, as I did many times in India, that the great yearning love of the missionaries was doing more to rebuild the spiritual and educational life of India than any other single factor. The Reverend G. N. Brown, my amazingly competent host, had advertised so well that he gathered one huge crowd after another.

On Monday morning at eight o'clock, 600 Hindus, Moslems, Jains, and Christians gathered in a public hall. That afternoon they were there again. The next morning at eight there were 700 present, that afternoon 600, that evening 1,000! The same 600 people had returned for five meetings to hear more and more and more, and still more. Fortunately, by this time I had accumulated enough convictions to make five speeches on literacy without repeating. I took the night train, tired but happy—and slept!

As the train pulled into Kosamba early Thursday morning, I was strapping my bedding in leisurely fashion when I heard the sound of Scottish bagpipes. I looked out the window to find a band of pipers in full Scottish outfit, bright plaid kilts and impudent Scottish hats—nothing was missing except the glowing pink complexions of real Scots. For these pipers were young Indians, and behind them as far as my eye could reach was a throng of people. The whole town was out to meet the train. What celebrity, I wondered, was arriving? Was it Gandhi, or the Viceroy, or perhaps the Gaekwar of Baroda himself?

My question was soon answered. In a moment a company of town officials filed into the train and approached me. "Is Gandhi here, or the Gaekwar?" I asked their leader, who proved to be Dr. R. D. Souri, representing His Excellency the Premier. "No," answered Dr. Souri, "we have gathered here to meet you and to receive you as a state guest of the government of Baroda." Then, following the recognized Indian custom of presenting an address of welcome on such occasions, he began to read:

> Our government as a mark of recognition to the services rendered by you for the whole country of India have commanded me to welcome you as a guest of his Highness' government on this March 30, 1939, at Kosamba, where you have so kindly agreed to lead a joint conference of the state government teachers, inspecting officers, missionaries, and their education staff. . . .

I was completely overcome by the honor and the fulsome praise contained in the rest of the address, but I smiled benignly and tried to look like a distinguished visitor! So we started from the station, the bagpipers leading, and behind us the school children of thirty-five schools, which had been dismissed for the occasion. As we reached the huge open space that had been decorated for the ceremonies, what struck my eye first was the side of a large building on which had fifty wives with him! If this poem is to become literature in Christian lands, it will need a little expurgating—although we have never expurgated the scandal about Solomon's seven hundred wives.

When you realize that the unwritten lyric and epic poetry sung by the Moros would make thousands of printed pages, you see that this work of recording becomes highly important to them. It is also important to anthropology as the only survival of the ancient Filipino literature. When Spanish friars reached the Philippines, they stamped out with fire and sword all the folklore of the Filipinos—but they could not stamp out the Moros or their culture. That this Moro folklore is ancient is proved by its strange obsolete language and by the fact that the ideas go back to a period long before the Moslem religion reached the Philippines. The heroes worshipped the spirits of rocks, clouds, and crocodiles and never mentioned God or Mohammed. So we are at last bringing to light something that has been hidden in Lanao for perhaps a thousand years.

June 1, 1930

Six months since I came to Lanao! How fast time flies when one is busy! And I am busy! For now that the Moros have become fast friends, I have little time to myself. They are here morning, noon, and afternoon—fortunately not yet at night. They are afraid of ghosts, and Galia and I are careful not to change that belief!

This forenoon after church, when I wanted to sleep for a few minutes, there was a rap at my door and in walked three distinguished *gooros* (teachers of Islam), and with them three other men. They came, so they said, to pay me a visit on Sunday because all my time was taken during the week and they were afraid I was working too hard. It did not strike them as rather funny to come and awaken me from sleep in order to tell me that they were afraid I was overtired. But I saw the funny side of it, for they were so kindly about it.

I told these religious teachers, "I am trying a little experiment with myself today to see how many minutes I can keep my mind on God, and how many minutes I forget Him in spite of myself."

One of the *gooros* replied, "Any man who tries to remember God all the time is not only a good Moslem but he is like Mohammed himself, and when he dies he will be carried up to the seventh heaven."

Then he added what to me was the most pathetic word of all, "We never heard anybody talk like this before, and so we have decided to make you our leader in religion because you are always giving us the loveliest things in the Koran."

"I learned all these things from Jesus," I said. "Jesus and Mohammed agreed that we must do God's will."

"Yes," said the delighted *gooros,* "they said the very same words."

Does it not seem to you that we are getting somewhere when we can have the strong moral backing of all the leading priests and *datos* in Lanao, and can tell them that these ideals are the ideals that we learned from Jesus? Doesn't this justify the method of approach we are trying?

Just at noon today a Moro from Togaya—where all the fighting has taken place during the past few weeks—came to ask us to establish a school there so that the people might learn good customs and stop fighting. Then, to my great surprise, he produced a New Testament and said he wanted to study it and that he wanted to have a copy in Maranaw. I promised that some day we would print it, and now we must make good.

Excerpts from letters written during the following year reveal the new problems that were arising and give the high points of our progress. I have not attempted to give their respective dates, for they form a running narrative of events.

Our problem is now going to be to print enough literature in Maranaw to keep up with the demand. This week a man came and asked whether the next issue of our magazine was out, and when I offered him a back number he said proudly, "I have read all the old ones and everything else your press has printed in our language." Is there another press in the world that can boast that anybody has read everything it has turned out? Here, many Moros have done so. But that is not saying very much, for our total output to date is about twenty pages!

When one sees the vile trash that appears in some of the books and magazines in English that reach these outposts of civilization, one feels sure we can make better Moros out of those who never learn to read English than out of those who acquire a taste for this low reading. So perhaps we may be able to mold this Moro nation far more than we realize through the pages we shall print and circulate among the people.

Two Moros just came in to show me how they are learning to read. Very, very slowly but correctly one read a paragraph; perhaps in another month he will attain fair speed. He has passed the first, and hardest, achievement, for he knows that letters can be so pronounced together that they form themselves into words and convey the ideas that he wants to express.

During the past months we have devised a system that is so easy that the brightest Moros can repeat every letter within ten minutes. We start with three words that contain all the consonants used in the Maranaw language. These three words are as familiar to them as "mother," "hand," and "work" are to us.

They are *Malabanga,* name of a town in Lanao; *ḳaratasa,* paper; *paganada,* study or learn. We cut the words up like this: *ma la ba nga, ḳa ra ta sa, pa ga na da.*

Then we begin with *ma ma,* which means man; *a ma,* which means father; *ma la,* which means big, and so on. The combination of these

a	ma	la	ba	nga
i	mi	li	bi	ngi
o	mo	lo	bo	ngo
u	mu	lu	bu	ngu

ma ma	a ma	la la	a la	ma la	la ma
man	father	to pat	God	large	yard
mi mi	a mi	li li	a li	li ma	li o
girl	our	name	name	hand	outside
mo mo	a mo	lo lo	a lo	ma lo	o lo
chewed	monkey	dull	hello	pretty	head
ba ba	ba ba i	la ba	ba la	ba li	ba lo
short	woman	profit	pair	a receipt	clang
bi bi	bi ba i	la bi	i bi	o bi	lo bi
duck	push	more	itch	a vegetable	cocoanut
bo bo	ba bo	la bo	bo la	bu la	bu l
to pour	aunt	prefer	ball	wide	smoke
nga nga	ba nga	bo nga	lu nga	ma nga	o nga
open mouth	island	fruit	plural	a fly	fruit
ngi ngi	la ngi	li ngi	lu ngi	lu ma	lu mi
corner of mouth	wait	to turn	allow	smooth	make flat

FIRST MARANAW READING CHART (LESSON 1)

consonants with the other vowels in the language is a simple additional step. Learning to read from the chart [p. 35] is so easy that the most stupid person can do it. And they love it so much they hardly give us time to eat.

It is like a miracle for a man who never knew a letter to walk out of our school in an hour able to read a whole page of his own language with Roman letters. We see that miracle happen over and over, every day. But the joy of seeing people learning ten times as fast as they expected to learn and all set up about their own brilliance does not lose its edge.

Mr. Galia says that he taught nine Moros to read in a half hour. That is better than any record that I have thus far made with a large group. A half dozen Moros interrupted this letter. They came in and said they could not wait until tomorrow but had to be taught right away! They had only an hour to spare and wanted all the education they could get in that time. So I have stopped this letter to teach them. While I concentrated on one of them, the rest listened. They have just left the house. I do not expect you to believe me, but here is the fact: this man had finished reading three pages of our newspaper, and could read everything I put before him with fair speed. One hour! Every time that happens I feel as though a miracle had happened. It is possible only because these people are hungry mentally and spiritually.

Nine-tenths of our job is sitting close beside the people who flock to us and getting thrills of delight with them as they emerge from ignorance. Just this morning we drove forty kilometers, stopping to teach crowds of Moros and to distribute the newest chart. The speed with which the people learned was even more astonishing to them than it was to me, for they had not had opportunity to see the thing happen before.

Yesterday an old *hadji* came to see me, and though he thought he was too old to learn to read a new way, we assured him that it was easy and he started. We kept him roaring with laughter and in fifteen minutes he knew every letter and could read. A letter a minute! When he went up the road he was still laughing and reading. This sounds incredible, yet we are doing it daily. Fifteen minutes is the time we expect a bright man who knows Arabic letters to require to learn to read Roman letters. Those who never knew how to read anything before require from an hour to a week.

One of the outlaws (I had better not name him for he's now my friend) came at five in the evening and I taught him in a half hour. He was unusually bright and very much pleased with himself, and I praised him and told him I wanted him to be a teacher in his village. When we had finished he took me over where nobody else could hear us and said, "You taught me to read, and you are the best friend I have in the world. I want to do something for you. Is there anybody in Lanao you want me to put out of the way?" I said, "No, thank you, brother. But you are certainly a very big-hearted man. Go home and teach others and that will make me happy."

I have been trying to teach a boy to read this afternoon, but his mind was so slow the task seemed like pouring water into a mosquito net. I often wonder when I am working with a stupid man whether he is worth all this effort. But then when that same man fondly runs his fingers through my hair and fairly beams with gratitude while he calls me "good uncle," I know that a little love is created. If, as we believe, this entire universe is a desperate attempt of love to incarnate itself, then "important duties" that cut us off from helping little people are not duties but sins.

On market day twice a week, I stand from seven to twelve before a chart in the market place while people crowd around trying to get near enough to learn to read, always threatening to push me off my stool in their eagerness to be next. I do not see how my teachers get time to record the names of their students; I seldom do.

As I finished breakfast about six-thirty and arose from the table there came a knock at the door. I turned the knob and there crowded into my little house sultans and *hadjis* and *datos;* sixty tried to get in, but some had to stay outside for want of room. They had hired a launch and had come twenty miles to be examined, for they had learned to read Moro with English letters. We marched down the road a mile to our school, and there we spent the whole forenoon in joyously throwing compliments at one another. Everybody in the province seems caught up with the same gladness. They think the whole world will be surprised at their achievement, and I think they are right! This thing may have had parallels, but I have neither seen them nor heard of them. On our school wall is a motto: "In five years, Lanao the most literate province in the Philippines." These men declared, "Less than five years, much less!"

But there is a price to pay for all this—one cannot get any time alone. Three men, very intimate friends and splendid workers, have just been here and in spite of my hints and insistences that I needed to work, they stayed a long time. One of them is writing a letter about our campaign to the President of the United States at this moment; and he did not relent until we promised to translate it into English and send it to President Hoover.

Any executive will say, "You ought to organize your time and have it understood that visitors are welcome only at certain hours." Something, at least, must be done about it; but not something that will nip our tender promising plant in the bud. What a beautiful frail thing it is!

The Moros know that we love them, but they do not realize what a gulf —at least historically—separates us. If they did, would they be so affectionate? Yes, if they knew all, if they knew the love of God in all its wondrous fervor, they would!

And to think that less than a year ago we were writing about "the most difficult place under the American flag, if not in the world!"

I think now that America is the most difficult place in the world, for there you demand ability, unusual ability, while here in Lanao they demand only love.

It is the end of a day as nearly perfect as any I have ever seen, and so I write about it at once. It has been exasperatingly busy, for Moros have come to the house from early morning to dark. They were all so loving and grateful that I think I never saw anything like it before in the whole world. As darkness approached, I sent them home, telling them I must walk off alone. As I climbed Signal Hill, God began to use my tongue to speak to me:

"My child you have at last struck your pace. Here in Lanao you will accomplish something with me for the human race. You will broaden the circle of their minds, which is good, and you will help them to a new comradeship with me, which is the most wonderful thing that can happen to any man. This very minute, while you are walking with me and listening to me, you are doing the last highest thing a human being can ever do. You must not fret because you have not done more in your life. Only live close to me minute by minute as you have done so much of the day today, and what you *are* will speak. You need not worry about what you do, but only what you are. And what you are depends upon whether you *are holding on to me.*"

The Moros come and watch our Sunday services with ever-increasing interest and appreciation. To our great delight we have found that they like Jesus. It is Christians they hate because Christians have mistreated and misunderstood them. They love Jesus and claim Him for their own. So we are going to try to write a series of tracts on "Jesus as a Good Friend," to be distributed in Maranaw in the market place. If we can untangle Christ from the terrible handicap of Christendom, which has kept so many millions from Him, we will be doing the Moros a priceless service.

When we came here in 1915 for the first time, we heard an officer say that the only good Moro was a dead one, and I have heard this very statement repeated by government officials this year. Perhaps the only good Moros they come in contact with are dead ones, but our program has attracted a group of young men who in my estimation are as big-hearted and as splendid as any young men you could find in any country. My heart is all bound up with them. I never had friends whom I felt I could rely upon to be more loyal and who understood my own motives better than these Moros. Neither they nor I feel that the boundary of religion or race can keep us apart.

A swift, wonderful year has gone by [I wrote in January, 1931], and yet it would not be counted much of a success in many mission circles. There has not as yet been a single baptism of a Moro. They do not even know that baptism is our custom.

On the other hand, we can claim one victory. Almost 100 per cent of the Moros are now our friends. It has been encouraging, too, to hear so many visitors in Lanao say, "This is what I call true missionary work!"

Some months ago the Sultan of Samoi collected over a thousand signatures of prominent *datos* and sent them along with a beautiful silver box to hold betel-nuts to Mayor Charles G. Phillips of Montclair, New Jersey. Today Mayor Phillips' reply arrived. I showed it to the men who are helping us make a dictionary, and they were so delighted they could not sit still. Mayor Phillips had pictured "a university to be established at your capital—an institution where boys and girls from all over the island might come for intellectual training, and then go back as teachers to their own localities." These men kept saying, "My goodness, that is just the thing. Just think what that would do for Lanao."

Sheik Bogabong, the very highest scholar of all the Moros, came this morning and this afternoon, followed by his retinue, to help us and to discuss religious problems. He is so genuine and friendly and so interested in the quest for God, which means everything to me, that I enjoyed the conversations greatly.

He said that the chief difference between Islam and Christianity was that the Moslem can pray anywhere, while Christians have to go to church! One of my fellow workers objected to this, and said that I prayed on top of Signal Hill at sunset. Sheik Bogabong replied, "That is just where Mohammed and Jesus liked to pray best—on a hilltop!" Then Campong, my helper, said, "Ah, the Bible and the Koran are much alike on the question of prayer."

Yesterday Effa and I went with Lieutenant Alviola and his wife to Ramain and visited a number of homes. Abolais, the teacher, had a *ba-i* or princess from the royal family read for us in each house. They all could read rapidly and beautifully. It was market day in Ramain and men were learning to read all about the market. Hundreds of men and about fifty women have learned to read here in the past two months.

We all wanted to know how Abolais had secured such a stampede of Ramain ladies to learn to read, so he told us his secret. He had a handsome young man write a love lyric to one of the young ladies who had already learned, telling her that her education made her the most charming lady in Lanao. She read the love song to the other young ladies, and the scramble to learn to read was on—a perfect illustration of the use of love as an educational instrument! When we told the other teachers how Abolais did it, they all declared they would adopt the same method and now we have to print a love lyric every week in *Lanao Progress*.

In the whole province 600 Maranaw women and girls have thus far been reported as having learned to read. Every week some high *dato* brings his daughter and asks us to keep her in our school, which we are not yet equipped to do. You see what a wonderful opportunity is opening here.

We now have twenty literacy teachers, most of them high school students and some of them graduates, scattered through the main districts. Their average pay is $10 a month. Besides these twenty who are in the employ of the *madrasa,* as our folk school is called, there are at least fifty others who are doing more or less regular teaching without pay. They reported having taught 930 this month, which is at the rate of 11,160 a year.

We have just come home from high adventure in Togaya, the home of notorious outlaws. It is our first visit since the soldiers destroyed their stone fort. Mr. McKinley, who was with us, tried to become friendly with one *imam* but received only black looks in return. This man was probably a close friend of the outlaws. As soon as we pulled out our lesson sheets there was a buzz of excitement. The old *imam* suddenly became friendly and said he had heard of the "American *madrasa.*" Every person in the party was soon surrounded by a crowd of Moros, all of them learning to read. When you consider that they burned down the only school they ever had, ten years ago, you can see what this new doorway to civilization may mean to them.

Campong Basman said, as we were leaving Togaya, "Our poor Moro people do not know in which direction to go and are in need of leaders. They follow anybody who knows what to do."

Campong is a keen-minded young Moro who graduated from Muños Agricultural College and began to teach, but was dismissed from the bureau of education for carrying firearms without a license. He is a tireless worker and a high-grade translator. He has just completed the translation of a little booklet on the care of babies, and has translated about a hundred pages of the Old Testament. From our pulpit on Sunday morning, he has been reading the stories of the Prophets to the Moros.

The Christian Endeavor meeting is just out. Down the street tonight goes somebody singing and whistling, "Out of the darkness into the light, Jesus, I come, Jesus, I come." It sounds like Campong Basman. Though still a Moslem, he takes a leading part in Christian Endeavor every week.

I think we could have imposing statistics in the way of church membership this year, but if we did so we might sacrifice the wonderful good will that now exists toward our enterprise. If we can be of great service to the Moros during the next four or five years educationally, medically, and in other ways, then they will think of our Christianity in terms of loving service rather than in terms of doctrine. Hitherto, Christians have seemed chiefly enemies of Mohammed and Islam. We do not want to be thought of as enemies of any other religion, but as lovers of all men.

Last Sunday was a turning point for our church here. We abandoned our room at the military camp and went to the Moro school in Dansalan to hold our Christian services. The windows were all filled with Moros listening to the service from start to finish. I spent a couple of minutes preaching to the Moros in their own language. What I said was about as follows:

"Friends, we use a different language and worship with somewhat different forms, but we worship the same God. These songs that we sing today could all be sung by you with as much earnestness as they are sung by us. The story of Joseph, which we read, is well known to you, for Joseph is one of your great prophets. Come in and worship with us if you wish. We call you our dear friends."

The life of the pioneer missionary can be thrilling! Never did I enjoy any other work as I do this. It is literally true that the missionaries on the very front lines are the ones who are getting the greatest fun out of their experiences. If anybody is going to be a missionary, let him plunge into the farthest frontiers. Never pity Livingstone again. Envy him, loneliness, malaria, and all!

Livingstone never had an experience like mine yesterday! We have five automobiles in Dansalan now, great curiosities to the people across the lake, where there are neither roads nor autos. Kakai (pronounced Cockeye) Dagalangit brought six of his thirteen wives, with their daughters and maid-servants, yesterday to see our auto and beg for a ride. So fourteen queens and princesses piled into our Ford, two or three deep, every princess saturated with perfume from Cairo. They giggled incessantly until we reached the corkscrew road down the mountain, when some of them began to get sick. A few got out, two leaned out, and one leaned on my shoulder. I did not hesitate for an instant to turn homeward, for there was a hole in one tire and I trembled for it every minute. Think of fourteen sick royal ladies, a flat tire, and no spare! Harems have lost their glamour.

Everywhere I turn I see people teaching each other to read, or else reading the papers that we have printed.

We have doubled our force of Moro typesetters, all inexperienced but eaten up with zeal. They are putting forced draught on our printing presses —we bought another old press—so that we may catch up with the rising demand for literature.

Yesterday a young man came and said, "We have now read everything you have printed. Are you finished with a new issue of the paper?"

"Not until next Monday."

He began to walk the floor in consternation as he said, "What will the young ladies do? They will be discouraged if they have nothing to read. They will finish this paper in a day. Then what?"

Then what! That is the question we are now trying to solve!

Lieutenant Carlton of the U. S. Army and Mrs. Carlton have been visiting Lanao for a week. They were deeply interested in our program and spent a long while watching us teach the Moros to read. They watched us make these large charts by hand, since of course our presses are too small for them. The day before they left, Lieutenant Carlton said, "Mrs. Carlton and I have noticed how much you need more charts, and how slow the present process is. If you will give us a sample of just what you want, we will make them on better paper than you have so that they will last longer; we will send you one thousand."

I visualized what it meant in an instant—a large lovely chart in every chieftain's house—and was so happy I felt stunned.

"Lieutenant," I said, "this means that we shall win! This will be the most literate province in the Philippines in five years—and perhaps the most literate in Asia." So every day has new wonders; God *is* doing this.

Before I opened my front door this morning I heard some men outside. One was a *dato* from Waw, a distant corner of the province. He said, "We have no public school in our district. The people are all ignorant, not even one man who can teach the rest of us. We want you to send us a teacher."

"There is no money to send you a teacher," I replied. "But Mr. Presidente (he was the mayor of his town), suppose you learn right now and go back and teach the people yourself."

So he went at it and in an hour he could read—slowly, it is true, but perfectly. Then he started in to learn to write. We teach them to print their letters, so they are easy to learn. He went away with a large, brilliantly decorated chart in his hand, a diploma under his arm, and a broad grin on his face. "I graduated from the *Madrasa* yesterday," he will say when he gets home. "Now I am your teacher."

This morning early a group of *datos* came to give us land. They wanted us to have a beautifully situated piece of land, which we had regarded as the most desirable in Dansalan, for a Moro girls' dormitory and school. They told me that they absolutely would not sell it to anybody else for it was too precious, but for our school they wanted to give it without a cent. And they were so excited about it that one of them said, "If anybody else ever tries to build a house on that land, we will murder him!"—and they meant it. These fellows have pretty tough ways with their enemies, but what marvelous friends they can be! The wife of one owner crowded up and cried in a high voice, "I told my husband if he did not give that property to you, I would cut his throat while he was asleep." The husband smiled proudly. It was his wife's gentle hint that she agreed with him entirely.

The financial situation in America has hit some of our supporters so hard that I shall have to cut my budget to less than one-half. I have gone over our meager resources and looked for money until I am about sick, but will have to drop twelve of our staff and cut the salaries of all the rest. This will reduce our total budget by $100 a month. I have worked over these names a hundred different ways to make the operation as painless as possible—they are such splendid, loyal fellows. Tomorrow they must be told; it will be a very critical day. If I fail in tact and wisdom everything may smash up, or worse. When one has a painful job like this to face, one needs to be alone. I am really scared about that meeting, and feel like a cur after all those boys have done.

I am so keyed up this evening that I cannot relax. It has been a wonderful and a terrible day. I have had nothing in all my life like it.

I tried to prepare our teachers for the shock by giving them the Friendship treasure chests filled with school supplies that were sent from the children in America. Then I told the teachers to write letters to those who sent the chests, explaining our terrible dilemma and the necessity of cutting our expenses in half. They all promised to write.

Then we heard the reports of their literacy work. Man alive, some of them made me weep! I know from experience what labor is involved in teaching fifty, sixty, eighty people, one by one, how to read. One man, Santos Gangawa, taught forty-one women and seventy-one men to read during this one month. How the crowd applauded his description! Something in my eyes would not behave, and all over that room I felt the same deep emotion almost ready to break out. The room became tense and silent as man after man came forward with his magnificent achievement for the salvation of his province.

I felt swept on by a power that I could neither explain nor control. I was a little part of it, and so were all the others. I know it was the spirit of God in a strange new form. At last the names of all who had learned to read were counted and there were 1,521, over 300 of them women. Then fifty-one young men arose and volunteered to be teachers, making 110 volunteers in all. I felt as though I were passing through an incredible dream. Somebody moved that we have a gigantic fiesta, and the sultans and *datos* who crowded that room voted with a mighty roar that a month from today Dansalan is to see such a fiesta as was never seen here in Lanao. And all that amazing morning a tragic secret was in my breast and I was afraid.

Then came the terrible afternoon. I had to call in the paid teachers and tell them one by one that I could not pay them any longer. These same magnificent fellows that had felt such a thrill in the morning had to hear that my money was exhausted. I told them the truth, that it would be much easier to jump in the lake than to face them with this news. I expected some of them, at least, to go into a rage, but they saw that I was suffering and so they rose to it like men. Some of them hung their heads and turned pale, but not a man showed any resentment. Because they saw how sick I was about it myself I think they learned a new sympathy, and we are better friends because of the things we are suffering together.

Kakai Dagalangit, a tall chieftain with fierce black eyes, stood up. He has thirteen wives and all he has to do is to look at them and they behave. He looked at me with those fierce eyes and said, "This campaign shall not stop. It's Lanao's only hope." Then he looked at those teachers with his fierce eyes and said, "I'll make everybody who knows how to read teach somebody else, or I'll kill him."

Everybody taught. Nobody died. Everybody liked it. I did not like the motto "teach or die" and so changed it to "Each One Teach One," and this method, started by the Moro chieftain, has gone around the world.

CHAPTER 3

1930-34: THE "EACH ONE TEACH ONE" IDEA SPREADS

IN THE TEN YEARS following the opening of the Lanao station the attitude of the Moros toward Christianity swung from one pole to the other. It was unmitigated hatred when we arrived; love, good will, and cooperation when we departed. As one after another of the younger generation was baptized during the last two years not a word of opposition reached our ears. The members of our church were trying to keep God in their thoughts every minute of the day so that, as they said, "the Moros will see Christ in us." This was why we developed the "Game with Minutes," which is our adaptation of Brother Lawrence's effort to practise the presence of God all day long. The daughter of the Sultan, who was attending our girls' school, said openly that she was going to be baptized. The Sultan himself had too many wives to become a Christian, but he always came and had his picture taken right in the center of our church photographs.

The beginning of this Lanao transformation had repercussions in other parts of the Philippines almost from the first. In 1930 the pastors of the United Evangelical Church of the Philippines came to Dansalan for a retreat to pray and plan. Before they left they made a Cebuan chart, like our Maranaw chart, and just as easy to learn. Our printer, Silvino Abaniano, himself a Cebuano, worked night and day to print the new chart so that every preacher could take a supply home with him. These preachers went away in high spirits and started literacy campaigns in other parts of Mindanao and in the central Philippines.

Then came one of those miraculous interventions that make me sure God is working for the forgotten illiterates. It happened (or did it just happen?) that my old friend Dr. Sidney L. Gulick, of the Committee on World Friendship among Children in New York, thinking I still lived in Manila, appointed me American representative to help distribute the 28,000 beautiful Friendship treasure chests sent by the children of America to the children of the Philippines. This was the third and last of Dr. Gulick's great friendly gift adventures. The first, in 1926-27, was when American children sent thousands of dolls to Japan. These were distributed in nearly every village in Japan amid a great wave of pro-Americanism. The second, in 1928-29, a shower of schoolbags from the children of America to the children of Mexico, had great influence in counteracting the Mexican's dislike for Yankee *gringos*. The Friendship chests for the Philippine children were very attractive. They were of metal, decorated with pictures of Washington, Rizal, Columbus, Magellan, gods of the sea, and maps of the world, in imitation of ancient Spanish treasure chests. Inside they were crammed with a variety of articles that the children of America had thought would please the children of the Philippines.

At the end of 1930 I spent ten days in Manila helping direct the formal reception of the chests and the great celebration before Rizal's monument on the Luneta. This responsibility brought me into contact with many officials from the governor-general to the director of education. All of them were interested in literacy.

It was while I was in Manila that Mr. E. K. Higdon, then secretary of the National Christian Council, arranged for me to make an exploratory literacy expedition through the northern Philippines. So the following October found me again aboard ship on the way from Mindanao to Manila. In the midst of a storm—and with everybody seasick!—I tried to write my father about the start of my voyage:

October 18, 1931

I am on my way to the northern part of the Philippines to help prepare lessons like those we made for the Moros in several Filipino dialects.

We are now out from behind the shelter of Mindanao and the waves are becoming uncomfortable. A sudden storm has struck us. Bump, rattle, bang go the doors. Good-by until it is over.

Three hours later: The tables are tied against the wall. The floor is streaked with rain, which is driving through the closed windows. At this moment a window was shaken loose with a loud clatter. There goes the hardest shock we have had yet. I wonder how much water poured into the lower deck of this little steamer.

Mindanao Sea is an ugly piece of water, because storms like this pile up against the tidal currents that pour in from the Pacific Ocean to the China Sea.

The wind howls worse every minute. I wonder whether the hearts of all the passengers are behaving as strangely as mine. I am reminded of Bob's remark after he was in an airplane: "I wasn't scared, but my stomach was." I wonder whom I shall see first in heaven if this ship capsizes or goes down. I read somewhere that if one prays for others he can forget himself. Can I pray for all the passengers on this ship while we toss about on this enraged sea?

Yes! It works! Praying for others has brought my heart back to its normal beat again. There goes a wave clear over the ship, but I have not stopped praying for the Filipinos and my heart behaves perfectly.

The captain has surrendered to the storm and is trying to keep it on our stern. We must be going at a terrific rate, yet the spray blows over the ship from stern to stem each time we pitch up, down, up.

Two hours later: Behind Siquijor Island—safe, and almost calm.

When we reached Manila, there on the dock was the energetic Mr. Higdon, who hurried me to Union Seminary, to the university, to the bureau of education, and to the newspaper reporters. The report went over Manila that we could teach people to read in a day—some said an hour; and an article entitled "Lightning Literacy" appeared in the best journal in the islands. It was a month before I had time to do any writing. Paragraphs from my next two letters to my father reveal what had been accomplished:

To date we have completed charts in nine languages—Visayan, Tagalog, Ibanag, Ilocano, Gaddang, Isinay, Pampangan, Pangasinan, and Bicol. It is proving easier than we had feared to find the key words for each of these languages. We have trained 150 young people to teach and have given them certificates.

A young Kalinga at the American Bible Society helped prepare a chart in his dialect. The Kalinga tribe lives in the northernmost mountains of Luzon. My curiosity was excited by the striking differences between Kalinga and all other Philippine dialects. It has no *r* as the others have; also, unlike the others, it does have the letter *j*. Governor Early, who lived among them for several years, has an explanation. He says that an ancient colony of Japanese was driven into the mountains and intermingled with the natives, introducing Japanese sounds. Certainly their features bear more resemblance to those of the Japanese than do those of any of their neighbors.

We are taking steps to teach illiterates in the leper colony on Culion Island. This will bring the Bible, and thus comfort and enrichment of life, to those pitiful unfortunates—there are six thousand of them—who are least able to care for themselves.

During this tour I felt more strongly than ever that we could sweep the world with this scheme of key-word teaching if it were not for one obstacle—the spelling of the English language! If we spelled English phonetically, American children could be taught to read in a week. We needed only a day with the Philippine dialects. I can see only one thing to do—start a strike against the way English is misspelled—become a spelling Bolshevist! I suppose that unless we revolt we shall be handing on this same accursed orthography to our children, and our children's children, to the crack of doom.

Back in Lanao, in the meantime, larger and larger numbers of Moros had been learning to read. We made a "literacy thermometer" to place on our school wall. It was ten feet high and recorded percentages from zero to one hundred. The left side showed the literacy percentages of the leading nations of the world; the right side, where Lanao stood each month. In 1931 the "mercury"—red paint!—showed a literacy of 20 per cent. It had grown steadily since our campaign had begun in January 1930, when we estimated the literacy of Lanao to be 4 per cent. A year later it had risen to 8 per cent, and during 1931 it increased at the rate of 1 per cent a month.

Several of the little boys became as expert in teaching as any of the men, and we could not refuse them certificates when their work was perfect. Besides, they were favorites with the women, who were timid about allowing any men except their husbands to teach them. Hundreds of women in all parts of the province were being taught by small boys, while thousands more were learning to read from other women. We knew that we could not get 100 per cent of the men unless we got 100 per cent of the women.

I have never found such genuinely grateful people as the Moros. We lived under a spell of continuous benediction. Nor have I ever felt so utterly safe in my life. I knew that if anybody tried to harm us, he would first have to deal with a hundred thousand Moros. They have qualities of fidelity and independence that every American honors. I am frank to confess that I lost my heart to the Moros.

Every Friday, in the Moslem mosques, Pambaya (now a *hadji*) preached the ideals that he learned in our mission. He told the Moros that God expected them to be honest; that it was God's will for every man to forget his own selfish interests and devote his life to serving his fellow man. The *hadji* returned from the mosque one day and told me that he had been pleading with the Moros to resist the idea of opening a cabaret, as some had planned to do. "We must not adopt everything we see in Western countries," he told them, "for many things there are bad. Though they call themselves Christian, some Western countries do not follow the teachings of Nabi Isa (Jesus). The Protestant mission is opposed to the cabaret. We are not going to admit that our religion does not have ideals as high as the ideals of these missionaries, are we?"

In the spring of 1932 I was filled with joy by the arrival of a staunch Moro Christian, and I wrote my father of what it would mean for our work!

March 13, 1932

The Moro Christian from Jolo, Matias Cuadra, whose story, you will remember, is in *Seven Thousand Emeralds,* is here with his family. He has come to work with us! Today he preached his first sermon. The church—the one that was once a saloon—was crowded, with more Moslems than Christians. Matias produced a profound impression as he talked about "Youth Movements Around the World." He made the babies cry with his mighty shout, while the rest of the audience gasped and trembled. As I sit tonight I can remember nearly every word he said—sure proof that he said it well.

The first day Matias arrived he began to mix with the people of the town. To the delight of the *hadjis,* he talked with them in Malayan, which is almost as sacred to them as Arabic. Mrs. Cuadra has a sweet voice, and is teaching the Moros Christian tunes. The new day has dawned for Lanao, and we are unutterably grateful.

Another very important event took place that spring. The new governor-general of the Philippines, Theodore Roosevelt, Jr., visited

Lanao and made a lasting impression upon the Moros and upon our school.

We went down to Iligan to meet him as he came in on the boat. Fine arches had been erected over the entrance to the dock, and the people of Iligan presented him with the "key to the city." He lived up to all their highest expectations for cordiality, making them feel that he was really glad to meet each person who came to shake hands with him. When he was given the key, he made a short but telling address.

The following day Mr. Roosevelt came to our school in Dansalan intending to stay only a few minutes, but he stayed half an hour. He showed deep interest and made some very helpful suggestions. He was enthusiastic about the eighteen Societies of Educated Youth that we had organized around Lake Lanao, and listened attentively while some of these young Moros told him that they were meeting every week to answer the question, "How can we help our town, our province, our country, and the world?"

"This is not mere theory," they told him. "We have found thirty needs in our province and we have set our shoulders with all our power to meet these needs. Each of us has charts in his home and has promised to teach as many people as he can. We are distributing seeds around the four parts of Lanao. We are showing people how to keep well. We are encouraging people to send their children to school. Hitherto we have thought the only use of education was to become a clerk or errand boy in a government office, but we have discovered so many ways to be useful to humanity that we are intoxicated with enthusiasm."

Their eyes flashed and their voices had a new ring. These boys were dreaming dreams far beyond the borders of Lanao. They were tingling with eagerness to do something for all the world. One day I had read to them from Professor Fleming's book, *Marks of a World Christian,* that "two out of three inhabitants of our globe have still to be taught to read and write. The United States may send its hundreds of teachers to the Philippines and make those islands a world model for educational progress, but there are a billion more who need this help."

"Boys," I had burst forth, "you and I are in the biggest undertaking we ever heard of. This book says that two-thirds of the people of the world cannot yet read. Let's start a world campaign! Tell the literacy teachers I'll have my eye on them and very likely some may be called to foreign countries to establish literacy campaigns like ours. Write to the *datos* and tell them that I believe that a world literacy movement is beginning in Lanao and I am on fire with the idea."

The boys had caught fire, too. We started at once to see what improvements we could make in our chart and in our methods of teaching. When we finished there was roaring in my ears the assurance that we were going to arouse the enthusiasm of many leaders in this literacy enterprise, and that it would sweep around the world.

We had made a large map of the world, with Dansalan, Lanao, Mindanao, in the very center. Whenever a letter came from some other part of the world, we would stick on a bright red silk thread running from that country to Lanao Province. The *datos* would come and ask what the threads meant, and while we explained to them, they would cluck their tongues and say, "See how important we are becoming all over the world! We'll certainly have to go and help those other people." How their eyes popped when Governor-General Roosevelt studied that map and asked me to send charts of Moro lessons to Puerto Rico, where he had been governor-general before coming to the Philippines.

At one of our meetings, called to enable the young men to explain to the *datos* about our dream of helping the world, Kakai Dagalangit stood up and said, "If we are going to do that for the world, we will first have to change our name. People think that Moros do nothing but murder and steal and spit betel nut. But now we have stopped being foolish and are getting educated. Why, most of us can read already! Please go to Manila and ask Governor-General Roosevelt to change our name. Tell him to call us 'Islam,' for that means we are trying to do the will of God."

Some of our young men wanted to be baptized, but we were leaning over backward in that respect to avoid fanatical opposition. So far we had baptized only one Moro boy and two Moro girls. We had achieved something, however, that should not be underestimated. There was a new friendliness toward our religious services so marked that the Moros came and watched us worship with open sympathy. I returned their visits by accepting their invitations to worship with them in their mosques every Friday noon. And after the prayers were finished, we would sit around in a circle in the center of the mosque, talking about the prophets and Nabi Isa Rokola (Jesus Christ)—ours and theirs!

In the autumn of 1932 I was off on another tour to the north, to the island of Luzon—a journey that lasted until almost Christmas. Early in my travels Mrs. Josefa Jara Martinez, one of those wonderful Protestant Filipina leaders, took me to Welfareville, where she conducted government homes for delinquent minors, orphans, and destitute aged. I trained about twenty teachers, and later they sent me a splendid letter, pledging themselves to teach four illiterate inmates each before I returned in two weeks' time.

At the invitation of Colonel Santos, director of prisons, I went with Dr. George William Wright to Bilibid Prison in Manila, where a large majority of the prisoners were unable to read or write. The director said the prison needed to teach literacy because it would give the prisoners mental occupation and make them better citizens when they were discharged. I stayed there over seven hours—my longest prison sentence to date!—and trained about forty prisoners, most of them Moros, to teach. One prisoner told me, "Half the murders in the Philippines are committed by your Moro friends!"

At the church in Cavite, I taught a servant girl to read, and the next day she taught the entire chart beautifully to another servant, in front of some thirty people. She was so overcome with joy that she wiped the tears from her eyes with her red handkerchief as she taught. The women who watched her wept, and the men turned their backs or bowed their heads and blew their noses. When the girl finished teaching, the pastor asked us to sing "Praise God from whom all blessings flow," and the meeting turned into a service of thanksgiving. Thereafter Pastor Cruz held literacy classes in that church at five every afternoon and evangelistic campaigns at night. "My little army," he boasted, "will teach 500 persons within the next year. You'll see!"

We had developed a splendid chart in the Ilocano dialect. The three key words we selected were: *carabasa*—"calabash" (squash); *mangalata*—"let us take it"; and *nagapada*—"they had a fight." We associated the three words with this story: "Two boys found a 'squash' and said, 'Let us take it'; but 'they had a fight.'" On the chart were pictures of (1) a calabash, (2) two boys running, and (3) pulling each other's hair. Everywere we traveled in northern Luzon people shouted, *"Carabasa! Mangalata! Nagapada!"* And we shouted back, *"Wen apo!"* which literally is "Yes, sir!" but has the flavor of "Oh, boy, you've said it!"

In Bangued, the capital of the province of Abra, the *presidente* was an ex-teacher and deeply interested in literacy. He himself learned our method, then he required his secretary, his clerks, his councilors, the captain of his constabulary, and a number of his lieutenants to learn. I taught practically all the government employees in the town. A map of Bangued with every house drawn in was prepared and hung on the wall of the big, dirty, old *municipio*. The *presidente* and his force, together with the constabulary, planned to visit all the homes, recording the number of male and female illiterates in each house, and then to send teachers to teach in every home. A gold star was to be pasted on each house that became 100 per cent literate.

At Lagangilang Agricultural School in Abra my heart went out especially to two boys of the primitive Apayao tribe of northern Luzon. They had black tattoos covering their bodies and wore bright red G-strings—a tribal custom. The boys were so eager to learn to teach their people that they would not let me go to lunch; they had heard that I was to leave in an hour and they felt that their learning to teach was infinitely more important than anyone's meal. They said that no one in their mountain tribe was able to read or write and they made me promise to go to those remote mountains above Baguio to prepare Apayao lessons.

At Baoguen, in Ilocos Sur, fifty people gathered from the hills and mountains, some walking thirty kilometers. We taught twelve who had never read before, and the second day passed six of them as qualified teachers. The whole community was abuzz with excitement. As we ate our dinner we could hear people in the neighboring houses repeating the chart—*carabasa* and all the rest, syllable by syllable. "Nobody in those houses knows how to read," said our hostess.

The *presidente* of San Fernando told me, "In all our family I am the only man who has been able to read. Think what a struggle it has been for me to get an education." He brought his own brother to be taught, and in an hour the brother knew all the syllables and could read very slowly. The man's face was radiant, and the *presidente* was astonished beyond measure. "It took me two years to learn to read even a little English," he said. We all laughed as I patted the young man on the back and said to the *presidente,* "See how much brighter your brother is!"

In all my life I have never engaged in work that brought to the surface so much genuine gratitude and such pathetic longing for help. For thirty years my heart had ached for these multitudes, and now that the way was opened to help them, I was most grateful to God.

I was introduced to the students of Muños Agricultural School by Professor Ambrosio Torres, a fine Christian gentleman, who said, "Boys, do you remember how our martyred hero, Dr. José Rizal, risked his life to return to the Philippines in order to cut the cataracts from his mother's eyes? You can be Rizals and cut the cataracts of illiteracy from the eyes of your mothers and fathers and neighbors." The effect of this speech was electric. To a man the students promised that when they went home for vacation they would try to teach their relatives and neighbors to read and write.

Upon returning to Manila from this tour through the Ilocos provinces, I found our leading Protestant layman, Jorge Bocobo, president of the University of the Philippines, intensely interested. He called in the hundred leading students of the university and looked on while I showed them how to teach the Tagalog chart. "I am going home tonight," said President Bocobo, "and teach our cook. I challenge these students to make somebody literate before I do." He said he was trying to put a bill through the legislature to provide for a department of adult literacy.

Dr. Bocobo, Representative Fabian de la Paz, and Dean Francisco Benitez took me to see Governor-General Roosevelt, who had been keeping in touch with our progress ever since he had visited Lanao. The governor-general said he had heard the fear expressed that our campaign would be used as Protestant propaganda. I replied that the only way to meet the objection was to take the movement out of missionary hands.

"At present," I told Mr. Roosevelt, "there is no government committee, and no non-religious committee of any kind, to which people can turn for information and literacy lessons. We have already set up five campaigns with municipal *presidentes* as their heads. For all their lesson material they must write to the National Christian Council, a Protestant organization. In Bangued the priest sent his principal teacher to learn our method. He must buy charts from the National Christian Council. Scores of high schools are taking up this cause with enthusiasm. They must write to the National Christian Council. Either the legislature or yourself should create a non-sectarian committee to study, stimulate, counsel, and coordinate the agencies interested in literacy and to furnish them books. I am sure that the Roman Catholic churches will cooperate with such a committee."

At the suggestion of the governor-general, the Philippine Education Company agreed to print and sell packets containing the necessary teaching material. We devoted several days to writing instructions for teachers and organizers in seven dialects.

Governor-General Roosevelt also sent me to see Dr. Luther Bewley, director of education. "We have started literacy campaigns in ten of your high schools," I told him. "If all your high school and intermediate students will learn this method and teach their parents, they can wipe illiteracy out of this nation."

"You are right," Dr. Bewley replied, "but it takes time to get a huge organization like ours to undertake such a tremendous task. Meanwhile I hope you will visit all the schools in the Philippines."

When I reached San José, Antique, on the island of Panay—the last stop in my two months' tour—the Reverend E. F. Rounds took me to visit his friend, the Dutch priest. The padre was extremely cordial, offered us his best wine and cigars, and took us to see the eight Catholic sisters in the convent. These nuns, six of them Spanish and two of them Filipina, were lovely, spiritual women with a deep eagerness to help the illiterates who, they said, were very numerous in the province of Antique. For two hours they studied our charts and methods with keen interest.

As I traveled toward Lanao once more I listed the languages in which we had prepared key-word lessons. I counted twenty-one:

Maranaw	Ilocano	Joloano
Cebuan	Ibanag	Subano
Ilongo	Manobo	Bukidnon
Tagalog	Isinay	Bontoc Igorot
Bicol	Gaddang	Ifugao
Pampangan	Samarino	Kalinga
Pangasinan	Magindanao	Visayan

This was the beginning of the Philippine literacy campaigns. "But," you will ask, "did they continue?" Indeed they did and for this the National Christian Council deserves much of the credit. It appointed Miss Maria Dayoan general director of literacy in 1935, and until she came to America in 1938 she achieved astonishing results. At one of her early demonstrations before a huge crowd at the Philippines Normal School, the leading teachers' institution of the islands, the illiterates learned to read so quickly that the crowd again and again broke into applause, and every student and teacher volunteered to teach. The Federation of Women's Clubs, one of the most powerful organizations in the Philippines, sent Miss Dayoan everywhere to train their leaders.

Her reports are full of happy experiences:

As I discovered how quickly people learned, I became more and more enthusiastic about literacy and was able to convince other people because of my own personal experience. Illiterates were taught far more rapidly than I had ever believed could be possible. In one demonstration before public school teachers, a woman was taught to read in twenty-five minutes. She was very much pleased and went home full of delight to tell her neighbors. Not long after she left, people flocked into the building. Many wanted to learn how to read and write, and others wanted to know how to teach their brothers, sisters, parents, or other relatives.

I have explained literacy and have trained teachers, not only in churches and women's clubs but also in parent-teacher associations, community assemblies, public and private schools, colleges, secondary and elementary schools, in lodges, municipal councils, dormitories, and student centers. The fact that I was representing the Federation of Women's Clubs enabled me to work with all sorts of organizations, with both Roman Catholic and Protestant groups as well as with those connected with no church.

The Moros themselves were becoming deeply concerned with the progress of their people, and soon after the first Independence Act was passed by Congress in 1932 I wrote of the hopes it had aroused:

January 27, 1933

I wish you could have been with me the other night as our head printer, Macaindeg, poured out his passionate longing to save his people. The passing of the Independence Bill by Congress is having a profound influence upon these young Moros. They know that their province is behind the rest of the Philippine Islands. Macaindeg realizes that unless the Moros put forth a tremendous effort to lift themselves educationally and economically during the next ten years, they will be ruined when independence comes.

Meanwhile, the governor-general took first steps toward a government department of adult education by instituting a series of community assemblies. Over a hundred lectures on vital topics were sent throughout the islands to be delivered in all important languages.

Just as soon as the Philippines became a commonwealth, the National Supreme Council established a division of adult education. This important development in the progress of literacy took place in 1936. Thereafter, the literacy campaign became a government enterprise and reached out to every province and village. Literacy wagons were sent over the islands to attract all the illiterate adults and give them reading lessons. Adult night schools were established nearly everywhere.

The March, 1940, number of the government publication called *Adult Education* announced that the prize for the greatest number of illiterates taught to read that month had gone to the Davao Penal Colony. "The prisons," it said, "are becoming universities."

Matias Cuadra eventually became a chaplain in the Philippine army, and because of his experience in Lanao was given full charge of the literacy campaign among the armed forces. He pushed the campaign with such vigor that the army was nearly 100 per cent literate when Japan struck.

No account of our Lanao mission would be complete without a tribute to the magnificent men and women who worked with us during those years. They had come to the Philippines for sheer love of Christ and the romance of this great literacy adventure.

First, in 1930, came Mrs. David Lund, who opened our Moro girls' dormitory, paying her own salary and contributing $50 a month to aid poor Moro girls. Mrs. Laubach came in 1931 to teach Moro women and keep our books, and with her came our thirteen-year-old son Bob and the Reverend and Mrs. Irving M. Channon, for years missionaries in the Caroline Islands and later at Silliman University, situated on Negros Island within sight of Mindanao. They gave us an extra year before retiring. Irving Channon could do more things than any other man I ever knew. With the aid of our Japanese neighbor, Mr. Matsui, he actually built us a home.

Late in 1931 the Woodwards, in whose home I had stayed on my first visit to Mindanao, moved to Lanao so that, while Mr. Woodward continued his evangelistic work along the coast of the island, his wife could help in the huge task of compiling a dictionary and translating the Bible.

In the summer of 1932 I was overjoyed to receive a letter from Miss Minnie K. Schultz in Pennsylvania. Her interest had been aroused by the magazine articles she had read about our literacy campaign, and she wanted to come out to help us. Friends in America contributed funds to cover her salary, and in January of the following year she arrived to act as secretary and librarian. She won our hearts by her splendid spirit and by the intelligence with which she grasped the work. She was the first person of our acquaintance to go out and secure her own salary before starting out into the field—a wonderful thing to accomplish during those years of depression.

Mrs. Pearl Spencer, one of the famous early government teachers—"best principal in the Philippines," the director of education told me—also joined our mission group for educational work at one-sixth of her previous salary. In 1941 she became the first head of our Moro high school.

In 1940 the American Board of Commissioners for Foreign Missions sent us the Reverend Alvin H. Scaff and his wife, both of them members of Phi Beta Kappa; and in the fall of 1941, when the situation in Japan grew tense and the Japanese Christian leaders urged the missionaries to leave, the Reverend Darley Downs came to our Lanao station. When the tragic war struck the Philippines, Darley Downs, Marion Woodward, and Pearl Spencer were still in Lanao, all three of them separated from their families, who happened to be in the United States. All of them were marvelous Christians, warm friends of the Japanese, Chinese, and Filipinos as well as of the Moros, and their influence was tremendous as they gave witness to the love of Christ in Lanao.

While our mission force was thus growing, there was coming over the Moros a change so profound that it was nothing less than miraculous. When we arrived in 1929 the atmosphere was tense with hatred between the Moros and the constabulary. The government was trying to "keep the boat from rocking" as much as possible. Everyone except the missionaries carried guns—even in the daylight in the military camps—in 1929. But in thirteen years this had nearly all disappeared.

And in 1942 these same Moros who had so hated us signed a solemn pledge that they would die rather than allow the Japanese to overthrow the good government established by the United States. Ten thousand Moros signed their names to this pledge—most of them men whom we had taught to read. They had stopped glorying in being outlaws and were proud of being good citizens. Fourteen years before they had burned fifty school buildings, determined to root education out of Lanao. In 1941 we left them clamoring for schools faster than the government could provide them, and sending girls as well as boys to be educated.

At the time of the Japanese invasion we still had the only press printing Maranaw literature. We were producing close to a million pages a year, although it had to be set up by hand or mimeographed. In the ten-year period preceding we had published booklets with stories of the Old Testament prophets, running both the Bible and Koran accounts in the same volume. We had printed Luke in Maranaw; and when the war broke out the American Bible Society was in the process of printing the Acts. We had printed three editions of an English-Maranaw dictionary, with definitions of ten thousand words. And we were issuing *Lanao Progress,* a sixteen-page fortnightly.

We had specialized in paper-bound booklets and pamphlets, which we sold and gave away by tens of thousands. The non-religious pamphlets were on such varied subjects as "Care of the Skin," "Motherhood and Baby Care," "The New Miracle Rice," "Moro Folklore in Prose," and "History of the World." The bureau of education took the entire edition of a hundred-page volume containing a compilation of Moro lyrics. The religious pamphlets besides the Bible were on such themes as "Life on Its Highest Levels," "Three Hundred Objectives of Character," "God Is Beyond Us All," "Why Does God Permit Suffering?," "Where Christians and Moslems Are Brothers," "Secrets of a Student's Success," "Game with Minutes" (later published in America), and sixty four-page tracts on "The Friendship of Jesus" for distribution in the Moro markets. In 1942 these tracts formed the basis for a book published by Harper & Brothers, New York, under the title *You Are My Friends.*

During all these adventures we were developing a science and technique in adult literacy that we believed would be distinct contributions to education. This was in part the art of building easy lessons, to be sure, but it was far more than that—more than anything that could be written on paper. It was a thing of the spirit—the art of applying to education that mysterious love power that held together the early followers of Jesus.

Experience has shown us that it is necessary to produce a congenial spiritual climate if a campaign is to flourish. So the training of teachers involves far more than teaching them to say the right words. It is helping them to be warm friends of their students, to pray for them, to rejoice in their progress—in a word, to radiate a Christlike atmosphere.

One day after I had taught a half-dozen women and children to read while fifty teachers looked on, the chairman rose and said, "I have watched this remarkable exhibition and I believe I have found the secret. It is love." He was at least 50 per cent right. The psychological principles that we explain to all our teachers are the "highest" secret, not only of the literacy enterprise described in this book, but of life.

We prefer to teach one by one so that we may sit down beside our students; a teacher of a class is too much like a superior person. Every illiterate has an inferiority complex—he thinks we feel above him. The very first thing is to remove the gap between us. When we sit beside him we disarm his feeling of inferiority. Then we proceed to treat him not like a student but like a rajah! We try to make ourselves humble and him important. He thinks he is too old to learn. We must prove that he can learn easily, quickly, and delightfully, no matter how old he is. Every step is so short that an ordinary man can take it easily. The chart provides for this; but occasionally the teacher must say just the right word to help a dull student over a hard spot. There must be no embarrassing pauses, never a question the student cannot answer, no examination to find out what he knows!

We must keep out of the student's way, neither pushing him nor retarding him. An illiterate is happy only when he feels free to take his own natural gait.

On every line of the chart the student finds himself saying something surprising. An atmosphere of expectancy is thus developed; we can see it in the bright, open-mouthed eagerness of our illiterate learner. The chart becomes a Pandora's box of glad surprises, appealing to the emotions and drawing forth peals of laughter.

There is never a frown nor a rebuke nor a loud tone of voice. Students remember a whisper better than a howl because it is pleasanter. In teaching an illiterate there must be no unpleasant moments. Never a gesture of impatience nor a yawn. Upon the slightest justification we pat him on the shoulder and say, "That's fine." The student strives to maintain this charmed spell, perhaps the most thrilling hour of his life! He is getting along much better than he had expected because the lesson is easy and we teach correctly. He attributes it to his brilliance. What everybody craves, of all things on earth, is to have some hidden genius discovered in him. If you become the discoverer of that genius, he is yours, body and soul.

We have seen hundreds of men and women going out from their first lessons wreathed in smiles, saying, "Very easy! He was surprised at my bright mind." And after that all the others in the village are eager to have their brilliance discovered! We never forget that while we are teaching one man we are selling the idea to his neighbors.

Then, when the student has learned lesson one, we set him to teaching somebody else. We look delighted at his teaching and say when he finishes, "You are going to be a splendid teacher. Teach about five more as you did now. Then I'll give you the next lesson." His teaching others has these obvious advantages:

1. The lesson is well fixed in his mind by the time he has taught it five or six times. We never really know a thing until we have used it.

2. He is at once given a new status in society, a new self-respect. He becomes a member of the teaching profession. It is astounding how his shoulders go back, his face beams, his eyes gleam—he has arrived!

3. By making every student a teacher, the teaching is done at small cost, and the increase in readers is very rapid. We educate by geometrical progression.

4. Our student comes to realize that he is learning in order to help others. The spirit of sharing is fostered.

Nothing I have ever seen begets friendship so effectively as thus teaching illiterates and sending them out to teach others; not even a doctor, caring for the sick, has quite the same chance. For while the doctor and nurse do something *for the patient,* they do not request him to *go and cure others.* On the other hand, when we teach we ask our student to pass it on. He goes out with the feeling that he has surprised us, and that now we expect big things of him. Warm with gratitude, he tries to merit our further praise, and there is established a bond of affection that will last a lifetime. The student emulates our warm kindliness, so that it begins to permeate the entire community like some beneficent contagion. The spirit of sharing is taught, not by talking about it, but by doing it, and—what is even more vital—recruiting others to do it.

CHAPTER 4

1935: A LITERACY TOUR ACROSS SOUTHERN ASIA

Malaya, India, Cairo, Turkey

OUR MORO TEACHERS kept asking, "Do you suppose we can really make lessons as easy as these in other languages?" We knew it could not be done in English with its hopeless spelling. But what we were all eager to know was how many of the languages of the world were spelled regularly enough to be taught by our method.

Matias Cuadra, our Moro preacher, had lived in Borneo for several years and fortunately spoke Malay. He went to work preparing lessons in our front schoolroom while a hundred Moros looked on with mouths agape. In two days he had a Malay chart completed and the whole Moro tribe clamored to read it, for they think Malay is nearly as sacred as Arabic. Cuadra almost became their god. Having tasted that triumph, we were all eager for more.

Many missionaries wrote us from India, men who had beaten their heads against the stone wall of illiteracy for twenty or thirty years. These men asked us to visit them, though one of them warned us to expect "a task about equal to shoveling the Himalayas into the Indian Ocean." "We shall never have a strong indigenous church in India," he wrote, "until more of its members can read the Scriptures; and so

I am keenly interested. Even though I fear that your visit will be a disappointment to you in the way of definite results, I do believe you will stir up interest in the subject."

It was our irrepressibly enthusiastic secretary, Minnie Schultz, who really pushed us over the brink into world literacy tours. She persuaded me to prepare a letter for persons along our route to America via India and Suez, which we would be taking when we left on furlough. Before I realized it Miss Schultz had mimeographed and mailed five hundred copies of this letter! Many of those who received it sent us most urgent invitations to visit them.

We wrote accepting invitations from Singapore, Ceylon, parts of India, Cairo, Palestine, Syria, and Turkey, and on January 20, 1935, I set out alone, half frightened at my own audacity! We had no resources except a furlough travel allowance, so, to save expenses, Mrs. Laubach, our son Bob, and Miss Schultz remained in Lanao two months longer and met me in Colombo after I had finished my visit in India.

On shipboard from Lanao to Manila I wrote to my father telling him all about the farewell celebrations the Moros had held for us:

January 20, 1935

At last I am on the way home. What a farewell we had! For days we had felt excitement in the air as we packed our baggage to leave, but we did not expect a *despedida* as overwhelming as those dear Moros gave us.

Five big trucks filled with them followed our car down to Iligan, the seaport twenty-five miles away. They swarmed on the ship and spilled over on the wharf. Every high *dato* in Lanao wanted to make a speech on how they were sending me to bring light to mankind and how this was to be the beginning of emancipation for the human race, the turning point in world history! At ten that night the captain blew his whistle to warn that he was about to cast off, but the Moros laughed and went on talking. The captain subsided for fear they would cut his head off. When every *dato* had made his speech the sheik said: "We are going to pray for you." They could not bow to the deck for they were crowded together like sardines, so they held out their hands and kept turning them over, palms up, palms down, while their highest *imam* prayed that this American friend, whom they had helped to make the easiest lessons in the world, should have the blessing of Allah as he went around the world introducing their method to the less fortunate nations. Then they kissed me and hugged me and one-eyed Hadji Kakairan cried on my shoulder as he said: "We will pray for you in every mosque in Lanao while you go around the world spreading the glory of Lanao." They declared they would have gone along if only

CHAPTER 11

1947: EUROPE AND AFRICA

London, Scotland, Sierra Leone

London

I DID NOT stay in the Philippines but went to London, arriving there on October 4, 1947. London, like the Philippines, was marked with the ghastly scars of war. These London scars had been cut by long-range German blitz bombs, streets were torn up and whole blocks were gutted by these predecessors of our present missiles. The plucky Britishers never said a word about their losses, nor did they complain about being half starved. They were clearly war-weary, but they were not defeated. They hung on to me and honored me with almost terrifying eagerness. On October 22 I had the honor of being elected a member of the famous Authors Club, and of dining with several famous British authors, including Sir James Marchant.

The Zenana Bible and Medical Mission, which works in Moslem lands, gave me a cordial welcome. They said that literacy was what they needed to go behind purdah to teach the Moslem women to read and to leave the gospel with them in their own language. Moslem women are not permitted to leave their homes without a veil.

At London University, I was invited to help prepare lessons in the Hausa language of northern Nigeria. There were perhaps fifty

Nigerian students at the university, and hundreds of other students from Africa and British colonies.

Cambridge University was also deeply interested in literacy. The crowning event of my experience in England was meeting the West African students attending Cambridge. There were 300 of them and they were so keen to help their countries with literacy that I found tears coming to my eyes and a lump coming to my throat.

Quite a different meeting was that with the students in another Cambridge college, where colonial officers of the British government were being trained. There, on Hallowe'en night after I had talked about "Literacy Problems in Africa," we engaged in the most unscholarly game of trying to bite apples suspended on strings while our hands were tied behind our backs. Thereafter all my fear of Cambridge was gone. The next morning one of the young professors made me walk what seemed to me to be at least twenty miles to see something of that stupendously spread-out university. No American should go to Cambridge without an automobile. The English students and professors use bicycles.

Scotland

I visited Scotland for two exciting weeks. In Edinburgh, 500 schoolteachers, many of them planning to be missionaries, were trained in teaching illiterates by the use of the charts we had made in Ethiopia.

At St. Andrew's University, a hundred miles north of Edinburgh, I found what was called the Ecumenical Group, which included students from British Guiana, Jamaica, India, Africa and Australia. St. Andrew's University is the original home of golf and the first golf course is still in use. One young man in that university followed me everywhere so that he could take literacy methods back to British Guiana, where his father is a wealthy man.

In Glasgow there were two great crowds, one on Sunday morning and the other in the evening. The Boy Scouts and the Girl Guides marched to the church with their flags and sat in the front seats. The spirit was so inspiring that thoughts seemed to come to me right out of heaven. The Scottish people have a way of drawing the very best out of you. The following day 3,000 schoolteachers met in St. Andrew's Hall. They had been released from school so that they could arrive at five o'clock in the evening. A huge chart of our lessons had been prepared from the Ethiopian Coptic textbook and I taught all the teachers this chart. I have never seen such interest and enthusiasm among teachers anywhere else. I left Scotland saying that the Scots are the greatest people on earth.

Sierra Leone

I flew from England to Sierra Leone, West Africa, where my son Bob joined me on December 11, 1947. The words "Sierra Leone" mean "Lion Mountains." It is a land of tremendously tall elephant grass, about fifteen to twenty feet high. We saw no elephants but we did see a lion and a leopard.

Sierra Leone is a land of diamonds. We visited the diamond mines and walked over large beds of white pebbles, some of them doubtless diamonds in the rough. You cannot tell the difference between a pebble and a diamond unless you are an expert. It is absolutely forbidden to pick up the pebbles in any of the diamond regions of Africa, which means that no African dares pick up his own diamonds.

Freetown is the capital of Sierra Leone. In this city the people speak pidgin English, so we made lessons in that language and another set of lessons in the language used by the fishermen. It is called "Kru."

Then we plunged into the interior, to the boundary between Sierra Leone and French Guinea. Here the United Brethren have their most remote mission. When they started this mission there was no road for the last sixty miles, only a jungle path through the tall elephant grass. Now, thanks to the diamond mines, there are very good roads in this remote region. One of the first missionaries to make that journey was a nurse, Miss Estelle High, who had been a classmate of my wife in the Presbyterian Nurses Training School in Philadelphia. Miss High was overjoyed to meet us and the stories she told of her adventures in Sierra Leone were among the most exciting we ever heard.

We made lessons in nine languages in Sierra Leone and began translating *The Story of Jesus* in the principal language. Bob did these lessons on the large type portable typewriter that we had brought with us. In each place the missionaries would gather five or ten people who spoke the language. On a blackboard we would write the consonants and the vowels they employed in that language. Then the natives and the missionaries would seek a word that began with each consonant and that resembled the consonant. For example: in the Kono language the word *da* means *pot,* so we stood a large spoon up on the side of a pot to make it look like the letter *d*. After we had selected these pictures we had to utilize anyone who could make an attempt at drawing pictures. Fortunately an English missionary, the Reverend R. A. Johnson, could draw pictures and he also had a printing press. It was he who published the lessons we prepared in all these languages and who has kept the campaign in Sierra Leone going steadily ever since.

There are more than 900 languages spoken in Africa. Primitive people live within very small circles and seldom have contacts outside their own tribes. This is why there is a new language across almost every river and over almost every mountain. For example, in the village of Binkolo, Limba is spoken, but a half mile down the road —ten minutes' walk away!—the people speak Temne.

The people of Sierra Leone never live in isolated houses as our American farmers do, because they are afraid of lions and leopards. They live in villages of from 500 to 1,000 persons and each village may have its own dialect.

The African languages are very easy to teach because they are all spelled phonetically with Roman letters. Nearly every language south of the Sahara desert has been reduced to writing within the last hundred years by missionaries. This is why the alphabets are free from the irregularities we have in English.

We found the women of Sierra Leone were at least as eager to learn to read as the men, and they took great delight in teaching other women all they themselves knew. For example, two women in the town of Kenema each taught fifty women and promised to make 150 literate within a year. None of the teachers received any pay at all! We were delighted with the enthusiasm of these women because, as the great African educator Aggrey said, "If you teach a man you teach only one person, but if you teach a woman you teach a whole family!"

In the village of Bumpe it was exhilarating to see the hands of 400 people as they volunteered each one to teach one. (It is easy to remember the name Bumpe after the bumpy road over which we had to travel to get there.)

At a mass meeting the paramount chief, Yavonni, of the Senehu tribe, said: "You have come to our country bringing us education for threepence (the cost of one booklet) for which we would gladly have paid 200 pounds. I promise you that my people will give full support to the efforts of my missionary friends."

Then the people came forward, each holding threepence in his hands to buy a primer. They looked quite downcast when we told them that the new books would not be ready for another month. The district commissioner, losing his customary British reserve, saved things by leading the entire assembly in three resounding cheers: "Hip! Hip! Hooray!"

Christmas 1947 found us in a fine Christmas celebration with all the missionaries of Freetown on top of a tall mountain overlooking the city. We blew enormous bubbles with bubble gum and fastened these together to make a Santa Claus, as we used to make snow men in America. Bob and I will remember that bubble gum snow man on the top of an African mountain to the end of our days.

CHAPTER 12

1948: DOWN THROUGH AFRICA

Liberia, Nigeria, Ghana, Belgian Congo, Rhodesia, South Africa

Liberia

ON JANUARY 1, 1948, Bob and I arrived in Monrovia, Liberia. This little country has a special place in the hearts of all Americans because after the Civil War our freed slaves were permitted to go there and carve out a country for themselves. No people in the world are more loyal friends of the United States than the Liberians. The reception we received fairly took our breath away. The minister of education told us that the policy of Liberia was to teach everyone English. I replied that this naturally thrilled me, but that the scientific approach was to teach their own language first, so that they would be able to learn English more easily through the eye-gate as well as through the ear-gate. He agreed that this was true.

Representatives of ten languages, missionaries and nationals, met with us in Monrovia. They included Methodists, Anglicans, Presbyterians, Baptists, Lutherans and Roman Catholics. This was the first time these denominational leaders had ever cooperated on any Liberian project. They made lessons in ten languages, and we immediately mimeographed 200 copies of the lessons in each language.

Bob worked night and day putting all these lessons on mimeographed stencils with our mammoth type typewriter.

President William V. Tubman was most enthusiastic and so was the minister of education. They accepted the entire program we proposed for Liberia: (1) literacy lessons in the vernacular, (2) *The Story of Jesus* in the vernacular, (3) *Streamlined English,* and (4) *The Story of Jesus* in English.

Two years later when we made a return visit to Liberia, President Tubman held a great "Literacy Day" celebration at which all the distinguished officials of the country made speeches. Airplanes flew overhead distributing handbills that announced the launching that day of the great campaign against Enemy Number One. The campaign in Liberia has been going on steadily ever since in ten dialects and in English.

Nigeria

On February 18, 1948, we arrived in Nigeria, the most populous country in Africa, with 25,000,000 people. Here, with missionaries and Nigerian educators, we made up lessons in nine different languages. The Reverend Nelson Ludlow and his wife, who is a physician, took us to two villages of the Ashanti tribe to try out our Bushanti lessons as soon as we had them prepared. We had the first lesson on a very large chart. In one village where 400 people were present we taught four men to read that first chart in fifteen minutes. The big chief was so excited that he shook hands with those four men and appointed them then and there as teachers of all the rest of the tribe. They were the only people in the tribe who could read their own language and they knew only one lesson! In fact, that language had never before been reduced to writing. Suddenly a hundred men all dressed in white came forward and amazed us by falling on their faces in front of me. I said to the Rev. Mr. Ludlow, "This is terrible. Tell them to get up and shake hands with me in the good American fashion."

At the next village a thousand people had gathered and though we were four hours late they were waiting patiently in the semi-darkness. They entertained us with some of the most remarkable acrobatics I have ever seen. Every feat was in perfect rhythm with music produced by pounding on huge round gourds covered with a network of shells. By the time these feats were finished it was too dark to teach by our big chart, but we taught them anyhow. They repeated after us each word without being able to see it and seemed to be perfectly happy. Fortunately we had no educational critics to see our bad teaching! Now we are making filmstrips for teaching at night. Nighttime is ideal because people have finished their work and are looking for some kind of entertainment.

The most widely used native language south of the Sahara desert is called Hausa. It is the language spoken by most of the Mohammedans of that part of Africa. It is written in Arabic letters. The missionaries had been trying to teach it the hard way. Some of them had tears in their eyes when we showed them how to teach it our easy way. Some of the best photographs Bob ever took show us teaching white-robed Mohammedans in northern Nigeria.

We visited the town of Jos where the people dress as Adam and Eve did after they were driven from the garden, with a bunch of leaves and a string tied around their waists. The missionaries there have never tried to change this scanty costume but allow the people to come to church dressed as usual. The natives were so reverent and so deeply interested that in a few minutes Bob and I forgot all about their scanty clothing. Bob took a few pictures but no mission board in America has wanted to publish them. The leaders of Nigeria are also unwilling to have these pictures published although I must say they are as modest as pictures of our bathing suits taken on any beach.

Ghana

We went from Nigeria to the Gold Coast (now called Ghana). This is one of the most exciting and colorful countries in all Africa and now it is probably the most progressive. The women of Ghana dress more gorgeously than anywhere else in Africa and the men are almost equally well dressed. The British have done a magnificent job in preparing young men to take over administrative responsibility. Achamoto College in the city of Accra is one of the best colleges in Africa. While we were in the Gold Coast the British were in process of handing the government over to the Africans.

We motored over to British Togoland on the east border of the Gold Coast and there we saw one of the largest churches in the world, with 50,000 members. As everywhere else the Christians seemed to show the effect of their religion in their faces and in their triumphant bearing. (There are other tremendous churches in Africa, for example, in the French Cameroons we encountered a church with a membership of 30,000.)

At Akropong, in the heart of the Gold Coast, is the famous Paramount Chief Nana Kwame Fori II. Seated on his throne under his royal umbrella, wearing gorgeous state robes, the paramount chief and his court watched us teach two members of his household. These illiterates learned so fast that the chief interrupted the teaching to ask if they were really illiterate and was delighted when he learned that they were.

At Kumasi, the largest city in the Gold Coast, we demonstrated our lessons in the Ashanti language spoken in that region. A crowd of a thousand brilliantly dressed men and women were so excited that every one of them marched forward to shake hands with us at the end of the meeting. Our hands felt as though they had been through a clothes wringer.

Belgian Congo

From the Gold Coast we flew to the Belgian Congo and motored for a few days on a third-class road to the great Methodist mission at Wembo Nyama in the very center of the Congo. There we held a full-fledged "each one teach one" campaign. First we prepared lessons in the Otetela language, the first language I had ever seen in which the letter *o* was the most important letter in the alphabet. We made a thousand copies of the primer on the mission mimeograph and then trained 120 church members to use this primer. One man from a distant village had walked for several days after he had learned that in Wembo Nyama he could get an injection for ignorance! The nurse, Miss Eye, laughed heartily and then brought him over to us. I taught him in front of 120 teachers whom I was training. When I told him that I wanted him to go back to his village and teach because he was so bright, he went stark crazy. He laughed and shouted until the place was in an uproar, everyone laughing or crying with joy. We had to dismiss the class until the next day.

At the end of ten days our 120 teachers had each taught one illiterate the whole primer and on Sunday morning we had a graduation ceremony. The teachers marched to the front of the church bringing their pupils with them and the Belgian inspector of schools (himself a Roman Catholic) gave each pupil a diploma and each teacher a certificate of Christian service. The big church was electric with excitement as it is so often when graduation exercises are held. "This," said one of the missionaries, "was the finest participation of Africans we have ever known."

In Africa they give every white man a nickname but they seldom tell him what it is because it is usually uncomplimentary. I am proud of the nickname the Africans in Wembo Nyama gave me. It is "Okombekombe," which means "Mender of Old Baskets." Baskets are among the most important articles in all Africa, so I felt highly honored.

We went to Leopoldville, where we held a literacy class for one hundred African women in the big church. Our stay in the Congo was nearly over and on the third day of the literacy class I told the interpreter to say "Goodbye" because on the following day we would be leaving. The women began to howl and to crowd toward me with anger and fear in their faces. I thought they would tear me to pieces. "What is the matter?" I asked, and the interpreter said, "They think you are stopping this class just when they were about to fulfil the hope of a lifetime, and they are frantic." I replied, "Tell them that you are going to continue the class and I am going away to find more teachers to help Africa to learn to read." But as I left that church the women were still howling and moaning. We shall never forget that sound for it represents the cry of more than two-thirds of the women of the world who are still waiting for a chance to come up out of their ignorance, poverty and despair.

Rhodesia

On June 2, 1948, we stood on the lower bank of Victoria Falls gazing down upon that infernal maelstrom known as the Devil's Cataract. Behind us was the colossal statue of David Livingstone, the first white man who ever saw those falls. He had discovered them in 1855. On the monument are these words, "Here Livingstone first saw the most awe-inspiring sight in the world."

But our party was even more awe-inspired by the statue of Livingstone than it was by those stupendous falls. Ten years previously, in Dar es Salaam in Tanganyika, I had seen the grave in which they had buried Livingstone's body after his faithful black companions had carried it from the heart of Africa. Only three weeks before visiting Victoria Falls we had made lessons and had taught illiterates in Stanleyville, which was named after Sir Henry M. Stanley, the man who sailed up the Congo river and found the long-lost Livingstone. He found Livingstone but he could not persuade him to leave Africa until his task was finished. Livingstone had come to free the slaves by exposing to the light of world opinion the horrors of the slave traffic, but he died of malaria and dysentery before his task was finished. In fact the Africans are not yet free from slavery of the worst kind, and they will not be free until the shackles of ignorance and superstition are cut from them and they know the freedom which Jesus Christ gives.

The memory of those brave missionaries who first penetrated darkest Africa, and who died like flies that the Africans might live, so overwhelmed me at the foot of Livingstone's statue that I could not repress the tears. I remembered seeing David Livingstone's burial place in Westminster Abbey, the only missionary lying in that sacred place among the famous kings and statesmen of England.

The British government demonstrated an ever greater interest in our literacy tours. They paid all our expenses in Rhodesia, where we were entertained by the British governor general. Indeed, our first visit to Africa was at the invitation of Mr. Arthur Mayhew, secretary of the British Foreign Office in London. In 1956 the British government extended to us a cordial invitation to come and help them with literacy in every one of their colonies.

When we made the trip through Africa in 1947 and 1948 we were accompanied by Mr. and Mrs. Svend Olsen of Denmark. Olsen is an entomologist and he captured about a thousand species of insects never before identified. Every night he would sit outside his tent with a bright light, drawing pictures until midnight. Beside him was his butterfly net and bottle of cyanide. While capturing insects he made 3,000 pictures for our primer!

We went to the Methodist mission station at Old Umtali in Southern Rhodesia. The missionaries from four other denominations gathered here and we all plunged into the preparation of lessons in five dialects. These dialects proved to be so nearly alike that we decided to make one set of lessons that would be useful for them all by using words common to every dialect. We tried them out on illiterates who spoke these dialects, and they worked. This was a landmark in our experience. We had never before been able to make one set of lessons that would cover five dialects!

But the thing that remained longest in our memories of Old Umtali was a student choir that sang a native song:

Give a thought to Africa
Breathe a prayer for Africa
Give your love to Africa
Tell the love of Jesus.
God bless Africa.

The look on their faces as they gazed toward the heavens and sang that song will never be erased from my memory.

Now we come to the ugly cancer in the heart of Africa, the wide gulf between the whites and the blacks. We had met it in Northern Rhodesia where a missionary refused to allow our best literacy teacher, a highly educated African, to sit beside us, but compelled him to sit on the edge of a board behind us while we drove for fifty miles. One young Scottish missionary in Northern Rhodesia revolted against this segregation and was thronged by the Africans; his church overflowed every Sunday.

South Africa

When we came to Johannesburg we found most of the missionaries and other white people were conforming to the general custom of rigidly segregating the blacks, but a minority of the white people felt that this was not Christian behavior and were daring to live in close contact with the black people in defiance of the general sentiment. Among these were Mr. and Mrs. Quintin Whyte, with whom we stayed while in Johannesburg. They were the directors of the South

African Institute of Race Relations. At the University of Johannesburg they called together Africans of six different languages and worked with us in preparing literacy lessons.

In these languages we encountered the "clicking" of the tongue that characterizes the languages of South Africa. The Xhosa language has three clicks and so does Xulu (which we usually spell Zulu). The Hottentots (pygmies) have twelve clicks and each click can be done three ways so their language sounds more like playing on rattle bones than like talking.

The missionaries who reduced these languages to writing had great difficulty at first in finding letters to represent the clicks. They used *x, xh, q, xq, c, cq, ts*. The international phonetic alphabet has a symbol for every click but only the very expert phoneticians know what these symbols represent, and the early missionaries were not expert phoneticians. Besides, our typewriters of the international alphabet did not have letters and the missionaries wanted to use their typewriters, with the result that there was a great deal of diversity in the early spelling of these strange sounds. At the present time phonetic experts are at work reconciling the various systems of spelling.

The tension between the Africans on the one hand and the Boers on the other hand grows more dangerous as the years go by. The principle of *apartheid* was just being developed when we were in Johannesburg. The Boer leaders were saying that all Africans should be confined to unskilled labor, leaving the skilled labor for the white workers. For example, the Africans might use a shovel because that is the tool of unskilled laborers but they should not be allowed to use a hammer or a saw for those are the tools of skilled laborers. Alas, this division has grown worse and worse as the years have gone by.

Dr. Ray Phillips took us to see the city of Negro servants about a dozen miles from Johannesburg, where 60,000 Negroes working in Johannesburg are compelled to live. There were no policemen in this servants' colony, and the general condition was the worst I have seen anywhere in the world. How callous and foolish can people be! Dr. Phillips also took me to the Orphan School, where Alan Paton had lived while collecting the material for his tremendous book *Cry the Beloved Country*.

One of the most unforgettable experiences in South Africa occurred in the gold mine area where thousands of African workmen lived. These men had been brought great distances, leaving their wives and children behind them, and were toiling in the gold mines in an effort to save a little money to take back home at the end of five or six years. The missions had churches for these homesick men, and when we held meetings in these churches we found the men wonderfully appreciative and eager to learn to read. They were groping hopelessly for any doorway leading out of the tragic inferiority that imprisoned them and literacy looked to them like their only hope.

A fine-looking Englishman, chief of the employment service for the gold mines, lunched with us and a few missionaries. I asked him for permission to teach the illiterate miners and he replied: "You have all the ethics on your side but we must be practical. Do you think these Africans would go 5,000 feet down in that hot hole if they could find a better job? If we allow them to become literate they will surely get better work and we shall lose them."

He said that in 1948; since then, I am glad to say, the managers changed their minds and now give their blessing to our literacy classes.

Many governments have also changed their minds about literacy since the Second World War and in ever-increasing numbers have asked our literacy team to help them. Altogether we have had invitations to help seventy-five governments; we have been able to respond to sixty-four of these invitations.

CHAPTER 13

1949: IN SOUTH ASIA

Thailand, India, Pakistan

Thailand

IN FEBRUARY 1949 we went to Thailand at the invitation of the Thai government, which paid for us to go all the way around the world—Phil Gray and his wife, my son Bob, and myself.

Thailand had become a member of UNESCO in January 1949. It was very much impressed by the fact that UNESCO had put adult literacy at the top of its list of objectives and had given favorable recognition to our method. This is why we had been invited. The welcome we received in Thailand actually frightened us; they expected so much. We were all the more frightened because we knew that the Thai alphabet was the most difficult alphabet we had ever seen. It has only twenty-one consonant *sounds,* but it uses forty-four consonant *symbols* for those sounds. Most terrifying of all, they had forty-four vowel symbols and you must know exactly when it is proper to use each of them.

In 1943 at Teachers College in New York, Dr. Paul Aiken and I had attempted to prepare Thai lessons but I found the alphabet so difficult that I gave up trying to learn it myself. And now here we were seven years later in Thailand with the government and people showing every confidence in us. I think I never prayed so hard in my life, and God answered that prayer in a remarkable way. Dr. Aiken had trained an unusually intelligent young Thai named Saram to produce Christian literature for the Presbyterian mission. Dr. Aiken and Saram together had worked for seven years to plan the lessons that fitted their difficult alphabet. The plan proved to be excellent. The ministry of education summoned 300 government teachers from their schools to meet every day in Bangkok and help prepare the textbook. In front of these teachers Saram wrote his ideas on a big blackboard and everyone liked them. The result was magnificent. The seemingly impossible had been made easy.

The government allocated 20,000 feet of film and a motion picture photographer to photograph us at work; every time we entered a building or left it this tireless photographer took pictures of us, wherever there was sunlight. He wasted at least 15,000 feet of that film on useless scenes but in doing so he revealed the eagerness of the Thai government.

American ambassador Edwin F. Stanton was a mighty aid to us during our stay in Thailand. In our honor he gave a reception to which all the chief Thai officials were invited. The prime minister also gave a magnificent reception at his home in our honor. The finest dancers of Thailand were there and gave their inimitable classic dances before the élite of Bangkok.

Government officials also took us on a private tour through the king's palace and the marvelous temples surrounding it on days when no other visitors were permitted to enter. Bob was granted permission to take pictures, which were forbidden to ordinary tourists. I have never seen such art as they have in those temples. The Taj Mahal is more graceful in its total design but these Thai temples are incomparably more intricate and delicate in their paintings and mosaics.

We held literacy classes in a village eighteen kilometers from Bangkok to try out our new textbook. The minister of education came out to the village and opened the course. Forty students worked every day for two weeks and finished the primer. Then we had a graduation ceremony, which was honored by the presence of Ambassador Stanton and his charming wife. Mrs. Stanton gave the diplomas to the graduates and certificates of patriotic service to their teachers. The rest of that day was devoted to athletics and dancing such as one can see only in Thailand.

Phil Gray and his wife and Bob and I went into the very heart of Thailand to Korat where we held another literacy class for two weeks. They celebrated our graduation day with an enormous festival at which 8,000 people participated. All the school children marched, all the soldiers paraded, all the athletes performed, guns were fired and drums were pounded. The crown prince, who had come to Korat for this occasion, distributed the diplomas. Thus ended in a blaze of glory the wonderful two months we spent in Thailand.

India

March 1949 found Bob and me in India as guests of the governor of Madras. We were housed all by ourselves in an enormous palace the British had built and the Indian government had now taken over. There were fifty servants keeping this huge palace in condition and Bob and I were the only guests. I stepped off the length and width of the palace and found that it was fifty yards across the front and 125 yards deep.

The former prince of Gwalior had been appointed governor of Madras. He and his wife were living in a much smaller house behind our own immense palace. In our honor he held a tea at which all of the important people in Madras were present. The Prince of Gwalior and his wife walked out to the tea on a long red plush carpet. It must have been fifty yards in length. Bob sat by the Prince and I sat by the Princess.

In Madras, and also in the other leading cities of India, there were conferences at which government officials took a leading part. This 1949 visit to India was in striking contrast to the visits which I had made between the years 1935 and 1940. In those earlier years very few men besides the missionaries had shown great interest in literacy and missionaries felt fortunate if the government officials honored them by appearing at all. But in the year 1949 the government officials were conducting the conferences and the Christian missionaries were in the background. India, like all the other countries of Asia and Africa, had become convinced that illiteracy was Enemy Number One and must be destroyed.

There was now a disposition on the part of missionaries and Christian leaders to say something like this: "Since the government is taking such an active part in literacy, we will devote ourselves principally to the production of Christian literature and Christian propaganda and leave the secular business of teaching illiterates to nonreligious agencies. Our part in this movement is to see that after they are taught to read they shall have good reading matter. Otherwise literacy will do them more harm than good."

Some Christian leaders said, "Our only obligation is to teach the Christians to read," while others went so far as to say: "Teaching people to read, unless they are also made Christian, is merely doing harm, for it is putting power into the hands of people without Christian principles and so making them more dangerous because they are more powerful."

All of these positions have appealed to some Christian leaders, and yet I believe they are mistaken. There is an ever-rising demand on the part of the illiterate people to learn to read and so come out of their poverty. The governments feel the tremendous pressure of their masses for better conditions and are in desperate need of help. In Asia and Africa, where only 10 per cent of the people have any money and where 90 per cent are practically penniless as well as illiterate, there is not enough money and there are not enough trained teachers to meet the demand of the masses for adult literacy or even to provide schools for all the children. The only hope they have is to employ the "each one teach one" method we missionaries have developed. This is why they are turning to us in such great numbers. They have no other hope. If missions join with the governments in developing "each one teach one" campaigns, they will find themselves in the forefront of education, and all the prejudices people of other religions feel toward Christians will tend to melt away. Here is where the old maxim, "A friend in need is a friend indeed," comes into play. The need of these governments is the most wonderful open door missions have ever known, if only they are wise enough to enter that door.

Since the Second World War twenty nations that were formerly under European control have become independent. The leaders of these nations have always blamed the Europeans for their backwardness, but now they have no alibi. They must make good or be repudiated by their own people. Our experience is that wherever we respond to this critical need, both governments and people are immensely grateful. My experience has been that when we help governments, they are so appreciative that they place no obstacles in the way of Christian witnessing. Indeed, they begin to feel that Christianity is a mighty asset to their country, and this is exactly what we want them to feel.

In some sections of India the Christians and the missionaries were alert to this opportunity and they have won thousands of friends and hundreds of Christians. In other parts of India they turned away from literacy and lost one of the best opportunities missionaries ever had to help the people of India to appreciate Christians.

Some missionaries lost interest in literacy because they found the first lessons we had made in India too difficult and so they gave up teaching. Our lessons needed improving, which required a great deal more hard research. No one knew this better than I, and so day after day and week after week I worked with educators in an effort to write easier lessons in these baffling Indian languages—lessons as easy to teach and as easy to learn as they were in Africa. No one will probably ever appreciate how many long hours of strenuous effort, of trial and error, went into the building of the lessons that finally emerged. I think that by the year 1950 our goal was achieved. The lessons that have been made since then are easy to learn and delightful to teach.

On March 27, 1949, the literacy workers of Madras held a big meeting in the Roman Catholic St. Mary's Hall with the archbishop in the chair and the minister of education making the principal address. The Roman Catholics in Madras, in Bihar Province, and in other parts of India, realized the intense desire of the government to help satisfy the hunger of the masses for literacy, and in these areas they plunged into the literacy campaign with as much zeal as the Protestants had shown. The Catholic archbishop on that day in Madras gave an impassioned speech in which he said that 350 million illiterate Indians were in the prison of ignorance, were blind, hungry, sick and in despair, and that the leaders of India must pull the bandages from their eyes.

We were back in Delhi in north India. Now we had an excellent Hindi primer and follow-up lessons we were proud to offer the government. The primer taught Hindi phonetics and 125 common words. A second reader was planned to cover eighty lessons on practical subjects about health, agriculture and home life. These two books together give the students 800 basic words. Then we planned a weekly newspaper containing valuable information and introducing ten new words on each page or 2,000 words in one year's reading. After this the student would have a recognition vocabulary of 3,000 words but he would not yet be able to read the difficult classical vocabulary found in Hindi books, magazines and newspapers. More simple reading matter had to be prepared. A conference was held at Delhi where fifty Indian men and women discussed the subject of writing for this ever-rising tide of new literates. Among other things, they wrote a letter to the editor of the *Reader's Digest* requesting him to send one of his creative writers to train Indians in the art of writing clearly and simply. They suggested that he might then begin a Hindi Digest like the editions he had started in many other languages. Two colleges of India, Hislop College at Nagpur and Osmanya College in Hyderabad, invited American journalists to come to India and start schools of journalism to train Indians to write with the powerful, clear style employed in the United States.

Pakistan

April 5, 1949, found us in Pakistan. The scars were still apparent from the terrible riots that took place during the partition of India and Pakistan. During those riots many millions of Hindus fled from Pakistan to India and many millions of Moslems fled from India to Pakistan. We found the boundary line closed except to foreigners. The railroad took us to the edge of India and we drove across no man's land, stopping nine times for police inspection and motoring ten miles in three hours. In Pakistan we found the interest in literacy as keen as it had been in India. Over 90 per cent of the people were illiterate. We were taken to Gakar Teachers Training School, fifty miles from Lahore. Here the teachers were going out to the wells, which are used for irrigation all over that area, and teaching the workers during their rest hours. As we traveled from village to village they put garlands of roses around our necks to show their gratitude. One man, seventy years old and with a red henna beard, had learned to read. With an affection impossible to describe he said to us, "You are saving Pakistan from despair. We were going down but now, thanks to your help, we are coming up again."

Forman Christian College in Lahore is the most important Christian school in Pakistan. Here we made Punjabi lessons employing Roman letters. A conference of about a hundred people, all of them Christians, was unanimous in wanting to change over from Arabic to the Roman alphabet because Arabic is so difficult. They agreed that the Roman alphabet could be taught in one-fourth the time and with far greater ease. But these are Christians; the Moslems, who regard their alphabet as sacred, are as averse to changing to Roman letters as we are to reforming our English spelling. So we made two sets of lessons, one in Arabic letters and the other in Roman letters. The first was for Moslems and the second for Christians. Many Christians in Pakistan now have the satisfaction of reading the Bible and their hymn books in Punjabi with Roman letters.

We flew from India to Australia and made lessons in four Australian aboriginal languages at Darwin in northern Australia. We had expected to find the most primitive people in the world near Darwin, but we were disappointed. Instead we found a city of white people and a few well-educated aborigines. Two missionaries came 1,500 miles from the heart of Australia by air, and another came 1,000 miles, to request our help in making lessons for the aborigines who roam through the deserts of the interior of Australia. A thousand miles is not as far in Australia as it is in most countries. They have airplane ambulances at Darwin and radio connections from the interior, so that if any Australian is sick he can be flown to the hospital in Darwin. Phil Gray worked like a slave, as he always does, on the 250 pictures that had to be made in those Australian primitive languages. Every time he made a picture his technique improved so it was not labor lost even when his pictures were not used, as sometimes happened.

CHAPTER 14

1949: IN NEW GUINEA

WE FLEW FROM Darwin to Brisbane and on to Sidney, where we were entertained by the mayor of the town and the archbishop. Then the Australian government flew us to New Guinea. Port Moresby is the capital of Papua, the southern province of New Guinea. To our delight, there were no mosquitoes in Port Moresby. The army had killed them all with DDT during the Second World War. We were entertained in the home of His Excellency Colonel Murray, the governor of New Guinea. We made lessons in the mission buildings of the old London Missionary Society, but we had real difficulty in finding any illiterates in Port Moresby. We found 400 natives in attendance at the Sunday morning service, and a choir of fifty men and women sang "God so loved the world that He gave His only begotten Son."

They sang it better than I had ever heard it sung anywhere else. I told them they should send that choir to sing all over America, only we would probably demand that the women wear more clothing because they were wearing nothing but grass skirts. We forgot all about that when they began to sing, for their faces were saintly. It was a very moving thing to realize that their grandfathers had been cannibals, and that we were witnessing the lifting of a race out of the dark Stone Age up to the beauty of Christ.

The next day, as I was teaching a group of young men to teach their own people to read, these young men told me that their tribe had eaten James Chalmers, the famous missionary of New Guinea, in the year 1901, and that the last man who participated in that feast had died the year before we arrived.

Governor Murray flew with us over the Owen Stanley Mountains to the town of Lae on the northern coast of New Guinea. Every time I inquire of any American audience how many have ever been to New Guinea, I always see the hands of two or more ex-soldiers, for there were thousands of them in New Guinea during the Second World War. Twenty-five missionaries from various parts of New Guinea and from the island of New Britain met us at the Lutheran mission in Lae. They had come to make lessons in thirteen languages. That meant that Phil Gray must make 1,500 pictures. Everyone who was willing to try to draw pictures was brought in to help him. By working night and day they were able to finish the lessons in every language. Bob kept a giant type machine hot, putting these lessons on stencils.

These new lessons worked so well that one Anglican sister exclaimed, "It is a miracle." To me it was a miracle that we were able to do so much work in such a short time.

On Sunday morning the big Lutheran church in Lae was crowded to the windows and doors with a thousand people. The pastor invited native Christians to come forward and speak, and they preached short sermons in five different languages, each in his own tongue. It sounded like Pentecost. One immense man from the plateau of New Guinea came forward wearing a ring in his nose and nothing below his neck except a leather belt and a brilliant red G-string around his powerful loins. He had a crown on his head that looked like the crown of King David. He was not a Christian, but he had come to make an appeal. This is what he said: "You have many white missionaries on the coast, and you have many bright teachers. I have been a bad man and my people have been bad because no one came to tell us what was good. We have eaten many of our enemies. We need the words of truth. Can words take legs and walk up these mountains alone?"

Somebody in the audience shouted, "No."

Then the mighty chief continued, "Come up to our mountains with your big bird planes and teach us what is good. Teach us how to worship God. You can fly over these mountains. You can come to my people."

This was translated into pidgin English, which is the language all the people can understand. It seemed to me that the very building trembled with the power of that man's appeal.

The singing in that church is something I shall never forget. The women began, then the men began to join in, more and more and more, until the bass sounded like thunder. Never have I heard singing so powerful or so soul moving. They sang in pidgin English and they made it sound beautiful.

Governor Murray was there at this service. He said he hated pidgin English because it violated every rule of grammar, and yet he was compelled to learn it because it was the only language the people could use in speaking from one tribe to another. So after we had made lessons in pidgin English, he sat down beside two illiterate policemen and patiently taught them to read. I think you would like to hear some pidgin English or at least see it in print, so here it is:

"I gudpela samting turu sapos yumi ken sijul kuik long rid na rait," which means, "It is a very good thing to suppose that you and I can quickly learn to read and write."

We had difficulty in suppressing our laughter in church when the minister in speaking of God called Him "Number one fellow belong top side," and when he called the Son of God "Pickaninny belong number one fellow belong top side." But this was not funny to the people who listened to the sermon, for it was the only language they all understood.

Accompanying the big man from the plateau was another man from the same tribe, the only man of the tribe who could read and write. He could not read and write English, only pidgin English. During the Second World War some Australian airmen had landed on this plateau and had brought one of the tribe to the coast where he learned to read and speak pidgin English. This was the man who now helped us make lessons in his language, which was called Medlpa. It had never before been reduced to writing. We found that it was easy to write and in a few days we had a primer written and 700 copies mimeographed.

Governor Murray sent us in a large plane over the mighty mountains to Ogelbeng, where lived the Medlpa tribe, 40,000 in number. We took the big chief with us. When we landed there were at least 15,000 people swarming around the airplane. Their faces were painted every color of the rainbow and black and white besides. Their handsome bare bodies glistened with fresh pig grease, which they use instead of taking a bath. They smelled terrible. A bundle of strings, six inches wide, fell from their waist, and that was all the clothing they wore except sea shells. Their ears and necks and noses carried all the shells they could afford, for sea shells are their money and they string them on their person wherever it is convenient. We were startled at the stampede that rushed in upon us when we put up our first literacy chart. Everyone wanted to learn that day. We put the chart on the outside wall of the missionary's home and made the people sit on the ground. The name of the missionary was Mr. Daring; I thought no name was ever more appropriate. We told them each word on the chart and they thundered back the answers. Then we selected one man after another to recite the whole chart. When he had finished the first lesson he was handed over to one of our party of forty persons so that he could complete the book. Half of us who had come were white and half of us were Christian natives from the coast. We scattered all over that huge level field and followed our usual plan of "each one teach one" while the rest looked over our shoulders. We hoped they would not get too hungry.

At the end of the week each of us had taught one person and it was time for that new literate to receive a diploma, for there was nothing else in the Medlpa language for him to read. When anyone has read all the literature in his own language it is time for him to graduate, so on Sunday morning we had a graduation service in the big crudely built Lutheran church. There were thousands of people sitting on the floor and crowded as tightly as sardines in a can. We distributed diplomas to thirty-six "graduates" and then appointed them as teachers to teach the rest of the tribe. After that graduation 20,000 people in the open field joined in celebrating the greatest event in their history. They danced and jumped and shouted all day. Six hundred big chiefs, with faces painted to look like the devil, wore birds of paradise feathers on their heads. New Guinea is the only place where the bird of paradise is found. Its plumes are more beautiful than any others in the world. The big chiefs, wearing these gorgeous plumes, marched round and round with their battle axes, shields and spears, bows and arrows. Twentieth Century Fox has made a film of this event and nothing in the world could be more colorful. After a while the big chiefs sat down for a long pow-wow. Then the king of them all came over and said to us:

"This is the new day for our tribe. We shall never be the same again. We are coming up. You have done more for us than anybody else who ever lived. We like your religion. It does so much for us. The chiefs have just voted to become Christian so go and baptize all those people right now—all except us chiefs. We are in trouble. They tell us that you Christians allow a man to have only one wife, but all of us have a great many wives and we can't think of any Christian way to get rid of them suddenly. But we're going to marry them off to other men and then we will be baptized too. We like your religion because it does so much for us."

The next morning as we were about to leave, a chief from a distant tribe came to speak to us. He pleaded with each one of us to come to his tribe instead of going home: "We people in our tribe do not know what good is and so we all have bad customs. Come and teach us."

Mr. Daring told us that this chief meant his tribe was still cannibalistic. We told the chief that all of us had to go home, and he said sadly, "Then go to the white man's country and tell the other missionaries to come and teach us what good is."

As we flew south across New Guinea we saw a tremendous clearing in the midst of the jungle, with a good many houses. "That," said the plane's pilot, "is the Kukukuku country. No one has ever gone into that area and returned uncooked." Somebody said, "Then Kukukuku is a perfect name for them."

When we returned to Sidney and told a large crowd, including the mayor of Sidney, that the big chief had said, "Go to the white man's country and tell the missionaries to come and teach us what good is," I saw tears in many eyes.

We wanted to go to Korea, but military restrictions meant very long delays so I sent a personal telegram to General MacArthur from Australia, and I have no doubt that is the reason our permit came the very day we were about to leave.

CHAPTER 15

1949: KOREA

JUNE 1949 FOUND US in Korea with a wonderful reception and wonderful cooperation from missionaries and the government. Mrs. Mabel Genso of the Presbyterian mission dropped everything else and devoted her entire time to helping us. She had read *The Silent Billion Speak* and had become convinced that literacy in Korea was her God-given task. She was nearing seventy years of age, but she drove her little jeep around the city of Seoul like a teen-ager.

We did not wait a day but started preparing lessons with the aid of Professor Kim of Chosen Christian College and Mr. Chung of the National Christian Council. It seemed to us that about half the people in Korea were named Kim and half were named Chung.

The Korean alphabet was invented a thousand years ago by a Korean genius and is one of the most beautiful alphabets in the world. We were able to make excellent lessons with the aid of these two brilliant Koreans and a roomful of teachers who came every day to help us and to be trained in our method. In one week the primer was completed and the United States Information Service immediately mimeographed 1,100 copies. The American embassy had an unusual number of deeply Christian men. Mr. Kinney, aide to the American ambassador, was Mrs. Genso's son-in-law. Mr. Stewart, head of the USIS was the son of a missionary and so was Mr. Caldwell who had charge of printing the lessons. So government and missions were working hand in hand.

We held a demonstration before 150 delegates who had come from every part of Korea. They were really jubilant when the illiterates learned with the greatest ease. Each of these delegates was asked to write an article for a "wall newspaper," and this newspaper was pasted up on the wall where everybody could read it. This is a way to get reading matter before people when they have no facilities or money for printing individual newspapers. We also started a second reader, full of information useful to the Korean people. Severance Medical College and the Nurses Training School sent us thirty articles on health for this new reader. The girls of the Methodist Ewa College wrote 150 articles they thought would be useful for our book. Our delegates were taught how to rewrite these articles with a basic vocabulary we had prepared in Korean. The enthusiasm of this conference was a joy to behold. Wherever we spoke and showed our charts in Korea the churches were crowded with from 500 to 1,200 people—as many as the churches would hold. The people kept saying over and over: "This is our hope. We must make all Korea Christian. We must convert the Communists. This is the Christian answer to the Communists." The Christians felt that they had been asleep while the Communists had been working hard, and they believed that literacy was the program that could carry on most effectively.

Out on the streets of Seoul there was also much excitement. On three successive days, as we were going to our classroom, the streets were blocked with marching people, all trembling with fear of the Communists. They marched to the American embassy to beg the United States not to pull her soldiers out of Korea without furnishing the people with enough arms to protect themselves. For one whole week while we were in Seoul 500 people stayed on top of the mountain above Seoul, praying day and night for a peaceful settlement between North and South Korea. On one day the students filled the streets marching with banners. On another day the labor unions marched, and on another day the Christians marched. We feared that this constant marching might work the Koreans into a frenzy to invade North Korea. I wrote home these words which turned out to be true: "I fear another tragic fraticidal war like that which has brought untold ruin to China."

That terrible war came less than a year after we left Korea. We had hoped that perhaps with our "each one teach one and win one to Christ" program we might channel this hot patriotism into constructive uses and save Korea from bloodshed. We trained the Christians to witness for Jesus while they were teaching, and printed a little book of seventeen pages to tell the Christians what to say about Jesus at the end of each lesson. In three different cities of Korea we trained theological students in this "each one teach one and win one for Jesus" campaign. We also worked on the translation of *The Story of Jesus* into Korean. Hundreds of copies of the English version of *The Story of Jesus* were already in use among those who wanted to read the Bible in English. We needed much more simple literature written in the Korean language.

One afternoon we called the writers of Korea into a conference, urging them to simplify their difficult style and to write for the common people. The customary style in Korea is classical and is aimed at highly intelligent readers. No one but the Communists had written simply enough for the masses to understand. When I urged these writers to use short sentences and simple words, one of them said: "If I tried to write the way you tell us to write my reputation would be ruined. People now read me for my style."

I am afraid all of those classical writers felt the same way. It is probably too late to reform them. We shall have to prepare an entirely new army of writers if we are to employ the channel that literacy provides to the minds of the average people.

We were especially perplexed because the classical writers in Korea insist upon using Chinese characters for half of their words instead of spelling them with the Korean alphabet. At a large meeting sponsored by the American ambassador, I told the minister of education and the other guests that they ought to be proud of the beautiful Korean alphabet and abandon the use of Chinese characters. The minister of education arose after my talk and in great excitement announced that he was convinced by what I had said and that he would do all in his power to prevent any further use of Chinese characters in government publications. This he said with a trembling voice and a shaking fist. The explosive temper of the Korean people at that time had been poured into his emotion over the alphabet. People were excited about everything because they were afraid of the war that might break out at any minute.

In the city of Taegu in the center of Korea 100 illiterate women came into a large Presbyterian church to be taught. Half of these women were over fifty years of age and two of them were more than eighty. The girls in the Presbyterian school were dismissed from classes and each one of them was set to work teaching one of these illiterate women on the floor of the church—they do not use chairs or benches in Korea. It was a stirring sight to see 100 little groups occupying every corner of the church. At the end of three days we had finished teaching the primer to these women and had a graduation ceremony at which we gave diplomas to ninety-eight. The emotion of these new literates went beyond all bounds. One of them stood up and said, "I was blind but you have given me eyes."

Another said: "All my life I have been despised because I could not read. Now I will go home and show them this diploma and read them this book. They will see that I am not so dumb after all."

Another woman said: "I am eighty years old and this is my first diploma." Then walking up to me she put her hands on my head, raised her eyes to the sky and said in Korean: "I give you my benediction in the name of the Father, the Son and the Holy Ghost, Amen."

Another woman said: "I walked many miles to this class and I slept every night in this church studying this book as long as there was light. Now I can read it all. Thank God that I came and that you came."

We visited President Syngman Rhee and found him delighted at the enthusiasm of the people. He said everyone in Korea was hungry for an education and that he would give them all the aid and encouragement in the power of his government.

As I left Korea I felt that here, if anywhere, the United States government was doing a fine job and I was enormously proud of American missionaries. I wrote to my friends in America: "If you know how to pray, pray now for Korea. Pray and then write to the President that you are praying; and write to your missionaries in Korea. Something has started here which might save this nation from catastrophe, so pray."

As I was going home at the end of this tour through Asia, with my heart burning and yearning for the American church to awaken, I wrote this letter, in August 1949:

My dear partners in God's great day:

Surely there were never in all history such stupendous spiritual wars as are going on right at this moment. I feel that God must be as excited about His world as those prophets were who wrote when the fate of Israel was at stake. Don't you feel that excitement with me?

If there were nothing we could do about the plight of the world, we might cringe with fear. But there is so much we can do, all of us, if we want to do it! It seems to me that one's power of doing is limited only by his willingness to be God's channel.

The way this world has broken wide open for literacy—far wider than we can find means for entering—just leaves one breathless, and but for the faith that God will supply the need, I should say frantic. They want our aid in starting literacy campaigns in Africa, India, in the Dutch East Indies, in French Indo-China, in Formosa, and we must make up our minds where to respond to the call first.

All of them want us to come because they are in the swirl of the stupendous world tornado, and they grasp now for every help they can get. I want to stay here in America to shake this nation awake, to make the call of Asia and Africa inescapable, but I must also go abroad to help meet that call. Everybody who knows the world probably shares with me the desire to be twins, so we can be here and abroad both at the same time.

Never was the church faced with such an opportunity, such critical need. Never was failure to see this and to respond as fatal as it would be today. For this is the situation: The whole world is in the throes of a titanic change. The sleeping multitudes are coming awake, like the seventeen-year locusts rising out of the ground. But they are not locusts, they are men and women. They don't know where they are going; they only know they are coming up—coming up out of poverty, coming up out of stagnation, coming up out of disease and oppression—coming up. They will take any hand that offers to lift them. He who offers to help is their friend. He who ignores or neglects them is their enemy.

Four-fifths of the human race are on the march somewhere, somewhere. . . . That is the meaning of strikes in America; that is the meaning of literacy campaigns thronged by tens of thousands; that is the meaning of communism. This vast multitude is not communist. It is just and only "come-up-ist." When Communists offer them a hand, they accept it.

These are the two great facts of our time: the world is fusing into one, and the masses are rising to our level. That is the reason for what some people call the "miracle of literacy." We saw the passion to learn in the

Moros in the Philippines twenty years ago, and we said, "Come on, we will help you." We have seen this yearning on every continent. The "miracle of literacy" is not a miracle, it is part of the birth pangs of a new world. We who have seen it, we tingle and are desperate at the same moment, because we could so easily lead these marching people to the feet of Jesus Christ if there were enough of us trained and going out to do it. Don't praise us, for we are like men with a gusher of oil, dipping it out with buckets, while most of it goes to waste forever. Blame us, urge us on, come and help us, pay the bills; but stop any praise, for we are thus far failing to meet that terrible multitude's appeal and so failing our Christ.

Praise torments us because we see what could be and is not. This is not the time for congratulations. This is the time to turn defeat into victory for the world and for the church of Christ. This is the time to help. There are thirty million literate Christians in churches scattered among the world's billion, two hundred million non-Christian illiterates who are determined to become literate. These thirty millions could be mobilized into a stupendous army, each one to teach one and win one. No government in the world has prevented them from doing this, and I do not think any government will try to prevent it.

All we need is to have the trained men and women who can go and help these native Christians learn the art of winning for Christ while they teach. As they teach and win others, there could be millions of new Christians a year. There could be a rising tide of the followers of Christ such as the world never dreamed possible. There could be, but there is not for one reason: we are not mobilizing our Christian army, not training them, not equipping them. Measure our petty results by that responsibility; then you see why we blush for shame for ourselves and for the church.

When this great hungry multitude marches into literacy we could furnish them with the kind of literature that would make them love Christ, make them love all things good, make them hate evil. For they tend to become like the things they read. If we were bigger, abler men, we would have the church ablaze with this stupendous call of hungry minds for something simple and good to read.

Our failure to meet this chance to evangelize and provide reading matter is not, I am convinced, the fault of the ordinary American people. They are burning to help when they see the opportunity. I think the fault lies with me and others who have seen the wide open door. My conscience torments me until Americans are shown not only what is needed, but also what they can do about it.

As we have tramped around through South America and Africa and Asia, we have seen how those awakening multitudes are groping for other things besides literacy and religion. They want a thousand things that make the difference between stupid defeat and radiant progress.

In the United States there are a thousand types of skills that the rest of the world must have and is determined to have. Both the United Nations and the United States see this. They are making a survey of the world to determine what the nations want and need.

The church in America ought to find and prepare Christian men and women to volunteer to meet these needs. Some form of a Christian employment agency should scour our technical schools and industries and professions for men and women with a Christian passion to serve. This agency ought to have contact with missions, governments, businesses and philanthropies, and be prepared to fill technical positions around the world with Christian know-how.

Technicians will not bless the world unless they are strong in Christian love and ideals. The world needs Christ more than it needs skills. It will not accept Christ unless we offer it help with these other things. But if we give skill without character, we make the world only more powerful to do itself harm. The really greatest thing we can export to the world is our best Christ-filled men and women, with the technical skills to help materially and spiritually.

We are foolish, incredibly foolish, not to help the world love Jesus Christ, when we know the way. We have the money, we have the knowledge, we have the magnificent people—more of each than perhaps the rest of the world put together. Yet we are losing the world! The atom bomb, communism and the rise of multitudes are all part of God's challenge. Awake, Christians, awake and join this mighty march.

God is calling us. It is we who must lead the world. Not rule it—serve it! And so lead it to Christ.

As I write ten years later, it seems to me that one of the greatest tragedies of all time is that the church has failed to do its best to meet the need of half the people of the world who are crying for education and deliverance from poverty and disease. Millions upon millions of these people have turned to communism during these past five years because we failed to recognize our day of opportunity. Is it too late? No, not too late, but alas, there is too little indication that the Protestants are awake to their challenge, even now!

CHAPTER 16

1950: BACK IN AFRICA

Liberia, Angola, Mozambique

Liberia

ON JANUARY 16, 1950, Dr. Maurice Hohlfeld and his wife, Phil Gray and his wife, my son Bob and I flew to Liberia. The lessons we had made in ten languages two years before had all been printed in large quantities at government expense. The president issued the following proclamation, which was posted all over Monrovia:

> I, William V. Tubman, President of the Republic of Liberia, do hereby proclaim an all-out Literacy Campaign drive, under the auspices of the Department of Public Instruction and the Committee of Reference and Counsel of the Liberian Missions. Beginning February 14, 1950, I call upon all civic, educational, and religious institutions, all officials of the government, all Paramount and clan chiefs, all citizens of the Republic, to cooperate in this drive, thereby contributing to the universal effort of reducing the percentage of illiteracy in this country.

The president appointed Miss Norma Bloomquist, a Lutheran missionary well trained in literacy, to coordinate all mission and government literacy work. The president called her "General Bloomquist" and treated her just like a member of the cabinet. Protestants, Catholics and government officials all worked together in complete harmony. Missions that had never before cooperated came together and made common plans. One missionary from the Swedish Pentecostal mission walked a distance of 270 miles in five days to attend our conference in Monrovia. Another woman, Jennie Davis, a Liberian by birth, walked eleven days through the jungle to get there. One hundred and forty-three missionaries and educated Liberians registered for the conference. Mr. Sam Smith, the personnel man of the huge Firestone Rubber Company of Liberia, was chairman of the meeting. He said that the Firestone Company planned to teach every employee and all members of the family of every employee—nearly 100,000 people! How to provide an adequate supply of literature was the chief concern of the conference. As in every other country, we faced the dilemma of making thousands, or millions, literate, and then of leaving them without good literature to read. In these primitive languages of Africa there was practically nothing good or bad because those languages have only recently been reduced to writing. Even more unfortunate are the people who speak languages in which all the easy reading matter is either doubtful or bad. The Bible has been translated into more languages than any other book, but alas, these translations are seldom easy enough for the new literates to read. It was agreed that *The Story of Jesus* should be put in every Liberian language.

In Liberia perhaps more than in any other place in the world the missionaries have a clear unobstructed path to evangelism and to education. If the churches seize their opportunity, they may have not only large numbers of church members but a very large percentage of literates in their churches. They may escape the unfortunate situation of many mission lands where two-thirds or more of the Christians are unable to read and write.

Before we departed from Liberia, President Tubman presided at a spectacular public gathering. He said that he was profoundly impressed by the literacy movement and that he was convinced that it was the embryonic start of an intellectual awakening that would usher in a new day for Liberia.

Angola

On January 22, 1950, we arrived in Luanda, the capital of Angola and its principal seaport. There we found 1,200 people packed in a church on Sunday afternoon. Dr. John Tucker, a wonderful diplomat as well as a wonderful missionary, taught the congregation to repeat many times in Portuguese, "Cada um ensina um e ganha um para Cristo," which means "Each one teach one and win one to Christ." That became the watchword for the Angola literacy campaign. Our first full-fledged campaign took place at Quessua, a Methodist station 250 miles inland from Luanda. Hundreds of people were waiting in Quessua to be taught. We prepared lessons in the Kimbundu language with the intelligent aid of Miss Cecilia Cross, and Phil Gray illustrated them with lovely pictures. Then we began to train our teachers. We also made lessons in Portuguese to please the Portuguese officials. Many of the people could speak a little Portuguese but none of them had learned to read it. When we tried the Kimbundu lessons with illiterates the results were so good that everyone was electrified. There is no more delightful experience in the world than to see the eagerness and joy of illiterates when they find that they can learn to read easily and swiftly.

We paired off about 140 teachers with that many illiterates. One hundred of them were studying Kimbundu and forty studying Portuguese. Miss Cross, who was managing the campaign, exclaimed with tears in her eyes, "Dear me, how they are learning and how they love it!"

At the end of a week our book had been taught and our students were ready for their diplomas. The governor of the province, who was himself a Roman Catholic, came and distributed the diplomas at the graduation ceremony. He was very much impressed and said that he would help the literacy campaign because it was the enemy of ignorance and superstition. It was a joy to see how he gave each student and teacher a kindly word urging him to teach someone else. The most touching experience of all, however, was to see boys of ten and girls of the same age bringing their old fathers and mothers up to receive diplomas, while the children received certificates of Christian service because they had taught their parents to read. Recalling that never-to-be-forgotten sight still brings tears to my eyes.

We were driven 350 miles southward across the Angola plateau to a mission station called Dondi. On the way we passed through the tsetse fly area. This fly carries the parasite that causes sleeping sickness. The tsetse fly comes at you straight as an arrow, takes his bite and departs before you have a chance to hit him. Fortunately, not more than one fly in a hundred is supposed to carry the parasite that causes this disease. We kept our windows closed, but in spite of this precaution a fly entered the window beside the chauffeur, flew straight at Mrs. Gray and stung her on the arm. We opened the windows to chase him out but he flew straight at my nose and I knocked my glasses out of the window trying to hit him. We had to stop the car while I went back through the tsetse flies and found my glasses. Fortunately there were not many flies and the glasses had not been broken. It is sleeping sickness that causes the central countries of Africa, south of the Sahara desert, to be sparsely settled. There are no domestic cattle or horses in this region because sleeping sickness gets them. It also kills tremendous numbers of wild animals and it is the cause of the death of millions of Africans. Happily, in the triumphant march of medicine against disease, a method of immunization has been found that prevents sleeping sickness from infecting animals or men even if they are stung by the tsetse fly. A method of exterminating the tsetse fly has also been found. This is to cut down the low bushes in which he breeds. Thanks to this medical triumph, central Africa will again be inhabited by millions of people and by domestic animals.

Our literacy adventure at the Dondi mission was one of the most thrilling experiences that we have had. Two large schools are conducted by the mission boards acting together, one for men and the other for women. Dr. Ralph Collins of the United Church of Canada wrote a song he sang for us when we arrived and it went straight to our hearts:

The Song of the Emancipated

Thanks to Thee, our God and Heavenly Father,
For the grace that came to us, revealing
That which makes the blind to see
And go their way rejoicing.

Thanks to Thee, our God and Heavenly Father,
For the light that shone upon our darkness;
Light of hope that brightly gleams
Upon the path before us.

Thanks to Thee, our God and Heavenly Father,
For the love that comes to heal and save us;
Love of Christ, who came to see
And save Thy wandering children.

Thanks to Thee, our God and Heavenly Father,
For kind hearts that know the love of Jesus
And for friendly hands outstretched
To help us in our weakness.

Give us now, our God and Heavenly Father,
Faith to tread this new and living highway;
That we may not miss the wealth of life
Thy love has willed us.

Make us now, our God and Heavenly Father,
Witnesses and stewards of Thy bounty;
Holding out the torch of life
To those still bound in darkness.

The news had gone around that part of Africa by grapevine telegraph that people were going to be taught to read, and for several days prior to our arrival illiterates began to drift into the mission—some of them after many days of travel. There were so many illiterates that the missionaries met in dismay and decided to announce that no one who had come less than twenty miles would be allowed to learn to read in this first campaign. Even then we had 1,200 people to house and feed every day. Since this crowd was for the most part neither disciplined nor civilized, it reminded one of a big circus. The large church in which we held our morning devotions could accommodate only 800 people, so the remainder of the 1,200 attending crowded to see through the windows and doors. Every seat contained two persons, although it was meant for one. The singing was magnificent. In three days we had finished making lessons in the Umbundu language. These we put on stencils and ran through the mimeograph machines as fast as they were made, a thousand copies of them. But the crowd was so much bigger than we had anticipated that we had to make another thousand copies immediately. Phil Gray and his wife made large charts for every page in the primer and we proceeded to train 400 teachers in the method of using them. As fast as teachers felt that they knew how to teach, we set them to work teaching illiterates—each teacher with two students. These teachers had been obtained by dismissing both the boys' and girls' schools and utilizing all the students. It was a marvelous sight. Under every tree as far as the eye could reach was a teacher with two pupils, one on each side. Every day we began with an assembly attended by over a thousand persons and then we divided up for an hour or two of study. At 2:30 in the afternoon we held another assembly, and then another hour of study, followed by the final worship assembly in the late afternoon. Toward the end of the week the teachers began to present their students for examination. We had five examining boards going all the time. Students who failed the first day were allowed to come back the next. When the student had passed his examination, his name was given to a missionary lady so that she could fill out the diplomas. Up to the very last moment before the graduation ceremony, desperate students kept coming for their examinations until 394 of them had passed. They and their teachers then marched in order to the table to receive their diplomas while a crowd of four or five thousand people beheld the astonishing spectacle. The emotion and the exclamations of those new literate graduates beggars all description.

It is difficult to describe the emotional impact of this great number of excited people, especially when they were trying to pass their examinations. One girl, who passed her examination after trying three times, lost control of herself, threw her head on the shoulder of her teacher, much to his embarrassment, and kept repeating over and over hysterically, "You helped me. Thank you, thank you, thank you."

All during this conference we discussed how to witness for Jesus at the end of each lesson. The Umbundu Christians were determined to use this literacy program to gather in a harvest of souls among the one million Umbundu non-Christians who surround them.

No one who has not been a missionary can appreciate the eagerness with which we missionaries receive letters from America, especially from our own home churches. While we were in Dondi a delightful letter came from our home church in Upper Montclair, New Jersey, offering to give the Dondi mission $500 for printing *The Story of Jesus* in Umbundu. The children in the primary classes of the Sunday school had built a railway out of cellophane, which they called the "Nickels for Knowledge Railway to Africa." They made this railway by folding over a long sheet of cellophane so that it would hold nickels. Each Sunday the children pushed their nickels into one end of this cellophane tube, to see how much of the track to Africa they could build that Sunday. They drew black lines across this cellophane to make them look like railroad ties. In two years they had brought 10,000 nickels, about 100 each Sunday. When we told the people of Dondi about this "Nickels for Knowledge Railway" and the gift the children had sent them for *The Story of Jesus,* they broke out in a big cheer and sang the doxology.

As we left these dear people in Dondi, we were torn between a feeling of gratitude and regret. Gratitude for what had been accomplished and regret that we could not stay there the rest of our lives.

Mozambique

Dr. John Tucker went with us around the southern end of Africa on a magnificent Portuguese ship, so that he could turn on his magic diplomatic charm in Mozambique Colony as he had done with such great success in Angola. The Protestant missions were having a very difficult time holding their own in Mozambique because of the opposition of the Roman Catholic archbishop. The Portuguese officials were friendly to the Protestant missions but they were afraid of the reports the archbishop might send back to Portugal, and under his pressure were depriving the missionaries of one opportunity after another.

The Portuguese settlers were doubtless unwilling for missionaries to see how they were oppressing the Negroes. In this far-off colony they were pushing the native Africans farther and farther back into the undesirable areas and taking the good land for themselves. We found here the same mistreatment of the Negroes that had made us shudder in South Africa. In the northern half of Mozambique, where more than a million Negroes live, not a single Protestant foreign missionary was allowed to work. That area is probably as illiterate as any place in the world.

In the southern part of Mozambique, the Protestant churches were jammed with people who looked upon Protestantism as their only hope. In four services in Lourenço Marques, we trained 2,000 people to teach by the "each one teach one and win one" method. Dr. Tucker taught them to repeat our motto, "Cada um ensina um, e ganha um para Cristo."

The Protestant mission in Mozambique had no printing press of its own, partly because it feared government interference. The lessons we prepared in six languages had to be printed in Johannesburg and mailed first class into Mozambique because the government did not open first class mail.

About a hundred miles north of Lourenço Marques the Methodists have a school at a place called Gikuki. Here we made lessons in two languages, Gitonga and Xitswa—pronounce that if you know how to click your tongue! At the Sunday morning church service 400 people said that they could read and promised that they would teach as many others as they could. We drove twenty-five miles to the large Methodist agricultural school at Kambini where 500 students are self-supporting. They raise their own food on a thousand acres of good land. This mission is remote and so free from the persecution the Protestant missions in the large centers are experiencing.

Dr. Tucker and Bob and I went up to Beira, a seaport in the central part of Mozambique. No Protestant missionaries are allowed in Beira but one Swiss went there as a businessman and held meetings in an old motion-picture house he had purchased. We found this house crowded every night with the laboring men who had been brought in from remote villages and who were very lonesome far from their families. They were boundlessly grateful to this foreign businessman who was giving them friendship and teaching them the gospel. One of the men rose at the first meeting we held in that motion-picture house and said: "We have had so much trouble that we had begun to think that God does not care. Thank you for the hope you have given us and for the chance we now have to learn to read."

We made lessons in the Shanga language for these lonely homeless men, and we purchased a mimeograph from a store in Beira and gave it to this Swiss businessman, so that he could print as many lessons as he needed.

Another man entered northern Mozambique as a businessman. He has a little printing press and is producing Christian literature for the people of this area. This man traveled by bus and railroad for eight days to meet us in Beira. We bought a mimeograph and gave it to him so that he could print the lessons for the people in his remote and terribly precarious mission station. Bob made the pictures for his lessons. We had not taken our artist Phil Gray and his wife to Mozambique because the missionaries feared that such a large crowd of strangers would attract the attention of the archbishop. So Bob had to do all the work—make the pictures, put them on the stencils and run the machine—but he never uttered a complaint, for he felt, like the rest of us, that we were meeting a tragic need. The Swiss missionary kept saying over and over, "This is exactly the right thing at the right time."

When the time came for us to say farewell to that pathetic group of Negro laborers who were holding secret church services in the motion-picture house, they tried to show the depth of their gratitude. The oldest man among them came up to the speaker's table after all the others had spoken and said with a trembling voice I shall never forget: "We cannot find words to tell you what you have done for us. We are like a dog which cannot speak but can only wag his tail. But every day we will thank God for you. May God keep you well and help you help the world as you have helped us."

The prayers that followed these heart-rending speeches were full of tragic fervor. How well these men illustrated the fact that literacy is the promise of a new day for this great unhappy continent of Africa, if it is accompanied by helpful Christian literature. They illustrated also the unspeakable consolation of the gospel for the multitudes of people who have no other hope in the world. The Communists accuse us of offering religion as an opiate for the masses but in Beira as we looked into the faces of those laborers and saw in their eyes a light "not seen on land or sea," we realized how our gospel brings hope to those who have no other comfort in this world or the next. I felt that those suffering men could understand the meaning of the suffering of Christ and of St. Paul as none of us in rich, comfortable America can.

One of the new hopes of Mozambique will probably come as a surprise to you. It is the fact that oil is being discovered. With the coming of the American oil prospectors, the light of publicity is shining upon the oppression those Africans have endured for many centuries. One American oil prospector saw a hundred Negroes tied together in single file and being marched to the coast to be shipped abroad for indentured labor. Outraged, he cut the ropes that bound them and ordered the police to go home. The government could not say a word because it knew that the United Nations was hot on the trail of African slavery.

CHAPTER 17

1950: THE LAND OF LIVINGSTONE

Nyasaland, Tanganyika, Uganda, Ruanda-Urundi, French Cameroons

Nyasaland

FROM MOZAMBIQUE WE traveled by train to Nyasaland, that remote little country on a high plateau where David Livingstone spent more time than in any other part of Africa. The mountain scenery beggars description. We crossed the enormous Zambezi river a thousand miles below the Victoria Falls over a bridge that was said to be about as long as the Golden Gate bridge in San Francisco. The train ran very slowly and the spans on the bridge seemed to be interminable. They told us that this railroad is the most expensive road of its length in the world because of the recent floods. For some mysterious reason, Lake Nyasa is rising a few inches every year and is converting the valley through which the railroad runs into a swamp. That is why each year they need to raise the roadbed and build more bridges. This railroad has also one of the steepest grades in the world. It climbed a mile in height while traveling thirteen miles with two engines puffing with all their might. When we left Beira in Mozambique we were hot and steamy, but by the time we reached Blantyre, the capital of Nyasaland, we needed a winter suit and an overcoat. No wonder Livingstone liked that climate.

At the Scottish mission, which David Livingstone had established a century before, we made our lessons and held our conferences. Those Scottish missionaries are magnificent people, every one of them.

The Dutch Reformed mission and the mission of the English Disciples were also bitten by the literacy bug; all of them joined together with zeal and energy to prepare lessons in the Nyanja language. They were so efficient that we had the entire book outlined at the end of the first day. The Adventist mission provided an artist. Before the end of a week, lessons had been run off on the mimeograph and we were hard at work translating *The Story of Jesus*.

With great enthusiasm the members of the churches of Blantyre learned to teach these lessons. I think the Seventh Day Adventists were the most excited of all. Bob and I stayed with the director of the Seventh Day Adventist mission and he told us how they managed to sell more books in Africa than all the other Protestant denominations put together. They train their own writers and have their own printing presses. They print their books with colored pictures and in very simple language the people understand, and sell them at a low price. They give their booksellers (*colporteurs*) 50 per cent profit. One enterprising *colporteur,* our host told us, gets a weekly commission as high as $250 which is more than the missionary himself was being paid by his board.

We had training classes for all the missionaries and Christians to show them how to teach illiterates. We brought two illiterate men and one badly scared illiterate woman before these teachers as a demonstration. The two men did well from the beginning, but the frightened woman refused to open her mouth for the first half hour. I began to think she was hopeless, but suddenly, to our amazement, she began to read the lesson and she knew all of it as well as the men did.

A lovely African girl, who was being trained as a teacher, taught four women between the ages of forty and seventy. They learned so easily that they all became hysterical and at the end of the lesson danced down the aisle, shaking hands with everybody and laughing and singing as they went out the door. One toothless old grandmother, who had learned to read as well as the others, was the "overbubblingest" of them all.

The government invited us to meet the paramount chiefs of Nyasaland, nearly all of them Moslems. They spoke the Yao language. I told these chiefs that I had as many Moslem friends in the world as I had Christian friends, and asked them whether they would like to help make lessons in Yao like those we had already made in the Nyanja language. There was a spontaneous outburst of enthusiasm, so without another word we plunged into making lessons on a blackboard while the chiefs gave everything they had to helping us. By five o'clock that evening we had selected the words we needed to illustrate our lessons in the Yao language. The biggest chief of them all arose and led that roomful of paramount chiefs in three lusty cheers. The three missionaries who accompanied me to this remarkable conference sat in open-mouthed amazement, for they had never had any contact with those Moslems before. As we went out of the room these missionaries were shaking their heads and saying, "We have seen a miracle today."

Everywhere in the world Christian missionaries have found Moslems difficult or impossible to convert, but there is one argument which no Mohammedan can ever resist and that is the argument of loving service. In at least twelve Moslem countries literacy is proving to be the open door to the people's hearts.

Tanganyika

Ever since I began literacy work in 1930, I have had a mystical feeling that God is ahead of us preparing the way, because He has a deep concern for the under-half of the world the rest of us know little about. This was illustrated when we wanted to go from Nyasaland to Tanganyika. The distance is only 200 miles, but there is no direct transportation and the round-about route we would have taken would have consumed at least three or four weeks of our precious time. Besides this, all the airlines were booked solid for there are never enough planes in Africa to meet the demand. To go to Tanganyika we would have had to go back down to Johannesburg and then up to Elizabethville in the Congo and then across to Dar es Salaam, a thousand miles out of our way. We did not have the time to spare and it looked as though we would have to give up Tanganyika altogether, but God was at work and He helped us out in startling fashion. He proved that He is in dead earnest about literacy as He had proved it a thousand times in the last twenty-five years. Superstition? O.K., then I am guilty! The very day we wanted to leave Blantyre, the air office phoned us that a new route was making its maiden trip. As usual, it was booked up full. We prayed that somebody would cancel and two people did the afternoon before the flight, so we flew on a new Viking plane on the exact day we wanted to go, straight to Dar es Salaam, the first flight that had ever gone that way. The mayor of Salisbury, Southern Rhodesia, was on board, wearing a big gold chain to celebrate this first flight. Bob took the mayor's picture, which he said we might publish. In honor of this maiden flight each of us received a large, handsome diploma granting us the degree of "Low Knighthood" from his "Imperial Divinity." Now comes the most amazing thing of all. This was not only the first trip that plane took but it was the last. For some reason or other it was discontinued. I am not claiming that my prayers had anything to do with this, but I do claim that God had planned this trip before we ever knew we would need it, because He wants the underprivileged people of Tanganyika to come out of their miserable existence and to know Christ. The remainder of this Tanganyika experience is just as remarkable.

We had been invited to come to Dodoma by Bishop Wynne Jones of the Anglican Church Missionary Society. Archbishop Ralph Banks, an expert in the Cigogo language and a few other missionaries explored the alphabet to discover which vowel should begin our lessons. Usually we try the syllables *ba, da, fa,* etc., to the end of the alphabet because the letter *a* (pronounced as in "father") is more frequently used than any other sound—except in the English language. But *a* did not prove to be the right sound for the first lesson in the Cigogo language. Then we tried the syllables *bo, do, fo, go,* etc., and found that *o* was not the right syllable for the first lesson. We tried the vowel *i* and the vowel *e* in the same way but they did not make good first lessons. Then we tried the syllables *bu, du, fu, gu,* etc., and found that *u* was a perfect vowel for the first lesson. This was the first time that we had ever started with that vowel. The remainder of the lessons unravelled so easily that it seemed as though the Cigogo language had been made for our method. We had a brilliant committee and so were able to insert more fun into the lessons than we usually do. For example, one story ended like this:

> The man saw the lion. The man ran away.
> The woman saw the lion. The woman ran away.
> The boy saw the lion. The boy ran away.
> The lion saw the boy. The lion ran away.

We mimeographed 500 copies of these Cigogo lessons and tried them out on ten illiterates, who learned to read in three days. At the end of that time they knew every word in this first book. Meanwhile we prepared *The Story of Jesus* to follow the primer. Miss Beryl Long, an Australian missionary, had shown perfect mastery of the language and unusual creative ability in making the lessons, so she was put in charge of the literacy program of that mission. She has been sending wonderful reports to us ever since. She wrote that she went to one village where no missionary had ever gone before, put her chart on a tree outside the village, and began to teach a man who was going by. He was so delighted that he began to whoop and shout and the whole village came out to see what was going on. They begged her to stay but she told them she would return in two weeks. On her return she was met at the edge of the village by the big chief and the entire population. The chief said: "We have built a church and we have built a schoolhouse and we have built a home for you and we have all voted to be Christians."

"No," said Miss Long. "You cannot be Christians because you have polygamy, you get drunk and you steal."

The chief replied: "We know you do not allow those things and we are going to give up everything that Christians do not allow. We like your religion because it will make new people out of us."

The Cigogo language is one of the richest languages in the world. They can express shades of meaning that are beyond our English language. They put several words together into one word and so have such surprising combinations as these:

mumagamagama—one who loses other people's things.
mumali lwa—an old person killed to put him out of his misery.
muwavi—a good-looking woman who can't cook.

murmizi—one who constantly grunts to show his endorsement of what people say; a yes man!
muwandoloci—one who growls when waked up in the morning.
mutolatoli—a man who is constantly putting away his wives to take others; à la Hollywood! (they really need that word in Hollywood).
muhonduci—a woman who leaves her husband in a fit of temper, and runs home to mother!

The Wagogo people who speak the Cigogo language are among the most picturesque people in East Africa. The men plaster their hair down with red clay and put clay on their faces; they look like a walking plaster of Paris model. Most of them wear wooden plugs in their ears. They are open to the gospel and are now coming into the church as rapidly as they can be trained.

Uganda

Leaving Tanganyika, we went north on a little boat on Lake Victoria to the British colony of Uganda, which is the best-educated country in Africa and in some respects the most progressive. It is the pride of British colonial policy. The idealistic British officials with a Christian conscience placed the welfare of the Uganda people above exploitation. This was partly because Uganda was too hot as an ideal climate for British colonizers, so those who were seeking new homes for themselves remained in Kenya, while those who had a missionary spirit stayed in Uganda. The director of adult education was using the lessons we had made for Kenya. These had been used by Uganda, but neglected by Kenya. He took us from one end of Uganda to the other on their excellent roads and showed us the results of the truly remarkable literacy campaigns that had been carried on all over that colony. Every few miles a booth had been erected in our honor. At each booth hundreds of people had gathered to wait for us and show us how they could read. After appropriate speeches they read for me and then I had the honor of distributing hundreds of diplomas. They loaded Bob and me with presents until we were embarrassed. They brought us dozens of eggs, dozens of pineapples, a dozen roosters, and one big sheep. We dared not refuse them and soon our station wagon was bulging with these evidences of their affection. One old man, who looked like Father Time with his long white beard, had learned to read and was now an energetic and indefatigable teacher. In fact, there were three generations of new literates who were now teaching other illiterates. The name they gave me in Uganda was "The Great-Great-Grandfather of Literacy" because I had made those lessons in 1937. Bob said I ought to grow a long beard so I could stand beside their old man, Father Time.

At the eastern end of Uganda, where Lake Victoria pours into the Nile river, we saw the workmen building a dam to raise the height of famous Ripon Falls. This dam will be used to generate electricity for both Uganda and Kenya. We also saw the superhighway the British were building from Kampala, the capital of Uganda, to Nairobi, the capital of Kenya. Here we saw the new Africa emerging from the shell of the old before our very eyes. As we gazed at this tremendous river, the second largest in the world, we realized that one thing Africa needs is more water. It is the biggest continent next to Asia, but the northern half of it is a desert and much of the other half is too dry. Here is where the coming invention for extracting the salt from the sea is going to have the most revolutionary effect, for if Africa can have water it can be the garden spot of the world.

Ruanda-Urundi

We flew from Uganda to the city of Usumbura on the northern tip of Lake Tanganyika, not far from the spot where Stanley found David Livingstone a hundred years ago. Lake Tanganyika is 400 miles in length, the longest lake in the world. We were met at Usumbura by three missionaries who took us up magnificent mountains to the American Quaker mission on a plateau 7,000 feet above sea level. We passed the great African watershed, where part of the water flows into the Nile and the Mediterranean, while a few feet away the water flows down the great Zambezi river over Victoria Falls into the Indian Ocean. We were in Ruanda-Urundi, the most picturesque part of all Africa. At the Quaker mission we found Free Methodists, National Holiness, and Danish Baptist missionaries, all joining with the Quakers to build lessons in the Kirundi language. We had but one week to give to that beautiful place, but our lesson committee was so brilliant that we were able to finish our primer in that one week and try it on several old men and women. They learned so easily and swiftly that the women gabbled and giggled and one man became so excited that we could not stop him. We allowed him to read the entire primer through in one forenoon. One of our teaching principles is never to hold a hungry student back. If only we could have stayed another week, I think we could have graduated several hundred new literates as we had done a few months before at Dondi, Angola.

In Ruanda-Urundi there are three main types of people. One type consists of very tall people, who look like the Ethiopians and are said to be of Semitic origin. They look like aristocrats, all of them. At the opposite extreme are the tiny pygmies, and in between these extremes are the ordinary Bantu Africans. The tall people rule the country. The king of Urundi came to celebrate the last day of our stay in Kivinda, the Quaker mission. He brought a thousand of his followers with him. His drummers baffled all description. They carried enormous drums on their heads, pounding them in perfect rhythm as they marched along. When they reached the mission buildings, they placed these four-foot drums on the ground and pounded them while they danced and leaped into the air, never for one instant losing the rhythm. Never before or since have we seen anything like it. As I remember them they remind me of what a scientist says about the particles in the atom—incomprehensible, impossible, unbelievable but true. Then down the mountains we went, to Usumbura, intending to take an airplane to the French Cameroons, but to our dismay found our plane had been pre-empted by Belgian officials (who always have priority) and we were compelled to stay in Usumbura for a week.

Reverend Carl Johnson of the Emmanuel mission at Usumbura said this was good enough for him because he wanted us to prepare a set of lessons in the Swahili language. Swahili is the most widely used language of central Africa. It is a mixture of Portuguese, Arabic, and African dialects. It originated when the slave traders were capturing slaves in central Africa and taking them over to the island of Zanzibar to hold them until sailing vessels came from all over the world to buy them. Although we had made Swahili lessons in Kenya colony in 1937, we had greatly improved our method in the intervening years and were anxious to make lessons according to our newer models. So we set to work in Usumbura and finished our primer before the week was up. We printed thousands of copies of this

Swahili primer with explanations in English as to how it was to be taught, and it has been used extensively throughout the world to train people in making and in using our lessons. We also began a useful graded series of books on such subjects as "Why Keep Flies Out of Your Baby's Eyes?", "Itch," "Lice," "Chiggers," "Witchcraft," "Gossip," "Worms," "Why Boil Your Water?"

Before Bob left Usumbura he wrote a letter to America too good to omit.

To be a successful literacy tramp three things are essential. First, a strong stomach; second, a strong love of your fellow men; third, an insatiable wanderlust.

Our literacy team saw very little of the wild life of Africa, although we passed near it and flew over it every week. The big game that we were after were these illiterate people; the guns we used were literacy lessons and *The Story of Jesus*. The hunters we left behind us were the missionaries and the native Christians, who sought to bring the minds and hearts of the illiterates to Christ through the printed word.

French Cameroons

Since we could not take the plane going directly to the French Cameroons, we flew to Leopoldville to see whether we could get a plane from there to the Cameroons. We had to wait a week in Leopoldville, and there I had the worst attack of African malaria I have ever had in my life. I still shudder to remember the fever and the upset stomach and shivers that came on me all at once. To think that half the world is subjected to this scourge of malaria, not only once but many times in a year, is to realize how far we still have to go in making our world healthy. But I took a big dose of aralin, and on the second day was weak but free from nausea and fever. I knew perfectly well that this malaria struck me because I had been neglecting my daily dose of the medicine.

Our plane flew over Lambaréné, made famous by the work of Albert Schweitzer, but there was no airfield and we would have had to stay at least two weeks in order to visit his hospital, so we had to give it up.

We reached Douala, the seaport of the Cameroons, a week late. We came to the missionary home unexpectedly and were frightened to see a big leopard, as we supposed, sitting on the doorstep. Just then the missionaries came out of the house and pushed the leopard to one side, explaining that it was a cheetah, which can be tamed, and they had it for a house pet. The cheetah can run, they say, faster than any other animal in the world. Dr. George Thorne, the Presbyterian mission doctor, put me to bed in the hospital at Elat and had me feeling like a new man in three days. We found that the Bulu lessons we had prepared a few years before in the Cameroons were printed in such small type that new literates could not read it, so we made a complete revision of these lessons, following our latest style, and Phil Gray printed large beautiful wall charts. The mission sent out an urgent call and soon fifty pastors and teachers had assembled to teach. We trained them from the big charts and set them to work "each one teaching one" with our new literacy lessons. One illiterate finished the entire book in two days, and six of them finished on the third day. Then they were able to read the newspaper in their own language. The excited missionaries wanted us to go right to work on the other languages of the Cameroons, so we made another set of lessons in Bassa and outlined lessons in five other languages, which we were not able to finish because we were a week late and had to leave with our work half done. The Christians all appreciated Phil Gray's splendid pictures and urged him and Mrs. Gray to stay on in Elat the rest of their lives.

The Elat mission of the Presbyterian Board in the French Cameroons has had an enormous influence. They had an attendance of 30,000 people every Sunday, but having no church big enough to hold so many people they split the congregation into twenty smaller congregations of 1,500 each. This has enabled the pastors to give the people much better personal attention and has saved them from walking so far to church. They had 2,500 present at the Sunday service when we were there. In one respect it was the most surprising service I have ever known. After every sentence the preacher asked, "Is that right?" and the entire congregation responded with a "Yea!" The pastor would start a verse in the Bible and the entire audience would complete it. He had discovered an equivalent for the ritual of the Roman Catholic Church in which everybody takes part. It seemed to me that he played on his people as a master violinist plays on his violin.

This was a healthy mission in another respect. It was interested in the economic welfare of the people as well as in their souls. They have an industrial school that teaches everything the simple African requires to improve his condition—carpentry, house building, blacksmithing, masonry and cement making, even tailoring. An American dentist had twelve dental students whom he was training. It was also this Presbyterian school that introduced cacao about fifty years ago. Now cacao is the chief product of the country.

The director of education told me that every child in that area between the ages of six and nine was in school and he said that this was due chiefly to the Presbyterian mission. Imagine a Roman Catholic French official saying that about an American Presbyterian mission!

The influence of this mission can only be realized when we recall that these lovely, well-dressed, cultured people were stark-naked cannibals a century ago. One of the Africans whom I heard pray in church said, "O God, we were once only animals, but now we are people. Once we thought the white people were ghosts, but now we know that they are people, too. We are all people and for this we thank Thee, we thank Thee, O God!"

For a long time these cannibals found Christianity too difficult for them. One man said, "I believed in God ten times, but it never stuck. Please remember me across the seas, for it is a shame in my heart. Now I have found it at last, and I hope it will stick."

It was here in the Cameroons that Miss Jean Mackenzie wrote her two famous books *Black Sheep* and *An African Trail,* which did more to make the world aware of Christian Africa than all the other missionary writings put together. Jean Mackenzie had learned to write before she went to the mission field and was therefore a hundred times more useful than she would have been if she had been unable to write so well. Every missionary ought to be required to take a course in journalism before he goes abroad, for two reasons: first, the most wonderful adventures in the world are lost forever because so few missionaries know how to describe them effectively; second, the missionary cannot teach the native people how to write unless he himself knows how to write. For example, in the Cameroons the missionaries have a thrilling story to tell about gorillas. While we were there, two Americans were collecting young gorillas and chimpanzees. Native Africans would kill the father and mother gorilla or chimpanzee, and bring the babies to the American collectors. These baby gorillas and chimpanzees would die in a day if they did not have a great deal of affection shown them, so a boy was employed for each baby, with nothing to do but feed it and show it affection. It was heart-moving to see those tiny gorillas rush to their owners and throw their arms around their necks and hug them. Each baby gorilla is worth $5,000 by the time he arrives in America, if he is alive, and he lives on love more than he does on food. The father and mother gorillas were affectionate too, but they are so strong that they would kill you with a hug when they thought they were being affectionate.

Bob kept saying, "This is Tarzan country," and it was. Most of Africa is a barren plain, sometimes covered with small bushes, but the Cameroons are covered with dense jungles and trailing vines, perfect for monkeys and Tarzans to swing from tree to tree.

Bob and one of the African teachers tried to teach a little chimpanzee to read our first literacy lesson. He seemed to be bright-eyed and intelligent and we are sure he would have learned to read, only he could not concentrate very well, and besides, he could not talk, so Bob had to concede that we had made our first failure in literacy.

By this time we had made lessons in ninety-six African languages. That sounds like a large number until one learns that there are more than a thousand languages and dialects in Africa, most of them spoken by very small groups of people. Everywhere we went in Africa we were impressed by the fact that the people are more restive, more dissatisfied, more eager for an education and more determined to better their condition with each passing year. Especially is this true of the young generation. One feels certain that Africans are coming up and will surmount all obstacles. If they can, they are coming up the education way, and if that fails they are coming up the bloody way of revolt. White rulers discount the importance of this rising passion but to discount it is very foolish. If the whites knew what the Africans are thinking and saying, they might be much more frightened than they are and much less arrogant. They would, I think, realize that the attempts being made in some parts of Africa to suppress the aspirations of the people may result in a tragic repercussion. Fortunately the British and Belgians now realize that they must satisfy the legitimate demands of the African illiterates or they will suffer the consequences, for education has become the leading passion of Africa.

Missions will be very wise if they satisfy this demand for education. In doing so they will reap a great harvest of souls. We did not find any government in Africa, or in fact in any other country thus far, that attempted to prevent Christians from teaching non-Christians to read, if they did it the "each one teach one" way in their own homes. In Peru there was a proposal to prevent anybody from teaching unless he was trained and had a certificate from the government, but I do not think that proposal was ever carried out. It would have been very foolish. Twenty African countries in which we worked not only permitted the church to make people literate but urged it to do so. Liberia not only wanted her population to be literate but also to be made Christian as soon as possible. One of the delightful experiences we had in most countries in Africa was to meet magnificent officials who have a sincere desire to lift the African people in education, in economics, in character, and in religion.

The reason the church ought to place literacy among the very highest priorities in its program is because literacy builds a bridge between the people of the world. Along this bridge those who know can communicate with those who do not know. We Christians believe that we have the religion they need, the laws of health they need, the knowledge about child-care and dietetics, agriculture, industry and a thousand secrets they need to escape from their misery. Literacy is the indispensable bridge across which we can share all the good they need.

CHAPTER 18

1951: AMONG THE ARABS

Algiers, Libya, Egypt, Jordan

Algiers

IN JANUARY 1951 we started on another trip to Africa. When Phil Gray and Bob and I landed in Paris, General Eisenhower was there organizing NATO and his name was on every tongue. We went to visit our friends in UNESCO and passed the hotel where General Eisenhower was staying. It was surrounded by a crowd and by soldiers stationed in front of the hotel. We went to Algiers and stayed at the St. George Hotel. Across the hall from us on a bronze plate were the words, "General Dwight Eisenhower occupied this room." We told the manager of the hotel about our experience in Paris and he said, "Eisenhower is the biggest name in Europe today."

But we did not hear his name sung among the Algerians. In fact, an air of gloom was hanging over that city. In my letter to New York from Algeria I wrote:

The papers here in Algiers tell us America's budget for war is fifty billion dollars, two thousand times as much for war as we are spending to help the backward countries through our Point IV program. Meanwhile poverty is stalking the streets of Algiers. It ought to be plain that we must lift the world out of its misery or we shall be destroyed by these angry suffering multitudes even though we pile hydrogen bombs as high as the tower of Babel.

Now as I write in 1959, with the terrible struggle going on in Algiers, the words I wrote in 1951 sound like prophecy.

The missionaries in Algiers were keeping on in spite of everything. They were true soldiers of peace. With hardly enough income to buy food because of drastic cuts in their salaries and a drastic rise in living expenses, they still refused to go home. This was especially heroic because they were living in a fanatical Moslem region where one might spend a lifetime without making a convert. The greatest virtue of a missionary on the north coast of Africa is dogged, unshakable persistency. Algiers presents a lesson from history for the Christian church. Here was the home of St. Augustine, the greatest of all the church fathers. Here the church flourished until the religion of Mohammed swept across northern Africa, converting the Christians at the point of the sword. The Moslems invaded southern Spain in the year 711 and held it until the Spanish Christians took the last Moorish stronghold, Granada, in 1492—the very year Columbus discovered America. Dr. Eric North, in his preface to *The Book of a Thousand Tongues* says that the reason Christianity succumbed so easily to Islam throughout Arabia, all the Near East and northern Africa, was because the church had failed to make its members literate. They were not well grounded in their religion and were easily persuaded to abandon the Christian church. There is a great need for the church to face this truth today, when communism threatens to take all of Asia and Africa with a zeal and fanaticism as powerful as the Mohammedans had in those early days of their expansion.

Wonderful heroes have labored among the Moslems of northern Africa. Here Raymond Lull was martyred, loving the men who killed him just as his Lord had done. Here Samuel Zwemer labored with tireless zeal, and here lived the saintly Canon Gairdner. Here also lived and died Lilias Trotter, a magnificent woman who is not well known in America, but is more famous in North Africa than any of the names I have mentioned. She was a marvelous painter and a close friend of John Ruskin. In North Africa, also, lived Oswald Chambers when he wrote *My Utmost for His Highest.* The selfless devotion and burning zeal one finds among the missionaries of North Africa does something to one's soul. I felt as we worked among them that they were doing far more for us than we were doing for them. North Africa is the home of heroic missionaries; no others have the courage to face insuperable odds.

We helped a dozen missionaries in Algeria prepare lessons in Kabyle, the language spoken by a large percentage of the people. We also made an Algerian version of the Arabic lessons because the Arabic of Algiers is very different from the Arabic spoken in Egypt. Then we prepared a graded series of lessons about subjects that are most urgently needed in Algiers. The themes proposed by the missionaries and Algerian Christians will surprise you. They included "How To Wean a Baby," "Mending Electrical Fixtures," "Interviewing Government Officials," "Evil in Cafes," "Truth About Demons," and "How To Dry Fruit." There were about a hundred such subjects proposed for our second reader.

We also prepared lessons in French. This was because Algiers was under French control and it was the French policy to attempt to assimilate the population by teaching them all to speak and read French. The government printed our French lessons and the mission boards printed the lessons in Kabyle and in Arabic.

We also made lessons in Spanish for the large number of Spanish Protestants who had fled from Spain when General Franco became dictator. The World Literacy Committee published these Spanish lessons and they have since been used in many parts of Latin America. In 1956, when we visited Spain, we carried this book with us and it was reprinted there by the Baptist mission.

As we were leaving Algiers, an influential French missionary declared: "This is the most important event of a century in North Africa."

In my notes I wrote: "It could be that important if the church would seize her opportunity in an adequate way."

Dr. Elmer Douglas, superintendent of the Methodist mission in Algiers, was especially elated by the influence of our literacy program on the Arab women. Here is a part of his letter:

Several illiterate Arab women and girls were introduced and taught in front of the charts. The veiled women learned the letters. They learned the words. They learned the sentences. They read the page. It worked! Praises were expressed and the women were congratulated. I received word from one station that had tried the new lessons on several illiterates and they were thrilled. The new literates wanted to teach others. One missionary wrote me that they had three grandmothers, two other old women, two girls in their teens and a man of thirty-five all being taught "each one teach one." The method is wonderful. One of the women is teaching her illiterate husband. Your twenty-three days in Algiers with missionaries and nationals of various church backgrounds was an unprecedented demonstration in Christian fellowship and harmonious cooperation for a common task. One missionary who has been here for twenty years said it was the most profitable month of his missionary career.

Dr. Douglas ends his letter with this pathetic question:

Where shall we find the money to carry on this program? We need a person with special training who will devote his whole time to head up this campaign.

Libya

Our team went to the city of Tripoli in Libya in 1951 at the invitation of the British department of education. Until the end of the Second World War Libya was under Italian Fascist control. Mussolini, the Italian dictator, made no effort whatever to train African men for government positions and schools for Africans were almost nonexistent when the British took over Libya from the Italians. Between 1946 and 1951 the British worked hard to establish schools, importing teachers from Egypt, Lebanon, or Palestine, because only a handful of Libyans were educated enough to teach.

Mr. G. C. Scott, the British director of education, assigned the Arab inspectors of schools to make lessons, which we found very easy because three-fourths of the words used had already been employed in Egypt and other Arabic countries. Phil Gray and an Arab artist worked with all their might to prepare the large literacy charts and the smaller textbooks. When we tried the first lessons, done in beautiful color, on two Arab messenger boys they learned so fast that the teachers declared it was magic. We had to do this literacy work in between many social events. On Monday we lunched with the assistant administrator of Tripoli, on Tuesday with the governor, on Wednesday with the commissioner of the United Nations, and on one day we all went out to a beautiful hidden retreat for a picnic dinner. Everyone felt that what we were doing for Libya was basic as a foundation for her independence. Mr. Scott was not only enthusiastic but extremely competent. He had our lessons printed in one of the most beautiful books we have had in all the world.

Libya was about to become an independent state under the supervision of the United Nations, which had fifty representatives in the country helping the government prepare for the event. In 2,000 years there could not have been a more perfect time to prepare for teaching illiterates, and everyone felt the importance of what was going on. Less than 5 per cent of the adult men and less than 1 per cent of the women could read. All of them knew that this was the big stumbling block to their success as a free government. After we left, the director of UNESCO took our beautiful lessons out into the desert and taught hundreds of people in the district known as the Fezzan. He was so enthusiastic that UNESCO has been one of our strong supporters ever since.

The busiest man in our party while we were in Tripoli was Phil Gray, for he was not only making pictures in Arabic but was trying to make 250 pictures for our lessons in French. We also began lessons in Italian at the Italian hotel where we were staying. These we finished in 1956 when we visited Rome.

Phil Gray and Bob took a day off to see the ruins of the immense Roman city Leptis Magna, which had been built by the Roman Emperor Domitian. Domitian, as Bible scholars will remember, was emperor while The Revelation was being written and was one of the most ruthless persecutors of the Christian church. It was he who destroyed Jerusalem in A.D. 70. At that time Libya was the garden spot of the Roman Empire. But during the last 2,000 years the sands of the Sahara have crept down upon the gardens of Libya, in some areas all the way to the Mediterranean. American agricultural experts told us that Libya had been destroyed by goats and camels. The goats ate the bark off the trees and the camels ate the leaves, and when the trees died the desert moved in. One of the big projects in Libya today is to replant the trees in an effort to recover hundreds of thousands of acres now submerged under the sands of the desert.

Mrs. Laubach and I went to see Wheelus Field, the largest American air base outside of the United States. Here is installed the only television in Africa. There were probably 10,000 Americans on the air base when we were there. We talked to the chaplains about training the soldiers to teach our lessons and allowing them to go among the natives with an "each one teach one" book under their arms. The chaplains thought it was a good idea but after we left it was forgotten. There are at least a half million soldiers stationed among illiterate people around the world. It is not at all fantastic to suppose that at least a hundred thousand of these soldier boys would gladly teach illiterates if they were trained to do so. The soldiers would like it; the illiterates would like it; and the governments would like it.

In all Libya there are only two missionary men with their wives, one a doctor and the other an evangelist. They live in semi-seclusion in the heart of the oldest part of the city. Because none of the Arab teachers could speak English, we invited the Reverend Norman Pearce, the evangelist, to help translate for us while we were making lessons. He was warmly welcomed—and this is the first time he and the department of education had ever met. There is not a single Christian in Libya. All the missionaries there can do is to hang on and hope and pray. Here, as in so many other places, literacy was the first opening wedge for the missionaries to contact the Libyan government and perform a useful service for them.

In A.D. 400 there were 40,000 Christian churches in Libya and it was inhabited by several million people, but when the Romans withdrew and the Moslems entered, the magnificent water works and streets and farms fell into disuse. Every trace of Christianity was obliterated by the irresistible advance of Islam, and now there are no Protestant Christians at all. Mussolini built a large Catholic Church, and a handsome hotel at which he occasionally stayed. He intended to restore the ancient glory of Rome in Africa, but alas, he became involved with Hitler and went down.

Egypt

Bob and Phil Gray and I flew on to Egypt. When we reached Cairo, my suitcase did not come off the plane. It had been left at Benghazi in Libya, and I had no clothes except those on my back. The airline made every effort to recover my bag and it arrived two days later. We stayed at the American mission of the United Presbyterian Church, as we have always done when in Cairo. Twelve men representing UNESCO were laboring in Cairo to prepare books for Egypt and they invited me to come and sit in with them. Then I met my old friend, Douglas McCaffrey, the American ambassador, a devout Roman Catholic; he goes to mass every morning. I had first met him in Brazil in 1943. He was as cooperative as any ambassador in the world. The American embassy offered to contribute all the paper for the first printing of the Arabic lessons we had prepared in 1947. This was a godsend because in Egypt they were having an acute shortage of paper. The American cultural attaché said to me jokingly: "You are responsible for this paper shortage, for you are teaching the people to read faster than we can get paper to print the books." We spent an afternoon with the Egyptian Inter-Mission council which had invited us to come to Egypt. (The Inter-Mission council supported literacy between 1947 and 1956.) They reported that the literacy campaign of the government had not progressed very rapidly, but that the church campaign was going vigorously and had resulted in a new spirit of cooperation between the Christians and Mohammedans. They said that the only obstacle to their campaign was the lack of paper and lack of money.

Jordan

My old friend, Halana Mikhail, was working among the refugees near Jerusalem for the United Nations, establishing literacy campaigns with wonderful results. The United Nations was anxious for me to see her work, so we hurried on to Beirut, Lebanon, and the United Nations took me on a long station-wagon journey of 600 miles over rather rough roads to see the Arab refugees from Israel. Since we could not cross Israel, we had to go by way of Damascus and Amman, the capital of Jordan. Amman hangs on the edge of a deep canyon. It was a tiny village before the war with Israel but had mushroomed into a large city because of the influx of Arab refugees.

My companions on this United Nations jaunt were educated Christian Arabs. They were my warm friends, and yet they tormented my conscience with questions like: "Why does America fight against aggression in Korea and yet support the aggression of the Jews in

Jordan, and tolerate the ejection of a million persons from their homes? What have the Arabs done to hurt America?" I found this difficult to answer.

The country of Palestine, where I had made lessons on previous occasions, no longer existed under its old name. Where Palestine formerly was there were now two countries, Israel and Jordan. There are Arab refugee camps at Bethlehem, north of Jerusalem, and along the Jordan river. UNRWA (United Nations Relief Work Administration) escorted me to these camps to see the thriving literacy campaigns under the direction of Halana Mikhail.

Halana had first started her work for UNRWA among the 200,000 refugees in the Gaza camp. There she astonished everyone by the campaign she conducted with the aid of volunteer teachers. Now her work in Jerusalem was equally effective. Her only obstacle was the fact that UNRWA did not have enough money to provide her with books. In fact, the cost of food had risen so much that they could hardly buy enough food to supply these refugees, so I wrote to Point IV asking them to give Halana $30,000 to meet this deficit. That money never came. I have learned since that one does not get $30,000 from the U. S. government merely by writing a letter. It takes an act of Congress and the signature of the President of the United States, and that is not easy.

Bob and I visited the Jordan river and the Dead Sea. It is the lowest spot in the world and even in February one is comfortable in shirt sleeves. In the summer months the heat is unbearable. There were two big refugee camps, one on each side of the Jordan, where the people live in little tents in temperatures that rise as high as 120° Fahrenheit. How the people survive is a mystery, but we found them carrying on a literacy campaign with great zest. One man fifty years old read to us after only two weeks of study. He had been taught by his twelve-year-old son. Neither of them could restrain his tears as I praised them for what they had done. As we returned on the trail from Jerusalem to Jericho, we saw the place where the Good Samaritan is supposed to have found the man wounded by thieves. Now it was Jerusalem that had fallen among thieves. The Jewish-Arab war left great areas of the city blasted and countless houses in ruins. Through the middle of the city ran an ugly scar. It was no man's land and was filled with rusty barbed wire. One of the finest Y.M.C.A.'s in the world stood empty and useless on the Jewish side, while the magnificent Jewish Seminary stood closed and idle on the Arab side.

A mile from Bethlehem, Halana Mikhail showed us a sickening sight. Five thousand Arab refugees were camped on black rocks where nothing will grow. They were within sight of the land of Israel from which they had been driven. The manager of this camp was a wonderful man. He showed us all of the ways in which he was trying to help the refugees forget their troubles. The boys were learning carpentry and shoemaking and the girls were attending sewing classes. But every drop of water for those 3,000 people had to be carried up a hill for two miles on the heads of the Arab women. A crowd of old men flocked around me, shaking my hand and talking excitedly. I could not make out what they were saying but I promised to do all I could for them. I had great trouble getting out of that crowd because they were so pathetic and so persistent in their pleas for help. When finally we got in our automobile my guide said they imagined I was the director of the United Nations.

We returned to Beirut and taught the girls in the American College how to use our lessons. They were burning with zeal to teach and to write for the new literates. It is among college students like this that we must find writers for the books and magazines that will make literacy a blessing.

CHAPTER 19

1951: IN INDIA, WRITING FOR NEW LITERATES

On February 21, 1951, we were flying across the desert of Arabia to Bombay. From Bombay we took a train to Poona. On the train we heard educated Indians discussing the American policy toward India. They said that India wants peace, and their great concern was whether the United States would join her in working for peace. These men were discussing a proposal America had just made to send India one million tons of wheat, with the understanding that India would release $70 million of Indian money for technical assistance to train farmers in raising their own food. They thought the idea was excellent because it would help India to help herself.

Then, as always, I was impressed by the rare idealism of most of the educated Indians. They are trying sincerely to make a success of their new freedom. Their postage stamps said at that time, "Republic of India inaugurated January 26, 1950."

Every Indian official was trying with might and main to make a success of their new democracy, but they had enormous problems, greater than any republic had ever had before. For one thing they had to get rid of hundreds of princely states and thousands of feudal lords who had been squeezing the lifeblood out of the illiterate masses. China got rid of her landlords the Communist way, by liquidating the lords and confiscating their property. The Indian government did not believe in liquidation, but it compelled the landlords to dispose of all large estates, paying them a fair compensation. These estates were then divided among the tenants.

At Nasrapur, near Poona, fifty Indian delegates met with us to prepare literature for new literates. We had learned many lessons during the campaign in India, which had flourished between 1935 and 1940. The first lesson was that millions of new literates had lapsed into illiteracy again because they could not read the difficult Indian books and newspapers and we had not provided them with literature that was easy and interesting. So this Nasrapur workshop devoted itself to the problem of writing graded materials for new literates that would carry them as swiftly as possible up to the newspaper level in their own languages.

These delegates were all devout Christians. We began our day with early morning devotions on the roof while the sun was rising. After breakfast we had a devotional talk and then divided into workshop groups to write letters. This we continued through the afternoon. The evenings were devoted to informal talks and to showing the slides that Bob had taken of literacy in other countries.

The first question we always discussed was "What to write." We agreed that because literacy is a means to lifting people out of their poverty and disease we must write about those subjects first. It requires unusual skill to make such subjects interesting. We knew that illiterates are not convinced by subtle arguments. Their *hearts* must be convinced. Therefore we aimed at writing articles that would touch their emotions, would make them laugh and cry and stir them to action. There is a saying in India: "Convince their hearts and their minds will listen."

But this is exactly what the books commonly written in India did not do. They sounded formal and unnatural and were often incomprehensible to new literates. We knew that the old writers could not be persuaded to write with simpler words—they could not do it if they tried. We faced the necessity of training a new school of writers to write as naturally and simply and interestingly as a good storyteller talks. Many Indians are wonderful storytellers, but for the life of them they cannot write the way they talk. We therefore tried making tape recordings of vivid stories as they were being narrated and writing these out exactly as they were told. We found that the new literates loved this style and that the educated classes of India would accept it if it was introduced by something like this: "George Prakasam is a wonderful storyteller. All the people gather around him to listen to his fascinating tales. This is the way he talks: 'Lucky learned to read. His teacher brought him books full of secrets. Every book told him something that made him wiser and happier. The first book told him that he was a foolish fellow because he did not eat the right food. There were weeds in his own yard that would make him well.' "

And so on and on the story would go in what the educated people would consider slang. It was the spoken language of the villages. The first book we wrote this way was a series of one-page stories about the life of Jesus, written exactly as a good Indian storyteller would tell them to a Sunday school class. All of our delegates attempted to write these stories, and they were left with a committee that was expected to refine them and put them in a book.

Then Dr. Gladys Rutherford came! She was a wonderful doctor who refused to work in a hospital and spent her time in Indian villages. She had done the health work in the Indian village service at Mahrera 100 miles east of New Delhi. I have never met anyone who could tell a health story so simply and fascinatingly. She told her stories while holding up "jet cards," which she had made herself using match-stick figures. The advantage of a match-stick man is that he is without color or nationality and can be used anywhere. While she gave us several of her inimitable health lectures with her "jet cards," we reported what she said so that we could put the exact sentences she uttered beside each drawing. She was a master of short, sharp phrases, terse, funny and to the point. Here for example is some of her lecture on "Itch":

(Picture of three people scratching) "Scratch! Scratch! Scratch!"
(Picture of many people scratching) "Everybody scratches!"
(Picture of mother and baby scratching) "Mother scratches. Baby scratches."
(Pictures of man scratching in bed) "Scratch all night. You don't sleep a wink."
(Picture of man taking a bath) "Take a bath. Plenty of soapsuds. Rub into every sore."

(Picture of man putting powder on his clothes) "Wash your clothes. Sprinkle gamexine on them."
(Picture of man sprinkling powder on his bed) "Sprinkle gamexine on your bed."
(Picture of man in bed) "Sleep sweet and cozy all night. Goodby itch!"

Dr. G. H. Towle came from the agricultural school at Vidala and gave us fascinating lectures on how to get more out of the land. Our fifty delegates tried to write these lectures for our new literates. Here are some of the titles of his lectures: "Soil Is Gold, Don't Let the Rain Steal It," "How To Make Soil Richer," "Plants That Enrich the Soil," "Rotating Your Crops," "Using Dead Leaves," "What Is a Legume," "Have More Sheep," and "How Buffaloes Enrich Your Soil."

Mr. Loy Long came from Bombay to tell us the remarkable story of the village industries he started. One of these industries uses sisal, a very strong fiber our American farmers use to bind wheat in the fields. Mr. Long said they had trained 150 women who otherwise would be begging, in the art of dying sisal fiber and making handbags, floor mats and napkin rings. He said that the social service center in Bombay was busy all day and late into the evening with classes in weaving, practical nursing and home economics. Loy Long's talks were also taken down on tape so that the delegates could rewrite them in simple language. Mr. Wilson Brown, one of the delegates, put every one of these lectures on a mimeograph machine and the delegates took them home, each delegate with a special assignment to write articles in booklets. These were to be sent to Miss Ruth Ure, the literacy secretary of the National Christian Council.

Bob and Phil and I went to Nagpur, capital of the Central Provinces. President Moses of Hislop College grabbed at our proposal to start a course in journalism in his college and prepare writers for new literates. The next year Professor Roland Wolseley of Syracuse University opened a department of journalism at Hislop College and this has been continued ever since. From Nagpur we went to New Delhi, the capital of India, and found the officials eager for every new idea. Professor Tara Chand, secretary of education, told us that he was convinced that our method of teaching phonics by means of pictures was the perfect method for the Indian language. We were delighted when Mr. Nehru came and sat beside us at a conference in New Delhi, at which he was the main speaker. Mr. Nehru has always been deeply interested in our literacy method. We have talked with him about it several times.

Miss Ella Griffin was in India representing UNESCO and our American Point IV. She had been sent there to prepare a number of useful books for India. The book she showed us was very attractive and beautifully illustrated.

The most exciting experience, however, of this visit to New Delhi, was meeting the wife of Dr. Spencer Hatch, famous for his village uplift work in Mexico, India and Ceylon. Mrs. Hatch took us to a *mela* about ten miles out of New Delhi. Here they had entertainment and exhibits very much like those of a county fair in the United States. After three days, when everyone's enthusiasm was at fever pitch, they began a literacy campaign. Within a few weeks, Mrs. Hatch told us, half the people of the nearby villages had been made literate.

CHAPTER 20

1951: AFGHANISTAN AND THE KHYBER PASS

We were approached by a representative of Afghanistan to come and help that country, and this ushered us into one of the most thrilling adventures of our literacy experience. Afghanistan has no missionaries and no native Christians. It must be entered by the famous (and infamous) Khyber Pass, which for thousands of years has been the haunt of bandits. Afghanistan is the gateway between India and Persia and was once the only way to enter Europe from southeast Asia. The fabulous riches that were carried by camels through Khyber Pass made fat prizes for bandit hordes. I had read about Khyber Pass when I was a boy, and now the dream of a lifetime was coming true. The British have suppressed the banditry, but the reminders of ancient conflicts are visible everywhere.

As we motored through the pass, only ten miles long, we counted 110 forts and blockhouses from which British soldiers were able to see every inch of the ten-mile road and to shoot bandits who dared attack the caravans or trucks. We met very few trucks and no automobiles while we were going through Khyber Pass, but we saw hundreds of camels.

The British built a fine railroad through that pass to protect Afghanistan from an invasion by Hitler's army, but Hitler was defeated before he ever reached that part of Asia and this first-class railroad remains entirely unused. When we were there, they talked of removing the track and converting it into a superb highway between Pakistan and Afghanistan. This idea was never carried out and we are beginning to see what a mistake it was to neglect it. The Communists are now building such a first-class road from Russia down to Kabul, the capital of Afghanistan. Moreover, they are paving the widest street in Kabul so that it will be as good as anything in India. It is exasperating to see how blind and stupid we often are.

Professor J. Christy Wilson of Princeton Theological Seminary had been given a visa by the Afghan government to act as my interpreter, since he was an expert in the Persian language, the official language of Afghanistan. So there were five in our party as we went through Khyber Pass, Christy Wilson, Phil Gray, Mrs. Laubach, our son Bob and I. We were met at the city of Peshawar by the director of primary education, Mr. Asif Mayil, and were driven to Kabul in a large station wagon. We drove 200 miles over a very rough road through stony river beds and over tremendous mountains with creepy hairpin curves and awe-inspiring cliffs. In spite of the indescribably marvelous scenery, none of us felt quite happy on the edge of those dizzy mountain sides because there were no fences between us and death. The road was narrow and the hundreds of sheep and camels that passed added to our troubles. Dr. Wilson spoke for all of us when he said, "Thank God we got over that safely."

The second day we reached Kabul valley, watered by snow from those immense mountains, and at the other end of that valley lay our destination, Kabul, the capital of Afghanistan. Here we were surrounded by snow-capped mountains, north, south, east and west. We were 6,000 feet above sea level and we shivered with the cold.

Mr. Jacob Hasan, one of the very few educated men of Afghanistan, was appointed by the department of education to help us prepare lessons. "I am your student," he said, "to do what you tell me to do. I want to learn all you know."

He was one of those rare geniuses whom one finds in nearly every country. After ten days of hard work we had completed the lessons in the Persian language, and Phil Gray had them on big charts with beautifully colored pictures. They were a joy to behold. The army sent fifty illiterate soldiers to be taught, so that they, in turn, could go and teach all the other illiterates in the Afghan army. So far as I know, every private soldier in the Afghanistan army was illiterate. Only the officers could read and write. But every private was burning with desire to learn, because that was his only doorway to promotion. This made an ideal class. The rigid discipline required them to attend every session and their own eagerness resulted in perfect attention.

The method always used before this in Afghanistan was to teach people to recite the entire alphabet before they could learn a single word. It was the Arabic alphabet and therefore they had to learn every letter with four different shapes. When we began to teach our charts, everybody was dumbfounded to see the students learn words even before they knew the letters. They were awe-struck by the rapidity with which these fifty soldiers learned, and were sold on our method.

It had taken us seventeen years to develop the type of lessons we now made in Afghanistan. Phil Gray had become a genius at associating objects with the shape of letters. He is a perfectionist, never satisfied with the work he has done, and always trying to lift better up to best. He paid the penalty for perfectionism by having frequent migraine headaches, but the good he has done in the world with his pictures was worth all his headaches.

There were no Christian churches in Afghanistan so on Easter we held a little service for five of us in our own hotel room. That evening the secretary of the American embassy held an Easter meeting in his home where thirty foreigners were gathered and Dr. Christy Wilson gave a good Easter sermon. Among these foreigners were several engineers who had just arrived in Kabul to set up an Afghan technical college. All of them were earnest Christian men—the type we need all over the world. Mr. Beck, representing the United Nations, was deeply interested in our literacy campaign and eager to help us with our graded follow-up books. He was especially anxious to have functional material in these books about health, agriculture, animal husbandry, home life, and child care.

Fortunately there was a very good German-made printing press in Kabul, run by a really expert German printer. This is why we were able to print the Persian lessons as fast as we made them. When we left Kabul, the department of education was printing 50,000 copies of our new primer and 500 sets of charts, six charts in a set.

I did not see a single Afghan woman while I was in Pakistan because they are required to wear a white gown that completely covers their heads and bodies down to their feet. They have two holes cut in the garment so they can look out, but no one can see in. On Sunday morning Mrs. Laubach went to a school for these women and found 600 of them learning embroidery and other home industries though none of them could read. The Afghan men were not sure that the women ought to learn, but after we left, the two daughters of the king not only went to school but became trained nurses—the most revolutionary thing that ever happened in Afghanistan.

The week before we left I received a gold medal from the king, presented by the minister of education, Abdul Majid. We took advantage of this opportunity to tell the minister that Christy Wilson, Jr., had just received his Ph.D. and wanted to come to Afghanistan as a teacher. The minister said he would telegraph for him to come immediately. Within a year Dr. Christy Wilson, Jr. was in Afghanistan. He won the hearts of everyone, although he was very conscientious about his Christian religion and would not teach on Sunday. They let him off, also, on Friday, because that was the Moslem Sabbath, so he had a five-day week. In spite of that they raised his salary. In 1955, after a furlough in the United States, he returned to Afghanistan with the permission of the Afghan government to be chaplain to the foreigners of that country. He is therefore the first person Afghanistan has permitted to act as a missionary in its borders.

CHAPTER 21

1951: BURMA AND INDONESIA

Burma, Singapore, Malaya, Indonesia

Burma

In Burma we plunged at once into lesson building. We used the headquarters of the Baptist mission and the Christian Literature Society of Burma. This had formerly been the site of Judson College. Missionaries came from all parts of Burma, some of them bringing illiterates with them. We prepared lessons, not only in the Burmese language, but also in eleven other languages: Thaung, Thu, Chin, Kachin, Lahu, Akha, Ganung, Karen, Pwa, Karen Sgaw, and Rawand. All these languages were easy to prepare, but we were particularly proud of our lessons in Burmese. That language was much more complicated and irregular than the other languages and it required a book of 120 plates, the longest primer we had ever made except *Streamlined English*. The Burmese letters are nearly all made out of segments of circles. Breaks in these circles distinguish the different letters. They are beautiful to see but rather confusing to remember. However, I believe we made one of the best primers produced in any language.

We were especially glad to prepare lessons for the Karens. About half of the Karen tribe had become Christians in the days of Adoniram Judson. Christianity stirred up ambition in the Karens to become the social equals of the Burmese. The result was an almost constant racial conflict similar to that which we have in the United States, only worse than anything we have had in this country since the Civil War. While we were in Burma we did not actually witness any bloodshed, but we were told that just before we arrived a Karen town had been obliterated by Burmese incendiary bombs dropped from airplanes.

Many other tribes were giving the Burmese government great trouble. Banditry was common in nearly all parts of Burma. The railroad was wrecked by bandits almost every week. Two empty freight cars were pushed in front of the engine so that when a bomb exploded they would be blown off the track and the engine would escape. One can imagine how slowly they had to run those trains.

The Burmese government was enthusiastic about our teaching the Burmese language, but very dubious about our making lessons in any of the ten tribal languages in which we worked.

In Burma we made graded series of books to follow our primer. They were called *U Sein the Wise Man*. Point IV gave us every aid and so did the Burmese director of agriculture.

We decided that in these books we would not write sermons such as "You should have a garden," "You should raise milk goats," but would convert our information into a story like *Robinson Crusoe*. Our story said that U Sein the wise man learned to read, and in each lesson he learned a secret that gave him more money, better health, and so made him happier, richer, and more famous. As the new literates read this book they said to themselves, "If U Sein could do this, I can too." So they were eager and ready for every help the agricultural and health workers cared to give them.

So this series of lessons killed "two birds with one stone," for while it taught people to read, it also lifted them out of poverty and disease.

Singapore

From Burma our literacy team went to Singapore. Here we had such a reception from the churches and the government that it fairly took our breath. We had meant to visit Singapore for two or three days as an incidental stopover, but the eager people there crowded those days to the limit. They wanted lessons in Malay and other lessons in Romanized Amoy Chinese, but they had so many meetings in between our working sessions that we had to pack every moment with work. There was an early morning meeting with the preachers, a tea and a speech at the University of Singapore with the governor of the colony in the chair; a talk to 500 Malay teachers, another to 1,000 English-speaking teachers, and a luncheon with the educational officers.

All of this unexpected cordiality was due to the fact that Dr. and Mrs. Paul Means had been in Singapore under a Fulbright scholarship for a year before we came, and had stirred up the zeal for literacy with such success that everyone was sold on "each one teach one."

Malay proved to be one of the easiest languages in the world to learn and also to teach. It has only eighteen letters. It was so nearly like the Filipino languages that we were able to prepare the textbook in about one day, so before we left Singapore we had this book mimeographed. We had also prepared a primer in Romanized Amoy.

Malaya

I left Mrs. Laubach, Bob, and Phil Gray in Singapore and flew alone northward to Kuala Lumpur, the capital of Malaya. Here I was entertained in the magnificent palace of Sir Henry Gurney, the commissioner of the Malay Federated States. It was the custom to wear a tuxedo for dinner every evening but I had no tuxedo with me. Fortunately I was invited out to dinner each evening and so evaded that embarrassment.

We tried the Malay charts Phil Gray had made in Singapore on one of the cooks in the home of the Reverend Gunnar J. Teilmann of the Methodist Mission. The assistant director of education looked on as the cook learned to read with incredible ease. At the end of the lesson, the assistant director said, "I have seen a miracle. I would not have believed it if anyone had told me." The next day, the Reverend Mr. Teilmann, in introducing me to the Rotary Club, said he had seen his own cook learn to read "like magic." In the simple Malay languages one can indeed teach illiterates with fantastic ease.

In Kuala Lumpur I found a surprising demand for *Streamlined English*. They wanted 1,000 copies at once, but were prevented from buying them by the dollar barrier. Mr. Newton of the USIS wrote to Washington, D. C., requesting them to provide these books as a public service.

This Malay campaign has been vigorous ever since I was there. In 1958, the Malay government wrote us that they were teaching 10,000 illiterates to read, over the radio. Dr. and Mrs. Paul Means returned to Malaya in 1959, supported by the Asia Foundation.

Indonesia

I returned to Singapore and on June 1, 1951, flew with Bob, Mrs. Laubach, and Phil Gray to Jakarta, the capital of Indonesia. We were met by two delegations, one representing the government of Indonesia and the other representing the National Christian Council. We were also met by Dr. Fred Rex, the new consultant of the World Literacy and Christian Literature Committee, who had arrived in Indonesia a week ahead of us.

At an opening reception we met Dr. Hendrik Kraemer, secretary of the World Council of Churches. He had been a missionary in Java for many years and was now visiting his daughter, who was living in Java and was a leading member of the National Christian Council of Indonesia.

The following evening we visited President Soekarno of Indonesia, who charmed us by his magnetic graciousness. Everyone this amazing man meets falls under the charm of his marvelous eyes, just as we did. He said that Indonesia was paying our expenses to come to his country ($30,000) because the government needed all the help it could get to overcome illiteracy. He said the Dutch government had left 93 per cent of the people illiterate, and then he added, "We all know that democracy without literacy is a humbug."

Soekarno invited us to attend a puppet and shadow play (they call it a *wayang*), which employs gorgeously attired puppets about three feet high, each puppet depicting an ancient epic hero. One man manipulated the puppets while he sang and spoke the parts for all of them—male and female characters alike. An orchestra of forty players accompanied the performance on gongs, xylophones and stringed instruments. The puppets were shadowed against a screen. The women sat on the side of the screen where they could see only the shadows, while the men sat on the opposite side where they could see both the puppets and the man that was manipulating them. The show lasted all night, but we could not understand the words, so excused ourselves before midnight and went home. This puppet show is so popular that thus far, motion pictures have never been able to attract a crowd in Indonesia. Everyone prefers the *wayang*.

The following morning we took a plane for Sumatra, one of the world's largest islands. At the eastern end is Lake Koba, and around it live the Batak people. A half million of these Bataks are Christian. In one respect they are the most remarkable Christians in all Asia. Their churches are not only totally self-supporting without aid from any country, but they actually send out missionaries. Never have we seen more Christian fervor than these people manifested when singing and praying and listening to the reading of the Bible. We were astonished to be told that one-fourth of the congregation that assembled to meet us were Moslems, who had no objection to participating in a Christian service in our honor. The service opened and closed with a Moslem prayer out of courtesy to the Moslems present. Here, indeed, was something new under the sun.

When we prepared lessons in the Batak language we were startled to find that it was more nearly like the Moro language of Mindanao than any other language we have found in Malay or even in other parts of the Philippines. The anthropologist, Professor Ottley Beyer of the University of the Philippines, says that the Moros came from Sumatra several centuries ago. When I told the Bataks that we in Mindanao were their first cousins they shouted their applause. Because of this happy similarity we found it child's play to make lessons in two of the Batak languages in one week. These two languages were Karo and Simalungun. In the Karo language there were only four books in print—all of them for children! The Bible had been translated almost a century before, but it had long since sold out and the Dutch Bible Society could not furnish money for reprinting. This, the only book for the Karo adults, had been out of print for a quarter of a century! I was greatly touched by their pathetic pleas that we leave the charts and the lessons for them to use, but the Christian Council Committee took them back to Jakarta and the poor Karo Bataks are not yet learning to read. One Christian leader, by the name of P. P.

Sukatendel, said pathetically, "If I can get a thousand copies of this new primer and *The Story of Jesus* in our language, we can make the Karo people literate in a few years."

My heart went out to these Batak people, and I wanted to leave our charts with them, but the Indonesian committee of the Christian Council objected for reasons they did not tell me. They took the lessons back to Jakarta, and never had them printed. And so the campaign among the Bataks ended in nothing.

We went from Sumatra to the southern part of Java, where they speak the Javanese language. At Jogjakarta, the ancient capital of Java, we prepared lessons in that language. It is one of the most difficult languages in the whole world for a foreigner to learn because of its grammar, but even more, because of the social castes. Courtesy demands that the Javanese use fifteen different ways of speaking to people, depending upon their rank. In the English language, we use only the words "you" and "thou," and some of us are polite enough to say "sir." But in southern Java, you address a man of very high rank with one very polite word, a man of a little lower rank with another word, a man with a still lower rank with another word. If he is of the same rank as yourself, you use still another pronoun. If he is lower than you are, you use another pronoun, and so on down the line, to the bottom of society. Fifteen pronouns for fifteen ranks in all! In America we do not have pronouns to distinguish our important people, though I am afraid that we do it with the tone of our voice!

Ancient Javanese once had an exceedingly difficult alphabet, but (fortunately for them and for us) they are now writing with Roman letters. Our primer to teach them these letters was easy to make. It is now printed by the government, and is in use in southern Java.

Leaving Jogjakarta, we flew to the famous island of Bali. But alas, the Christian Council had not set aside any time for us to see the famous Bali dancers! After an exasperating stop of only two hours, we reluctantly flew northward to the city of Macassar, on the island of Celebes, famous for its spices. The Portuguese had discovered it four centuries before. Here we found six missionaries eagerly waiting to make lessons in six different languages, all at one time. Fortunately we had a large blackboard, at least twenty feet long, and at this blackboard we had a six-ring circus, with about a hundred nationals and a dozen missionaries all talking at once. One missionary had brought some illiterate Dyaks from Dutch Borneo, so we made lessons for them also, and they have been in use in Borneo ever since.

The island of Celebes looks small on the map of the vast Pacific ocean, but it is a big troublemaker. It contains several tribes that are hostile to the Indonesian government; indeed, it is in a state of almost constant rebellion. I was not able to learn what the trouble was, but it did not seem to be caused by the Communists. There had been a bloody uprising in Macassar just before we reached that city, and it broke out again soon after we left, but we saw no fighting while we were there.

We found that these languages were remarkably like those in the island of Mindanao. In fact, the Dyak language from Borneo was so similar that we were able to make a book in their language in a day. They have only sixteen letters, and a Dyak child or man could learn in two days to read better than an American child can in two years—so easy is Dyak and so chaotic is English spelling!

The leading missionary on the island of Celebes was the Reverend Walter M. Post of the Christian and Missionary Alliance. Thanks to his efficient leadership, a vigorous campaign has continued in Macassar ever since.

The National Christian Council of Indonesia did not publish any of the lessons we prepared during that trip. The government, however, was eager; they sent a man to our headquarters and persuaded me to give them copies of the lessons we had made in Javanese and Indonesian. Both of these books were published by the Indonesian government. They have been carrying on a vigorous literacy campaign under government auspices ever since.

CHAPTER 22

1952: INDIA—*ANAND THE WISE MAN*

In January 1952 we were again in India. We found the Indian people unusually friendly. The reasons were obvious. First, the government of the United States had sent two million tons of wheat to India, and it had just arrived. Second, Chester Bowles was ambassador, and his complete freedom from racial bias had captured the imagination and affection of India. His daughter Cynthia rode her bicycle every day to the Indian public school, and there she studied in a tent being used provisionally while the government built a permanent school. She was the only American girl in a wholly Indian school.

There was still a third reason for this beaming hospitality. The United States had given India $54 million in Point IV money for technical and economic assistance. The Indian Congress had scrutinized this gift with extreme care, and it had reached the conclusion that it had no strings attached, and that America had no motive except to help her new sister republic. It was the most unselfish gift America had made to India up to that time, and the Indian people were both astonished and grateful. "After all," they concluded, "America understood India, because 170 years ago America had herself become free from Britain, just as India had become free this decade." This is the reason why, when we reached India, the customs officials *apologized* for even looking at the outside of our baggage, and one government official loaned me five rupees so that I would not need to get any money changed at 3 A.M. Here was a vivid firsthand demonstration of how easy and how delightful it is to make friends with other nations.

India was feeling proud of herself; she had just started a free election—the most stupendous free election in the history of the world. One hundred eighty million men and women had voted—more than twice as many voters as we have in the United States. In fact, more women voted in India than all the men and women voters in the United States combined. India has two and one-half times the population of the United States.

There was surprisingly little talk of corruption in India. Everywhere we heard people talking about the major issues—and even more, about the major candidates. In this country, so lacking in transportation and communications, it was impossible to finish an election in one day, as we do in America. It took three months to finish that election.

India has freedom of speech and freedom of the press. In fact, she is much more tolerant than we are in the United States. The Communists are permitted to speak and write freely, and they were printing many untruths in some of the Indian papers they controlled. I asked a man why India allowed these untruths to go out among the people, and he said their constitution gave every man the inalienable right to lie if he wanted to.

We returned to Marehra where Dr. William Wiser had carried on a remarkable village improvement program for many years. This village had once been occupied by Moslems, but during the riots that accompanied the separation of Pakistan from India, these Moslems had been killed or had fled to Pakistan, leaving their homes empty. While we were in Marehra, we lived in a large Moslem house that contained a half-dozen small anterooms. These, we were told, had been occupied by the wives of the Moslem chief—one small anteroom for each wife. It was our first experience in actually living in a harem. Phil Gray and his wife, Ewing, occupied one of these harem rooms, and used another one for Phil's art gallery. His floor was as soft as any rug—it was made of dry cow dung.

Mrs. Laubach and I occupied another of these harem anterooms. It was in this Moslem house that we made a revision of our Hindi lessons, while Phil and Ewing drew the pictures. We took the lessons to an outcaste village on the edge of Marehra, to try them out each day. While we were doing this, a topflight photographer by the name of Colonel Arnold M. Maahs, took pictures that were later used for the motion picture film called "Each One Teach One."

Maahs took the pictures while we were doing the teaching. Though the picture "Each One Teach One" was filmed as fiction, it was based on actual experiences that occur not once but ten thousand times every year in India. Because they do not know how to read or to keep books, illiterates are swindled by landlords and moneylenders every day. One of the blackest tragedies in the world is the way millions of helpless, ignorant peasants must live on the edge of starvation, year after year. They do not own the land, and their landlords take from one-half to two-thirds of the crops they raise. What they have left lasts them six or eight months, after which they go to the moneylender and borrow from him at the rate of about 300 per cent a year, and with that money they buy back food which they had given to the landlord! If the crop is bad, there is nothing for them to do but to starve to death, and seldom did one find either landlord or moneylender who had any mercy on these starving millions.

One of the main reasons we are teaching these people all over the world to read is to enable them to defend themselves from "man's inhumanity to man."

This is why, as soon as we had our phonetic primers finished, we started a book designed to teach these illiterates the secrets that would enable them to come up out of their poverty and disease. We resolved that the graded books should not merely entertain the illiterates, but that they should teach them how to help themselves.

So we began at Marehra a graded series of lessons, similar to those we had made in Burma. We called our book *Anand the Wise Man*. Anand learned to read, and in every lesson he learned a secret that made him healthier, wealthier, wiser, happier and more respected in his community.

Dr. Gladys Rutherford provided all the information for the chapters on health and hygiene. Her aid in preparing *Anand the Wise Man* was priceless, both because she knew the villagers better than any other doctor in northern India, and because she knew *their own words* for all diseases.

Our information about farming and care of animals was provided by several professors who came to Marehra from Allahabad Agricultural College. It required ninety stories to tell to the Indian peasant the priceless secrets that make our own farmers so incomparably superior to the illiterate peasants of India.

Here are some of the chapter titles in *Anand the Wise Man:*

Anand Learns To Read
Anand Reads About Itch and Flies
Anand Makes a Latrine
Anand Learns To Grow Better Crops
Anand Gets Seeds from the Government
Anand Reads How To Make Sore Eyes Well
Anand's Wife Is Revati
Anand Reads About a Safe Well
Anand Reads About Malaria
Anand Reads How To Kill Mosquitoes
Revati Learns What To Feed a Baby
Revati Reads How To Make Tomato Chatni
Anand's Daughter Has a New Baby
Anand Buys a New Plough
Anand Plants Fruit Trees
Anand Learns About Vaccination
Anand Learns How To Raise Better Chickens
Anand Reads About Leprosy
Anand Reads That India Is a Republic
Anand and Revati Cultivate Their Souls

Here is the translation of the first lesson in *Anand the Wise Man.* It shows how we build up a vocabulary, using about ten words to a lesson, and repeating each word five times. The words repeated here were not found in the Hindi primer.

Anand learned to read.
He learned to read.
Anand learned to read books.
He learned to read books.
Anand learned to read good books.
He learned to read good books.
Anand was wise.
He was a wise man.

Anand was good.
He was a good man.
Anand said to his wife:
"These are good books.
The things in these books are good."
Anand's wife was good.
She was a good wife.
Anand read to his wife.
He read the good books to his wife.
Anand said to his wife:
"We will do these things.
We will do these good things."
Anand's wife said:
"Yes, we will do these things.
We will do these good things.
We will do the good things in these books."
Anand was wise.
Anand's wife was wise.

We carried our new primer and *Anand the Wise Man* back to New Delhi, and showed them to Mr. Humayun Kabir, the director of education. He was charmed by Phil Gray's new charts, with their lovely colors, and agreed that they ought to be on the walls of all the villages in India. He was agreeably impressed by the useful material we had put in *Anand the Wise Man*.

We took our primer to Calcutta and had it printed beautifully by the Baptist Press. It is now the most used literacy primer in India—more used, in fact, many times over, than all others put together.

We went to Katpadi, in Madras State, which we found tortured by a terrible famine. They had not had a good monsoon rain for five years, and the water table had gone down thirty feet. Farming had ceased; not a single field was under cultivation. Fifty per cent of the people had left the area in a desperate search for food, and thousands of them lay along the roads dying of starvation. When we arrived, three-fourths of the trees had withered and died for want of water.

Here was a perfect scene for Communist agitators. There were a great number of them among the people, promising both food and water if they came into power. Here was ghastly proof, before our very eyes, that the lack of water was one of India's chief problems, and that unless this was solved India might go Communist.

Jack de Valois, the head of the Katpadi Agricultural Institute, had suffered with the rest of the people. Half of his beautiful fruit trees were already withered and dying. He had kept men digging down, down, down, day after day, to find the receding water table, and thus had been able to save half of his trees and most of his magnificent goats and cattle. But the unfortunate illiterate villagers lacked both money and machinery for saving their animals and trees, and so they faced nothing but starvation. We saw long lines of men, women and children coming to the mission for half a cup of "meals for millions" mixed with water, and that was the only barrier between them and death. It was a horrible sight—spindling legs, thin arms, protruding ribs, sunken cheeks and deep, bloodshot red eyes.

Jack de Valois was desperate. He wanted to invite experts to come to India from Texas because in western Texas they employed the techniques learned in drilling deep wells for oil, and had thus been able to reclaim great areas of waterless land. We talked also about the possibility of harnessing the sun's rays. At that time the temperature was running as high as 110° in the shade every day. Some day, when we care as much about saving the human race as we now care about getting ready for a war to annihilate the human race, our scientists will take the salt out of the ocean and pour great rivers over parched India and over the deserts of Arabia and the Sahara. With one-tenth of the money we now spend on the military we could make the deserts blossom like the rose.

Twenty-five delegates, who believed that we must help illiterate people to help themselves, met at Katpadi and worked in the terrific heat to write Tamil and Telugu versions of *Anand the Wise Man*. These have since been printed and are now in use in south India, bringing new hope to the despairing, hungry multitudes.

We must not leave the impression that water is the only important pressing problem in south India. Equally important is a fair distribution of the land. Three-fourths of the people have no land of their own and would still be destitute even if water were plentiful. Everyone in Katpadi was talking about the Indian saint, Vinoba Bhave, who was then walking through India, persuading each landowner to donate a part of his land to the poor. The success of this saintly *sadhu* was great, beyond all belief. In six months he walked 900 miles and was given

300,000 acres of land. Today, he is the greatest landowner in the world, for it is proving easier to get the land than to redistribute it wisely. Almost no landowner in southern India had dared to refuse Bhave, because the desperate people were ready to kill the landowners and take the land for themselves. Nehru himself had given Bhave part of his land. Like Saint Francis, Vinoba Bhave went about penniless, barefoot, always walking. He never rode in an automobile or a train or even an oxcart. Thus he identified himself with the poorest peasant, and they adored him.

From this sickening scene of starvation in Madras, we flew back to Bombay. Because of the terrific heat, there were enormous heat waves rising all over the land, and our airplane bobbed up and down, like a cork on rough water. Perhaps it was not dangerous, but it was a ride I do not care to repeat.

Meanwhile, a new movement to lift India out of her poverty had been launched by the Congress government. It was called the "Economic Development Plan." The Indian government, American Point IV, and the Ford Foundation were pooling their resources to provide the money. Horace Holmes was an American farm agent who had gained renown by doubling the production on one estate called Itawah in northern India, and he had been employed by the Indian government to teach his method all over India.

It is interesting to note that he had borrowed his ideas from the pioneering experiments of Dr. William Wiser at Marehra, where we had just been making our lessons.

Horace Holmes was excited about the charts and lessons we made at Marehra, and had the large charts photographed to show to the government. The government then ordered 3,000 copies of our primer and asked me for the names of Indians who were able to teach them properly. I was able to give them the names of sixty Indians who had been teaching the method—all of them Christians.

On April 20, 1952, the leaders of Point IV in India sent a telegram to their headquarters in Washington, D. C., saying that they wanted me to assume responsibility for the literacy part of the Village Development Project. It was agreed that we should return to India under the contract made between the United States government and

World Literacy, Incorporated. Our plan was to complete our work between July 15, 1952, and January 15, 1953.

World Literacy, Incorporated, had been organized that very year to contact governments like India. In fact, this new corporation came into being because each year more and more governments had been calling for our help. The World Literacy and Christian Literature Committee of the National Council of Churches felt that there would be greater freedom if these governments could deal with an organization that was not church-related. Thus the trustees of Lit-Lit created this non-sectarian World Literacy, Incorporated, so that the separation of church and state might be complete.

Because the call of these governments was in the nature of pioneering and because I was the pioneer going from country to country, I was loaned by Lit-Lit to work for World Literacy, Incorporated. And it was with this new organization that the contract with the United States government to work in India was consummated, to begin on July 15, 1952.

CHAPTER 23

1952: PAKISTAN, MALAYA AND THE PHILIPPINES

Pakistan

We had three months before this Point IV program in India was to begin, so we went up to Pakistan where we spent two weeks in April. During the first week we joined a literacy institute at Raiwind, with nearly 100 delegates. The Reverend Earl Rugg had built a beautiful school at Raiwind, where previously there had been nothing but desert, and here he was doing one of the finest jobs as a missionary that I have seen in many years.

The heat was terrible, but our 100 delegates were filled with enthusiasm and seemed never to get tired. The Indians have become immunized to heat, and never complain even when we are near nervous prostration. We made a revision of the Urdu literacy primer and of the Punjabi primer at the same time. Phil Gray made breathtakingly beautiful pictures for our phonetic charts, and everyone was enraptured. We trained those 100 delegates to go back to their homes and organize their congregations into teaching armies, with the motto "Each One Teach One and Win One to Jesus."

We spent the second week at Raiwind studying the question of writing follow-up books for new literates. Every year it becomes more clear that unless we have such books, literacy is valueless and can even lay us open to subversive or demoralizing literature. And so we made long lists of the books that needed to be printed and started several delegates on the way to writing these follow-up books.

When our conference closed at the end of two weeks, we loved one another enough to weep at being separated. We had been away from Raiwind only one week when we learned that our Christlike Earl Rugg had been burned to death while trying to light his kerosene refrigerator. The kerosene did not work, and so he had been mixing it with gasoline. He had done it many times, but he tried it once too often.

The big problem in Pakistan, as in all of Asia, was to find women who could write helpful and interesting books and magazines for newly literate women. At Kinnard Girls College in Lahore, we tried to train the girls to do this writing, but we did not make much headway because we faced an almost insurmountable obstacle in the crowded curriculum. The government of Pakistan laid out the curriculum every college had to follow. It was overloaded and lopsided; almost all of it was cultural. There was no effort to teach the practical subjects, like home-making or cooking or child care or journalism or stenography or typing. Following the Asiatic idea, these girls were being educated to live like princesses without doing a stroke of work.

The principal of the college was as unhappy as I was about this overloaded program, but he was compelled to prepare the girls for examinations sent out from the Central Bureau of Education. We found education throughout the Orient unrelated to life, except the life of idle luxury, which only princes were able to live. We also found many educators ready to revolt, because this impractical curriculum crowded out everything else, including literacy. The minister of education said, "Frankly, we have been disappointed with our results in literacy, and we appeal to you to tell us what to do. We need your help."

The Pakistan government was indeed trying to do one of the most difficult things in the world. The people of Pakistan speak Punjabi—even the most educated men speak Punjabi to their families. And yet the Pakistan government was trying to teach illiterates Urdu!—although the illiterates knew almost nothing of this language. It was as difficult as though they had undertaken to teach English to the Pakistan illiterates. This difficulty was compounded in Pakistan by the fact that the government insisted upon using the Arabic alphabet, with a dozen special letters added for the peculiar Urdu sounds. This Arabic alphabet is terribly difficult for people who have never read anything. Every letter has at least three different shapes—one for the beginning, one for the end, one in the middle of a word; and one letter has twelve different shapes! One must identify many of these letters by a mere dot.

So it was pathetic and frustrating to meet these desperate educators. When we showed them Phil Gray's attractive charts they were overjoyed and wanted lessons as quickly as possible.

Some of the missionaries in Pakistan had the courage to teach Punjabi with Roman letters, and they found that it was child's play. The trouble was that, after the people had been taught to read, there was almost nothing printed in Roman Punjabi for them. In addition, these missionaries faced government opposition and the constant threat of being deported because the government wanted only Urdu with Arabic letters. Every Moslem believes that Arabic letters are sacred.

These heroic missionaries kept on fighting for their convictions, in spite of every threat and discouragement. If you want to find the true successes of the early church that was founded on the blood of martyrs, you have to go out to these remote areas where the missionaries are still fighting. In Pakistan it was a battle of alphabets.

The longer I engage in literacy the more I am amazed at the stupidity of us all in clinging to difficult orthography and difficult alphabets. We in America are just as foolish as they are in Pakistan. We forge chains of difficulty about our own necks and about those of our children that impede their progress in school and our own efficiency through life and cost billions of wasted hours and billions of dollars we cannot afford to lose. The English-speaking world deserves the booby prize (we do not even have the excuse that our alphabet is sacred); but the users of Arabic are a close second.

Malaya

Leaving Pakistan in May 1952, we returned to America by way of Singapore and Malaya. My family and the Grays remained in Singapore while I paid a return visit to Kuala Lumpur, the capital of Malaya. The year before I had stayed in the home of Sir Henry Gurney. Now he was dead, killed by Communist bandits while on a tour of inspection. The murder had stirred all England. The British government sent one of its foremost generals, Sir Gerald Templar, who had commanded British troops in Germany during the Second World War. Sir Gerald acted with vigor and thoroughness. He immediately removed half a million Chinese from the villages near the Communist-infested jungles, and built new villages for them near the seacoast. These villages were surrounded with barb and a heavy guard. The soldiers explained that this was not to keep the Chinese in, but to keep the bandits out.

The government took us forty miles from Kuala Lumpur to a region where the bandits were constantly causing trouble. We were preceded by an armored car with four soldiers ready for instant action. Fortunately we had no violence during that trip.

Sir Gerald Templar was enthusiastically outspoken in his praise of literacy and of our mission work in Malaya. He said he believed the only hope of Malaya was, not military suppression, but conversion of the people to Christianity. I was present when the Reverend Mr. Teilmann of the Methodist Mission told Sir Gerald that a law existed which forbade American doctors from practicing in British countries, and this prevented the missions from bringing in medical missionaries to those refugee villages. Sir Gerald replied like a flash, "That's a foolish law! You get the doctors here and by the time they arrive the law will be changed." He made good his promise, and now any American doctor can practice in those villages.

Eighty per cent of the people of Singapore and 90 per cent of the people of Malaya are Chinese, who have migrated from China during the past thousand years. However, on the east coast of Malaya there is a strip of land where 90 per cent of the people are still Malay. Very few of these are Communist sympathizers. The government sent us over to Kota Bahru, the largest city in that part of Malaya. These Malay people have the same language as the people in the Philippine Islands, and it was extremely easy for us to make lessons. In fact, they were almost the same lessons we had made in Singapore.

The educators were dumbfounded to find that I knew more about making lessons in their language than they did. We told them how our work had begun in the Philippine Islands, and that those people were their first cousins. Never shall I forget the enthusiasm, and warm-heartedness of their love for us.

We mimeographed the lessons and started to teach eighty illiterates, while 150 schoolteachers who had been released from their classes looked on and learned how to teach. By the end of the week all of those illiterates had completed our primer, and were able to pronounce every word in their language—something no one can do in the English language after a lifetime of study—no, not even in Harvard! The secret of the success of these eighty illiterates was that their language had only sixteen letters, and only one sound for each letter.

On graduation day, the prime minister invited the teachers and the new literates to his magnificent palace. Here, the crown prince presented diplomas to the new literates, in person. The prince then made a speech, in which he said that this was one of the greatest occasions in the history of Kota Bahru. It is probably the first and last time these literates will come that close to their prince and it was unquestionably the greatest event in the lives of the teachers and of the literates. They would be telling their grandchildren about it as long as they lived.

As we were leaving Kuala Lumpur to return to Singapore, the American consul and other American and British officers thanked us over and over again for what we were doing for freedom. The Reverend Mr. Teilmann told us that he had never seen Malaya so excited about anything else. I am happy to say that this excitement has never subsided. As I write these words, the latest report has arrived from Malaya stating that this year 50,000 people have learned to read and that 10,000 are being taught by radio.

One of the leaders who traveled with me through Malaya was a young graduate of the American University in Beirut. His praise of that institution was so great that I could hardly wait to tell its president and my Princeton classmate, Bayard Dodge. Bayard had been this young man's teacher.

The American University in Beirut has had an enormous influence throughout all of the Orient. It is more responsible for the intellectual and political awakening of Asia than any other single institution.

Philippines

From Singapore we flew to the Philippine Islands, and this proved to be the grand climax of the year 1952. We were greeted in Manila by eight telegrams and many letters from Mindanao, saying, "Welcome; come back home. We love you." At the airport there was a crowd of old friends, newspaper reporters and camera men, trying to get between us and our friends so they could write a long story for their papers. Next morning, they had published two columns.

The superintendents of schools from all the provinces of the Philippines had been called to Manila to meet us. The Philippine government was proud of the fact that the Philippine method of teaching illiterates had spread to almost every country of the world. The next morning we met with the heads of the department of education and the superintendents of schools, who had come from every province to discuss adult education. It was such a homecoming as we had never had in all our years in the Philippines.

Every morning and every afternoon for five hours a day, we held literacy conferences with the superintendents of schools, making lessons along the new pattern we had learned from our travels around the world. Our lessons had undergone a great evolution since we left the Philippines in 1941.

We were greatly surprised at the stupendous recovery that Manila had made from war's destruction in the five short years since our last visit. In 1947 Manila had been the most sickening sight that had ever met our eyes. But in the intervening five years the University buildings had been repaired or torn down, and three-fourths of the residences of Manila had been rebuilt—almost as beautifully as before the war. This had been made possible by the vast war damages paid by the United States government to the Philippines. This American generosity was also part of the explanation of the warm reception we received when we reached Manila. One can always tell when our government is popular.

There was a new spirit of optimism and progress in every Filipino.

They are "go-getters" in the best sense of the word. Everyone seemed young, healthy, friendly, vibrant, and full of laughter.

Bishop Proculo Rodriguez had become the leading literacy expert of the Philippines. He had come up from Mindanao to participate in this revamping of the lessons for the southern Philippines. My heart was filled with gladness for Proculo Rodriguez because when I had met him in Surigao in 1915, he was a boy just out of high school looking for a job and I persuaded him to go into the ministry.

A large part of the success of this visit must be credited to Miss Doris Hess, a Methodist missionary who was promoting literacy. She had been one of the first graduates in the School of Journalism at Syracuse University, where my son Bob was a professor. She took us to the printing plant of the United States Information Service in Manila, the best equipped press in the whole Far East. Mr. Earl Wilson, who headed the USIS, offered to print lessons for us in every language of the Orient.

One result of this visit to the Philippines was the publication of a simple newspaper in several of their main dialects. In English this paper is called *The Light of the Philippines.* It is written simply enough so that new literates can understand it.

This return to the Philippines was especially joyous to me, because 27 years before (in 1925) I had printed a book called *People of the Philippines.* In that book I had made a daring prophecy. I had written that the Philippines was destined to become the example of democracy for the Orient. "Perhaps," I had written, "the success of the Philippines may become a factor in settling the fate of the world."

That sentence had brought guffaws from many Americans when the book first appeared. One American newspaper had talked about my "fantastic exaggeration." But now, in 1952, the Philippines with all their defects were beginning to fulfil my prophecy of twenty-seven years before, and what I had said was becoming a reality.

As I write, the Philippines are even more truly the model of Christian democracy for Asia than they were in the year 1952. Every American knows the name of Carlos Romulo, former president of the Assembly of the United Nations and now one of its leading delegates. He is a good illustration of the progressiveness and brilliance of Filipinos.

I believe that the importance of the Philippine Islands as a beach-head of democracy will increase as the years go by. Right now, World Neighbors has a school in the Philippines to train village workers, and is inviting nationals from all over the Far East to come to this school and be trained, so that they can return to their own countries with literacy, agriculture and the other skills their illiterate peoples so sorely need.

CHAPTER 24

1952: WITH POINT IV IN INDIA

MRS. LAUBACH AND I returned to the United States in June 1952 and remained five weeks. We then returned to India to begin our work with the Indian government, preparing literacy lessons for the Village Development Project. The American and Indian representatives who met us at a large reception said, "This is probably the most important assignment you have ever had."

They were right. India, with the largest population outside the iron curtain, is fighting a crucial battle of ideology that may determine the fate of the world. The fate of India hung largely on the success of the Village Development Project. The masses of India were determined to come up out of their destitution. They would come up rapidly by way of "know-how and peace" or they would come up by the bloody revolutionary path of communism.

James Michener, the famous newspaper correspondent, said: "India is of inestimable importance to the world—the second largest nation, the key to the Indian Ocean, and the best remaining link between the Western world and the mainland of Asia . . . If I were directed to spend the rest of my life overseas, doing what I could to help America, I should not need a moment to choose. I would go to India."

The government's plan was to train young Indians to do everything that a village needed to have done; these especially trained young men would go down to the villages, live among the people, and show them how to help themselves. Our task was to provide the literacy lessons for this program. We needed a good artist so the government employed Philip Gray. S. K. Day, director of the Village Development Project, declared that he would make literacy the top priority in the list of his objectives.

Each province had to give us a special invitation, for Indians are as jealous of state's rights as we are in America. Thanks to many previous visits to India I am well known, so we received invitations from every province. In fact, we got more invitations than any other branch of the Point IV program. Following these invitations, we went from one province to another, working with educators, to prepare primers in Telugu, Kanarese, Tamil, Malayalam, Marathi, Gujerati, Bengali, Oriya, Punjabi, Urdu, and Assamese—just like the primers we had made in Hindi the year before. Our first few weeks were crowded with flying from city to city and province to province, through all kinds of weather.

Happily, we found a press in Lucknow directed by a wonderful, public-spirited Indian named Chowdry. He was enormously enthusiastic about the Hindi lessons we had made and printed them 10,000 at a time. He also printed *Anand the Wise Man,* but his little press was not equal to the demand that rose beyond all our expectations and constantly exceeded our supply.

While in Lucknow we visited Isabella Thoburn College for Women. Miss Sarah Chakko, principal of the college, was enthusiastic about opening a writer's workshop, and so were her students. The following year Margaret Lee Runbeck, a wonderful story writer, came to Isabella Thoburn College and opened the first course in writing ever given to the women of India. From Lucknow I flew to Bombay to deliver a lecture on literacy in one of their principal colleges. For an hour we flew through clouds and rain, and had one bump so bad that it sent the pantry dishes all over the floor.

I interviewed the *Times* of India, the leading newspaper of Bombay, about printing our colored Hindi charts. I wanted charts large enough to display on the walls of Indian villages. The paper agreed to undertake this task. Later we chose the Fine Arts Press of Bombay, which did about the finest work of this kind that I have ever seen.

On Sunday evening in Bombay I spoke to a large crowd of Hindus about the relationship of food, health and literacy. When I told them that America loves India and admires her as the largest republic in the world today, the applause continued for a whole minute. I was quite astonished, because as a rule the Indians give about three gentle taps with their hands and the applause is ended.

Madam Sayani, a progressive Moslem woman who owned a newspaper of her own, came forward and pledged the whole-hearted cooperation of her newspaper for this campaign. She promised to discontinue using the old classical style in her paper and to attempt to write so that the new literates could understand. Only those who live in the Orient can understand what a daring innovation that was! She risked the danger of losing all her old subscribers because they might consider her paper too "infantile."

From Bombay I flew back to New Delhi, bumping through the rough monsoon all the way because our two-motored plane could not rise above the storm. From New Delhi I was driven by a representative of Point IV to Nilokheri, about seventy-five miles north. Here was a tremendous resettlement program for the Hindus who had fled for their lives from Pakistan during the riots seven years before. Mr. S. K. Day had become famous as director of the local rehabilitation program, and that is why he was made head of the Community Projects Administration for all India. It was amazing to see what new industries and comfortable little homes had been built in Nilokheri for these totally penniless refugees.

We trained fifty of their village workers in the use of our charts. Some of them who had taught the ABC's in the ancient fashion were reluctant to give up what they called the "Indian way" and adopt what they called "foreign style." Fortunately, I was able to tell them that this method had actually been invented at Poona in the province of Bombay. So far as I know, the first "association pictures" to teach Indian letters were introduced by Mr. S. R. Bhagwat, the mayor of Poona, for teaching Marathi. This information won over nearly all of them, and a successful demonstration in teaching illiterates won over the rest.

Some of the delegates at this conference despaired of conquering the immense illiteracy problem and they did not think literacy much mattered. They thought that the illiterates could be taught how to farm by demonstrations, and perhaps by lantern slides, and that they might even be happier if they never knew how to read, for they would not "get big ideas which they could never fulfil." I told them: "Literacy can become the most powerful aid in your program of improving villages. Illiterates are conservative and afraid to try the unknown. Custom is their law. But when they read, they believe everything in print. They do not know that occasionally an inaccuracy slips into print. They believe it, and are willing to try it if they see it in a book. So if we include in our lessons the things we are trying to teach these illiterates, they will believe them and will be eager to cooperate with us. After they read about improved plows and better seeds and fertilizers, they will ask the village worker to help them get these things, and all he will need to do is to say 'yes.' Thus his problem of persuading them is solved. They will ask to do the very things he was intending to persuade them to do."

The Community Projects Administration had the whole of India divided into blocks of 100 villages each. At the center of each block was a Village Development Headquarters where lived an agricultural expert, a health expert, a road building and house building expert, a veterinary expert, and two social workers. This staff kept in constant touch with the multipurpose village workers, who actually went out to the 100 villages and worked in cooperation with the village people. With these experts was the American Point IV man, not as a boss, however, but as a counsellor. This was the setup of the vast Indian Village Program.

The chief defect of this ambitious plan was the lack of trained specialists. The Ford Foundation built thirty schools to train these specialists and at my suggestion later started five more schools to train *literacy* experts to go and work alongside the other experts in these blocks of 100 villages.

There are 250 million Indians over five years of age who are unable to read and write. You may well ask, "What can a few hundred literacy men hope to do with a population of illiterates almost twice as great as the total population of the United States?" The answer is found in our slogan "Each One Teach One." Our literacy experts conducted model campaigns, hoping that others might imitate them and that the eagerness of the masses and the enthusiasm of provincial governments might carry literacy on and on and on to the ends of India.

The first great problem was to provide these centers with charts and primers, and with the kind of simple follow-up reading matter the new literates could understand and enjoy. We saw that within three years they would need two million copies of each textbook in eleven languages. That was the enormous order for all of the presses of India! If, in addition to this campaign for *adults,* the provinces of India decided to use our books for *children* in schools, the number of textbooks in each language would have to be ten or twenty times as great. These were the considerations that kept us gasping, but all of us remembered that an even bigger literacy job had been done in Russia and in China, and that this work *could* and *must be* done in India.

Our most unfortunate handicap was the indifference of the Hindu and Moslem men to the education of their women. The illiteracy of women in India is at least twice as great as that of men. I talked with Mr. Chester Bowles and to Madam Pandit, Mr. Nehru's sister, about this problem. The only school in all India that was really attempting to solve this problem of supplying women teachers was Isabella Thoburn College. But the trouble with that college was that it was made up of the daughters of the highly educated, aristocratic families of India, who had little or no contact with the masses.

How important this problem of the women was may be seen by the fact that in the election in 1950 there were 50 million women voters but only two and a half million of them could write their own names or read the ballots; the rest voted by pictures—a cow for the Congress party, and a hammer and sickle for the Communist party.

Point IV officials permitted me to go to Moradabad and hold a Christian literacy conference for the teachers of illiterates. The government was desperately in need of all the aid it could get from Christian teachers. Christians active in literacy had come to Moradabad from every corner of India. Their deep dedication brought tears to our eyes. We realized that quietly and unknown to the rest of the world, hundreds of Christians had been conducting "each one teach one" literacy programs ever since we visited India in 1935. There was no ballyhoo, but there were really impressive results. These results were revealed by the Indian census, which reported that 36 million more people in India could read in the year 1951 than in the year 1931.

The significance of this can be appreciated only by comparing the figures with the previous twenty years. Between the year 1911 and 1931 there had been an increase of only 5,000,000 new literates, but between 1931 and 1951 the increase was 36,000,000! These figures are accurate. The Indian census is recognized the world over as one of the most careful censuses taken in any country. The reason given by the educators of India for this jump from 5 million to 36 million was the scores of literacy campaigns that took place between 1936 and 1941, and which were never destroyed by the Second World War. Ninety per cent of those 36 million illiterates who learned in India used the method we had helped prepare.

One often sees the statement in print that our literacy methods have resulted in the teaching of "sixty million new literates in the world." That is a pure "guesstimate" because we have never felt we could spend the money needed to make a survey of our results. But I am convinced that this "guesstimate" is far under the truth.

On January 22, 1953, we went to the Delhi airport, but were grounded because of a fog that delayed us for five hours. Prime Minister Nehru was also delayed, and Dick Cortright and I had a long conference with him about the literacy situation. Margaret Lee Runbeck was with us. Nehru was delighted to meet her, and quite excited at her attempts to train women to write for women. He was also excited at our idea of challenging every student in every college to teach at least one illiterate a year.

Another miracle happened that week. Chester Bowles had brought Leigh Danenburg over from Connecticut to India to help solve the problem of cheap literacy publication. Danenburg owned the Bridgeport *Herald* and was printing 50 million comic sections for newspapers all over the United States. He offered the Indian government to print a million copies of our textbooks in each language and in color, delivered in India, for two and one-half cents a copy! He said that his four-cylinder duplex presses would make it possible to print these books and sell them at that price without losing money, and that he would provide any quantity to India without any profit!

I wish that I could report that the Indian government accepted this offer; but Indians burn with as much loyalty to home enterprise as we do in the United States, and the government decided to pay fifteen cents each for home production in preference to two and one-half cents for those produced in America. And so Leigh Danenburg's proposal was rejected.

Point IV now employed Dick Cortright and Betty Mooney, and both of them proved to be exceedingly valuable. Cortright could learn a new language more quickly than anyone I ever met. He was talking with them delightfully and amazingly in a day or two in each new language area.

The most formidable obstacle we were encountering was the reluctance of Indian writers to abandon their difficult classical vocabulary and write with a limited word list understood by the new literates. To them it sounded just as bad as our English might sound if we wrote as Amos and Andy talk. It is more serious in India than it is in the United States because about half of the words printed in newspapers and books are not used by the common villager. Before he can learn to read these books and newspapers, he must acquire this new vocabulary. It was to meet this problem that we brought not only Margaret Lee Runbeck to India, but also Harold Ehrensperger and Professor Roland Wolseley of the School of Journalism of Syracuse University, who started a school for writers at Hislop College in Nagpur. Professors O'Dell and Conger of Indiana University also opened a school of simple journalism at Osmania University in Hyderabad. Dr. and Mrs. Paul Means came to India from the University of Oregon, principally to develop Indian writers.

I wrote to America in January 1953, "We are in the birth pangs of a new Asia. Yesterday, Mr. Nehru spoke to the World Council of Churches in Lucknow. He did not believe in proselytizing, but he begged the church to help India out of her tragic illiteracy and poverty. I pray God that the World Council may grow big enough soon enough for this terrible, wonderful opportunity in India!"

I prepared a little book called *A United Attack on Illiteracy* and sent it to Mr. Nehru. After reading it he gave it to his daughter, and I had a long interview with her about it. Ambassador Bowles also read it, and wrote a note saying, "I enjoyed your report very much.

Would you prepare a somewhat shorter version spelling out the steps which must be taken if the program is to succeed, together with a statement of the techniques which must be used?"

Requests like this were coming in far greater numbers than I was able to meet without a secretary. Two American churches sent Miss Jean Dohse to help us prepare the reports and programs that were needed.

CHAPTER 25

1953: THE BIRTHPLACE OF MAHATMA GANDHI

Rajkot, Literacy House and Literacy Village

Rajkot

IN FEBRUARY 1953 a party of six of us went to Rajkot, in the province of Saurashtra, the most western of all Indian states, and Mahatma Gandhi's home. We visited the high school where Gandhi studied. The people of Saurashtra are exceedingly proud of their fellow citizen, and are more nearly like Gandhi in their viewpoint than the other people of India. Our party consisted of Phil and Ewing Gray and their daughter Jane, Dick Cortright, Margaret Lee Runbeck, Betty Mooney and myself. We all went to the Hindu temple where Gandhi had worshipped, were received with open arms by the Hindu priest, and were thoroughly indoctrinated in Gandhi's ideas. They told us that Gandhi believed:

1. Resist wrong, but always love the man who wrongs you.
2. Never injure another person, but accept the injury yourself.
3. Have compassion for the needy multitude.
4. Give your life—all of it, and die if necessary, for others.

These ideals are taking more and more possession of the Indian people. All of us knew that Gandhi had derived them from the New Testament, but we were too polite to ask the priest if he knew it.

Later, when we described this interesting experience with the priest of that Hindu temple, a missionary told us that Gandhi had done more harm to Christianity in India than any other Indian, because he had persuaded people they could be Christlike without being baptized and without joining the Christian church. When I heard this startling statement I remembered the words of Jesus, "He that is not against Me is for Me." No one has ever dared to say that Gandhi was against Jesus. All of his major convictions came from the New Testament through C. F. Andrews, one of the saintliest missionaries that ever lived. Gandhi read the New Testament and had it by his side every day, all day, until the day of his death; I saw it beside him, myself. Gandhi often said that he would have called himself a Christian, if the Christian nations had not betrayed the Christ they professed to follow. Who can deny that church membership has all too frequently been a cloak for selfishness, and that nearly all of us have found a way to evade the stark uncompromising demands of Jesus? Gandhi never evaded those demands; they carried him to his death, and to immortality! He was killed while trying to reconcile the Hindus and the Moslems, during the great riots.

Through C. F. Andrews and Mahatma Gandhi much of the spirit of Christ has entered Hinduism. The Brahma Samaj, a very Christlike movement within Hinduism, is striving to eliminate all the non-Christian elements from the Hindu religion. This is easer in Hinduism than it would be in any other religion of the world, because Hinduism is nebulous, without any creed, and with no fixed god. They have at least two million gods—some say 50 million—but it is not necessary to believe in any of them.

Professor Robert Hume used to tell his classes that a good Hindu "could believe anything, deny anything, say anything, and do anything, so long as he venerated a cow." But since the days of Gandhi the Hindus have lost their veneration for the cow, and so there is nothing distinctive about Hinduism, except that you were born in a Hindu family. If the Gandhian movement and the Brahma Samaj succeed, Hinduism will end by being as Christlike in its spirit as the best in Christianity.

While some Christian missionaries think this is tragic for the Christian church, others think it is a demonstration of the fact that all Christians are too small for the Lord they profess to follow, and that He is forever reaching out to wherever hungry hearts are willing to receive Him.

We finished making the lessons in Gujerati at Rajkot and returned to Allahabad to hold a conference with the teachers of the United Provinces—all of them Hindus. They helped us prepare a third graded book to follow *Anand the Wise Man*. I have never been with a more brilliant group of educators. Dick Cortright pounded the typewriter while the Indians translated into Hindi the lessons I gave them in English. We used every new word five times. One of the Indians kept score on the blackboard. What amazed me was to see how quickly and accurately Dick Cortright could hear and remember these words.

With these educators we also translated *Anand the Wise Man* into Hindi before sending it to Lucknow to be printed. There they needed to do nothing but transliterate it from Roman letters to Sanskrit letters.

Our team crossed India to the Bengal province and reached Burdwan, about 100 miles north of Calcutta. The school there had been established by the Ford Foundation to train multi-purpose workers. Here we celebrated Independence Day for India, January 26, 1953. The celebration was an event none of us will ever forget. The students sang improvised songs about how the British had come to India, how Indian taxes had increased, and their poverty had grown worse. They sang about how the British had put down every revolt until Gandhi came with his program of non-violence, non-cooperation and love!

They sang how Nehru had been thrown into prison; how the Indian Congress had been created by the leaders who were in prison. They sang how India had remained true to the ideal of loving, passive resistance. They sang about the coming of liberty at the end of the Second World War, about the framing of the constitution, and about the Five Year Plan of the Community Projects Administration that was lifting the terrible load of poverty and ignorance off the backs of the Indian people.

As these boys sang, the tears rolled down their cheeks, and my heart went out to them with a great understanding love. I told them that we Americans, too, became free from England, and that our Independence Day was on July 4. I told them that we glory in their new republic, and I could see the love and understanding and joy beaming in their tear-filled eyes.

Two charming young men came down to India from Nepal to see us. They watched us at work translating *Anand the Wise Man* and then told us that Nepal needed us. The story they gave us of illiteracy in Nepal was so incredible that we thought they must be exaggerating. Nepal, nestled up against the Himalayas, surrounded by mountains and without a single road connecting it with civilization, has for thousands of years not only resisted the invasion of one conqueror after another, but has also resisted the invasion of modern education.

These two boys told us that in District One of east Nepal there were 100,000 people, of whom only three could read! One other person, besides the two young men who had come to see us! These two boys kept saying over and over, "We will work and we will gladly die if we can help our people. If you will show us how to teach them, you will be the saviour of Nepal."

These boys had come to see us because Point IV had agreed to send us if we received an official invitation from the Nepalese government. We told them that we would be glad to go, and they wrote back to their government to invite America to send us. Six months later we went to Nepal.

But I must tell the story of what happened in the meantime. I was very anxious to get Phil Gray's wonderful color charts onto the walls of every village in India. The villagers could learn their letters as they passed these large charts going back and forth to and from their work every day. Then when they began to learn their primers, they would find it much easier.

The Fine Arts Press of Bombay did a perfectly splendid job in making these four-color charts in Hindi, Marathi, Gujerati, Telugu, Tamil, Malayalam, and Kannada. The big problem was the cost. There were 500,000 villages, and each set of charts, usually five or six in number, would cost at least a dollar. That meant at least $500,000 as a minimum charge for printing those charts.

In addition, we had the immense job of placing them in suitable protected spots where the illiterate villagers could see them. I visited the Lever Soap Company in Bombay, which offered to put these charts on the walls of the villages on condition that the company would be permitted to advertise its soap. It seemed to me that nothing could be more perfect, because next to godliness and food, soap was what the villagers needed. But when I proposed this to S. K. Day, the director of the Village Development Project, he said that he did not want to be involved in advertising of any kind. If the government of India were to do it, it would cost about $6,000,000 and this the government was not willing to spend.

The refusal of the government to accept the offer of Leigh Danenburg to print lessons for two and a half cents each, and its refusal to allow Lever Brothers to put these charts on the walls, were two of my greatest disappointments and very serious blows to the literacy of India. Both of them, however, are very understandable. India is going through a period of intense patriotism, and she wants neither printing nor soap from abroad. I suppose, under similar circumstances, the American Congress would have done the same.

Literacy House and Literacy Village

In March 1953 we opened a school at Allahabad to train workers in literacy and simple writing. Mrs. Welthy Fisher came from America to take charge of this school. It was started in a house belonging to the Agricultural Institute, which had been started many years before by Sam Higginbottom and had become the most important agricultural school in India.

The Ford Foundation had given $1,000,000 for an extension program of this Agricultural Institute, where multi-purpose workers were being trained and where 400 villages were being transformed by the Village Development Project. It was in connection with this extension department that we were conducting our literacy center. We trained all the students who were studying in the extension school to become expert teachers of our literacy books. Besides these, scores of other students came to us from the missions in India, from the Gandhi movement, and from many of the provincial governments. About half the students were Hindus or Moslems, and the other half were Christians.

Margaret Lee Runbeck, who had been teaching journalism in Isabella Thoburn College, came to Allahabad and conducted a really wonderful course in simple writing. She told writers how to introduce a villain and a hero and how to keep the reader in suspense. She contributed her genius to the preparation of a new series of stories for *Anand the Wise Man,* and made them highly readable thrillers. She introduced a villain, as well as a hero in every story. Sometimes the villain was a disease like malaria, or Japanese beetles, or drought, or poor seeds.

Everyone in this exciting school was required to write stories. After a story was submitted, we all worked together with a blackboard, so as to introduce only ten new words each day. Each word was repeated five times, and Miss Runbeck helped us put in the excitement.

Every evening the students went out with their flashlights to teach illiterates in three nearby villages. Here, with very dim little oil lamps, or even dimmer candles, men and women would gather on the ground around the teachers. It was a miracle that anyone could see or learn, in that dim light. The reason we held the classes at night was because these men and women had to work hard from sunrise to sunset. They got up at daybreak and worked until seven in the evening. Yet so eager were they for literacy that they came to these classes every night.

When the primer was completed we gave the students an examination, though the lighting was so bad that we were not quite sure whether the students were really reading or whether they had memorized these books by heart. The grand finale of this literacy campaign was "graduation night." Everyone in the village and from neighboring villages attended. You could not see how many people there were, reaching back into the darkness. Thirty persons who had passed the examinations received diplomas. There were many fervent speeches of appreciation. The speech that received the real applause was given by Dick Cortright, who spoke to them in slow, but excellent Hindi. The old chief of the village, who had a long white beard, put his arm around Dick's waist, pointed to his own heart, and then made the final speech of the evening. We had brought a loudspeaker, which blasted the speeches and songs far down the streets. As the thirty graduates came forward to receive their diplomas, a garland was thrown around their necks in true Indian style.

The most heart-touching of all the experiences that evening was to see a number of "untouchable" women come forward for their diplomas and to have a high caste chief throw a garland around their necks, the first and probably the last time in his life that he would touch an outcaste!

There was a puppet show about a man who contracted smallpox because he could not read a health poster that told him to get vaccinated. The smallpox destroyed one of his eyes, and his fiancee refused to marry him because he was so ugly. The moral of the show was obvious. The graduation ceremony ended with gorgeous fireworks provided by the Indian government as a surprise for us all.

The literacy center at Allahabad began to send letters to America, appealing for money to provide Coleman lamps, which would give a light almost as bright as our electric bulbs. The center also appealed for money for a one-foot library, which consisted of 100 booklets in a Standard Oil can containing insect powder to keep out cockroaches, silverfish and white ants. Twenty-five dollars would provide a library, including a Coleman lamp, and a tin trunk of one hundred simple books. Thousands of American people and churches contributed $25 apiece for these libraries, which were given free where the people of a village were learning to read, providing they, themselves, built a library room where they could go and read around the Coleman lamp. It proved to be the kind of gift package people liked to make.

Margaret Lee Runbeck, writing back from India to the World Literacy Committee, told the excitement she felt while working in Allahabad:

> This is just ending one of the most wonderful, exciting, difficult and enriching months I have ever lived. We have written six little books, writing and re-writing fifty of the chapters which our students had written. Welthy Fisher wrote a splendid chapter about community projects. Betty Mooney has been tireless in checking words to make sure we had the right number, and that they were used often enough. It has been a terrific task. I have never in my life written so hard and so much, in such a short time. This project in Allahabad is wonderfully worthwhile. You have grand people here, but they are not miracle workers. Please do not let this wonderful start lapse.

Miss Runbeck was herself such a radiant Christian that she inspired everybody else with her spirit. She was planning to return to this work in 1956 when she died of a malignancy. All who knew her said that she was a beautiful soul, too good for this world.

Literacy House was doing two things: (1) training men and women to use "each one teach one" literacy techniques, and giving them practical experience in teaching villagers; (2) providing a workshop where the students and teachers were writing simple materials for new literates. Under the direction of Betty Mooney, students and teachers examined more than a thousand books that had already been written in various dialects of India, and they rewrote more than a hundred of these in simpler language and printed them in Hindi.

On the staff at Literacy House at that time was the Reverend George Prasad, who was probably the most expert teacher of illiterates in all India. He was constantly called from all directions to train other teachers. It was George Prasad who appeared in the motion picture "Each One Teach One" as the beggar boy who later became the teacher and benefactor of his village. Other members of the faculty were Mr. Comfort Shaw, a graduate of the School of Social Work at Delhi University, and Mr. T. G. Telang, a graduate of the new department of journalism at Hislop College.

Welthy Fisher described a typical year:

> The weather is fiendishly hot. I have never lived through so long a period of heat in my life but it is worth it. In addition to our night classes, we are teaching sixty farmers to read and write in the daytime, since the ground is too dry for them to work in their fields. On our veranda every day, in the blistering hot shade, our sixty trainees are teaching these farmers. Thirty of these trainees are from the Indian government. On our back veranda sits Alfred Moses, a talented Indian artist, illustrating our literacy stories.

Literacy House in Allahabad was the first one of its kind in the world. It was setting a pattern for other countries to follow. Many people, not only from India but also from other countries, including representatives from UNESCO, are making pilgrimages to find out how they also can train teachers and conduct literacy campaigns.

Literacy House continued to grow in importance each year. It soon outgrew the accommodations available at the Agricultural College in

Allahabad. In 1956 it was transferred to Lucknow, and is now called Literacy Village. This was done at the urgent request of the governor of the United Provinces, who pointed out that it was better for the village to be at the capital city of the United Provinces where he could give it his personal assistance, and where it would be accessible by airplane.

Literacy Village has been growing, and it is now the most important literacy center in the whole of India. In 1956 the Indian state governments sent 800 workers, from every province, to be trained in literacy and simple journalism.

CHAPTER 26

1953: IN ASSAM AND NEPAL

On March 30, 1953, the graduation of the class in simple journalism, so far as we know the first in the history of India, took place at Hislop College in Nagpur. Professor Roland Wolseley had started the course the previous June. The purpose of this course was threefold: to make the writing of newspapers and magazines more interesting and comprehensible; to help young men and women learn religious journalism; to prepare simple, useful, interesting material for new literates.

A great handicap at Hislop College was its very inadequate buildings. Though it was Christian it was not a denominational school, and so it would fail to get money from either a denomination or from the Indian government. In my opinion, this college presents an opportunity to help India with a program that is badly neglected.

One permanent result of the effect of Professor Wolseley's year in Hislop College was his writing of a manual for Indian writers, the best manual yet prepared in India for this purpose.

Assam

In April 1953 our team moved to Assam, in the extreme northeast corner of India where India touches Communist China. On the way to Assam we took an excursion to Darjeeling, 7,000 feet above sea level, close up against the tremendous Himalayas. Here we could see two of the highest peaks in the world, Mt. Everest and Kanchenjunga. On the way, our automobile ran into a storm that left three inches of hail on the road. The hailstones were as big as your thumb. Our windows must have been made of good glass and the roof of the car of good steel. The noise of these hailstones as they hit the car was so terrific that no one could hear himself talk.

Then we ran into a fog that looked like milk and had to creep along, hoping that we could stay on the road. We ran into a telegraph post, which was fortunate because there was a precipice 1,000 feet down just behind the post! The Lord takes care of fools, missionaries and children! We finally reached our hotel by wading through hail up to our ankles. The next morning we were rewarded by a wonderful view of Kanchenjunga, which is only 600 feet lower than Mt. Everest. The next day when we went down the mountain, rain had washed the hail away.

When we reached Assam we had a glorious welcome. An excellent committee of Indian educators worked with us at Gauhati University. *Gau* means "cow," and *hati* means "elephant"—so we were at "Cow-elephant University."

The educational attainments of this board of literacy workers was formidable. Dr. Borkakoty was formerly director of education; Dr. Borua was a trained phonetician; Dr. Da Gupta, formerly of the University of California, was a psychologist. But the most brilliant man in the party was Shri Chaudhry, under-secretary of the legislative department of Assam. There were a dozen such top-grade men, who prepared lessons far more rapidly than Phil Gray could draw the pictures. After he had made the first chart, a gathering of Indian educators and a half dozen missionaries came to see the first test with illiterates. The teaching worked like magic, and everyone was not only convinced but thrilled. The Assamese government printed these lessons and has been carrying on a vigorous campaign ever since.

The missionaries of Assam were also enormously interested. Mrs. D. L. Swanson, for many years a missionary in Assam, had retired and was living in America, but she returned to Assam just to make these lessons and to participate in teaching them. It was through Mrs. Swanson's influence that the government had invited us to come. Another missionary, Miss Julia Rose, had come down from the foothills of the Himalayas. We helped her make lessons in the Kabui Naga language. Phil Gray made beautiful pictures for the lessons of both languages.

Nepal

We went from Assam to Nepal, one of the most secluded countries in the world. Arrangements had been made for us to work with Point IV there, and with the Nepalese government. Because there was no road into Nepal from any country we flew over the mountains to Katmandu, the capital.

Between India and Nepal is a great mountain range 10,000 feet high, and between Nepal and Tibet is the mightiest mountain range on earth. In fact, the twenty-nine highest mountain peaks in the world are on the northern boundary of Nepal.

At the head of the Point IV program of the United States government was Mr. Paul Rose. He was a man with a big heart, so democratic that everyone who knew him loved him, and he was a natural born diplomat. He had entree to the king, the royal family, and all the government officials, and they all did almost exactly what he recommended. What he had accomplished in eighteen months was little short of miraculous.

We made our home with Mr. and Mrs. Floyd Dowell, very earnest Christians who had volunteered to go out from America as a direct result of reading my book *Wake Up or Blow Up*. In fact, all of the Point IV men were devout Christians; one Catholic and five Protestants. Their families held Sunday school services just for themselves, since no Nepalese was a Christian.

Nepal had two rival royal families. When one family was in power, the other family took refuge in Paris, leaving their palaces empty. The American Point IV men were able to rent two magnificent palaces for only $300 a month, and these two palaces were large enough for all of the Point IV men, with plenty of room to spare. Some people have criticized Point IV men for being extravagant, but these men were getting their rent for $50 a family—and living in such luxury as few people enjoy in America, as far as the palaces were concerned.

The first day we arrived in Katmandu Paul Rose took me to see the king's advisor for education, General Shamshere. He himself is a prince and his home is another magnificent palace. There are about a dozen such palaces for the two royal families; all the rest of the people of Nepal are wretchedly poor and the illiteracy is somewhere near 98 per cent. All the homes we saw, except the palaces, were shabby, and thousands upon thousands of them were pitifully wretched huts.

At the suggestion of Paul Rose, General Shamshere at once appointed a committee of three men to help make lessons and two other men to help Phil Gray draw the pictures. One of these lesson makers was a well educated ex-teacher named Chakar Das. Another had been brought up from India at my suggestion, Mr. D. B. Sharma. His birthplace was Nepal but he had been an educational officer in Bengal for many years and now was back in Nepal for the first time in forty years.

With this brilliant committee we completed charts and a primer in the Nepalese language in one week and had our Nepalese *Anand the Wise Man* finished within a month. The American agricultural experts gave us splendid help; they selected the subjects to be used in our Anand books. Each of these men prepared digests based upon his knowledge of Nepal's needs, and our committee simplified their materials. I doubt whether any textbooks in the world are better adapted to meet the crucial needs of the people than these books we prepared in India and Nepal with the aid of our Point IV agricultural experts.

Paul Rose was always invited to every royal party and to all the receptions of the Indian and English embassies, and he always took us along with him. I had left my tuxedo in Delhi, little dreaming that I should be plunged into this social whirl in Nepal. But fortunately Floyd Dowell had a tuxedo that exactly fitted me, and he was so unselfish that he stayed home from several parties so that I could go. We did not meet the king because he was ill—he died a few months later. But we met the queen and the princesses and all the members of the royal family who were not in exile.

When Phil Gray had his Nepalese charts ready, General Shamshere arranged for a demonstration to be held in the royal reception hall of his father the king. Here were marvelous chandeliers that rivalled those in Versailles; beautiful rich ornaments, tapestries, pictures; and a magnificent throne for the king.

We had arranged for five illiterates to be brought in for our demonstration, but the guards on the outside refused them entrance until Paul Rose went out and conducted them personally into this hall, the like of which these illiterates had never seen before and I am dead sure will never see again. Here were gathered the king's counsellors, the governors of the states of Nepal, and all the aristocracy of Katmandu. And up in the front seat sat the queen and the king's daughters.

The terror on the face of the young man who was supposed to teach these illiterates in front of this group of celebrities filled me with a lot of compassion, and a little terror myself. He was trembling and hardly able to talk out loud. I watched him for fear he would run away, but by the end of some preliminary speeches about the importance of this occasion the teacher had regained a little of his composure. Fortunately, I had drilled him over and over in exactly what to say until he could have said it in his sleep. It worked! The illiterates learned very rapidly. Indeed, so quickly that several persons suspected a fraud, but Mr. Sharma stood up and convinced them that these five illiterates had been totally illiterate when he had tested them outside, that they had never read a letter or a word before. Then the guests became excited and went forth to tell the city of Katmandu that they had seen a miracle!

Shortly before we left Nepal we attended a farewell party given by the commanding general of the Nepalese army. All the royal family except the sick king were there. Mrs. Laubach and I talked with the crown prince, who is now king of Nepal, and he was profuse in his expressions of gratitude for the great help we had given to the education of his country. The lessons were published at once and now Nepal is the scene of a flourishing literacy campaign.

The American government is now providing money and machinery to help Nepal build a road in from India over tremendous mountains. Up to this time men have found it necessary to carry everything on their backs, including refrigerators, grand pianos, jeeps, and even large automobiles. Lowell Thomas visited Nepal at the inauguration of the new king and has shown in his Cinerama this astonishing way of carrying automobiles over the mountains. There is an overhead trolley from India to Katmandu, but it cannot carry anything heavier than 300 pounds.

When we returned from Nepal we visited one of the Ford schools at Delhi, where men are being trained in literacy. Then we attended a reception given by the new American ambassador, George V. Allen, for Adlai Stevenson. We were pleased to find that both Adlai Stevenson and George Allen were so well acquainted with our literacy work. Even more gratifying was the statement of Mr. S. K. Day, the head of the Community Project Administration, that our series of readers, especially our Anand reader was, to use his own words "Wonderful! Simply wonderful."

CHAPTER 27

1953: THE TEAM LEAVES INDIA

OUR CONTRACT IN India was up and we were leaving with reluctance and much misgiving, for our task was not finished. Our primers had been made, and some of them had been printed, but the campaigns themselves had hardly begun. Phil Gray stayed on to finish the publication of these primers, but unfortunately he fell sick with infectious jaundice and influenza soon after we left and had to return home.

Three Americans were able to remain and they provided continuity for the India program. Welthy Fisher carried her Literacy Village to a very successful finish. Dr. and Mrs. Paul Means did a splendid job in south India in promoting our lessons among the Village Development projects. And Betty Mooney did prodigious work in promoting the writing of follow-up material and the preparation of the one-foot libraries for India.

President Eisenhower has said "there is nothing so futile as regret." And yet one of the regrets of my life is that I did not ask for an extension of my contract and remain in India one or two years longer.

On the way back to America Mrs. Laubach and I visited Rome and found Dr. Anna Lorenzetto, a very highly educated and public-spirited woman, heading an Italian literacy campaign. Her organization was teaching 10,000 students in 500 different classes, chiefly in south Italy where the illiteracy rate is the highest. We prepared lessons with her aid in Italian, and these have been printed and are very beautiful.

At Geneva we had the thrilling experience of eating dinner with Dr. John R. Mott, probably the greatest Protestant leader of the twentieth century. Dr. Mott was still vibrant with his old stupendous vision for a Christian world that had made him the most dynamic religious leader of his time. This was the last time I ever saw him.

When we reached London we were met at the airport at 2 A.M. by Dr. and Mrs. George Appleton. Dr. Appleton is the general secretary of the London headquarters of the International Missionary Council. We had three solid days of conferences with the United Christian Literature Society and various groups of Christian laymen. Sir Alan Lane came to see us about offering a publication for the Penguin book series. This seemed like a call from heaven, because the biggest unsolved riddle we have is how to produce books in vast quantities for the impoverished multitude who cannot afford more than a few cents for a book.

Dick Cortright had remained behind in India to help Point IV carry on literacy work. In September 1953 he returned to America. When he reached Cairo on the way back, the quarantine officer found that he had not had a cholera booster before leaving India. So Dick spent five days behind barbed wire at the airport. Davida Finney and Dr. Elder of the American mission came out to console Dick, but had to talk to him through the barbed wire fence. Dick tells his adventure with a delicious sense of humor, and ends it with these words: "When they finally came to set me free, at the end of five days, I thanked God for freedom."

Dick then went to see the magnificent literacy program being carried on at the village of Hirz, 100 miles south of Cairo. It was a Christian village of about 1,000 inhabitants, and they held a huge festival in honor of literacy while he was there. Hundreds of people received literacy certificates presented by Dick Cortright. Then they took him to a second village called Hur, where again scores of people received certificates. Every Moslem was given a picture of Mr. Naguib, who at that time was prime minister of Egypt.

The Christian students were given *The Story of Jesus* in Arabic. *The Story of Jesus* had been prepared originally in 1944 at the Biblical

Seminary in New York with the aid of Betty Mooney and other workers. Mrs. David Cook of David C. Cook and Company, provided both the pictures and the printing of *The Story of Jesus* and in 1956 her son, Mr. David C. Cook, Jr., reprinted 20,000 copies of a revision of that book. This deed of generosity resulted in *The Story of Jesus* reaching around the world, for it has been printed in ninety languages, and we are hoping that it will ultimately be printed in a hundred more. The first story in this book illustrates how easy it is for new literates:

Lesson One, The Story of Mary

This is the story of Mary,
This is the story of the angel,
This is the story of Jesus.
The angel said to Mary,
Mary you will be a mother.
The angel said to Mary,
Mary you will have a child.
Mary said to the angel,
I have no husband; I cannot be a mother.
Mary said to the angel,
I have no husband; I cannot have a child.
The angel said to Mary,
You have no husband but you can be a mother.
You have no husband but you can have a child.
You have no husband but God will give you a child.
God will give you His child.
God's child will be Jesus.
Jesus will be God's child.
Mary sang, I will be a mother.
Mary sang, I will have a child.
Mary sang, God will give me a child.
Mary sang, God's child will be Jesus.
Jesus will be God's child.
Mary sang and sang and sang and sang.
This is the story of Mary,
This is the story of the angel,
This is the story of Jesus.

Each lesson in *The Story of Jesus* has not more than ten *new* words, and each new word is repeated *five times,* so that it will be remembered by the student. There are ninety lessons covering the entire story of Jesus' life.

In December 1953 Mr. Alfred Moore, executive secretary of the World Literacy Committee, visited India. There he encountered Mr. Steward Meacham, a Methodist missionary, and employed him to make a survey of literacy in India. In this survey Mr. Meacham found that the various state governments were more active in their attack on illiteracy than the missions of India were. This was also true in at least twenty other countries of the world.

In addition to the work that was done in ninety countries by missions, we have worked officially with sixty-four governments in making lessons and starting literacy campaigns. The names of the countries that officially invited us to help their departments of education will be interesting:

Afghanistan
Algeria
Angola
Australia
Basutoland
Belgian Congo
Bolivia
Brazil
British Guiana
Burma
Ceylon
Colombia
Cuba
Dominican Republic
Egypt
Ethiopia
French Cameroons
Ghana
Greece
Guatemala
Haiti
Hawaii
Honduras
India
Indonesia
Iraq
Iran
Italy
Jamaica
Jordan
Kenya
Korea
Lebanon
Liberia
Libya
Malaya
Mexico
Nepal
New Guinea
Nicaragua
Nigeria
Northern Rhodesia
Nyasaland
East Pakistan
West Pakistan
Paraguay
Peru
Philippines
Portugal
Puerto Rico
Singapore
South Africa
Southern Rhodesia
Spain
Sudan
Tanganyika
Thailand
Trinidad
Turkey
Uganda
United States
Venezuela
Vietnam

CHAPTER 28

1954: STREAMLINED ENGLISH

DURING THE SUMMER of 1954 I was in the United States traveling from one missionary training school to another, spending a few days in each school to train missionaries in the proper use of our lessons. We had made primers in 250 languages but the training of missionaries to teach these lessons had lagged far behind. Where missionaries without proper instruction went abroad and tried to teach our lessons they were not successful and they blamed our method instead of blaming the fact that they did not use the method. The chief trouble with their teaching was that they "talked" our lessons to death. The ordinary primers used in schools of America require constant talking on the part of the teacher, but our "each one teach one" textbooks are as nearly self-teaching as we can make them. They require very little talking by the teacher and a maximum of participation by the student. In the ordinary primers the pupils had to be told each word, but in our phonetic method the pupils could pronounce every new word after a week of teaching.

We were convinced that the opposition to our lessons, which we found among many teachers and educational leaders in America, was due to the fact that they did not understand our reasons. We were teaching phonetics from the very beginning, whereas the orthodox method in America was to teach stories, sentences, words, but not letters. Phonetics was out of favor, in spite of the fact that the story method had produced millions of poor readers and tens of millions of poor spellers. During the years 1954 and 1955 I spent many hours with teachers who were going abroad to convince them that it was wrong to use the American word method to teach languages with very regular alphabets, like those in mission countries. Rudolf Flesch came to my rescue with his best seller, *Why Johnny Can't Read*. He brought the wrath of the conservative educators of the United States down upon his head, as all heretics do, but he did not suffer in vain, for the educators of the United States are swinging in ever larger numbers toward the teaching of phonetics, even in English with its lunatic spelling.

We began to establish more and more schools for training foreign missionaries and for those who desire to teach illiterates in this country. Prior to the year 1954 we had only three schools teaching our method: the Kennedy School of Missions in Hartford, Connecticut, where literacy was taught by Professor Maurice J. Hohlfeld; Syracuse University and its extension course at Chautauqua, New York, where my son Robert Laubach was teaching literacy and journalism; and Koinonia Foundation, where Miss Betty Mooney was teaching literacy techniques.

When we decided to establish these courses in other schools we found many of them eager to begin. At Asbury College, Kentucky (Dr. E. Stanley Jones' alma mater), Miss Ruth Fess began a course. At Carver School of Missions in Louisville, Kentucky, Richard Cortright began a course and later established a year-long department of literacy at Baylor University. Courses were subsequently started at San Francisco State College, Upland College in Southern California, Denver University, Biblical Seminary, New York, and at WKNO-TV, Memphis, Tennessee. New ones are springing up in all parts of the country —"each one teach one" has become fashionable.

Besides the out-going missionaries who ought to be taught, there are 48,000 foreign students in the United States each year. All of these foreign students ought to have at least the beginnings of our literacy course, so they will understand its value and be able to participate intelligently when they return to their homeland. If both missionaries and foreign students, qualified to direct "each one teach one" campaigns, scatter around the world, the bottleneck of a scarcity of properly trained teachers will be broken.

The need of literacy in America is also greater than most people suppose. Dr. William Gray, a foremost authority on adult education, says that 10 per cent of the people of the United States are functionally illiterate. That is to say, they do not read well enough to make any valuable use of it. The migrants who came from Puerto Rico and Mexico were more than 50 per cent illiterate.

One day in the summer of 1954 while we were in New York we were visited by a delegation of German Jews. They said, "We came to ask you to make lessons for the Yiddish-speaking people of this city." I then learned that Yiddish is nothing more than the German language written with Hebrew letters. In New York there are two Yiddish newspapers; almost every line they publish contains at least one English word because most of the Jewish people of New York know English as well as they know German. A young woman told me that her mother-in-law spoke Yiddish but could not read it, and she wanted me to prepare lessons so that her mother could read. We made these Yiddish lessons with German words, but then we discovered that New York Jews spoke English better than they spoke German, and they wanted Yiddish lessons using only English words written with the Hebrew alphabet. So we made these lessons and called them "Engliddish."

To our surprise we found that Engliddish had two uses we had never anticipated. In the first place, it turned out to be useful as a means of demonstrating to English-speaking people the value of associating the shape of a letter with a picture. Some of our critics kept insisting that this association was not necessary, that the student could learn without it if he worked a little harder. But when these teachers were confronted with this English lesson written in Hebrew letters they realized how it feels to be illiterate, and they also realized how wonderful it is to have a hook to hang your letters on and so aid your memory. For the first time they understood why our lessons are sometimes called "lightning literacy." By the use of these associations any person with average intelligence can learn the entire Hebrew alphabet in twenty minutes. One minister who had learned Hebrew and had forgotten it, exclaimed after taking one of these lessons, "I learned more about Hebrew from you in twenty minutes than I did in the theological seminary in a year."

Just to show the reader how he can learn one-fourth of the Hebrew alphabet in five minutes, here is the first chart. Start on the right side of the page and read left.

Point to the man's ear; say "ear." The letter to the left of this picture looks like an ear; say "ear." Now run your finger under the word with two letters. The word is ear; say "ear." Now cover the left-hand letter of that word with your finger. The first sound of the word ear is *ee;* say "ee." Say "ee" again, again, again. That finishes the first row.

Now begin with the second row on the right side. Point to the picture of the girl; say "girl." This letter to the left of the girl looks like a girl. See her head and her knees; say "girl." This word with three letters is "girl"; say "girl." Cover all but the first letter. The first sound of girl is *guh;* say "guh," again, again, again.

On the third line is a picture of a dog, with a big head and a long ear; say "dog." Point to the letter left of the dog. This letter looks like the big head and the long ear of a dog; say "dog." Here is the word "dog"; say "dog." Cover all but the right-hand letter. The first sound of dog is *duh;* say "duh," again, again, again.

This is a nose with a bump on it—a baseball hit him. Say "nose." Point to the letter left of nose. This letter looks like a nose with a big bump on it; say "nose." Point to the word nose. Say "nose." Cover all but the letter and say the first letter of "nose" is *nuh;* say "nuh," again, again, again.

This is an open mouth with a finger in front of it. Say "mouth." Point to the letter. This letter looks like an open mouth with a finger in front of it; say "mouth." Point to the word; this word is "mouth"; say "mouth." Cover all letters but the first one. Mouth begins with *muh;* say "muh," again, again, again.

This is a swollen lower lip—a wasp stung her lip; say "lip." This letter looks like a swollen lower lip; say "lip." This word is *lip;* say "lip." Cover the last two letters of the word. Lip begins with *luh;* say "luh," again, again, again.

You have learned six letters; one-fourth of the Hebrew alphabet in less than five minutes. In twenty minutes you could learn it all because the other three charts are just as easy as this one.

We have made lessons with association pictures, similar to these, in more than 100 languages, and all of them are just as easy as that

ENGLIDDISH CHART

shown above. That is why millions of people are finding literacy so easy. It would be just as easy in English, if it were not for our irregular spelling. But even in English, children and older people, by using our Reading Readiness Charts and *Streamlined English* learn to read in a fraction of the time they require when they use other methods.

Another problem to be solved around the world is the shortage of printing presses. Whenever possible we use the commercial presses because we have neither the capital to buy presses nor the skilled men to run them. But we have found that small presses like the multilith or the rotoprint are necessary in areas where there are no commercial presses. Mr. Andre Clerc of Laurenço Marques wrote to us appealing for a printing press for his mission. They had been doing all their printing in Johannesburg, South Africa, a thousand miles away. When I was in Baton Rouge, Louisiana, in 1954 I told the people about the need for this printing press and they sent $1,200. The first dollar came from a young Filipino girl who was studying at an American university. None of it came from people of wealth. It was collected from the working people of Louisiana and they were giving sacrificially. After the press had been purchased the big problem was how to get it into Mozambique despite the opposition of the local Roman Catholic archbishop, previously referred to in Chapter 8. A Swiss merchant, a friend of Mr. Clerc, got it through by importing it as merchandise, and it arrived in five large packing boxes. Because of the inexperience of a poorly educated African helper the machine was soon broken, but it was fortunately repaired. In February 1954 there appeared a sixty-page booklet, the first of its kind ever printed in Mozambique, and this was swiftly followed by primers, new readers, and other material.

Mr. Clerc wrote back to the delighted givers in Louisiana:

> The Laubach method and the printing press are beginning to produce a minor revolution in Mozambique. You would never have suspected when we began that there were so many illiterates right among our Bible students! It is making an enormous difference to them, when they do not have to listen to the preaching of the Gospel for all the religion they can get, but can now read it with their own eyes. This is especially important for the women. Some of their husbands and children know how to read, and their own illiteracy was like a dead weight hung around their necks. As soon as we had lessons ready, 129 women began to read. They are no

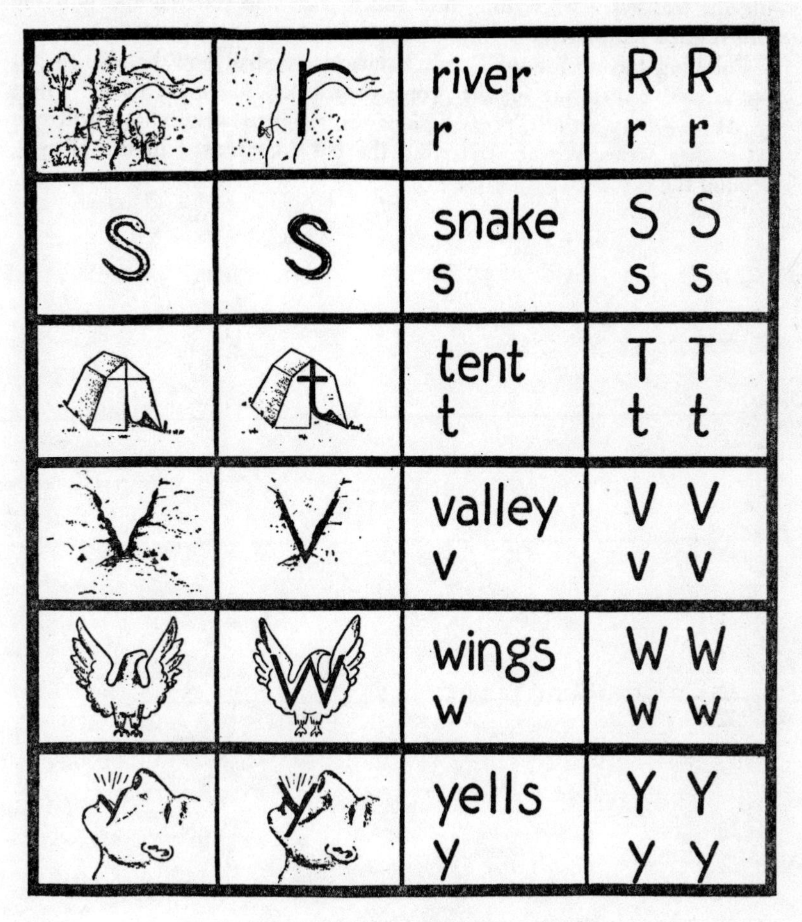

AN ENGLISH READING READINESS CHART

longer isolated human beings who know nothing, but persons who can really help others to know Christ.

The lessons taught in *The Story of Jesus* bear their own fruits. One woman who had read several of these stories said she was ashamed of the life she had led, after reading how much Jesus had suffered and how He had resisted temptation.

Fulfilling the dreams of Frank Laubach, we shall now be able to put out attractive literature for the people themselves. There are many writers in Africa—story writers, poets, visionaries, religious writers. We will edit what they write. We are collecting the old tales recited in the villages, around the evening camp-fires.

CHAPTER 29

1954: LITERACY AND COMMUNISM

IN FEBRUARY 1954 Mr. Garner Hoyt and our artist Phil Gray went to Algiers to help revise literacy lessons and to build graded follow-up books. In every country where we had gone, our material had never reached up to the level of the ordinary newspaper, and it was now necessary for us to build a bridge all the way from illiteracy to the newspaper-reading stage. The definition of "literacy" that we adopted was, "The ability to read a simple newspaper."

Here, as in other countries, the revisionists selected the most useful information for the people of Algiers and incorporated it into the story of *Achmed the Wise Man*. They also employed the art of Margaret Lee Runbeck, building a plot into the story, holding the reader in suspense until the hero sank down and down to the black moment, and then when everything seemed hopeless, having the hero suddenly bring forth the answer that solved his whole dilemma.

The French lessons we prepared on our first visit to Algiers were remade. The French language requires more lessons than most other languages because there are so many groups of letters that stand for a single sound, like *eau* pronounced "o," meaning water. It is necessary to teach every one of these letter clusters. And yet French is not as difficult as English because there are very few exceptions. Once you know that *eau* is "o" there are no exceptions.

English, on the other hand, has a booby trap in almost every word. Here is a foolish phrase, "though a tough cough and hiccough plough through me." There are six different ways to pronounce the letters *ough*.

The French in Algiers were more interested in teaching French than they were in teaching Arabic, because they hoped to assimilate the native population and make them true Frenchmen. There is little racial prejudice and no color bar in France. Several highly educated and influential men of Algiers helped our team prepare the best possible French lessons, and then the French government had them printed.

Iran

When the team reached Teheran the members were invited by the Near East Foundation and the government of Iran to help build lessons geared to the agricultural programs then going on and to such industrial programs as machine repair, irrigation and tree planting. How careful one must be in making lessons is illustrated by some of the pictures Phil Gray made in Iran. He had one picture of a pig and another of a guitar. The Moslems vigorously rejected both of these because both pork and music are forbidden by the Mohammedan religion. Our team included in their lessons in Iran such practical information as "How to spray storage tanks to prevent weevils from eating the grain stored in the tanks," "Why it is better to take a shower bath than to get into an unclean pool," "How to make bread over a sheep manure fire without spoiling the bread," "How to have credit when Mohammedans forbid charging any interest on money."

This functional reader pleased the Iranian government and the Near East Foundation so much that they asked Dr. Hohlfeld to remain for a year. Miss Runbeck joined the team that March and took charge of writing up this material in the most attractive English style. It was then translated by Iranians into the Persian language.

When our team reached India they heard a very shocking report. A young Indian told them that he had been on the train with a Communist who said, "I know the Laubach method well. It is excellent. My job is to follow up his campaign printing Communist propaganda." One encounters people everywhere who fear this will be the result of our literacy campaigns, but we have not yet encountered any Communist literature that we considered very readable. It is cheap and it is written in an easy style but is nearly always as dull as a government bulletin—and that is dull! In fact, it is all printed by the government. Much of it is an attempt to interpret the philosophy of Karl Marx. We in America write so vividly and convincingly—especially our advertisers—that we grip people's attention and sell them articles they do not need and in many cases should not buy. Our trouble is that we are aiming our magnificent literary style at one another instead of trying to use it to help and to save the people in illiterate areas. America has been an introvert, interested in herself and neglecting the world until the two wars, sputniks, threats in Korea, Vietnam and the Near East compelled us to stretch our horizons.

Contacts with Communist literature in various countries convinced the World Literacy and Christian Literature Committee that it must put a larger proportion of its efforts into the writing and printing of Christian books and also books to counteract communism. Much thought was devoted to printing a book called *The Christian's Handbook on Communism*. Since its publication in 1954 this book has been distributed around the world in other languages.

Miss Ruth Ure conducted a nine-month's project in India to find out what the Indian attitude toward communism is. She found that many Indians believe that Christian communism is possible. They say that the first church was Communist, by choice and not by compulsion. Mr. A. K. Thampy, a young Christian in south India, was enthusiastic about bringing communism and Christianity together until he found that he could not remain loyal to the party line and retain his Christian convictions. He found that the Communists believed in resorting to deception, murder and intrigue in a way wholly incompatible with Christian ethics. So he joined a group called the "Christian Institute for the Study of Society" and soon became its director. He circulated more than a dozen pamphlets among Christians to warn them against the illusion that they could be both good Christians and good Communists at the same time.

In India and in all other countries where literacy has been thriving, hundreds of thousands of people are clamoring for something to read. In fact, they will read anything because there is not a page of reading matter in their own language in most of their homes. After they have finished our primer and our graded readers, they come to a jumping-off place. They are still unable to read the difficult, classic language ordinarily used in the newspapers. It became evident that we must find ways to print editions, not of five or ten thousand books, but of fifty or a hundred thousand books. This need grew more insistent in a hundred languages. It became more evident each year that we must train a small army of writers who would be able and willing to write for the new literates in the fascinating style employed in the United States. They had to make the Christian way of life more attractive than the Communists were making their way of life. The battle for men's minds was becoming the battle of the books.

Many missionaries have often appealed for a stronger missionary program around the world on the theory that if they could make the people Christian they would be immunized from communism, but it has not worked out that way. Travancore, now called Kerala, is almost half Christian and it is the only Communist state thus far in India. It has become clear that Christianity stirs up people's ambition and makes them aspire for a more abundant life and that this attracts them to communism unless we have fulfilled those aspirations. In the last few years the best missionary strategists have come to a sharp realization that a missionary program anywhere must not only stir up people's aspirations but also help fulfil them. We see that our lopsided missionary program in the past has made many Christians unhappy by indoctrinating them with Christ's "good news for the poor" without relieving them of hunger or ignorance. One of the greatest missionaries who ever went to China said that he and other missionaries did not know what they were doing, but they were really preparing China for communism by inspiring in them infinite aspirations and through their health program multiplying the number of mouths to be fed, leaving them hungrier for food and also hungrier for a better life. Hindsight is so much more wonderful than foresight! I know of no missionary who understood this fifty years ago, but many of them understand it now.

In 1954 Betty Mooney reported that Literacy House in India had trained 257 teachers and that these teachers had taught 800 nearby villagers to read. These teachers in training had prepared for each village where they had taught the one-foot libraries referred to in Chapter 17. Mr. George V. Allen, at that time American ambassador to India, went to Allahabad for the graduation of these 257 teachers in training and presented the diplomas, not only to the teachers but also to the 800 villagers whom they had taught while in training.

Literacy Village so wound itself round the hearts of teachers in training that they did not want to go back home but rather, to remain in that wonderful atmosphere. Two of these teachers in training, Ravindra Lal and J. D. Mangogher, were so heartbroken at leaving that they petitioned Ambassador Allen not to allow them to go away. A young girl who was herself a Brahman, was so eager to learn to read that she went out and joined a class of outcaste illiterate women. When her father learned of it he beat her for contaminating herself with untouchables, but she went out and joined another group and persisted until she was able to read.

Once a year there is a stupendous pilgrimage of Hindus to the sacred Ganges and Jumna rivers. These two great rivers meet five miles east of Allahabad and here is where millions of people gather each year to bathe in the sacred waters and have their sins forgiven. The name of the place is Kumb Mela. Here one of the leaders from Literacy Village set up a literacy tent. There were probably two million people in that gathering who could not read, and every last one of them wanted to learn. As they tried to push their way into the sacred river to be purified the crush became so great that hundreds of them were drowned, pushed and squeezed and crushed to death by the crowd behind them. This resulted in a horrible stampede. Betty Mooney wrote back:

> This black day will never be forgotten. Although we in Allahabad were not there when the crush occurred, we realized the meaning of it. India on the march, millions of people, tired, hungry, poor, but ready to undergo unspeakable hardships to make their religious pilgrimage. Solemnly we Christians kept asking one another as we ate our meals, "Are we willing to undergo that much sacrifice for our religion? Are we able even for a few hours to forget our food and physical comforts in order to seek the highest we know?"

CHAPTER 30

1954-55: IN PAKISTAN

IN DECEMBER 1954 Mrs. Laubach and I were headed for Pakistan. In Zurich we were joined by Mrs. Elizabeth Baity, wife of the director of the World Health Organization. She went with us to Pakistan to help write about child care, health and home life. In Cairo we picked up Dick and Mabel Cortright and in Karachi we were joined by Phil Gray and Warren Webster.

In Karachi the minister of education was very cooperative. He requested us to make a plan like that we had written for India two years before. The Urdu primer we had made on a previous visit was working well and the ministry of education did not want to change it.

While we were in Karachi six delegates from East Pakistan came to see us. They had traveled 2,000 miles all the way around India by boat to get from East Pakistan to West Pakistan. These two parts of Pakistan are separated by a thousand miles of land; the inaccessible Himalayas on the north and the unfriendly Indians on the south. Travel between these two parts, whether by rail or by road is extremely difficult. The only really practical mode of transportation is by air or by water. These six delegates from East Pakistan had come to beseech us to come over to their country and help them learn to read. They had been sent by the Ansars of East Pakistan, an organization of a quarter of a million young men and women dedicated to the service of their country. Seldom have I been so touched as I was by the earnest appeal of these men.

In Karachi we were staying with Mr. and Mrs. J. Baird. He was the head of Point IV. Through him we had every social courtesy our government could provide. There was a tea party on the lawn of the USIS attended by the aristocracy of Pakistan. In the middle of my speech the lights went out, but it was not my first experience of this kind so I talked twenty minutes in the dark. From that reception Mrs. Laubach and I went over to the home of our American ambassador where a huge reception was being held in honor of his daughter who had just married a prominent Pakistani.

The government adult education authorities took us from one school to another to see how well they were teaching the lessons in our new primer. I had to demonstrate the best way to teach our book in the government training school, in the UNESCO Social Service School and in churches. We had a class of illiterate outcastes in a sweeper colony on the outskirts of the city. The director of education took us to the grave of Jinnah, the first prime minister of Pakistan, and we placed wreaths upon his tomb. We had demonstration classes at the Parsee High School and at an all-Pakistan Women's Association meeting. Mrs. Laubach and Mabel Cortright were as busy as I was those four days.

We went from Karachi to the city of Hyderabad Sindh where the Sindhi language is spoken. A great change had taken place in the attitude of the Sindhi people since 1937 when I first came into contact with them. In 1937 a group of Sindhi merchants told me that their language was not written—only spoken—and they did not allow anyone to learn Sindhi except themselves. But now in 1954 they were eager for help. They had dismissed their schools and had brought all their teachers together at Hyderabad Sindh to help prepare a primer that until then had never been written.

The schoolteachers who had come together to help us worked with incredible zeal and sometimes with such heat that they nearly came to blows. This never worried me for I found it was characteristic of Mohammedans everywhere. They were ready to fight one moment and became excellent friends the next moment—if they survived. While we were preparing those lessons in Sindhi, a conference of Christians from all parts of West Pakistan was studying how to teach the Urdu lessons. The Catholic sisters from a nearby school brought their girls to learn how to teach these lessons. The most enthusiastic person in that city was the principal of the school where we were meeting each day. He was a rare man full of compassion and progressive ideas. Every morning he took down the news from his radio concerning world affairs, copied it on a blackboard, and placed it in front of his school building so that everyone who could read got the news and everyone who could not read wished he might.

Our literacy team moved on to the mission at Montgomery, Pakistan. One hundred and fifty delegates met in freezing cold weather, without any fires, wrapped in every coat and overcoat they could get. We trained everyone in this conference to be letter-perfect in teaching our Urdu charts. We drove out to several villages near Montgomery and tried the lessons and the teachers with illiterates.

One day Dick and Mabel Cortright and Mrs. Laubach and I crowded into an old car to visit an all-Christian village. A tire went flat two miles from the village and we had to walk ingloriously across the fields of rice and sugar cane. But when we reached this village and found 2,000 people waiting for the greatest celebration in the history of that village we forgot all about the hardships on the way.

At the Montgomery conference was a Moslem boy with a horrible facial tumor. He was completely illiterate. No one liked to look at him and no one taught him. But he watched the teachers as they taught other illiterates and one day he came to announce that he was ready to teach. Everybody laughed. But he stood up and taught the first chart perfectly. Everybody said, "Miracle," because two days before he had not known one word. We have since received information that about half of the tumor was removed surgically from his face and that by tying off the blood vessels the doctors were able to shrink the rest of the tumor until his face was almost normal. Now he spends all his time teaching anyone and everyone.

After we left Montgomery, Mrs. Janet B. White, the missionary with whom we stayed, wrote to her own mission board:

> Dr. and Mrs. Laubach and Dick and Mabel Cortright were our Christmas guests and Mrs. Laubach honored us by having her birthday on Christmas.
>
> The local government helped us in many ways. They gave us a large tent for our meetings with three hundred chairs and a squad of men who came every day to clean the premises. The Rotary Club gave a dinner in their

honor and Mrs. Laubach and Mrs. Cortright spoke at the local Women's Club. About 125 delegates, nearly all of them Christians, came to our conference. We have never seen delegates go home from anything more enthusiastic. Dr. Laubach has often described Jesus going about showing compassion and doing good, creating in everybody a longing to do the same. This was motivation at its highest level.

There was a daily training period in the teaching method. Mr. Cortright's charming spirit in this training was much appreciated. One delegate later reporting the conference referred to him and his wife as Mr. and Mrs. "Quite-right."

The local government provided buses for carrying the delegates out to the distant villages, and every day these delegates came back with garlands around their necks and paper flags to express the joy of the villagers.

We all remembered Dr. Laubach's cautious warning to the whole conference that we would not know whether this were a great conference for at least one year. It would depend upon what the delegates did after the conference was over.

It is now six weeks since the conference was finished. We have been out living in tents and touring among the villages. We have put on little Laubach conferences in numerous places and have carried on campaigns in our larger mission schools, training the children so they could go back home and teach their own relatives to read. Illiteracy is very high but in nearly every village we were able to find at least one literate person who was willing to learn the method and to teach the rest. We have been busy providing primers and follow-up books.

We thank God for the tremendous help and inspiration the team has given us.

Janet B. White

When we reached Lahore everyone went to work training teachers to use our lessons properly. Mrs. Laubach and Mabel Cortright showed the women in the Lady McLagen Training College how to teach their 2,000 children. The minister of education beamed with enthusiasm. He wanted us to send somebody to teach the prisoners, who crowded the jails to the breaking point. In America we look down upon prisoners with disapproval, but it is no disgrace to be a prisoner in Asia. In fact any Indian who was not a political prisoner during the years when they were striving for independence from Britain was almost ashamed to admit it.

Dick Cortright and I went to the social service classes at the University of Lahore and trained many students whom we urged to go out to train others. You may wonder whether they actually carried out these instructions. We have never made a scientific survey to answer this question, but the letters that come to us convince us that a large percentage of those whom we have trained continue teaching in their communities without pay, and without ever expecting any glory. The liquidation of illiteracy has become a patriotic duty in the eyes of the educated people of Pakistan.

When I talked to the students at Forman Christian College they sat on the edge of their seats in their eagerness to be shown how to fight illiteracy, which they regarded as enemy number one to the progress of their country.

At the request of the ministry of education we prepared a filmstrip of our Urdu lessons with a script telling what a teacher should say. We were helped in this by the brilliant daughter of Dr. Spencer Hatch, whose name is known to experts in social reconstruction all over the world. The Lahore ministry of education gave us a special letter of thanks for the filmstrip and for the other work we were doing in Pakistan.

From Lahore we took a plane to the frontier city of Peshawar, which is the gateway to Afghanistan. If there is a rougher frontier on this earth I have never seen it. The trainees of the Village Development Project met with us daily to prepare lessons in the Pushtu language. It sounded like a prize fight. Nearly every day we expected someone to get killed. Everyone shouted and everyone disagreed with everyone else. They would fly into a rage at one another and then subside as quickly as they began. Those Pushtu boys were tough! This is the country of the famous Pathans, the notorious robbers who for 2,000 years infested the Khyber Pass. Every day you could see Pathans going through the streets of Peshawar carrying the longest guns in the world. They carry these guns because they have perpetual blood feuds and must be ready to shoot their enemies on sight. I am not quite sure whether we were relieved or disappointed when we heard no shots during our stay in Peshawar.

When at last our rough and tumble sessions were finished, the lessons we had made were as fine as any we had ever done with Arabic letters. The governor of Northwest Frontier Province gave us a special reception and was profuse in his expression of gratitude. He said he wanted literacy campaigns in the prisons (which are always overflowing in Peshawar) and in the industrial mills.

The most unforgettable event during our stay in Peshawar was a visit with the minister of education, Mr. Mian Jafar Shah. He was one of the biggest men in Pakistan, big in weight and in influence. His enthusiasm knew no bounds. He said he had got out of bed with a temperature of a hundred and three and had come to his office just because we were going to be there. He said the thing we were doing was the most important service, in his judgment, ever performed for his province. It is expressions of gratitude and appreciation like this that provide us with our greatest reward.

Leaving Phil Gray to make pictures for these Pushtu lessons, we took a train to a small town called Lalamusa. Here the Ford Foundation had built a few buildings for the village aid trainees of the Pakistan government. Eighty men were in training at this place and we trained every one of them in the use of our lessons. Each afternoon the government brought in twenty-five illiterates from nearby villages and the trainees taught them while we looked on. Dick Cortright spoke to the 1,200 students at Gujrawala College. One of the professors at that college was named Mr. Sidiqui. He had studied journalism at Hislop College under Professor Harold Ehrensperger. Mr. Sidiqui was burning with zeal for the illiterate people of his country. We found that he was translating into Urdu the Anand books, which had been written in India in Hindi letters. It was easy because the Urdu and Hindi languages are almost identical except that the Moslems use Arabic letters to write Urdu and the Hindus use Sanskrit letters to write Hindi.

From Lalamusa we journeyed for four hours on a slow train to Narowal. It was wholly without electric lights. We were met in the rain by a brass band and a company of soldiers and their commanding officers. They were Mohammedans, but with them were many Christians who had come to throw garlands around our necks and to welcome us to their city. Two hundred Christians and twenty Mohammedan officers of the Pakistan army met every day at our conference. They learned to teach with an enthusiasm I have seldom seen equaled anywhere. Here we began to appreciate, perhaps more than ever before, the organizing ability of Samuel Iftikhar, who was with us all during this tour of Pakistan. It was his genius as much as any other one factor that resulted in Christians and Moslems working here in such perfect accord. Sam took Dick and Mabel Cortright with him to visit the village where he was born. In that village Sam is the conquering hero, the greatest man that has ever come out of that village, for now he was working for the Pakistan government! Their great man had come home and he was greeted by sky rockets and fireworks. Sam has since become the Pakistan representative of UNESCO.

On Sunday morning the Narowal church was bulging to the doors with perhaps 500 people. Their excitement ran high as we told them about the literacy drive destined to emancipate their country from ignorance and the poverty that goes with it. At the end of a week we examined 200 delegates to see whether they could teach our lessons properly; nearly all of them passed the examination. In fact, we had twice as many graduates as we expected. We ran out of the diplomas Sam Iftikhar had prepared and had to distribute blank sheets of paper to half of the graduates. This cold page cannot reveal the fervor of that conference. Here is a resolution they gave us, truly expressing the gratitude in their hearts:

January 27, 1955

We, the delegates to the Narowal Adult Literacy Conference held at Mission High School, Narowal, from 21st January 55 to 26th January 55, unanimously express our deep sense of gratitude and resolve a vote of appreciation to the World Literacy Team for the valuable training that they have imparted to about 250 delegates from several Districts of the Punjab.

Your lectures, Dr. Laubach, have been very inspiring and your love for an illiterate and a keen desire to save him from the clutches of the demon of ignorance is catching.

We are in no way less indebted to Mrs. Laubach, who through her personal magnetism has been a source of inspiration to all and especially to our women folk. We also express our heart-felt gratitude to Mr. and Mrs. Cortright. Mr. Cortright for practical demonstration and for practical training in the methods of teaching adults and Mrs. Cortright for her gracious presence and her pleasant ways of talking to lady delegates.

We shall be failing in our duty if we do not express our heart felt gratitude to Mr. S. Iftikhar for his consistent and untiring efforts through which he has mobilized all the official and private resources of the country in organising this literacy campaign. His devotional messages and his practical instructions in the methods of teaching have been very encouraging.

In the end we want to assure Dr. Laubach and his colleagues of our sincerest efforts which we will put forth to fight the greatest enemy known to mankind "The Illiteracy." We have all caught the spirit and the zeal which you have been so keen to engender in us. We shall follow your method of "Each One Teach One" and with the spirit of the Lord to guide us, we shall proceed on and on and will go on adding to the Army that will wage a war against ignorance and illiteracy in our motherland "Pakistan," which is so dear to us and which we all cherish one day to stand high among the Nations of the World.

The war against Illiteracy "ZINDA BAD" and Pakistan "PAINDA-BAD."

Proposed by Safari, Major Saiyid Musa Jafai.

Seconded by Manohar Lal, B.A.B.I. Headmaster, C.M.S. High School Narowal.

CHAPTER 31

1955: TURKEY, EGYPT AND SUDAN

Turkey

ON FEBRUARY 1, 1955, Mrs. Laubach and I found time to visit Turkey for two weeks. The director of education in Istanbul knew that we were coming. In fact he had sent a man to America to invite us to help them. He immediately appointed five men, the best he could provide from Istanbul. They were released from their job as teachers to help us make a new set of lessons in Turkish. Only one of these men, Ahmet Atilgan, was able to speak English. He acted as interpreter for the rest. But despite this handicap they immediately understood what we were doing and we made a splendid set of lessons in just one week. I shall never forget the zeal and the loving spirit with which these men worked. They were working with patriotic fervor for their own country. We took these lessons to Ankara, the capital of Turkey, and showed them to the educational consulate of Turkey and to the minister of education. He was a new minister, extraordinarily gracious and full of enthusiasm for these beautiful lessons, which he promised to have printed at once.

Although the Christian church in Turkey received a near fatal blow from Ataturk when he was dictator twenty years ago, and there are now almost no Turkish Christians, yet the friendliness of all Turks toward America is so wonderful that it would be difficult to exaggerate it. The Turks are more friendly and more loyal to America than any other people on the entire continent of Asia. The reason is not hard to find. To offset Russian influence, our government not only gave Turkey arms but also made every effort to cooperate with Turkey in developing her natural resources—the same great effort that we made to befriend the countries of Latin America. Today Turkey buys more machinery per capita from the United States than any other country in Asia and it is the most prosperous country on the mainland of Asia. If Americans need any proof that compassion pays big returns, they ought to go to Turkey.

While we were riding on the train from Istanbul to Ankara a well-dressed Turkish gentleman pointed out of the window at the fields being plowed with tractors and said: "Until last year, this land was all barren and had never been plowed, but this year it will produce a magnificent crop of wheat. It was American tractors that did that. Turkey owes all her prosperity to America and we love you!"

Egypt

Mrs. Laubach and I went from Turkey to Egypt and were there during the last two weeks of February 1955. At Minia, about a hundred miles south of Cairo, Dr. Davida Finney and Halana Mikhail had organized a Literacy House and were working out from that center to first one village and then another. Halana had helped me make the adult textbooks that the Egyptian government printed in 1947. From that time onward she had been working with Davida Finney in promoting literacy in Egypt. For two years she had worked with the United Nations teaching illiterates and organizing classes. Her first work was among the refugees from Israel who were living on the Gaza strip. After organizing Gaza she moved on to other refugee camps in Lebanon, Bethlehem and the Jordan valley. She and her impassioned colleagues taught 30,000 refugees to read and write. Then a long-standing tubercular lesion in her lung grew worse and sent her to bed for one year. The campaign went on and the United Nations purchased 50,000 copies of the book we had prepared for Egypt in 1947.

But now in 1955 we found Halana Mikhail back in Egypt completely well. She and Davida Finney and a dozen Egyptian Christians were hard at work at Hirz. They had first made a survey of this village of a thousand people. They found that 310 were children under six years of age or else were so old and blind that they could not see. That left 690 persons who were eligible for literacy. By the time we arrived the team had taught 400 of them to read and write. Some of them they found too stupid to learn. Some others were prevented by their husbands who thought that an educated wife would be a nuisance.

The campaign had been going five months when we arrived. The chief secret of its success was the Reverend Mr. Menis and his congregation who gave their time and their money. First of all the church members were taught how to teach the primer expertly to illiterates. These church members in turn trained other people until there were 100 ready to teach. There were five supervisors chosen to direct and to coordinate the campaign. A census was taken of the village, street by street. Each house was numbered for identification—the first time any village of Egypt had ever had its houses numbered! The name of every man and woman who could read was recorded and he or she was trained to teach.

Then the campaign began. The five supervisors each had two streets as their responsibility. They visited the teachers who were under them and ironed out any difficulties encountered with the pupils. Since the primer took about three weeks to teach, a graduation ceremony was held every three weeks. At the first graduation twenty-seven persons received diplomas. The mayor was invited and attended in a skeptical frame of mind. When he heard every one of the graduates read, he was not only convinced but almost hysterical with enthusiasm. Thereafter he attended every one of the graduations and distributed diplomas to 400 graduates. The enthusiasm of the people of the village rose higher and higher. Those who had learned to read went around the town reading what they could and asking the educated people "What is this word? What is this word?" until they had pieced out every word in their books.

The literacy campaign produced a profound change in the outlook of the people. The Christians and Mohammedans had never before worked together but now they cooperated as though they were one religion. They all began to read how other people were doing things and they planned to do the same. For example, they bought a Jersey bull from the agricultural school at Assiut to improve their local breed of cattle. They read about the chicks that Heifers Inc., an American organization, had sent to Egypt from the United States and ordered a large supply. They made a school for their children by walling in a courtyard behind their church; they built a club, a reading room and a library for the Arabic books the mission provided; and they built another room for a nurse and a clinic. These rooms were all made of mud and did not cost a cent. They would look primitive to us who are accustomed to million-dollar church schools but they stood for a tremendous advance in civic pride in the village of Hirz. They bought a "taxi," an American jeep sold to them second-hand for almost nothing. This was almost their only contact with the outside world. The road was horrible beyond all description, punctured with holes two feet deep; but the people began to fill these holes until they had a fairly smooth road. That is what literacy did for their village!

When everyone in Hirz had been taught, the Literacy Committee began a campaign at the village of Gaawir. They trained six supervisors for that campaign, four of them Moslems. The Christians taught illiterates in their church but the Moslems taught one another in a room the Christians rented to them at a cost of $1.50 a month.

Mrs. Laubach and I were present at the graduation ceremony in Gaawir. It was a sight to make the heart sing. A hundred and ninety-four certificates were distributed. Half of the graduates were Christians and half were Moslems. The women were separated from the men by a partition, but we on the platform were able to see both the men and the women. The Christian graduates received New Testaments with their diplomas but the Moslems received books that would help them in their agriculture and homelife. The mayor of Gaawir made a speech in which he said, "Never in the history of Gaawir has there been such wonderful friendship between Moslems and Christians as there has been during this campaign. I never thought that my eyes would behold a sight like this graduation, where Moslems and Christians sit together in one church like brothers and sisters." It was indeed a miracle that the Moslems were willing to go to a Christian church to receive their diplomas.

Then the fanatically zealous church members of Hirz invaded a second village called Diijab, with the same results. Mrs. Laubach and

I arrived just as they were starting another campaign in the town of Manhari with 13,000 inhabitants. When we reached that village on Sunday, February 20th, we were met at the wall of the town by a large crowd that shouted "Hurrah" in a hundred different ways as their hysterical leader led them. It reminded us of a college football game. The cheer leader would utter a short sentence and everybody would repeat the same sentence as loud as he could. The guard shot off guns, which made us jump and nearly broke our ear drums. Impeded by this mob of people and by the rough, narrow, crooked streets, barely wide enough for an automobile to pass, it took us a half hour to travel a half mile to the church. After the church service was over the crowd was bigger than ever as they led us out to the village gate. This noisy, hysterical reception made us two hours late in reaching two more nearby villages, where the people waited patiently until we came.

The following afternoon we returned to Manhari from Minia and settled in a house provided by the wealthiest man of the city. The twelve young men who accompanied Davida Finney and Halana Mikhail from village to village were supervising a campaign. In the afternoon 200 women were teaching 200 other women in the church building or out in the church yard. One of these women, who was carrying one baby in her arms and was soon to have another, had learned the primer in five days. When we arrived she was reading *The Story of Jesus*. It would take her three months to finish the book and then she would be able to read the gospel in Arabic.

That evening we found the church full of men—about 300 of them—each one teaching one. They had worked all day in the fields but no one would suspect it from the enthusiasm they showed for learning. One of these men had finished the primer and *The Story of Jesus* after only one month of study, and he was now reading the Bible. The trouble in Manhari was that there was such a demand on the part of illiterates to learn to read that it was impossible to provide them with enough teachers. They had to wait patiently until some of their friends had been transformed from illiterates to teachers. Mrs. Laubach and I wanted to stay and teach the people of Egypt the rest of our lives. There is only one thing we did not like—flies! The Bible says Moses sent a plague of flies to Egypt—it is a plague they have never been able to get rid of. The Rockefeller Foundation tried to kill the flies with DDT, but these Egyptian flies developed immunity and now they are bigger and more voracious than ever.

On Washington's Birthday, February 22, 1955, as a demonstration for the mayor of Manhari, we held a class for four men who had never read a letter. They learned a whole page like "lightning" and were wreathed in smiles, almost beside themselves with delight. One of them said, "I thought it would take me a hundred years to learn, but here I have taken two lessons in one morning." The mayor was much moved by this miraculous demonstration and by the four men who learned to read.

The next day was graduation, one of the most uproarious hilariously hysterical ceremonies that I have ever seen. Everyone was in the mood for applause and applauded everything that was said. When we began to distribute the 200 diplomas one exuberant young graduate shouted "Hip Hip Hooray!" in Arabic and he made the whole crowd stand up and give three cheers. The next man who came to receive a diploma thought he had to do better, so he turned to the audience and made an impassioned speech. The third recipient of a diploma made a still longer speech. When the pastor of the church took hold of his clothes and tried to stop him he grew angry and wanted to fight the pastor. I turned to Mrs. Laubach and told her, "Take over. I can't control this crowd." So she gave away about 150 diplomas and managed to get her delighted graduates off the stage without any more speeches or "Hip Hip Hoorays." But the noise was so great that very few people noticed when the pastor was pronouncing the benediction as loud as he could.

On the evening of that graduation day they had a strange kind of religious service. A man of fifty-five years who had taken only twenty literacy lessons but who had studied at home a great deal in the meantime, stood up and read the Bible fluently. I felt sure he had it memorized! Eleven other graduates read from the Gospel of Mark.

Then the crowd escorted us to the town gate, shouting incessantly and shooting off guns entirely too near our ears for comfort. When one leader had shouted until he was hoarse, another took over. The old mayor of the city, who sat beside us in our station wagon as we drove through the streets, was trembling with emotion. These polite soft-spoken Egyptians can become tremendously demonstrative when their emotions are aroused. Mohammedans are wonderful friends but I should not want to be their enemies.

Inspired by these remarkable demonstrations seventy-five Christian ministers in Egypt have already requested Davida Finney to open campaigns in their towns. The literacy team has selected 130 villages it plans to teach and to provide with village libraries, clubs, better livestock and schools for the children. Mrs. Laubach and I were in Cairo when twenty ministers came forward at a large conference and said, "We are ready for you to start a campaign in our churches and we pledge you to give five months of our time exclusively to organizing our congregations and leading them in teaching brigades." But they will have to wait their turn because Davida Finney and Halana Mikhail want to take their team of experts with them to make sure that every campaign is organized along correct lines.

On February 25, 1955, just before we left Egypt, Minia Literacy House was formally opened in the presence of a hundred leaders of the churches of Egypt—Roman Catholics, Copts, Episcopalians, Plymouth Brethren, Canadian Holiness, Y.M.C.A. and Y.W.C.A., United Presbyterian, Evangelical Church of Egypt, the Nile Mission Press and the literacy committee of the Near East Christian Council. Also present were the mayors of the towns and villages in which these literacy campaigns had been held, and they were the happiest men in the crowd.

This Egyptian campaign has been going strong ever since. Dr. Floyd Shacklock of the World Literacy and Christian Literature Committee paid another visit to this same area in 1956 and wrote a glowing report about the campaign in the World Literacy news letter. He told how the campaign had moved on to the village of Deir Abu Hinnis. That village, he said, had been torn for many years by a feud between the Protestant and Coptic churches. The literacy campaign had brought them together. In fact, the entire town, Moslems and Christians alike, cooperated in beautiful harmony. In each campaign the literacy team is learning new methods which it applies in succeeding campaigns. Dr. Shacklock says that in this town of Deir Abu Hinnis the eight supervisors kept careful notebooks, listing the names of teachers and of pupils, and recording absences very much as we do in ordinary schools. From these notebooks they could tell how far each student had progressed each day.

Dr. Shacklock attended another graduation ceremony and one elder of the church read the Scripture lesson to prove that he was literate. Then he added, "In *The Story of Saleh* I learn that flies bring germs on their feet and poison the food so that we become sick. We must keep our food clean. In fact, we must clean up our dirty village where the flies are breeding. I also find in *The Story of Saleh* that charms and amulets do not accomplish anything. So give up your charms now that you have learned the secrets in these books."

Dr. Shacklock discovered that literacy makes people eager to try new things. One man who was newly literate was buying a Jersey bull and another was buying chickens. The people were preparing rooms for a clinic and were asking for a Christian nurse to come and help them. "So," said Dr. Shacklock, "literacy has got this ancient village on the move." He told of one big burly farmer who, a few months before, had said he was afraid to enroll for fear he was too old to learn, but who had done so after some persuasion. When graduation came around he was one of the ninety-five who received diplomas. He and the other graduates stooped to kiss Dr. Shacklock's hand and touched their hearts as a gesture of gratitude. On the front seat, sitting side by side, proudly clutching their new certificates, were two men who had once been bitter enemies. Literacy had made them friends.

A splendid literacy campaign has been going on in Egypt ever since 1952. It is supported by a grant from the Committee on World Literacy and Christian Literature of the National Council of Churches of North America. This Committee financed the training of Samuel Habib at Syracuse University and of Miss Marjorie Dye at Hartford Theological Seminary. Since the retirement of Dr. Davida Finney, they have shared the responsibilities of the vigorous campaigns which still continue in the middle of Egypt. In 1957, the Committee on World Literacy and Christian Literature invited Halana Mikhail to tour through America telling the thrilling story of literacy in Egypt. During this visit she was given a well-deserved honorary doctor's degree. In 1959 Dr. Finney was given a citation by the Committee for her distinguished service in the literacy campaign of Egypt.

Sudan

We have jumped ahead a little in order to finish the story of Egypt. Now we will return to the year 1955. In March of that year our literacy team went to Sudan. This country is sharply divided into two classes. In northern Sudan the people are Arabic-speaking Mohammedans. They rule the country, though not more than 10 per cent of them are literate. But that is far better than south Sudan where not more than 1 per cent are literate. The people of south Sudan are naked or nearly naked Negroes with primitive customs and animistic gods. Our team went to the southern part of Sudan to work among these primitive tribes. It is exceedingly hot, being only about five degrees north of the equator.

Juba is the principal town of southern Sudan. There is a government school in Juba with a magnificent young Arab as the principal. He had been teaching these Africans the Arabic language although they were not Arabs. He invited us to visit his school to train his students in teaching our primer. A half dozen old illiterate Arabs who were working around the school premises were brought in to act as guinea pigs so that the students might practice teaching. We could see that the air was electric with excitement, but I did not know what a revolutionary thing I was doing until one of the missionaries who was present told me as we returned home. "This," he said, "was the most astounding sight of my life. Do you realize what you did today?" "No," I said, "I haven't the slightest idea." "Then get ready for a surprise," he said. "The Arabs for centuries swooped down upon these primitive Africans, killed the weaklings and carried the strong men and women away as slaves. Some of that is going on in the southern Sudan to this very day. But today you have asked these children of slaves to teach the old Arabs who no doubt have captured their parents and sold them! Didn't you see the excitement in those boys? Didn't you see the fire in their eyes? Now they see that education is turning the tables. Didn't you see it?"

I had! But I did not realize the fierceness of this feud until months later, when, after we left southern Sudan, a horrible insurrection took place and every Arab who did not escape to northern Sudan was killed, leaving that area temporarily without a government. This insurrection was carefully screened from the newspapers and we would never have known of it if letters from our friends had not informed us. The insurrection has been suppressed but the old hatred between the slavers and the former slave-tribes will not perish for many a year.

While Mrs. Laubach and I were making lessons at Juba in the Bari language the rest of our literacy team made lessons in Moru, Zande, and Nuer in the villages of Mundri and Yambio. Dick Cortright reports an interesting fact common among primitive people. They have trouble recognizing pictures. When they saw the first pictures to illustrate our lessons they thought they were dead men because they were flat—two dimensional—and because the Moru word for pictures is "spirit" or "shadow." Dick Cortright exclaims, "What a truly frightening experience it must have been for them to see ghosts on those pages. Here we learned a lesson: that when making primers for primitive people we must test not only the words but also the effect of the pictures upon them for they do not know how to read pictures until they are taught."

The members of our team parted company in Sudan. Mrs. Laubach and I returned to America. Mrs. Baity went back to her home in Geneva. Phil Gray went for a rhino hunt in Uganda and then traveled on to Hongkong and Korea, making pictures for the missionaries in both of those countries. Dick and Mabel Cortright went to the Philippines where they held conferences with literacy workers from Manila to Mindanao.

CHAPTER 32

1956: NEEDED—MORE WRITERS

As the literacy program expanded around the world it became necessary for us to increase the number of well-trained writers who could prepare primers—a very difficult thing to do—and also to write follow-up literature that would be interesting and helpful and properly graded for new literates.

We have been told by hundreds of people that literacy could be harmful and even dangerous unless the new literates had something to read that would benefit them. The fear was expressed time after time that the Communists would take advantage of our campaigns by pouring in communist literature. We did not need to be told this for it was the most obvious thing in the world and it is on our consciences all the time. In fact, my son Robert has dedicated his life to teaching people to write simple, valuable reading matter because he was obsessed by the conviction that good simple material for new literates is the great unmet need. He was invited in 1953 to teach simple journalism and literacy at Syracuse University in connection with a new department called Religious Journalism. Since 1956 more than twenty schools and colleges in the United States (as noted in Chapter 20) have been teaching simple writing and literacy.

This is a good beginning but far more must be done not only in the United States but especially in foreign countries to prepare writers who will write simply. Especially in Asia there has been a classical style using hundreds of words never used by the illiterate people. When we try to persuade these writers to use a vocabulary understood by the illiterates they nearly always revolt. They say they would be despised if they wrote like that. It has been the custom to impress the reader with as much erudition as possible in the ancient languages of Asia. The writer seems to feel that he must impress his reader with his knowledge of ancient sacred words, words which no illiterate ever heard in his life. So as a rule we have found it necessary to train new writers who have never acquired the habit of using the classical language. This requires a long time and not more than one person in a hundred turns out to be a competent writer. That is true of course in every country including America, for writing requires more creative imagination than most people possess.

It is difficult also to find persons who really understand the village life. Most of the students in the colleges of India come from the cities. The things they write are likely to be uninteresting or valueless to the village people. This is why the writing being carried on in Literacy Village in Lucknow is especially valuable. The students there came from villages themselves and plan to return to the villages as workers. They will be able to try out what they write among the village people where they will live. The Ford Foundation appropriated $70,000 for a journalism building at Literacy Village, Lucknow.

The literature production at Jamia Milia College near Delhi excels any other in India. It covers every type of production, including literature for new literates. It is wholly Indian and aims at the improvement and perpetuation of the best in Indian culture. Though not aimed primarily at the new literates, its contribution to literature suitable for them is important. This may also be said of Santanikitan, the college of the glorious poet Rabindranath Tagore. An entire chapter could be devoted to the contributions of these and many other purely Indian centers of learning. But since neither I nor any of my American associates deserve any credit for what they are accomplishing, it has no proper place in this book on my literacy adventures. I must deny myself the desire to print a thousand titles of books and booklets written in India, because this book is too long.

We have already described the other courses which were established at our initiative at Hislop College, Nagpur, at Osmania University at Hyderabad, and at Isabella Thoburn College in Lucknow.

Writing for new literates is pioneer work. There are no guideposts to follow. The nearest writing in the world to this simple material is published by American newspapers and by the *Reader's Digest,* but this is still far more difficult than writing required by new literates. Some of the popular magazines published in the United States are about the level needed by the new literates, but of course the content of these magazines is almost always useless for them. It may be that we ought to imitate comic books like those now being used to rewrite children's classics. But this entire field is largely uncharted and needs much more exploration. We need many more studies in readability for new literates.

In 1955 Dr. Hohlfeld made a study of the textbooks used in Iran. He found that the Persian primer *How We Can Live Better,* developed by Miss Runbeck and Ann Brink and Mr. Jadidi, was four times as easy for the illiterate to read as another book written for the purpose of helping farmers.

The Committee on World Literacy and Christian Literature has placed ever increasing emphasis on the preparation of simple Christian books. Dr. Shacklock, executive director of Lit-Lit, says: "Men and women who have been kept in ignorance for centuries are demanding something better. Everything depends upon the kind of books they get. They read everything they get their hands on which may be about better farming, better citizenship or home and family life. If they are fed propaganda and lies they will be confused, misled and betrayed. That need not happen. We have the Gospel with its message of God's love of spiritual freedom and of human worth. We know how to write simply for new readers and we know how to teach illiterate adults to read and to help them teach others. Each one teach one is self-propagating. It is 'love thy neighbor in action.' "

In general, two types of literature are being prepared. One type is religious for missions, and the other is functional, for governments. "Functional" literature is useful in everyday life, for making a living or improving one's health or one's standard of living. Examples of the religious literature are *The Story of Jesus* and the *Inspired Letters of the New Testament. The Story of Jesus* is already in print in ninety languages and the *Inspired Letters* are now being translated into several languages. Examples of the functional material that we have written for governments are *Anand the Wise Man, The Story of Saleh* and similar graded books for other countries.

CHAPTER 33

1956: AROUND THE WORLD FOR WORLD LITERACY, INC.

Portugal, Spain, Italy, Libya

From 1946 onward governments in increasing numbers kept requesting our aid in preparing textbooks and follow-up literature. It seemed to the trustees of the Committee on World Literacy and Christian Literature that there ought to be two corporations: one to deal with the missions and churches of the world, and the other to deal with the governments and non-Christian organizations. Accordingly in the year 1952, they organized World Literacy, Incorporated. This new corporation contracted with the United States government to help literacy in India. It was under that contract that our literacy team worked while preparing lessons in eleven Indian languages. These are the lessons now being used almost wholly by the Community Projects Administration throughout India as they seek to make the people literate. World Literacy, Incorporated sponsored and financed the Literacy House in Allahabad, now known as Literacy Village and located at Lucknow. It also financed the literacy program of Judge Hugh Bivar in East Pakistan.

In 1956 World Literacy, Incorporated received a gift of $10,000 from a woman with a world vision. She requested that it be used for a survey tour around the world to study literacy needs. Dick Cortright and I made the trip. We had been invited by thirty-five governments to come and hold conferences or prepare lessons in their countries, but we were able to visit only twenty-one of these countries that year.

Portugal

The first was Portugal. A tremendous change had taken place in that country since I visited it eight years previously. When in 1948 I interviewed a leading official in Portugal he replied bluntly, "We do not want any more literate people than we have. Literacy gives people ambitious ideas they cannot fulfil and then they create trouble." That is the way officials felt in Portugal in 1948, but during the subsequent eight years Portugal had turned a complete somersault and on my second visit was eager for literacy. Portugal was not the only country that reversed its opinion. Almost every country in Asia and Africa has become deeply concerned about its illiterate people. Twenty years ago they all thought that illiteracy and hunger could continue alongside prosperity, but by the year 1956 they had all become convinced that illiteracy was the cause of poverty and that poverty was the cause of communism. They were frightened at communist inroads and clamoring for any method to save their people from violent revolution.

Dr. John Tucker, the most influential missionary diplomat of Portugal, wrote to us in 1955:

> A great literacy campaign sponsored by the Ministry of Education is going on here in Portugal. Night schools have sprung up all over the country and there is much enthusiasm. The government has decreed that only those who are literate may occupy lucrative posts. Your visit in 1948 awakened interest, and in my opinion, much of the credit for the present campaign is due to your former visit.

I do not know how much influence my first visit had, but I do know that very often one plants seeds in the most unpromising soil, sometimes even in the midst of hostility, and a few years later these seeds break out of the ground and yield great harvest. One often hears the saying quoted that in the field of education it requires twenty-five years for a new idea to be accepted.

It was in response to Dr. Tucker's letter that we were in Portugal in February 1956. We found that this campaign was indeed vigorous! The ministry of education wanted more books like the Anand series from India, even though the Portuguese themselves had written and printed 200 different titles to be used by new literates. The enthusiasm of the under-secretary of education as he told us about the progress and hopes of Portugal was something I shall never forget. The minister of education requested us to send an expert to Portugal to help them conduct their campaign in the most scientific fashion. But alas, this was only one of twenty such requests and we did not have the experts in sufficient numbers to meet those needs.

Spain

We went to Spain at the invitation of the minister of education. We had never been invited before. Spain was beginning to feel the sting of criticism because her illiteracy was about 50 per cent. General Franco had ordered the ministry of education to get going with the campaign. They wanted help from us in doing four things: (1) providing them with a good, easy Spanish primer for adult illiterates (they were delighted with the primer we had made in Algiers in 1951), (2) they wanted us to prepare a graded series in Spanish like *Anand the Wise Man,* (3) they wanted us to send a man to Syracuse University to learn our literacy techniques, and (4) they wanted us to establish a School of Literacy and Simple Journalism in Madrid. This greatly astonished us for we had supposed that Spain was utterly indifferent to literacy, and I felt weak in the knees, for where could we find the men and money for these needs?

Italy

From Spain Dick Cortright and I flew to Italy, again at the invitation of the Italian government. We found Miss Louise Wood of American Friends Service Committee overflowing with enthusiasm for the Italian literacy campaign. We visited the headquarters of the National Union for the Battle Against Illiteracy, which is waging a literacy fight in the mountains of southern Italy where 40 per cent of the people are illiterate.

We found the assistant director of adult education alive with optimism and eager for bigger and better literacy campaigns. He told us he had heard a great deal about the Laubach method and wanted to give it a thorough test in Italy. The Anand reader made a tremendous hit with him. He asked us to help or send someone to Italy to help them set up a truly scientific literacy campaign. His secretary, a vivacious and attractive young woman, exhausted her English vocabulary as she tried to express the great love Italians have for us Americans.

Dick Cortright was a delightful companion on this trip. He always hunted up the most interesting restaurants and took me to a different one every meal. I shall never forget Alfredo's Restaurant, famous the world over for its spaghetti. Alfredo himself comes to your table and mixes the steaming hot spaghetti with cheese and spices until it makes the most delicious mixture one can possibly imagine. On the walls of the restaurant were pictures and autographs of the world's great men and beautiful actresses. Among them were Dwight Eisenhower and several Hollywood stars.

I do not know whether I dare leave Italy without going into raptures about St. Peter's and the Coloseum, but we had seen all of these before. There is just one other spot in Rome I think I shall long remember. It is the dungeon dug out of black rock where St. Paul was supposed to have spent his last months before being thrown to the lions. He was let down through a hole about a yard in diameter. The dungeon itself was about ten feet in diameter and ten feet deep. At one end is an ancient post with a rusty iron ring where his feet were chained and another iron ring where his hands were chained. A stairway has been chiselled out of the solid rock so that visitors can now go to the bottom and see the posts and the rings and the ancient Roman lamp. This is where Paul may have written some of his prison letters. Seldom in all history have we had such an illustration of a Christian soul vanquishing tragedy with his glorious faith. To me, that was more meaningful than all the glory—and the "gory"—of ancient Rome.

As Dick Cortright and I left Italy, Dick was full of exclamation marks. The English language was scraped to the bottom and he had to invent a few new words to express his emotions, "Gorgeous! Exciting! Dramatic! What an opportunity for literizers!"

Libya

We flew to Tripoli, which we had previously visited in 1951 (Chapter 10).

The most exciting experience Dick Cortright and I had on our 1956 visit was meeting Mr. Hussein Moagzaran, the head of UNESCO in Libya. He was an Indian, and before coming to Libya for UNESCO had taught our lessons in one of the tribal languages of India; he was therefore an enthusiastic rooter for the Laubach method. He carried a supply of the lessons we prepared in 1951 into an area called the Fezzan, in the heart of the Sahara, where 20,000 nomadic Arabs lived in tents. Mr. Moagzaran taught hundreds of these nomads to read with our books. It was this long thorough trial that made him one of the most convinced protagonists of our method in all of UNESCO. He wanted us to prepare the entire graded series. A talented woman named Mrs. Bahia Gulick, a member of the American Point IV, stood ready to make this series of lessons and welcomed our suggestions about how to write a useful secret in every lesson.

We needed technical advice about hygiene and sanitation so I proposed to them that they call into consultation Dr. Patrick McCarthy of the North African Christian Mission. Nothing in this whole trip gave me a greater sense of satisfaction than to bring him and Point IV together. Libya is a fanatically Mohammedan country and this North African Christian Mission has operated in seclusion in the narrow streets of the old walled city under almost unbearable restrictions. The mission is not permitted to sell Bibles or to hold any open meetings, though it can carry on its clinic and tiny hospital without being molested. Now Dr. McCarthy for the first time was able to help prepare lessons for the government of Libya to use! It was a triumph that gave me great satisfaction.

These missionaries who are willing to go and bury themselves where they are subjected to perpetual persecution, as they are in many countries, touch my heart more than anyone else in the world. I cannot understand the self-sacrifice and devotion that leads them to these fields, but I can admire and marvel. And long after I leave them they still haunt me. Those two missionary men with their wives are still secluded in terrible heat and almost intolerable persecution behind the mud walls of ancient Tripoli. Only God understands and appreciates that.

Dick and I went to the Wheelus Air Base of the United States government. It is a veritable American city with every comfort and every attraction any soldier could possibly desire to keep him from getting homesick. How many men they had there was a secret, but I should guess it was 10,000. We told the head chaplain of Wheelus Air Base that we had been to the Pentagon in Washington after our 1951 visit to the field and had found the educational committee of the Armed Forces interested in training soldiers stationed abroad to teach illiterates. We had suggested that Wheelus Air Base would be a good place to begin. Miss Anita Ayala, a teacher of English, volunteered with enthusiasm to train any soldiers who desired to teach Arabic. I do not know why that program has not yet been carried out, for it seems to me that our armed forces scattered across Africa and Asia could do boundless good and make thousands of friends if they taught the people to read. The Pentagon is definitely interested in the idea and it may materialize before this book is printed.

CHAPTER 34

1956: BIRTH PANGS IN THE NEAR EAST

Greece, Turkey, Lebanon, Jordan, Egypt, Sudan

Greece

DICK CORTRIGHT AND I flew to Athens on March 9, 1956. We arrived just when the island of Cyprus was in ferment and there was danger of a war between Greece and Turkey. That evening we were attending a meeting at which one of the archbishops was present. He was called to the telephone in the middle of our meeting and informed that Archbishop Makarios had just been exiled to the Seychelles Islands. Our meeting was in a turmoil. It seemed to the people there that this meant war with Turkey and with England. As we went home that night the streets were crowded with mobs who were shouting every imprecation in the Greek dictionary against the British and hurling stones into the windows of the Hotel Britannica. We thanked God we were in another hotel.

But we did not let this war atmosphere interfere with our work. The Greek ministry of education appointed two extremely competent Greek women, Dr. Estella Xeflouda of the University of Michigan and Dr. Antonakaka of Columbia University to help prepare these lessons along our "each one teach one" lines. Dr. Kyrios, a cultured gentleman, also from Columbia University, helped us part of the time. These assistants were so brilliant that they had selected all the words we needed for our pictures in the first forenoon. Then Dr. Xeflouda started making pictures for these lessons. In three days all the primer and half the pictures were completed. Large charts were prepared by the USIS. As always everywhere, the United States government gave us every possible cooperation. On the fourth day we took our charts to a rural school where 150 teachers had gathered to watch us experiment with three illiterate women. These women learned with the greatest ease and with deep emotion. When we had finished teaching them the applause was thunderous. Those 150 Greek teachers had taken us to their hearts and the three professors trained in America who had helped us make the lessons were overjoyed. We made a second reader following the lines we had used in other countries, filled with secrets that Greek illiterate men and women needed. As we flew away from Greece Dick Cortright said: "Wow! The cooperation of the American government was enough to make you weep for joy."

Turkey

We went from Greece to Istanbul, which we had visited in 1955. Our reception was like heaven—in spite of the fact that we reached the air terminal through a driving snow storm. On the way from the airport our bus got stuck on a muddy unsurfaced road and we finally came into the city by another route. This was our firsthand proof that Turkey does indeed need the roads she is building with American money. As we drove through the streets of Istanbul and saw more old buildings than we ever saw in any city, we realized what an enormous task of rebuilding still remains to be done. That is the feeling one has all over the Near East, all over Asia, all over Africa . . . the almost paralyzing magnitude of the task to be accomplished.

It was the lovely reception by Ahmet Atilgan which reminded us of heaven. Mr. Atilgan had been the head of the committee which in 1955 helped us prepare the literacy primer. The printing of the primer had been delayed, due to the appointment of a new minister of education and failure of the government to provide the necessary money.

It is difficult to exaggerate the sweetness of Atilgan's nature. Although, like all Turks, he had had next to no direct Christian training, he has every quality one could expect to find in a saint. I said to Dick, "I love that man" and Dick replied, "So do I. He's a darling."

From Istanbul Dick and I took the train to Ankara. We were also delighted by the cordial reception we received at the American Embassy. They told us that we were doing one of the most important good neighbor projects in the world. We saw the American Turkish Cultural Center, a school conducted by the American government. It is teaching 1,700 students to speak English and it has another thousand on the waiting list! The English teacher told us, "All of them hope to go to America some day."

There is an enormous madness in Turkey to learn the English language. Indeed, we found this same madness wherever we went. Educators were eager for copies of our *Streamlined English* because they said they needed phonetics and could not get a good system of phonetics in any other book.

The American cultural affairs officer arranged for us to see the Turkish president of the educational council, Bey Kadri Yorukoglu. He called in two of his assistants who were deeply interested and they asked many questions about the Laubach method. Mr. Yorukoglu said that they had been told that our method and the story method were different, that they had sent a man to America to study this question in 1955, and that they were anxious for an explanation. I told him that we had met this gentleman and that his invitation was one of the reasons for our coming to Turkey. We invited the minister of education to send people over to America to be trained in our method and he promised to do so. In 1957 Nurettin Sezerkan was sent by the Turkish government with a scholarship to study Laubach literacy methods in the United States, and while here he prepared a new revision of our literacy lessons.

On March 13, 1956, the entire Turkish council of education was assembled from all parts of the country and discussed plans that seemed certain to make Turkey completely literate. The council showed me a graded series of books on which it had been working. The first ten of these books it hoped would be off the press within two months. I cannot find words to express the warmth of friendship we felt while among those Turkish people. In my notes I find this sentence, "Thus ended what may be the most fruitful visit we have yet had on this tour."

Lebanon

From Turkey we flew to the island of Cyprus on March 21, 1956. Again we were in an atmosphere of fear. On the airfield as we landed stood a British plane that had been blown up the night before, and we heard that two British soldiers had been killed that morning. Military curfew had settled over the beautiful island, and no civilians were allowed to visit the airport. "We prayed for peace as we boarded our plane. Suddenly our spirits were lifted. The sun began to shine; the Lebanese stewardess offered us a Coca-Cola. We landed in Beirut, the cross-roads capital of the Middle East. We had entered a new world." In those graphic words Dick Cortright described our entrance to Beirut.

We spent two days interviewing the heads of the many organizations that have their headquarters at Beirut. We found the director of United Nations tremendously concerned about the 750,000 Arab refugees who had fled from Israel and were now living in camps along the Mediterranean, the Jordan river, Bethlehem, the Gaza strip and elsewhere. He said that almost all of the refugees were unwilling to leave the camps because they still hoped that Israel would be overthrown and that they would be able to return to their homes in Palestine. Nearly all of them are idle, eating the food (seven cents' worth a day) provided for them by the United Nations at a cost of $20 million a year, and griping perpetually—who wouldn't! They were whispering among themselves that communism would some day come and liberate them. The director thought that these people could be bribed to go to Iraq and take up government land where a vast irrigation project was under way. He said that he thought that for $2,500 per family it would be possible to provide a home and working animals and farm implements and seeds and enough food to last the family one year. Assuming that there are 100,000 families to be resettled, the total cost of this resettlement project would be $2.5 billion. He thought that an investment of that size would be one of the greatest contributions toward peace that the world had ever made. I asked him if those refugees would be willing to go to Iraq. He said: "Supposing a man drove up in a Cadillac to the refugee camp at Bethlehem and said, 'I will give you a free ride to Iraq and show you the home and the implements, the animals, the seeds and the food you will get without any cost and twenty acres of land that will be yours if you want to stay. But if, after seeing it, you prefer to return to Bethlehem, we will bring you back without any obligation to you,' do you think," asked the director of United Nations, "that very many families would refuse such an offer?"

Jordan

Dick Cortright and I flew on to the Jerusalem airport where we were met by Graham Leonard, who was carrying on our literacy program among the refugees in Jordan while acting as chaplain in the Quaker School at Ramallah.

Mr. Khalil was also at the airport to meet us. He was in charge of the Palestine branch of UNRWA. These two men were working hand and hand with the Jordan government to teach the illiterate adults in the refugee colonies. Bad as those camps are, there is one redeeming feature—every child of the refugees was in school and had a good teacher! Indeed, one of the Jordanese teachers told me that because of these refugees, Jordan has a larger percentage of children in school than any other country on the mainland of Asia—13 per cent of the population. The saturation point for schools in any country is supposed to be 15 per cent of the population, so Jordan has almost reached the ideal in school attendance.

Graham Leonard was a dynamo of energy. He had prepared a bone-breaking program for us. We had to make speeches in the schools and to hold interviews with literacy teachers, educational leaders and government officials. Every hour of the day and evening was occupied.

Testing illiterates in four camps showed us that the literacy classes were going well and that many people were learning to read. This program was begun in 1950 when Halana Mikhail headed the literacy campaign among the refugees. Although she was compelled for health reasons to quit and return to Egypt, her campaign has never stopped. It is a truly "each one teach one" campaign, for most of the teaching is done without any pay. We were especially delighted to see boys and girls teaching older men and women.

Within sight of the ancient ruins of Jericho is the largest refugee camp in Jordan. It had 10,000 people. There we visited a literacy school. The tears filled our eyes as we saw how eagerly old men and women were learning to read. While we were teaching two illiterate men, one of them as old as myself burst out into hysteria and trembled with joy, talking in Arabic so vehemently that we had to stop the class. If I had had my choice I would have stopped in that camp and spent the rest of my life teaching those dear old men.

Something very unusual happened while we were in that camp—it rained! They told us that sometimes it does not rain for a year, but while we were there it seemed to be trying to make up for lost time. But Dick Cortright was expecting a baby in his family so he did not allow the rain to prevent him from driving seven miles down a muddy road to the Jordan, to get a bottle of holy water to baptize their first baby when it should arrive. Richard Junior is now two years old and he will always have the satisfaction of being baptized with the holy (if very muddy) water from the Jordan river.

We drove over to the ruins of the ancient city of Jericho. It is now a mound from fifty to a hundred feet above the rest of the country. We could not climb up to the city because the pouring rain had converted the mound into mud. It is said that twenty-six cities have been built one upon another, every one of them built of clay! If the walls of Jericho were built of the mud we saw that day it is not hard to believe that Joshua could shake them down with a blast of trumpets.

The most memorable experience of our whole trip in Jericho was a visit to the spot where the famous Dead Sea scrolls have been discovered in recent years. Here we saw the monastery of the Essenes, a religious order thriving in the days of Jesus. We saw the big tanks in which they immersed their believers. We also saw three of the caves in which the scrolls had been buried when they anticipated the coming of the Romans about A.D. 70. New caves and new scrolls are being discovered by the Bedouins every year.

Fortunately for us, two first-class archeologists were living with Graham Leonard. They took us to the museum the Rockefellers have built for studying and preserving these Dead Sea scrolls. Mary Gray knows more about Nabataean, the language spoken in the famous ancient and mysterious city of Petra, than anyone else in the world. She herself had visited the site, which can be reached only through a narrow gorge between almost impassable mountains. It is said that this city had 70,000 inhabitants before the Romans captured it by a clever subterfuge. Long after that it was the refuge of Ali Baba and his forty thieves.

The experience that touched our hearts most while we were in Jerusalem was a visit to the tomb in the Garden of Gethsemane outside the walls of Jerusalem. Many Protestants believe that this was the tomb from which Jesus was resurrected. Here on March 20, 1956, a few days before Easter, twenty-five missionaries and other Christians sat on chairs and benches facing the empty tomb while I read to them the story of the risen Lord meeting Mary Magdalene, perhaps on the very spot where they were sitting. We entered the tomb where the Lord may have lain for two nights, and stood in reverent silence gazing at the place where His body may have come to life.

Egypt

The next day Dick and I flew to Cairo where more exciting experiences awaited us. It was Friday. Egyptians are Mohammedans and Friday is their Sabbath. That Friday noon we heard the Moslems chanting their call to prayer from the high minarets of Cairo and I wrote in my notes, "That call makes me homesick for the days twenty-five years before when I went every Friday to the mosque in Mindanao and prayed with the Moslems. I feel more like praying now than writing this report."

I wanted desperately to visit the literacy team a hundred miles up the Nile but there had been a heavy rainfall just before we reached Cairo and some of the railroad up the Nile valley had been washed away. In spite of this flood I took the train southward to see whether I could get through. There were buses running the few miles around the broken railroad track, so it was possible to get to Minia the same day. Here I learned that the literacy campaign was going on thirty miles farther up the Nile on the opposite bank of the river. We ferried across the famous Nile at a point where they told us Cleopatra had once entertained Cæsar. On the east bank of the river was the village of Deir Abu Hinnes where the literacy team was carrying on its campaign. A delegation met me at the river's edge and escorted me to the home the village headman had set aside for Davida Finney, Halana Mikhail and a dozen Egyptian workers who were cooperating with them to direct the village campaign. It was a delightful experience but all too brief. I had time only to visit the pastor of the Protestant church who took me to visit the pastor of the Coptic church. Formerly, these men had been hostile but literacy had made them warm friends. The entire town was working together in wonderful cooperation.

Upon returning to Cairo I found that we had to make some swift changes in our plans. We had been invited to Arabia and Yemen but found that there was no regular airplane service to Yemen. It looked as though we might waste a month getting transportation to that remote country. And a letter had come from Arabia saying that it was inconvenient for them to work with us at that time. Our government had just refused to send a consignment of military equipment to Arabia, and relations between the two governments for the moment were strained. This was no doubt the reason why they had cancelled their invitation for us to come. Meanwhile a very urgent invitation had arrived from Iran. We decided to go to Sudan, Ethiopia, Kenya, and Iran and to omit Yemen.

Dick and I were called to the UNESCO offices in Cairo. The director general of UNESCO, Dr. Luther Evans, had sent a contract over from Paris that he wanted me to sign. The contract said I would remain in Egypt and work with the UNESCO officials at Sirs al Layyan, the beautiful UNESCO experimental center fifty miles north of Cairo. UNESCO wanted to try a control experiment comparing the Laubach method with the story method and wanted me to stay as long as necessary to complete that experiment. I was very reluctant to refuse UNESCO, but on the other hand it seemed impossible to break faith with World Literacy, Incorporated. I suggested they ask Halana Mikhail to come to Sirs al Layyan. She visited them and offered to stay six weeks, but this was not satisfactory to UNESCO and so the control experiment has never been tried. Perhaps both Halana and I did wrong, because UNESCO is enormously influential all over the world.

The relation between our own government and Egypt was not very cordial while we were there. The American embassy suggested that we visit the Egyptian officials as private citizens without any aid from our government. Dick and I had a most delightful visit with Mr. Naguib Hashim, the under-secretary of education who had been in Washington D. C., five years before. He was profuse in his appreciation of the work I had done for Egypt in making literacy lessons. Then we visited Dr. Hasan Hussein, the head of the permanent council of public welfare. His cordiality could not have been greater. He insisted on taking us to see the "liberated lands." When King Farouk abdicated, his land was confiscated and divided into small farms for the landless fellahin of Egypt. Each family had been given a home, animals, tools, seeds and food enough to last for one year. They had the advice of expert agriculturalists to make sure that their methods were the best. "This," said Dr. Hussein, "is the finest project in rural reconstruction in the whole wide world. We want you to see it because we hope to use the Aswan Dam to irrigate a million hectares of land never yet used, and give all that land to our landless peasants, for we have the greatest poverty on the face of this earth. The Aswan Dam will be Nasser's everlasting monument, far greater than the pyramids."

Dick Cortright and I left Egypt with the impression that Nasser and the Egyptian government were burning with a vision of social service as noble as that of Nehru and the Indian government. Whatever anyone says about Nasser's ambitions, I think no one can deny that his sympathy for the hungry masses of Egypt has never been equaled since the days of Joseph.

Sudan

From Cairo Dick Cortright and I flew southward for several hours at 200 miles an hour to reach Khartoum, the capital of Sudan. We caught one of the big British planes that fly from London to Johannesburg and arrived in Khartoum four hours before we were expected.

Following our usual custom we visited the American embassy immediately upon arrival. We found that our embassy was only three weeks old and there was no ambassador. Sudan had become independent on January 1, 1956, only four months before we arrived. The American in charge of our embassy said we must be careful to go through the Sudanese premier as a matter of protocol. We waited a couple of hours but the premier could not be found. I said to Dick, "Let's forget this 'protocol' business. Let's go straight to the ministry of education. We don't need any announcement. They invited us to come." I could see that Dick was scared, but he came along with me. To his amazement—but not to mine—two men greeted us at the door with beaming faces, and threw their arms around me with tender affection. "We were just about to go to the airport and meet you," they said. "How did you get here ahead of schedule?"

We related our flight experience, and they were profuse in their apologies for not being mind readers and for permitting us to go all the way from the airport to the Khartoum Hotel without an escort. They told us that ever since we had left the Sudan in 1955 the campaign had been going fine. They said that masses of people were clamoring for an education and that they thronged the literacy classes. We learned that the latest model of lessons was being used. The textbook followed our suggestions very closely and the people were delighted with it. There was being printed (circulation 7,000) a simple magazine that could be read after our primer. They were eager to send somebody to Syracuse University to learn simple journalism.

We regretted that we had such a brief visit in Sudan. We had not expected to visit it and had squeezed two days out of our Egyptian visit in order to be there. But after all, Sudan did not need us!

CHAPTER 35

1956: THE NEW ETHIOPIA AND THE NEW KENYA

OUR NEXT COUNTRY, which was also an afterthought, was Ethiopia. I almost dreaded to return to Ethiopia because in 1947 the Coptic priests had compelled the emperor to reject the book we had made at his request. At that time we had reduced the alphabet from 260 symbols to only 35 letters with the approval of the emperor, but after I left the Coptic priests said that the Coptic alphabet is sacred and that it must not be changed one iota. Since the priests make and unmake emperors and are the most powerful people in Ethiopia, Haile Selassie had to submit although he had ordered 10,000 copies published. So now I dreaded meeting him.

But all my fears were groundless. They welcomed us in the ministry of education with open arms. Dr. Ato Zaude Gabre, a very progressive educator who had just returned from New York University, held the position of coordinator of the ministry of education. It seemed certain that he would soon become the minister of education. He told me that he was entranced by our simplified alphabet and by the lessons we had made, and that he was going to get our lessons "out of mothballs" and use them to teach illiterates. It will be interesting to see whether Dr. Gabre can stand up against the Coptic priests or change their minds.

Our most exciting experience in Ethiopia was meeting the American ambassador, the Reverend Joseph W. Simonson. He had been a Lutheran minister before his appointment as ambassador and had heard me speak in Minneapolis. He invited us to his home, had a dinner in our honor and moved heaven and earth to open all the doors we desired to enter. The emperor was out of the city and could not be reached by telephone. I suspect he was ashamed to meet me. But everything else that the heart could desire was accomplished. We met all the departments of Point IV and found that its work in Ethiopia was very effective. There is a wonderful era of goodwill between Ethiopia and America. The director general of education began laying plans to send a man to Syracuse University to be trained in literacy and journalism. This was done the following year.

Another exciting experience in Ethiopia was meeting Mr. Merlin Bishop. In five years this remarkable man had developed a truly splendid Y.M.C.A., all the money coming from Addis Ababa. Mr. Bishop told me that he had formerly been in China, where he had been captured by the Japanese who had tried to extract some secret information from him. When he refused, they put him before a firing squad.

"But," said Mr. Bishop, "I was playing the 'Game with Minutes' which I had learned from your book. I was praying and loving that firing squad every second of the time. Suddenly one soldier gave a shout and rushed at me with a bayonet. I jumped to one side, threw my arms around him and held his gun. When he looked at me I was smiling and praying. He smiled back. So," said Bishop, "my life was saved by your 'Game with Minutes.' "

Kenya

Dick Cortright and I arrived in Kenya in April 1956. This was the first time I had been in Kenya since 1937. The change in the attitude of the British government was startling. When I visited Kenya in 1937 I was not invited to meet the minister of education. The director of education said, "I suppose we shall not be able to refuse the rising demand of the Africans for education much longer." But in 1956, what a contrast! I was welcomed by the minister of education, who said with great enthusiasm, "We want the best literacy expert that you have ever trained to come here and teach the Kikuyus to read and write. We are convinced that the uprising among them was due to our neglect."

I found that this was the opinion of the other British officials with whom I spoke. Mr. J. L. Porter, headmaster of Jeanes School, showed me a report he had written for the United Nations on this point. I said: "The Mau Mau uprising ended the reactionary and restrictive policies of the British and has led to the adoption of democratic ideas of literation and racial cooperation."

This statement was not altogether true. The hunting down of Mau Mau insurrectionists was still going on. Because of the Mau Maus, no Kikuyus were allowed to remain in separate farmhouses as formerly, but were now gathered into villages surrounded by barbed wire and "protected" by soldiers. There was a fort beside every village, always on the alert for a surprise attack. We were taken to one of these Kikuyu reservations and had to get a clearance from a blockhouse full of soldiers before we could enter.

But the British were ashamed of this situation and determined to win the confidence of the Kikuyus by any and every means. In America our newspapers attributed the Mau Mau uprising to the Communist agitators, but in Kenya the government officials were honest in saying that it was the reaction to long continued neglect and to the constant pressure to push the Kikuyus off their land and give it to British farmers.

The new policy was to convince the Kikuyus that they could win their way to equality faster by partnership and cooperation than by violence. The British officials wanted to waste no time in convincing them that this was true. There was great fear of disillusionment, if the people were not guided in campaigns of self-development. In the words of Porter: "The surge toward the new civilization cannot be held back. Go out to meet it! Help African society to find the techniques and skills it needs in order to build its own economy quickly enough."

This statement is so important because it is exactly what is being realized by fifty other countries that are running a race between a new concern for the masses and an unthinkable era of bloodshed. In America our wrath is directed toward communism without realizing that communism itself was the revolt against starvation, just as the French revolution had been a century before.

The educators in Kenya saw this and begged us to help them; they hung on our words, took notes and were delighted when we promised to find someone who could guide them as they attacked the problem of illiteracy. They at once appealed to the United States government. The government offered three American educators, one of whom was a Ph.D., but the British turned them all down and demanded some expert whom I had trained. I recommended Betty Mooney, perhaps the best trained expert in the Laubach method in the world. She was accepted by the British, sent by the American Point IV in 1957, and for two years did a magnificent job in Kenya. She had a thousand Kikuyus in her classes and was writing the kind of books that will help them progress the "know-how" way.

CHAPTER 36

1956: PAKISTAN AND IRAN

Karachi, Iran, Lahore, New Delhi, East Pakistan

Karachi

To RETURN TO our story in 1956, Dick Cortright and I flew from Nairobi to Karachi, the capital of West Pakistan. We were met by Sam Iftikhar who took us at once to see the deputy secretary of education, Mr. Inidad Hussein. Mr. Hussein was fascinated by our proposal to write a graded series of textbooks that would be packed full of useful information. This idea has now been accepted by the United Nations and the senior officer of the United Nations in Karachi offered to put his office at our disposal to help us prepare these lessons.

We went to the American embassy and there met the director of the Ansars of East Pakistan who had come to West Pakistan by air to meet us and urge us to return and see how their Ansar literacy campaign was getting on. We were invited to a dinner for the president of the Pakistan Republic. Both the president and the prime minister of Pakistan were exceedingly cordial and expressed their deep interest in our literacy plans. Equally exciting was the visit to the president of the Women's Clubs of Pakistan. Her name is Begum Tazeen Faridi. She was about to visit America to find out how to educate the women of her own country. As in other Mohammedan countries the education of women had been wholly neglected until recently and 95 per cent of them could not read or write. Begum Faridi was enthusiastic about sending a woman to Syracuse University to be trained in literacy and simple journalism. Here and in other places we found that the high tuition of the American colleges is a big obstacle. The Fulbright scholarships take care of transportation of foreign students to America and return, but they do not provide for their expenses while in this country.

One of the most poignant experiences of our 1956 tour was a visit to the greatest poet in Pakistan, Faiz Jallandhri. I had seen him two nights before reciting one of his poems before a large crowd at the president's reception. Now I came to realize what a noble idealist he was. He told me that his heart was with the underprivileged people. From his lips there flowed bitter condemnation of the exploiting classes of Pakistan, who, he said, were responsible for the terrible condition of the illiterate masses. I loved the man for his vision, his courage and his sympathy for the underdog. He was a Moslem and I a Christian, but our hearts beat as one, at the point of compassion. When shall we discover that the meeting place of the great religions will not be at the point of intellectual agreement about theology, but at the point of heart agreement about compassion for those whom Rabindranath Tagore called "the poorer, the lowliest and the lost"?

Iran

From Karachi we flew to Teheran over the Iranian desert, bumping and rolling in one of the most unpleasant air trips I have ever had. The Iranian airways were so poor and dangerous that until recently Americans had been forbidden to travel on them. They flew small planes that could not get above the boiling hot air rising from the burning deserts. We stopped at a desert town on the border of Iran and waited in the sun for four hours while they took all the baggage out of our plane, let it lie for three hours, then gave it a cursory glance and put it back again. Perhaps they wanted to see if it would blow up in the hot sun. The whole thing could have been done in a half hour. When our plane started off again the heat waves were rising like a rough ocean and half the passengers were losing their meals.

We reached Teheran at sunset and found a large crowd waiting at the airport. A few of those waiting had come to meet us, but the great majority was there to greet members of the Bagdad Pact. A meeting was to be held that week and leaders were coming from all over the Middle East. Not realizing this meeting was to be held, we had not made any hotel reservations. There were no rooms available except in a luxurious and expensive hotel six miles from the city where, we were told, "the big oil men always stay." I am glad we had this experience because the hotel was located at the foot of the magnificent glacier in the mountains north of Teheran—one of the most glorious sights I have ever beheld. Beneath the hotel rushed a mountain torrent from the melting glacier to the city. This water runs through the streets of Teheran in open ditches into which all the refuse is thrown. It is not as unsanitary as it sounds because people drink this water. Sanitary experts insist that the water rushes down through the streets so fast that it kills the germs, but Dick Cortright and I took no chances. That snowcapped mountain is the lifeblood of Teheran and of the beautiful green fields that surround it and feed it. Beyond the reach of the glacial water Iran is largely a desert, but underneath the desert is water. In ancient times tunnels were built for hundreds of miles across the plateau of Iran to carry the glacial water to irrigate the fields. Thousands of these tunnels have fallen into disuse since the days of Persian glory. Now Point IV is helping Iran to restore these tunnels and to put down deep wells. Around these wells the desert is again beginning to "blossom like a rose." Here and all over the Middle East and all over northern Africa one is reminded every hour of the fact that water is among the chief needs of the world. Not a day passed that Dick Cortright or I did not wonder how soon it would be possible to extract the salt from the ocean water and pour it out over those deserts. If that water could be made sweet it would be just as easy to send it to any part of Arabia or the Sahara as it is to build pipelines two thousand miles across Arabia to carry oil.

On Sunday morning we attended the English service in Teheran and met at least twenty missionaries whom we had known either in Teheran or in some other country. There was the Reverend Frank Woodward, Jr., the son of Frank Woodward, who had been our colleague in the Philippine Islands for twenty years. Also, there were Dr. and Mrs. John Elder, who invited us to come to their home instead of staying at the Glacial Hotel six miles away. And there was Dr. Gladys Rutherford who had just driven in from India with her station wagon. It was she who had helped us write all the health lessons for our Indian primer *Anand the Wise Man*. When I asked Dr. Rutherford what kind of road she encountered between India and Iran she replied, in her usual terse way, "Not so good, but it might have been worse." She is the only woman I have ever met who had made that trip. She had two missionary men from India with her. They were planning to continue the long drive all the way to England.

Twice we visited Dr. Mehran, the minister of education; the first visit for an hour and a half alone and the next visit for two hours with his educational council. He said that we had come at a very opportune time because he was on the point of signing a contract for literature to be used in a literacy campaign. The minister took notes during all of the three and a half hours we were with him. He arranged for us to speak to a large gathering of 1,700 teachers who had volunteered to teach illiterates.

We also visited the personal representative of the shah who told us that the shah was dividing his own crown land among the common people, hoping that the landlords would follow his example. Alas, there are very few landlords in Iran with the social vision of their king. Landlords are not only the worst curses in Iran, but also in all Asia and all Africa and most of Latin America.

We visited the offices of the Near East Foundation where we found Dr. Shamsol Molous Mossaheb, a highly cultured woman, engaged in a word study to discover what words were known to the illiterate people and how they differed from the words used in magazines and newspapers. This project had been started by Dr. Hohlfeld the previous year. His work was very much appreciated and he was urged to return to Iran but was not able to do so.

Lahore

Dick Cortright and I flew from Teheran to Lahore on a modern airliner far above the turbulent heat waves from the desert. In Lahore we visited the minister of education, who said that he had risen from the village level himself, that he realized the hardships of poverty and that he wanted easy lessons to help the people to read. He was delighted with our idea of packing each lesson with a useful secret. When he requested us to send someone from America who knew how to organize literacy and we announced that Sam Iftikhar, whom we had trained, was about to join the Department of Education, he was delighted.

Iftikhar took us to see Mr. Wahad, the leading publisher of Lahore and a member of the Commission of the United Nations on Human Rights. He had visited New York three times and Geneva twice. This dynamic man said that just as soon as Iftikhar had the graded material ready he would publish them free as a public service!

New Delhi

From Lahore we went to New Delhi on April 3, 1956. Dr. and Mrs. Paul Means had flown up from southern India to meet us. They were filled with enthusiasm as a result of the response they were getting in the states of south India and assured us that "Literacy in that part of India was going over big." They were using our lessons in Telegu and Tamil, which had been published by the government and sent to southern India, and were hard at work training teachers to use them. Mrs. Welthy Fisher also came to tell us about the progress of her Literacy Village in Lucknow. The government had sent 800 multi-purpose workers to be trained in literacy and writing, and The Ford Foundation had just promised $70,000 to build a special school at Literacy Village for training writers. Some of the leading men of India had agreed to serve on Mrs. Fisher's board of directors. Comfort Shaw was its secretary-general.

Mrs. Fisher was staying at the home of Mr. Thomas Keehn, the representative of Mr. Nelson Rockefeller in India. Mr. Keehn lived on the edge of New Delhi, which is expanding in all directions with incredible rapidity. New homes are being erected by embassies of all the countries of the world. One gains the impression that India, with the second largest population in the world, has aspirations of one day becoming the world's cultural center. Everything the officials said indicated that they believe that they are already leading the world in the paths of peace and reconciliation. The spirit of Mahatma Gandhi still marches on.

The Community Projects Administration is making a heroic effort to lift the masses. The results are tremendous just as the problems are tremendous. In fact, everything in India is on a stupendous scale. The success of this village uplift project is terribly important. It is probably true, as many people say, that as goes India so goes Asia and the world. We ought to be doing far more to help its literacy, for that country contains one-half of all the illiterates of free Asia and one-fourth of all the illiterates in the world.

The most delightful experience in Delhi on this tour was a visit with Mr. Saiyadain, who had become the director of education for all India. He had always been a very warm friend of mine and greeted me like a long-lost brother. He was eager, also, for an American expert whom I had trained to come and take the place of Dr. Means in south India. I told him that there was some thought of establishing a television program for teaching illiterates at Lucknow, and he said this was the most exciting good news of all. He said that if we could harness television to a literacy campaign we might really make India literate.

East Pakistan

Dick Cortright and I went to Calcutta where we were met by Judge Hugh Bivar who had come over from East Pakistan by air. Judge Bivar is the director of our fine literacy program for East Pakistan, with headquarters in Dacca. The Judge escorted us to Dacca and then we began to open our eyes in delighted astonishment. We had never dreamed that Judge Bivar was such an important leader in that state. He took us to visit Governor Fazul Kuq, who threw his arms around Judge Bivar and exclaimed: "Judge, with this literacy campaign you are the hope of East Pakistan!"

I never heard any governor in the whole world go so all-out for literacy as did this governor of East Pakistan. Our opinion of Judge Bivar rose every hour as we went with him from place to place. He took us to the home of Begum Hasmuddin Ahmed, the president of Apwa, a women's organization. This remarkable woman has written two textbooks that are now in use in East Pakistan for beginners in English. She writes poetry, and everything about her corroborated her statement when she said, "I'm in love with life!" Her husband is the minister of Agriculture. When we spoke of someone going to Syracuse to learn simple writing, she said without a moment's hesitation, "I will go myself."

Judge Bivar took us to see the cultural affairs officer of the USIS, Mr. David Garth. Mr. Garth has written sixteen novels. He volunteered to provide Judge Bivar with a first-rate artist to make pictures for the textbooks that their literacy campaign needed, and he promised to try to start a course to train Pakistanis to write interestingly and clearly. David Garth was a good example of the magnificent men who represent the American government and are deeply interested in the welfare of the people.

We were impressed by the unusually great ability of the other fine Americans in Pakistan. Perhaps the most useful of them all was Mr. David Somers. Certainly he was the most useful man to us. He held a huge party in our honor on the lawn outside his house. He invited several hundred villagers who lived near his home to come to the party. We taught them the first lesson in the Bengali language by means of lantern slides prepared by Mr. Somers.

One night Somers took us to a village fifteen miles from Dacca. We walked in pitch darkness for half an hour and one could not help wondering when we might step on a cobra. When we reached the village we found the room packed with people. Patriotic young Ansars were doing the teaching. These Ansars are an organization of 250,000 young men originally organized to help free Pakistan from England. After Pakistan became free the Ansars continued to fight "the other enemies of Pakistan—disease, hunger and ignorance." They pledged themselves to introduce "Each One Teach One" to every family in Pakistan. We attended the second annual meeting of the East Pakistan Adult Education Cooperative Society, which also joined in the fight against illiteracy.

We met Prime Minister Mohammed Ali at a reception, and found him not only interested in our literacy plans but also greatly excited about them. He was also delighted to meet Judge Bivar, whose sincerity and earnestness impressed him greatly. The minister of education was equally enthusiastic. We left East Pakistan feeling certain that a great advance in literacy would take place there, if Judge Bivar could find the resources to carry on his campaign.

CHAPTER 37

1956: BURMA, THAILAND AND VIETNAM

Burma

May 6, 1956, found Dick Cortright and me in Rangoon, Burma. The Burmese government had rejected the Point IV aid of the United States because America was supposed to have aided the army of Chiang Kai-shek in north Burma when it was planning to invade Communist China. The Burmese want to remain neutral. Much as they need American aid, they are unwilling to accept it at the price of taking sides.

The Burmese were very eager for private aid, however, and they invited the Ford Foundation to prepare literature for Burma. Mr. Seth Spaulding of the Ford Foundation was the publications consultant for the Burmese government and he developed a really splendid library and book store.

The government of Burma seemed to us to be shaky and inefficient. In fact, it hardly governed Burma except in and near the city of Rangoon. The railroad running northward from Rangoon was still as unsafe for travelers as it was on our previous visit in 1951. Dick and I visited Pat McCoppin, an old friend from Syracuse University, and her husband U Thaung Win, who was construction engineer on the railroad. They told us about the hazards and excitement of repairing the railroad after the outlaws had left. They said that these rebels were not Communists, just tribal people who hated the Burmese.

We wasted hours upon hours trying to see Burmese officials because they were on the job only three or four hours a day. The telephones were inefficient and the transportation was poor. The minister of education was on a vacation and it seemed to us that his office was also on a vacation. However, U Khin, director of social welfare, came to our hotel and examined a primer we had made at the Baptist mission in 1951. He said it was excellent. One thing that U Khin said was characteristic of highly educated Orientals: "The professors in Oxford and Cambridge remained aloof from politics and did their work superbly. For this we loved them. On the other hand, your American Point IV officials get their hands into politics and try to control us. That we will not have. That is the reason Point IV is no longer with us in Burma."

He said this with such an ingratiating smile that we neither contradicted him nor pushed the subject further. We were delighted that he was so hospitable and that he welcomed our assistance. He was a good illustration of the gentlemen of leisure who now head the Burmese Government. They are as far from the rigid, cruel dictatorship of China and Russia as they could be. Yet, because they are so easy-going, we wondered how Burma could escape the infiltration of the Communists.

In Burma were two delightful American women who perfectly illustrated how American tourists can win friends when their hearts are right. One of these was Dr. Laura Bolton of the University of California. She was gathering religious music from all the religions of the world in the hope of publishing a book. The Buddhist priests were helping her with great enthusiasm. It happened that they were holding an immense Buddhist convention a few miles from Rangoon, so Dr. Bolton was able to gather music from every Buddhist country. She had already visited almost all the countries of Africa and Asia. With her was a pianist named Jacob Feuerring, who had collected instrumental music from all nations. He played the piano before a large spellbound audience in the Rangoon hotel and I agreed with everyone else that it was "out of this world." Dr. Bolton and Jacob Feuerring had discovered the perfect approach to foreign lands. There is nothing the people of the world want so much as to be appreciated for their achievements. In fact they want it even more than they want to be helped.

The most heartwarming experience of our stay in Burma in 1956 was the splendid cooperation of the United States government, which was eager to get back in the good graces of the Burmese at almost any price. Mr. Tony Pia, assistant director of USIS, heard that the lessons we had made in Burmese five years before were out of print. He called in his Burmese associates and agreed to print 100,000 copies of those lessons if the Burmese would accept them. It was like lightning out of a clear sky. God's lightning!

Thailand

Dick Cortright and I reached Bangkok the capital of Thailand on May 10, 1956. We were four hours late and did not expect anyone to meet us. But there was our old friend, Charoon Chamchareon, who had helped us make our textbooks in Thailand in 1949. Waiting four hours from 10 P.M. to 2 A.M. was a real test of loyalty. He took us in the car marked "Ministry of Education" and saw us settled in the Park Hotel before he returned home at 3 A.M.

The following afternoon we visited Minister of Education Promyoti, who had presented us with a beautiful silver tea set in 1949. He was as friendly and cooperative as ever. After we had talked to him for about two hours I said I thought we had stayed too long, but he replied with true Oriental courtesy: "No, stay longer. I see you so rarely."

He said he had tried to find us when he was in New York but that we were out of the country. He sent us over to the director of primary and adult education, Abbai Chandavimol, a very smart young man, realistic and down-to-earth in all his plans. These were the things he wanted from us as soon as we could get them: (1) a scholarship to send a man or woman to Syracuse University, (2) a high-grade writer to come and teach the Siamese how to write more simply, and (3) better printing presses.

That evening we were escorted by our friend Charoon on a visit to forty literacy classes for adults in Bangkok. We received a formal bow of courtesy from the students in every classroom and a glass of orangeade from every teacher. They had been carrying on their campaign for five months, had finished the primer and were reading the Siamese version of *Anand the Wise Man*.

The members of Point IV were delighted with the reception we had in Bangkok and agreed to try to get all the things the government had requested. The USIS was especially cooperative. The American in charge of the Fulbright scholarships said he would try to get a scholarship for Thailand. Dr. Luther Ambrose of ICA (International Cooperation Administration) told us to ask the minister of education to send a proposal direct to him. He thought that all the suggestions of the ministry of education were good. Dr. Ambrose is from Berea College, Kentucky, and is a perfect example of the splendid spirit of that institution.

I was especially interested in Dr. Anthony, a phonetics expert from the University of Michigan. Dr. Anthony was exploring the difficulties the people of Thailand have with the English language, and how to overcome those difficulties when teaching English. Everyone knows how much trouble the Chinese have with English, and the people of Thailand have just as much trouble. No one before Dr. Anthony had made such a serious attempt to discover exactly what causes these difficulties and exactly what to do to overcome them.

We are close allies of Thailand and they love Americans. This is one reason the Thai government is friendly to Christians and offers no obstacle to the missionaries. It is a perfect example of the tremendous influence our governmental policy has on missionary efforts; and it needs to be added, missionaries have an equally great influence upon the acceptability of our government. Today more and more missions are sending missionaries to Thailand.

Vietnam

Dick and I arrived in Saigon, Vietnam, on May 14, 1956, and were met at the airfield by Mr. Robert Kennedy, cultural attaché of the American embassy. He took us at once to visit the minister of education, a cultured gentleman who spoke excellent English. He told us that among the Vietnamese-speaking people literacy was not a serious problem because 80 per cent were literate. They had good schools and good books almost everywhere. Whatever we may say against the

French administration of Vietnam we must admit that they emphasized education in that country. The minister of education said that The Macmillan Company had notified them of our expected arrival, and had aroused their interest in *Streamlined English*. Since France had left Vietnam, the demand for English had skyrocketed and the schools teaching English were bursting at the seams.

There was also a vast hunger for more books. The minister of education wanted us to help him get the latest offset press because every press in Vietnam was old-fashioned and inefficient. The pictures were especially poor. You can imagine the breathless delight with which we left the presence of that enthusiastic minister of education. Delight, but also frustration, for we lacked the resources to meet these demands.

When Dick and I returned to the hotel two young women came up to us and said: "We have walked 300 kilometers out of the jungle to get your help. We are Christian Missionary Alliance missionaries working with jungle tribes and want you to help us make a primer to teach the Koho language. There are more than a million primitive people who speak Koho or one of the other hill-tribe languages in Vietnam. We received a letter from Mabel Cortright, written to the Christian Missionary Alliance, saying that you were coming and they wrote to us so that we should be ready for you."

We began making lessons without losing an hour and by the end of the following day had our primer finished. It was an easy language with only about twenty letters. Mr. Kennedy, the cultural attaché of the American embassy, was delighted and promised to print the lessons as a contribution to Vietnam. This the United States government did with beautiful colored pictures, and now the Koho-speaking people are on the trail to literacy.

Three more missionaries of the Christian Missionary Alliance arrived the third day and we helped them make lessons in the Raday and Jarai languages. Just two days before we were leaving, another Christian Missionary Alliance man named George Tubbs arrived from Laos to ask for help in making lessons. He said that not a single Christian in that province was able to read; so we went to work with George Tubbs to prepare lessons in the Laos language. The language in Laos resembles the language of Thailand and the letters are the same, so we were able to make rapid progress. George Tubbs said: "God brought you here just at this moment when we needed you. The government of the United States is giving me every assistance in Laos and I'm sure it will print these lessons." It did.

Then came another of those miracles that seem to be waiting for literacy workers all over the world. Mr. Robert MacAlister of the International Rescue Committee, which is trying to care for the 800,000 refugees who fled from Red China to Vietnam, came to see us. With him came Do Trong Chu, who was teaching 2,000 Vietnamese to read but did not like the lessons. So with his assistance we prepared a set of lessons in the Vietnamese language.

Thus, Vietnam turned out to be full of surprises, full of unexpected needs. When we first arrived it seemed to us that it was so literate that we would be wasting our time, but before we left we had made lessons in five languages. I was especially proud of the American missionaries in the Christian Missionary Alliance. In Vietnam and in fact in all parts of the world I found them to be magnificently self-sacrificing Christians. Everywhere they penetrate into the remote corners of the world where others have never gone. In Laos, Vietnam and Cambodia they are among tigers and cobras, and they never know at what hour the Communists or outlaws may rush in on them, destroy their work and perhaps kill them.

There are hundreds of dedicated missionaries of all denominations out on the firing line where the real need lies. In God's eyes these quiet, patient, kindly, dedicated men and women are infinitely more important to the world than are the men and women whose pictures usually make the front covers of our magazines. The only missionary, so far as I know, who ever made one of those front covers is Albert Schweitzer. The things that are great in the eyes of this world are an abomination in the eyes of God, while those who are known and despised in this world are the stars in heaven. One of the great joys of my work has been to be with missionaries with whom it was as natural to pray as it was to work.

CHAPTER 38

1956: SINGAPORE, INDONESIA AND THE PHILIPPINES

Singapore

DICK CORTRIGHT AND I reached Singapore on the night of May 17, 1956, and were met by Miss Betty Townsend of the United States Information Service. She proved to be our guardian angel while we were there, taking us wherever we wanted to go and finding all the information we asked for.

Singapore is 80 per cent Chinese. They or their ancestors had migrated from China during the past hundred years and had a warm attachment for their homeland. There was fear of a riot or uprising while we were there, an unknown number of the Chinese being Communists. The British government had never dared have an election in Singapore because of the high probability that if the Chinese were allowed to vote, the government would go communist.

Mr. Tan Bah Chee, assistant secretary of the Adult Education Council, said that they have 373 classes in English, 94 in Chinese Mandarin and one in Malay. No one wants to learn Malay, he said, because it has no economic value. He took us to see about a dozen of their literacy classes. The Communists have established a university in Singapore and it is crowded with Chinese students.

In the evening we had dinner with Dr. Olin Stockwell, author of the famous book *With God in China,* in which he describes how as a prisoner he had to endure the ordeal of "brainwashing." He gave me a copy of another of his books, *Meditations from a Prison Cell.* Stockwell's marvelous experience in prison reminded one of St. Paul, John Bunyan and countless others who down through the centuries were imprisoned for their faith.

As we were leaving Singapore Dick Cortright said: "Singapore is just as dangerous as Israel, or Jordan or Egypt or Kenya or Cyprus or Algiers or Indonesia or Malaya, though it does not get into the limelight."

Indonesia

We were off for Indonesia on the KLM airline. When we reached Jakarta the people were all talking about President Soekarno, who was visiting the United States, making magnificent speeches before Congress, and spellbinding every American. At least this is what the Indonesian newspapers said. The people believed it because he had been spellbinding them for twenty years. It was only through the magnetism of Soekarno that the diversified and antagonistic elements of that sprawling country had held together. The invitation to President Soekarno to come to the United States was a magnificent stroke of diplomacy. It demonstrated how easy it would be for us to have good relations with every country if we leaned heavily upon kindness and refrained from using the big threat.

This astonishing new friendship produced by Soekarno's visit to the United States was a great aid to our visit to Jakarta. Every Indonesian was radiant with smiles. One of the men most responsible for the popularity of our country was Mr. Jay Baird, head of Point IV. It was his cooperative spirit and his ability to make friends with the Indonesians that laid the foundation for a new friendship between Indonesia and the United States. Dick and I stayed with Mr. Baird while we were in Indonesia and are indebted to him for much of our success while there.

We went to the Mass Education headquarters without any previous announcement, but the welcome we received was a joy to our hearts. They at once summoned all the workers in their department and also the representatives of UNESCO to meet with us and work over a revision of our lessons.

This new set of lessons was better than any we had ever made in Indonesia. Secretary of Education Hutasoit was the most important man in the ministry of education from the point of view of making decisions. It was a delight to watch the eagerness with which he grasped for aid. He wanted two men to go to Syracuse University, an expert in simple journalism, a school to train people in organized campaigns such as they have in Lucknow, a writer's workshop, film-strips to teach illiterates, and he wanted us to prepare a course of graded lessons filled with useful information. He wanted it *all* right away.

His criticism of the United States government was that there was so much red tape that it took two or three years from the time a thing was begun until it was finished. "So," he said, "we would much rather have you do it."

Philippines

When Dick Cortright and I arrived in Manila on May 24, 1956, we were at once caught in such a whirlpool of activities that we scarcely had time to breathe. At the airport we were met by many old friends. We were also met by four newspaper men. The first thing they asked was whether I thought that José Rizal's novels ought to be required reading in the public schools. Those two novels had been prohibited during the Spanish regime. I said I thought they ought to be required reading because they were the best picture of the birth of the Philippines.

When we went down to breakfast the next morning we found that all four Manila newspapers carried my picture on the front page and my opinion of Rizal's novels. In 1925 I had written a book called *Rizal, Man and Martyr*. The reading of his novels in school had become a very hot question. The Catholic church in the Philippines was attempting to suppress the memory of Rizal because he had been the foremost opponent of the evils in the old Spanish Catholic hierarchy. The Filipino people were burning with indignation at this attempt to obliterate the father of their country. Rizal's statue is in the plaza of every town and city in the Philippine Islands and he reigns in the heart of the people. The attempt of the Catholic church to destroy his glory was both unwise and impossible.

As always, I found the American embassy eager to cooperate. The Asia Foundation, which has useful programs in many parts of southeast Asia, was sparkling with ideas. The Philippine Federation of Churches represented by Mr. Yap, asked us to find money and a man who could devote his entire time to literacy. Bishop Proculo Rodriguez had offered to give his full time but had been prevented because there was no money to support him. This was unfortunate because Rodriguez is the best man in the Philippine Islands for literacy work and he loves it with all his heart.

The head of UNESCO in Manila was Mr. Krishnamurti. I had worked with him in India and he was zealous for our method. Indeed, he was publishing the lessons I had helped make in the Philippine Islands with the name of UNESCO on the cover. UNESCO was training teachers to use our method in their center at Bayambang. The government also had a literacy program for all schoolteachers who were willing to give extra time at night to teach illiterates.

One of the keen joys of this visit to the Philippine Islands was meeting Dr. Luther Bewley, former director of education of the Philippine Islands. He is now retired and is one of the patron saints of the Philippines. In 1932 he had given me a letter which I had carried to all the principals of high schools in the Philippines. On the strength of this letter they had opened their schools and had helped me make literacy lessons in twenty Philippine dialects. They had also arranged for me to train all the students so that they would know how to teach these lessons. And I think Dr. Bewley was as happy as I was when the Manila newspapers named him and me as the most loyal friends of the Philippines. We were two happy old men as we recalled those days a quarter of a century before.

Dr. James Yen, famous for his social reconstruction work in China before the Japanese invasion of that country, was then living in the Philippine Islands, unable to return to China now because he was not a Communist. He had organized the Philippine Rural Construction Movement, which resembled the movement he had organized in China. He had his headquarters at the Manila Hotel and was anxious for us to cooperate with his movement.

Meanwhile there were so many calls by telephone from friends throughout Manila who wanted to come and see us at the Manila

Hotel that we had to have a strict time schedule. Even then many were disappointed.

Dick Cortright was on "pins and needles" to hurry home to America in the hope of reaching South Bend, Indiana, where his wife was "expecting the arrival of the first Cortright heir—age zero." So he took a plane for America.

I went to Baguio to attend the annual meeting of the United Church of the Philippines. There were gathered more of the dear old friends of long ago than I could ever have found anywhere else in the Philippines. In all this year's tour I was not so moved by any other experience as by this meeting. Cirilo del Carmen, who had become a Christian as a boy when I was in Cagayan, Mindanao, was now nearly sixty years of age. He had gone through such terrible hardships during the Second World War that he looked older than he was. There was Bishop Enrique Sobrepena, who had been co-pastor with me in Manila between 1923 and 1927. But I was proudest of Bishop Proculo Rodriguez, for I had found him in Mindanao when he was uncertain what he would do with his life and I had challenged him into the ministry. Now, while I was at that convention, he was elected head bishop of the Protestant church in the Philippines! I was invited to make the final address to the assembly instead of Bishop Rodriguez, and I told them I was just as proud of him as though he had been my own son, for he was indeed my own son in the faith, and I know how Paul must have loved Timothy.

En route to San Francisco I stopped off at Honolulu where the government was conducting a driving literacy program using our *Streamlined English*. They also used the Tagalog lessons we had made in the Philippine Islands and the Portuguese lessons we made in Africa—for there are many Filipinos and almost as many Portuguese in Hawaii.

Thus ended one of the most encouraging tours that I have ever taken. In every country that we visited literacy was very much alive. The masses were beating at the doors of the governments demanding literacy and the governments were eager to help. Letters that flow into our office every day from all over the world indicate that in at least three-fourths of the ninety-seven countries for which we have made lessons, literacy is moving ahead.

CHAPTER 39

1957: ATTEMPTING TO AWAKEN AMERICA

We had many requests for experts to come to a dozen countries and help them, but we did not have properly trained experts to send nor the money with which to send them. We also needed money to print books and to provide scholarships. It seemed to be unwise to go abroad and arouse any further hopes in foreign countries until we could meet the requests they had already made. The time had obviously come to awaken America. I was convinced that the American people were neglecting Asia and Africa, not because of any ill-will nor because of indifference, but because they did not know the facts. So instead of making a tour around the world I devoted the entire year of 1957 to an attempt to challenge the churches and the people of America to hear the call of Asia and Africa.

Although I was, and still am a strong advocate of the government giving economic and technical aid to foreign countries, it was all too obvious that the U. S. government was not reaching the illiterate people firsthand. Our embassies never touched the illiterates, nor did our soldiers. Our Point IV experts worked in the higher echelons and seldom came into direct contact with the hungry illiterate villagers. So our government was failing to contact, except indirectly, the people who needed us most, and we were losing as many as 100 million of these hungry people every year. The Communists were said to have 400,000 well-trained missionaries working among the very people whom we were losing. Our government realized this.

On September 11, 1956, the President of the United States summoned to the White House seventy-five leaders and pleaded with them to start what he called a "People to People Movement." He and Mr. Dulles both indicated that unless we could do more to win the allegiance of the billion who were being alienated from us, all the money we were spending to defend ourselves with arms was being lost. As the President put it, this military expenditure was merely negative, holding the line, giving us time to do the positive thing. He pleaded with the people of the United States to reach beyond governments down to the underprivileged masses of the world and win their friendship with a "person to person" program of helpfulness.

As I spoke to the American people about this call of the President I found them eager to respond but bewildered as to how to begin. The people did not want to be told that things were right. They knew that things are not right and they appreciated a forthright explanation of why we are losing the world, even though it pained them to hear the truth. They seemed actually to want to be hurt, if only they could be told what to do. I found them bewildered, frustrated because they felt so helpless, disgusted because the world was turning against us, frightened at the threat of the atom bomb, and desperately eager for someone to tell them how to go in a new direction. The thing that exasperated them most was to be told that a hate wave around the world was rising higher and drawing nearer. They themselves hated nobody, certainly not the people of Asia and Africa, and they wanted to know why they were hated. I spoke at many minister's meetings during the year and found that ministers could be stirred as I had never been able to stir them before. Many of them actually wanted a crusade to stir their own churches out of the luxurious lethargy into which they had fallen. One minister said: "You are the salvation of my church. I have not been able to persuade my people to meet their budget because the only thing they could think of to do with their money was to build a bigger church they did not need or to have more colored glass windows. But you are challenging us to save the world and my people are thrilled."

I found also that young people in schools and colleges were eager to offer themselves to world service when they realized how critical the situation is. They were healthy, overflowing with energy and lacking only one thing—a vision. They were seeking a cause bigger and more noble than merely making money in order to spend it on luxuries. America needed a challenge and a crusade big enough and gripping enough to save its soul.

Telling this story of the world's call over and over was also helpful to me, for it enabled me to see around the total world problem better than I had ever comprehended it before. I began to understand that our retreat in southern Asia and in Africa is not an accident, it is because the Communists have been persuading these people that they are emancipators while we are interested in maintaining the status quo. The Communists were winning them by promising the two things that they needed and wanted most—freedom from hunger and freedom from ignorance. The Communists told them that they had liberated the hungry masses of Russia and China from want and ignorance and that they would do this for the whole world. This good news electrified the hungry multitudes.

I found that the people of America were unaware of the tremendous educational strides that both Russia and China were actually taking. They did not know of the immense literacy campaigns going on in both of those countries. They were inclined to look upon Russia and China as countries still in the age of barbarism. When the first sputnik was shot into the air in the fall of 1957 this country had a rude shock, for we suddenly were awakened to the realization that Russia had five times as many men and women studying science and engineering as America had, and that they were unquestionably ahead of us in some branches of engineering, science, and especially in nucleonics. But Americans still did not realize that Russia and China were building a broad base of education for men, women and children. They have taught or are teaching a billion people within their orbit to read and write. Americans did not know until I told them, that Russia has more books, magazines and newspapers in process of publication than America has. Our country needed to be told that we are neglecting a billion people on our side of the iron curtain and spending all our money and effort upon educating 170 million people within the boundaries of the United States. They did not realize that the billion whom we are neglecting are desperate for education and that if we do not offer them what they want they will turn to communism. This is why tens of millions of people every year are changing over to faith in communism. If we allow this situation to go on for ten years the entire world will see what will have happened. The Communists will educate all of the billion within their orbit while we are educating only ourselves and neglecting the billion within our orbit. This will appear as proof of what the Communists claim, that they are out to save and lift the world while we are interested only in helping ourselves.

As I told these things large numbers of Americans were agitated and some wept. Many came forward after my talks, asking what they could do. There was one proposal that always struck more fire than anything else I had ever proposed. It was simply this: That in every church 100 persons agree to give a dollar a week ($52 a year) and thus provide $5200 for the support of a technically trained missionary. This money was to be offered to their own mission board for that special purpose, with the understanding that the people were giving this money over and above their other church gifts.

The mission boards were all pleased at the response that came to them. Some leaders doubted whether we would be able to find enough technically trained Christians who had the health and other qualifications needed for this task. Personally, I believe that we have exactly the type of technicians in our churches and communities that the world requires. When they hear this challenge thousands of young college graduates will have to be shown where to apply. The bottleneck is in finding suitable channels. Most mission boards have made some unrealistic requirements for their candidates, many requiring a theological course for educators or agricultural experts or engineers.

There is also a tremendous army of retired people who are still strong and eager to be of service. Many of them have accumulated enough money to last the rest of their lives. They have stopped making a living and now they have time to begin to live! Their rich lifelong experience in their chosen profession is far better than theoretical knowledge gained in college. Some of these retired people would be able to finance themselves abroad. Thousands with the mellow kindliness that Chistian compassion develops would find a wonderful welcome in foreign lands. Asia and Africa reverence age and they do not think a man knows much until he is gray. An ideal team would consist of a younger man and an older man. The first could provide the leg work and the second could provide the—shall we say "practical experience"?

Then there are ten million young people—a very low estimate—who are straining every nerve to come to America, and who could be trained here to return and help their native lands. In many cases they would do a better job for their countries than we could do because they know their customs and prejudices and weaknesses and needs as we can seldom understand them.

No, the bottleneck is not lack of money nor lack of manpower, nor is it lack of *generosity*. The American people give more generously than any other people in all history. But we give nearly all of it in our own communities and our own country. We have made the slogan "charity begins at home" a part of our religion—although it was invented by a Roman pagan, and is directly contrary to the teaching of Jesus in the story of the Good Samaritan. Charity begins where the need is greatest and the crisis is most dangerous. I believe that each month more millions of Americans see where that crisis is—in south Asia and in Africa.

If 40 million Americans see it and contribute an average of a dollar a week, that will be a grand total of $2 billion a year, enough to support 200,000 American technicians, or a million nationals. If we mobilize this army of compassion, we shall no longer be fighting merely to save the world from communism. We shall be fighting to save the world from the intolerable hunger that breeds communism and all other councils of desperation. We now have enough scientific knowledge and technical skill so that the educated people of the world working in harmony can easily and swiftly lift the entire human race up out of poverty and ignorance and despair to a high level of abundance. Then America, instead of being surrounded by a starving world jealous of her wealth, will find herself the most beloved country the world ever saw. If we go in this direction of compassion we shall intervene in history, which is now going against us, and we shall change its very direction. We can then call upon the Communists to follow us in a glorious crusade to build a new world—a world grander than any utopia ever dreamed by the men of old. Then we shall emerge from this nightmare of fear, and feel at peace with all humanity and with God.

CHAPTER 40

TEACHING LITERACY ON TELEVISION

In the spring of 1956 I made a speech in Memphis, Tennessee, and told the audience that, no matter how fast we were teaching illiterates, the booming population growth was outstripping us. After the meeting a tall young man came forward and introduced himself as Keith Nighbert, the director of an educational television station that the city of Memphis was running. "This is just what we've been looking for!" exclaimed Mr. Nighbert, "for we need a program to catch the imagination of this city, and to do the community a real service."

In the same audience was Mrs. Pauline Hord, with years of experience in teaching reading to school children. She and Mr. Nighbert immediately formed an enthusiastic team—one with the technical know-how and the other with compassion for the people learning to read. They carefully considered many methods of teaching reading, and settled on our *Streamlined English*. I was thrilled, and said I would help them as much as my busy schedule would allow, and offered to send Betty Mooney to Memphis. Betty had helped make the original lessons of *Streamlined English* back in 1945, as well as helping to write *The Story of Jesus*.

Betty went to Memphis from Koinonia, where she had been helping in the teaching, and was soon followed by a small host of other Koinonia-trained persons—for the job of adapting the book *Stream-*

lined English to TV teaching was staggering. But the small army of dedicated workers moved into the already overcrowded WKNO television station and began the job, aiming for a September opening of the new literacy classroom of the air.

Right from the start, Mrs. Hord realized that just telecasting the programs wouldn't do the job of making adults literate. So she and Betty and Mr. Nighbert started out to mobilize the entire community behind the project. They spoke in churches, civic groups, high schools, sports clubs—anywhere and everywhere they could get a hearing. "This is a wonderful chance for every good citizen of Memphis," they would say, "to help the 60,000 people within range of station WKNO to learn to read."

The Memphis radio and television stations and newspapers got behind the coming program. The Chamber of Commerce officially endorsed literacy TV, and the project became Memphis' very own. The first part of the plan was to sign up the prospective students by "Each One Bring One." Most of the illiterates were too embarrassed to reply to a radio invitation, but one good friend would tell another about the classes, and even offer to take him to the first one. In this manner, hundreds were "signed up." The second part of the plan was the setting up of dozens of TV classrooms all around the city, and out into the country. A room in a club, church, schoolhouse, or private home became the classroom. Television dealers, civic clubs and persons with spare TV sets donated them to the classrooms, or centers, as they were called. (Memphis' rock-'n'-roll singer, Elvis Presley, gave a brand-new TV set.)

In each center there was to be an assistant teacher, whose job as a volunteer was to come about a half-hour before the 7 P.M. broadcast to help the students find their places, and answer questions about the previous lesson. Then, for another half-hour after the televised lesson, the assistant teacher stayed to help get the students started on homework for the next lesson. The Memphis section of the Council of Jewish Women pitched in and sent dozens of ladies to be assistant teachers in the three-nights-a-week program; they have to this very day contributed countless thousands of hours in the WKNO center, where papers have come in to be graded.

Finally, the stage was set for the first real experiment anywhere that

I know of in teaching people to read by television. One evening in September, 1956, the program started. The first teacher was a soft-spoken southern lady, Ruth Knowlton, who charmed everyone in the sixty or so centers throughout the city that night. Close to a thousand students had registered for the first course, "Improve Your Reading on TV" (the word "illiterate" is never used among sensitive nonreaders in Memphis).

The Center for Educational Television, at Ann Arbor, Michigan, granted WKNO $5,000 to make a thorough study of its literacy program. Some students were selected and a careful chart of their progress was kept. Much background information was collected on other students. When the study was completed and the report sent to Ann Arbor, Mrs. Hord and her colleagues knew more about more people in Memphis than anyone had ever known before.

I was invited down to Memphis in the spring of 1957 to participate in the world's first TV literacy graduation. No one who saw the 300 graduates file past the spotlight where they were being televised will ever forget the look on their faces and the exclamations of sheer delirious delight. The Reverend Dr. Wingfield, who led the prayer at the opening of the program, was so overcome that he went outside and cried like a child. "This," he said, "was the greatest sight of my life."

The leading citizens of Memphis saw tremendous possibilities in the success of the first program, not only for Memphis, but for the whole nation and world. The program had attracted national attention, through articles in *Life* magazine and several educational journals. Inquiries from every city in the country poured in: "How can we start TV literacy in our city too?" Clearly, the job was bigger than WKNO could do alone. The Memphis Chamber of Commerce sponsored a Conference on Literacy for the World Through Television. Among the 200 distinguished educators, businessmen, and radio and TV executives who came to that conference was Dr. William Gray, a foremost educator in the United States, who is regarded by UNESCO as the leading authority on fundamental education.

Dr. Gray proposed, at the closing session of the conference, that a Foundation for World Literacy be organized for promoting TV to teach the illiterates around the world. As this book is published, the first offices of this Foundation have been established in Memphis, and plans are being drawn up for the erection of a permanent training center there, so that trainees from many parts of the world can learn TV literacy know-how, and return to teach illiterates in their own languages by television.

The work at WKNO has gone right ahead. The first year's course has now been recorded on ninety-eight half-hour "kinescopes," or movies, so that TV stations and theaters around the nation may lease them for use. Mrs. Helen Brown, whose accent is universally accepted and whose TV classroom manner is just the right combination of pleasantness and efficiency, is the teacher on the kinescopes. So, the experimental stages of TV teaching are completed, and Memphis has demonstrated conclusively that success in teaching hundreds (or thousands) to read can be achieved by any community through television. Ahead lies a tremendous potential in television's "Ray of Hope," as the program has been called, for the entire world.

An opportunity to explore the possibilities of educational television in other countries came in September of 1958. The United States government asked me to go the Trade Fair in Tunis and hold a demonstration literacy class, so that people could see the illiterates learning and would want to join the classes. Our government prepared a special section of the Fair for this purpose and another section where writers might be seen working out the simple books which illiterates would require. I went to Tunis and found our American Embassy enthusiastic. But when the Tunisian minister of education learned about it, he vetoed the project, because he said people would be humiliated to be seen learning in front of large crowds. "Come back after the Fair is over," he said, "and we will welcome your help."

I was really relieved at this decision, for I discovered that they lacked the facilities for making a TV film in Arabic, which was now my heart's deepest desire. So I returned to Paris and had an interview with Dr. Luther Evans, then director general of UNESCO. He gave me a letter to the Egyptian branch of UNESCO called AZFAC at Sirs al Layyan, sixty miles north of Cairo. In this letter he suggested that perhaps they would like to help me prepare a television lesson in Arabic. Mr. Khadri, director of AZFAC, did like the idea, so during the next month I cooperated with UNESCO and the Egyptian government in preparing an Arabic lesson for TV, using the Arabic lessons which we had prepared for the mission classes in upper Egypt. It was a really formidable undertaking. It happened that Mr. Mahmoud Mohamed had been trained by one of our Point Four Americans to make motion picture tape, and he was irrepressibly eager to make use of this experience. Without him the film never would have been made. The Egyptian government had marvelous equipment in visual aids, and they were eager to cooperate in making this film. The sound track had to be put on by the use of magnetic tape, which Mr. Mohamed happened to know could be added to the film by a private firm in Cairo. So we managed to get our first lesson finished in a month. When we showed it to the Egyptian educational leaders they were excited as well as delighted. Literacy is not increasing as fast as the population in Egypt, and they saw in TV the hope of getting them out of this predicament.

I took this film down to Khartoum, Sudan, and showed it to the minister of education and all the Sudan educational leaders. They were enthusiastic about it, and wanted copies as soon as possible. I showed it in Kenya, and although they did not understand Arabic, they were excited about the *Streamlined English* film which I had brought with me from Memphis, Tennessee. They too faced the problem of population rising faster than literacy.

In fact this "population bomb" has become a more serious menace than the hydrogen bomb. Recent U.N. figures give the population of the world as 2,790 millions; but in forty years from now it will be 6,300 millions at the present rate of increase. The highest rate of increase is in Asia, Latin America and Africa. The hydrogen bomb might explode, but the population bomb *is* exploding right now. There must be a vast program of family planning or the world will soon be overrun with starving, dangerous hordes. But the illiterate people cannot be trained in family planning. The strenuous efforts in India and Egypt have failed. The people have no money and they cannot read instructions. Japan, on the other hand, while she has reached the saturation point of population, has been able to reduce her birth rate since 1950 because she is one of the best-educated countries in the world. Literacy has emerged as a necessity so that we can save our world from the disaster of overpopulation. And TV is the most promising medium for spreading literacy rapidly—it is the only mass medium that can reach all the people.

I took the films to Somalia and found the same excitement among government officials. They had never printed their language in Somalia, so while there we made the first primer ever made in that country at the Mennonite mission headquarters. The Point Four officials of the United States government offered to print it for us.

When I reached Jidda (forty miles from Mecca) in Arabia, my films were confiscated and held until I left Arabia. Pictures are regarded as violation of the Second Commandment: "Thou shalt not make unto thee any graven image. . . ." The Arabs boast that they keep the Law of Moses far better than do the Jews or Christians. I was told while I was in Jidda that they have no prisons. If a man steals, his hand is cut off and he is allowed to go free. If he steals again or commits adultery or murder, his head is cut off. This is done at the public market, so all the people will know what happens. They say they have solved the problem of juvenile delinquency!

In Beirut, Lebanon, the government and UNESCO were equally excited about the possibilities of TV. UNESCO made a copy of the film which I had prepared in Egypt. One man from Iraq was especially eager, for they have educational television in Iraq.

For me the greatest thrill came when the foreign relations officer from Yemen followed me to Beirut and spent a whole evening imploring me to come to Yemen and help them with literacy. "We have a new minister of education," he said, "and he wants to lift Yemen out of the dark ages up to our modern level in one generation. You must come!" The miracle of this is seen when you know that up to this time not a single American citizen has been allowed to remain in Yemen. They have several dozen Communist engineers, but when I go I shall be the only American. And *I am going!* This is the most inaccessible place in the world. Lowell Thomas wrote asking me if I could not help him get into Yemen to take pictures. That, I fear, will be impossible, for they are like Arabia—they are ultraconservative Moslems, and regard all pictures as violations of the Second Commandment.

I must skip back to Kenya for a moment and tell of the magnificent work of Betty Mooney for the illiterates of that country. We worked on primers in four new languages and on *The Story of Jesus* for those languages while I was there. Helen Roberts, a retired schoolteacher from California, had come to help Betty, at her own expense. She wrote a play which was translated into Kikuyu. While I was there they showed that play to a thousand Africans in one of the university halls, and it was an immense success. All of us were in tears and laughter. Then four hundred of these Africans came up to the platform and received diplomas from the director of education. This was one of the most moving events of my whole life, and a fitting climax to this book.

But this is a book without an ending. In fact it seems to be the introduction to a literacy program which is breaking open all over the world. The Memphis Rotary Club is making literacy a major objective, and this may spread to international groups. The Red Cross has asked whether we can make our lessons available for them to distribute all over the world with a red cross on the cover. WE CAN! The Women's Clubs have voted to make literacy a major objective, and have a special director for that purpose. America from coast to coast is beginning to believe that compassion will save the world!

This book is not a history—it is an announcement! I believe we shall abolish the war of missiles and atomic bombs. I believe we are right now declaring the war of education and world progress. We see that for our side of the world to progress with ever more abundance as the underprivileged world sinks deeper into hunger and ignorance is not only suicidal for us all, but it is the world's blackest sin. And the Army of Compassion grows greater every day.

INDEX